LEAPS OF

D0712028

"Houses of the Spirit"

A single mother indulges her six-year-old son's wish to go to church for the first time to "see if God's there" and feels the tug of faith herself. Moved by the sight of her son receiving communion, she experiences a conversion of sorts: "Some window in my head flew open, and the light poured in."

"What Faith Is" by Lisa Vice

The death of a beloved cat named Tommy reawakens the grief left by the loss of a life partner in this beautifully told account of love and loneliness.

"A Tale of Seven Sisters" by Sandy Boucher

A spiritual journey leads Boucher to a nunnery in Sri Lanka to study with the German-born nun Ayya Khema and a conflict between demands of the inner and outer worlds.

"In the City Ringed with Giants" by Barbara Kingsolver

Kingsolver describes a search for a new spirituality when the old talismans fail in this powerful poem filled with stark imagery and passion.

And many more divine works by today's literary women

AMBER COVERDALE SUMRALL is the co-editor of several anthologies, including *Touching Fire: Erotic Writings of Women* and *Women of the 14th Moon: Writing on Menopause.* She lives in Santa Cruz, California.

PATRICE VECCHIONE is a poet, editor, and radio host for KUSP, the National Public Radio station of California's central coast. She lives in Del Ray Oaks, California. Together, they edited *Catholic Girls* and *Bless Me, Father* (both Plume).

Also edited by
AMBER COVERDALE SUMRALL and PATRICE VECCHIONE:

Catholic Girls
Bless Me, Father: Stories of Catholic Childhood

STORMING HEAVEN'S GATE

*An Anthology of Spiritual
Writings by Women*

EDITED BY

Amber Coverdale Sumrall

AND

Patrice Vecchione

A PLUME BOOK

PLUME
Published by the Penguin Group
Penguin Books USA Inc., 375 Hudson Street,
New York, New York 10014, U.S.A.
Penguin Books Ltd, 27 Wrights Lane,
London W8 5TZ, England
Penguin Books Australia Ltd, Ringwood,
Victoria, Australia
Penguin Books Canada Ltd, 10 Alcorn Avenue,
Toronto, Ontario, Canada M4V 3B2
Penguin Books (N.Z.) Ltd, 182–190 Wairau Road,
Auckland 10, New Zealand

Penguin Books Ltd, Registered Offices:
Harmondsworth, Middlesex, England

First published by Plume, an imprint of Dutton Signet, a division of Penguin
Books USA Inc.

First Printing, July, 1997
10   9   8   7   6   5   4   3   2

Copyright © Amber Coverdale Sumrall and Patrice Vecchione, 1997
All rights reserved

Pages 475–477 constitute an extension of this copyright page.

 REGISTERED TRADEMARK—MARCA REGISTRADA

LIBRARY OF CONGRESS CATALOGING-IN-PUBLICATION DATA

Storming heaven's gate : an anthology of spiritual writings by women /
    edited by Amber Coverdale Sumrall and Patrice Vecchione.
        p.   cm.
    ISBN 0-452-27621-7
    1. Women—Religious life.   I. Sumrall, Amber Coverdale.
II. Vecchione, Patrice.
BL625.7.S76   1997
291.4′082—dc21   97-1990
                                                              CIP

Printed in the United States of America
Set in Bitstream Carmina Medium
Designed by Stanley S. Drate/Folio Graphics Co. Inc.

Without limiting the rights under copyright reserved above, no part of this
publication may be reproduced, stored in or introduced into a retrieval system, or transmitted, in any form, or by any means (electronic, mechanical,
photocopying, recording, or otherwise), without the prior written permission of both the copyright owner and the above publisher of this book.

PUBLISHER'S NOTE
Some of these stories are works of fiction. Names, characters, places, and
incidents either are the product of the author's imagination or are used ficti-
tiously, and any resemblance to actual persons, living or dead, events, or
locales is entirely coincidental.

BOOKS ARE AVAILABLE AT QUANTITY DISCOUNTS WHEN USED TO PROMOTE PRODUCTS OR SER-
VICES. FOR INFORMATION PLEASE WRITE TO PREMIUM MARKETING DIVISION, PENGUIN BOOKS
USA INC., 375 HUDSON STREET, NEW YORK, NEW YORK 10014.

Contents

HEART OF COMPASSION

SACRED PLACE

LEAPS OF FAITH

SPIRIT BREAKS INTO SONG

THE LONG JOURNEY HOME

INVOCATION

Acknowledgments

To the following we extend our appreciation: Rosemary Ahern, Linda Fox and Kelsey Ramage of Bookshop Santa Cruz, Gloria Wade Gayles, Stephen Kessler, Charlotte Raymond, Ken Weisner, and Alison Winterle.

Our gratitude to those who have given us abiding faith, especially Kim Beecher, Ali Bermond, Sister Bernice, Les Breese, Ruah Bull, Patricia Mathes Cane, Nellie June Coverdale, Nanda Currant, Cybele, the Friday evening writing group, Father Richard Graham, Sister Ann Lenore, Michael Mason, Virginia Mayer, Maude Meehan, Audrey Mendoza, Nancy Norris, Wally Parham, Joseph Milton Park, Michael Stark, Wendy Traber, Gina Van Horn, and the women of WomenCARE.

For the places they take us, Patrice would like to thank her bicycle and Amber, her encounters with sacred substances.

For the everlasting gift of friendship we are grateful to each other.

All of the larger-than-life questions about our presence here on earth and what gifts we have to offer are spiritual questions. To seek answers to these questions is to seek a sacred path.

—LAUREN ATRESS

We are not human beings trying to be spiritual. We are spiritual beings trying to be human.

—JACQUELYN SMALL

The liberating encounter with God/ess is always an encounter with our authentic selves resurrected from underneath the alienated self. It is not experienced against, but in and through, relationships, healing our broken relations with our bodies, with other people, with nature.

—ROSEMARY RUETHER

The expression of women's spiritual quest is integrally related to the telling of women's stories. If women's stories are not told, the depths of women's souls will not be known.

—CAROL P. CHRIST

Introduction

At a certain point you say to the woods, to the sea, to the mountains, the
world, now I am ready. Now I will stop and be wholly attentive.
—ANNIE DILLARD

Writing is the only way I know how to pray.
—HELENA MARÍA VIRAMONTES

Writing, for me, is an act of faith, a hope that I will discover what I mean
by truth.
—AMY TAN

As girls who had grown up embracing Catholicism, we gradually became aware of the Church's profound failure to recognize, honor, and include women, an awareness that grew until, as young women, we felt forced to abandon our religion. What we didn't leave at the church door is that which sustains us still, a reverence for ritual and mysticism, an attention to beautiful detail: voices praying in song; the waft of frankincense; votive candles, their blue and yellow light; the immensity of sacred darkness.

In the profound silence of the church, we learned to listen, within and without. And what we found, despite the Church's intentions otherwise, was an emerging feminism, the realization of the power and freedom of our imaginations that opened onto a world, vast and illuminating, replacing the idea of a God and salvation as being at a distance, outside our ourselves. This led us to a faith centered in nature, women, and creativity. And ultimately, we were both led to poetry as a spiritual vocation.

From Catholicism to Buddhism, from Judaism to paganism, within the framework of religion as well as separate from its structure, women today are creating religion anew, reclaiming the feminine principles of compassion, cooperation, and reverence for the earth and its creatures. Many women who participate in organized religion are re-visioning their traditional philosophies and practices. And others who have left the churches of their childhoods or grew up without religion are being called to create lives that honor the sacred.

Historically, women have not been validated or represented by the models of traditional religion that have frequently been used to establish and validate male hierarchical power, control the people, stifle creative thought, and provide a moral imperative for obliterating those who dissent or believe differently. Many religions also ask us to relinquish responsibility for our lives, surrendering to a "Higher Power" or to those who claim to be God's messengers.

Faith is larger than anything that tries to undermine it. Audre Lorde writes, "For each of us as women, there is a dark place within where hidden and growing our true spirit rises." Faith exists within the realm of spirituality. It implies uncertainty, is creative, intuitive, known through the senses and emotions, as well as the mind. Faith allows for the awakening of grace in our lives. In the words of Lucille Clifton, "i had no model./born in babylon/both nonwhite and woman/what did i see to be except myself?/ i made it up. . . ."

In part, it is the search for what has been lost that is currently motivating women to redefine their own spiritual beliefs and practices. And many women are finding a link to God through the feminine.

The prominent Buddhist teacher Joan Halifax writes about her years of practicing, working, and living with the traditions of both Buddhism and shamanism, and the discovery of her own "fruitful darkness"—the healing nature of both suffering and compassion. "We complain about the state of the world and are fearful of the state of our bodies, our families, the economy, and the Earth. Over the years, we have become lazy, complacent, and depressed and, like the gods, have forgotten to tend the hearth of the Fire of our awareness and to enter the Waters of the Feminine.''

Women are healing themselves from illness, emotional loss, sickness of the soul, despair for the earth, and fear, through spirituality. Recognizing the imperative of healing their lives, which are often disparate, hardworking, demanding of body, heart, and mind, women are seeking and finding solace through the life of the soul.

The writing in *Storming Heaven's Gate*, a compilation of memoir, fiction, and poetry, serves as testimonials to the ways in which women currently define, bear witness to, honor, and celebrate God and spirituality in their lives. The source of these words is faith.

More than three hundred years ago, Saint Theresa said, ''Words lead to deeds. . . . They prepare the soul, make it ready and move it toward tenderness.'' May the words that follow tend you and further you along your path.

INVOCATION

Joy Harjo

Eagle Poem

To pray you open your whole self
To sky, to earth, to sun, to moon
To one whole voice that is you.
And know there is more
That you can't see, can't hear,
Can't know except in moments
Steadily growing, and in languages
That aren't always sound but other
Circles of motion.
Like eagle that Sunday morning
Over Salt River. Circled in blue sky
In wind, swept our hearts clean
With sacred wings.
We see you, see ourselves and know
That we must take the utmost care
And kindness in all things.
Breathe in, knowing we are made of
All this, and breathe, knowing
We are truly blessed because we
Were born, and die soon within a
True circle of motion,
Like eagle rounding out the morning
Inside us.
We pray that it will be done
In beauty.
In beauty.

SOURCES

*Attend me, hold me in your
muscular flowering arms,
protect me from throwing any
part of myself away.*

—AUDRE LORDE

Adrienne Rich

Sources, Part II

I refuse to become a seeker for cures.
Everything that has ever
helped me has come through what already
lay stored in me.   Old things, diffuse, unnamed, lie strong
across my heart.
                    This is from where
my strength comes, even when I miss my strength
even when it turns on me
like a violent master.

Brooke Medicine Eagle

The Rainbow Bridge

I found some dry, bleached bones today,
and gathered them to put into a bag
for casting to ask the future,
when modern means have failed me.

The vision quest that I have done was with my teacher who is a Northern Cheyenne woman. She is eighty-five years old and is known as The Keeper of the Sacred Buffalo Hat. Her people call her The Woman Who Knows Everything. She and a younger medicine woman took me to a place called Bear Butte, South Dakota; it's plains country that goes up into the Black Hills. That's the traditional fasting, vision-questing place of the Sioux and Cheyenne and has been for centuries and centuries. What is usually done among the Cheyenne is that you fast and cleanse yourself bodily, emotionally, and psychically. Then you go atop a mountain for four days and nights with just a breechcloth on and a buffalo robe, and you stay there without food or water, praying for vision. This is the kind of quest that I did.

The younger medicine woman took me up the butte. She prepared and blessed a bed of sagebrush on a very rocky hill halfway up the mountain. This was to be my bed. After we smoked a pipe and offered prayers, she left me. So I spent the time there fasting and praying for vision.

It was just getting to be dark. Up on the mountain, I can look down over the country: There's a lake down below me; in the far-off distance are the Black Hills, and I can see the lights of Rapid City. I'm hoping it won't rain because I really don't want to be rained on up here. A few little clouds are flitting across the sky, but it is relatively warm, the late fall. I'm just lying here very peacefully. And beside me there comes a woman, older than me, but not really an old woman. She's dressed very simply, buckskin. And I'm surprised that she doesn't have beading on her dress. She has raven black hair with long braids. And she stands beside me and begins to talk to me. As she talks to me, her words come, but not in my ears; I don't really hear her say anything. It's as though she's feeding something in at my navel, and it comes through me, and I can interpret part of it in words but not all of it, like she's giving me something through my stomach and letting it come up. So the words that I put to it have to be my own, and I have discovered more and more of what she told me as time has gone on.

Just then the little clouds that were over the moon move off, and as they move away, the moonlight shining on her dress creates a flurry of rainbows, and I can see that her dress is beaded with crystal beads, hundreds of tiny crystal beads; the slightest movement she makes sends little flurries of soft rainbows all over. About this time, something else starts to happen. Down off the high part of the mountain, it starts to become light, and I hear soft drumbeats begin, very soft. There's a kind of dance that the women do that is very soft. And down off that mountain in a slow, soft, and gentle step come the old women, spirits of that land, that mountain, old gray-haired women, Indian women, dancing down. They either *are* light or carry light. They wind down the mountain and then circle around the hill I am on. And as they dance around in a circle, very quickly, into that circle comes another circle, this of young women, of my age and time, young women that I know, and they, too, are dancing. Those two circles are dancing and moving, and then they begin to weave in and out of each other, sway in and out of each other. And then inside of that circle comes another circle of seven old grandmothers, white-haired women, women who are significant to me, powerful old women.

In the Native American tradition, there is an amazing amount of humor. And the humor comes when all this very solemn, very slow, and very beautiful ceremony is taking place. Running off the mountain, with her hair flying, is this friend of mine. She's always late. She is a very high person, but she is very unstable. Into the circle comes Dianne, flying, with her hair streaming, late as always. And on her hand she is carrying a dove. The Rainbow Woman looks down on me and says, "Her name is Moon Dove," and she smiles. Dianne then lets the dove fly. The circles around me disappear, and I am again alone with the Rainbow Woman.

She said to me that the earth is in trouble, that the land is in trouble, and that here on this land, this Turtle Island, this North American land, what needs to happen is a balancing. She said that the thrusting, aggressive, analytic, intellectual, building, making-it-happen energy has very much overbalanced the feminine, receptive, allowing, surrendering energy. She said that what needs to happen is an uplifting and a balancing. And because we are out of balance, we need to put more emphasis on surrendering, being receptive, allowing, nurturing. She was speaking to me as a woman, and I was to carry this message to women specifically. But not only do women need to become strong in this way; we all need to do this, men and women alike.

Women are born into that kind of space. It's more natural for us to be receptive and nurturing. That's what being a woman in this body is about. But even the women in our society don't do that very well. None of us has ever been taught how to do that. We know how to *do* something; we know how to *make* something, how to *do*, how to *try*. But we need to allow, to be receptive, to surrender, to serve. These are things we don't know very well. So she told me that women especially need to find that place, to find the strength of their place, and that also the whole society, men and women, need that balance to bring ourselves into balance.

Another thing she said to me was that we on this North American continent are all children of the rainbow, all of us; we are mixed-bloods. And especially me she was speaking to, saying that she felt that I would be a carrier of the message between the two cultures, across the rainbow bridge, from the old culture to the new, from the Indian culture to the dominant culture, and back again. And in a sense, all of us in this generation can be that. We can help bridge that gap, build that bridge into the new age of balance.

Those are the kind of things that she talked about, about cleansing ourselves so that we can allow love and light and surrender to come through us. And when she finished talking, she stood quietly for a moment. Her feet stayed where they were, but she shot out across the sky in a rainbow arc that covered the heavens, her head at the top of that arc. And then the lights that formed that rainbow began to die out, almost like fireworks in the sky, died out from her feet and died out and died out. And she was gone.

When I woke up the next morning, on the other side of the sky was the completion of the rainbow that had started the night before. And for days and days after that, rainbows kept appearing in my life.

There are very few women who are on the path of the shaman, and yet, this is my way. I was raised on the Crow Reservation in Montana. My blood is Sioux and Nez Percé. The Indian tradition was very much hidden when I was growing up on the reservation. However, I am getting back, more and more, to the tribal way. This happened as I began to have visions; I was drawn back to the old ways by my visions. I did not choose it outwardly. It just came about.

One of the things that I feel about the quest for vision:

The traditional Indians, when they prayed, their prayers were always "Not only for myself do I ask this, but that the people may live, the people may live." Any of us can dream, but when you seek a vision, you do this not only for yourself but that the people may live, that life might be better for all of us, not only for me but for all people.

I feel my purpose is to help in any way I can to heal the earth. I feel that we are in a time when the earth is in dire need of healing. We see it everywhere, the droughts, earthquakes, storms, pollution. Yes, the earth itself is in need of healing. And I feel that any way that I can help, that is my mission: to make it whole, to pay attention to that wholeness, not only in ourselves but also in relation to the earth.

The Indian people are the people of the heart. When the white man came to this land, what he was to bring was the intellect, that analytic, intellectual way of being. And the Indian people were to develop the heart, the feelings. And those two were to come together to build the new age, in balance, not one or the other.

It has been only a couple of hundred years now, and I think we're beginning to see the force of this land, that receptive force, come back again, and that balance is beginning to happen. And I feel that what we are is that land. We are those children Rainbow Woman talked about. We are the ones who are going to have to do it. We are that blend.

In the philosophy of the true Indian people, Indian is an attitude, a state of mind; Indian is a state of being, the place of the heart. To allow the heart to be the distributor of energy on this planet; to allow your heart, your feelings, your emotions to distribute your energy; to pull that energy from the earth, from the sky; to pull it down and distribute it from your heart, the very center of your being—that is our purpose.

Several different traditions talk about four or five different worlds and say that the Creator made all these worlds with one simple law: that we shall be in harmony and in balance with all things, including the sun. And time and again people have destroyed that harmony; we have destroyed that harmony. And we have done it again needlessly. Unless we bring about that balance again, this is our last chance.

We need to achieve a clarity and lack of resistance before we seek vision—a surrendering, a relinquishing. If you are unwilling to be in your experience now, then vision will not open for you. You need to get on that circle where there is no resistance, no up, no down, where there are no square corners to stumble on. Then, someday, you become that circle.

Madeleine L'Engle

Healed, Whole and Holy

Along with reawakening the sense of newness, Bach's music points me to wholeness, a wholeness of body, mind, and spirit, which we seldom glimpse, but which we are intended to know. It is no coincidence that the root word of whole, health, heal, holy, is hale (as in *hale and hearty*). If we are healed, we become whole; we are hale and hearty; we are holy.

The marvelous thing is that this holiness is nothing we can earn. We don't become holy by acquiring merit badges and Brownie points. It has nothing to do with virtue or job descriptions or morality. It is nothing we can *do*, in this do-it-yourself world. It is gift, sheer gift, waiting there to be recognized and received. We do not have to be qualified to be holy. We do not have to be qualified to be whole, or healed.

The fact that I am not qualified was rammed into me early, and though this hurt, it was salutary. As a small child I was lonely not only because I was an only child in a big city, but because I was slightly lame, extremely introverted, and anything but popular at school. There was no question in my mind that I was anything but whole, that I did not measure up to the standards of my peers or teachers. And so, intuitively, I turned to writing as a way of groping toward wholeness. I wrote vast quantities of short stories and poetry; I painted and played the piano. I lived far too much in an interior world, but I did learn that I

14

didn't have to be qualified according to the world's standards in order to write my stories. It was far more likely my total *lack* of qualifications that turned me to story to search for meaning and truth, to ask those eternal questions: Why? What is it all about? Does my life have any meaning? Does anybody care?

To try to find the answers to these questions, I not only wrote but read omnivorously, anything I could get my hands on—fairy tales, the brothers Grimm, Hans Christian Andersen, Oscar Wilde, the story of Tobias and the angel, Gideon and the angel. Very early in my life the Bible taught me to care about angels. I also read about dreams in the Bible, and so I took dreams seriously. I read and reread and reread *Emily of New Moon*, by L. M. Montgomery, author of the more famous stories about *Anne of Green Gables*. I liked the Anne stories, but especially I loved Emily, because she, too, wanted to be a writer, a real writer; she, too, walked to the beat of a different drum; she had a touch of second sight, that gift which allows us to peek for a moment at the world beyond ordinary space and time.

My lonely solitude kept me far more in touch with this world of the imagination than I would have been had I been off with the other children playing hopscotch or skipping rope. It was this world which gave me assurance of meaning and reality despite the daily world in which I was a misfit, and in which I knew many fears as I overheard my parents talking about the nations once again lining up for war.

If I found this world in *Emily of New Moon*, in books of Chinese fairy tales as well as in Andrew Lang's collections, I also found it in the Bible stories. I was fortunate (in the strange way in which tragedy brings with it blessings as well as griefs) because my father's deteriorating lungs dictated an unusual schedule; he worked best in the afternoon and evening, and slept late into the morning. Therefore there was no one to take me to Sunday school. I have talked with such a surprising number of people who have had to spend most of their lives unlearning what some well-meaning person taught them in Sunday school, that I'm glad I escaped! All the old heresies of the first few centuries—Donatism, Manicheism, Docetism, to name but three—are still around, and Satan doesn't hesitate to use them wherever possible.

In the world of literature, Christianity is no longer respectable. When I am referred to in an article or a review as a "practicing Christian" it is seldom meant as a compliment, at least not in the secular press. It is perfectly all right, according to literary critics, to be Jewish, or Buddhist, or Sufi, or a pre-Christian druid. It is not all right to be a Christian. And if we ask why, the answer is a sad one; Christians have given Christianity a bad name. They have let their lights flicker and grow dim. They have confused piosity with piety, smugness with joy. During the difficult period in which I was struggling through my "cloud of unknowing" to return to the Church and to Christ, the largest thing which deterred me was that I saw so little clear light coming from those Christians who sought to bring me back to the fold.

But I'm back, and grateful to be back, because, through God's loving grace, I did meet enough people who showed me that light of love which the darkness cannot extinguish. One of the things I learned on the road back is that I do not have to be right. I have to try to do what is right, but when it turns out, as happens with all of us, to be wrong, then I am free to accept that it was wrong, to say, "I'm sorry," and to try, if possible, to make reparation. But I have to accept the fact that I am often unwise; that I am not always loving; that I make mistakes; that I am, in fact, human. And as Christians we are not meant to be less human than other people, but more human, just as Jesus of Nazareth was more human.

One time I was talking to Canon Tallis, who is my spiritual director as well as my friend, and I was deeply grieved about something, and I kept telling him how woefully I had failed someone I loved, failed totally, otherwise that person couldn't have done the wrong that was so destructive. Finally he looked at me and said calmly, ''Who are you to think you are better than our Lord? After all, he was singularly unsuccessful with a great many people.''

That remark, made to me many years ago, has stood me in good stead, time and again. I have to try, but I do not have to succeed. Following Christ has nothing to do with success as the world sees success. It has to do with love.

Mary Karr

Houses of the Spirit

When I asked my six-year-old son, Dev, why he wanted to go to church for the first time that Sunday morning, he gave perhaps the only answer that could have nudged me into folding my newspaper and moving toward some faith I'd never bothered with before. He wanted to go, he said, "to see if God's there."

The wish caught me up short. In my two years as a single mom, I'd indulged Dev's curiosity in all other realms—bass lessons, computer camp, tae kwon do. I'd stood in soccer fields stiff with frost all fall and cheered from the sweltering T-ball bleachers come summer. But should I—or could I, even—provide him with a God in whom I'd absolutely no belief?

I'd grown up agnostic in a swampy corner of the East Texas Bible Belt. My own parents were religious outlaws, although in different ways and for wholly different reasons. My oil-worker daddy figured religion to be another rich man's trick to steal his wages. He swore never to set foot in church unless toted there in a box.

Mother sporadically showed spiritual leanings, but then only for the most unconventional sects. She flirted with yoga and theosophy. The Christian Science church she took me to a few times appealed to her in part because it demonized the medical profession, as she did. Otherwise, she preached against organized religion with all the ardor of a fire-and-brimstone evangelist. Her own strict Method-

18

ist upbringing had schooled her against premarital sex, a restriction that had led her to marry seven times—twice to my daddy, who was numbers five and seven.

The chaos these marriages wrought in my early life made me a wary child, scared of loss and inclined in most situations to presume the darkest possible outcome. Above all, I feared looking foolish. By the time I reached high school, my pose as world-weary realist certainly precluded my going to church. So I never walked on sacred ground except to marry or bury my beloveds. The pessimism I'd cultivated all my life as a hedge against disappointments had seemed clear-eyed and permanent, somehow woven into the very fabric of my skin. My son's hope challenged that view, maybe for the first time.

He stood before me, fiercely blue-eyed in his Power Ranger pajamas. Though his barely literate mind had gone unpreached to, he was professing a native belief in God, as if some circuit hardwired into his brain's pathways led him to stare out the window at the pale autumn sky and innately view that sky as some mask for heaven. I'd parted with my own hope so glibly. Dev's seemed dearer.

For his sake, I embarked on a journey of churches, not in God's name but in the name of love, out of some instinctual need to protect his belief that God existed. We spent two years at it. In that time, my motives underwent a radical and wholly unexpected transformation. The search I started for Dev ultimately became my own. But I'm getting ahead of myself.

In picking the first church (or mosque or zendo or temple; we weren't die-hard Christians, after all), I had to suspend all judgment. My disbelief proved so enormous that I had to abandon it utterly, approaching God as I'd approached dating after my divorce, when friends had lined up innumerable blind dates. So, too, with church. Anybody who'd take my son and me to a religious service could have us. Dogma didn't interest me. Neither did politics.

That first Sunday, I called a close friend who was active in the Episcopal Church. Dev's father had been confirmed in that faith; he'd also gone to an affiliated prep school but had never—in our ten years together anyway—bothered with services. Still, his history in that faith made it sound more palatable. Plus the 10:00 A.M. service my friend attended exactly matched our 9:00 A.M. decision to go.

It was a capital-*C* church, its gray stones like those of some horror-movie castle. It sat amid red maples at the intersection of two streets—one leading to the university where I teach, the other to a cinder-block housing project.

Dev bolted for the huge oak doors as soon as I killed the engine. His loafers slapped on the leaf-strewn walk. I'd never seen him actually wear that sport coat, a hand-me-down. With his green clip-on bow tie and wet-combed blond hair, he looked like a refugee from a 1950s wedding. Church seemed the perfect place for him to be loping to. Me, I was edgy. For no apparent reason, the whole enterprise made me watery inside.

In the foyer, I expected to find some *Ozzie and Harriet* episode in progress—the women in pillbox hats, white gloves, and pearlized ear bobs; the men in lizard-green jackets and hard-buffed wing tips; everybody held in that old fluorescent light the color of celery that makes white people look so seedy. But half this parish was black. And their clothes involved khaki and flannel, denim even. Even the ancient blue-haired ladies had pants on.

Organ music started in the sanctuary. The room Dev and I drifted into was vast and barnlike, with tall stained-glass windows on which saints I didn't know were doing saintly things I couldn't decipher. We stood and sat and prayed for more than an hour. People took turns talking at the granite altar, which sat dead center. I moved my lips to the hymns that Dev belted out in his brassy, tuneless soprano. Afterward, people ate pastries in the foyer. Kids streaked around. A few parents from my son's school walked over smiling. Strangers introduced themselves. Someone brought me coffee like I like.

This uninvited niceness made me uneasy. A memory flitted through my head to fuel the paranoia: an airport scene in which a Hare Krishna devotee had once given me an incense stick with a sweet bow, then pestered me for a "donation" all the way to the baggage claim. In short, I could view the Episcopal coffee only as some sneaky prelude to commerce.

Yet Dev's experience wholly opposed mine. When I half-jokingly asked him in the car whether God had been present in church, he cocked his head at me and winced, as if I'd missed the obvious. "Where were you?" he said.

My criteria in choosing a parish were at first entirely practical, without spiritual tint. We stopped going to the Episcopal church after a few months because I found the place too cold, not emotionally but physically. To heat that vaulted space would cost a fortune, I guess. Still, the scalding baths I took after services felt like penance.

Most of the subsequent places of worship got just one visit from us—the synagogues, for instance. The Hebrew that mesmerized me at the Conservative temple only frustrated Dev, who preferred the Reform service, which to me sounded—with its talk of Middle Eastern strife—too political. In truth, I now realize, I'd begun to yearn for some spiritual nurture from such visits, and politics seemed to undermine that. Dev and I both adored the Southern Baptist church, with its hand-clapping gospel choir and hugely active Sunday school. But its four-hour service was a bigger time investment than I cared to make each week.

Oddly, the two superliberal Protestant parishes, whose lack of dogma should have appealed most to me, instead put me off church entirely. The first one we visited—let's call it Church X—had a strangely sterile quality from the outset. For one thing, its Sunday school disbanded every summer, so few kids were in evidence when we visited in August. This kept Dev squirming while I fussed at him to sit still. The sermon, on justice toward one's fellows, had been so squeezed of reference to God or Jesus—perhaps in order to modernize the language or to free the parish from washed-out doctrine—that any sense of history was lost. The pastor asked for peace and gave thanks for plenty, yet showed not the faintest strain about the facts of war and rampant want. I asked the pastor if I hadn't missed something in his talk, a reference to evil. "We don't believe in evil," he said, smiling broadly. To my taste, it was like a Rotary Club meeting, where everybody had agreed on the agenda in advance and only waited for the chicken lunch to appear.

To Church Y I brought high hopes because so many of my friends from the university belonged. That sense of fellowship was new. Other places, we'd been virtual strangers. But whereas Church X had avoided all talk of God, Church Y saw gods everywhere, all more or less interchangeable. This ubiquity, in my view, made these "gods" no more potent than the rabbit's foot Dev carried for luck. This second church's spiritual dilettantism had a random quality; like the first church, it seemed without ritual, sadly untethered to any tradition.

We stopped going to church for a while after that. In eighteen months we'd failed to find a spiritual home, though Dev continued with evening prayers, a practice I came to envy. Here's one verbatim: "Thank you, God, for my pets and these warm covers." Listening to him, I began to hope that prayer might do for me what church couldn't—cultivate some internal sense of calm acceptance, a rightness between myself and the world. Left to improvise my own prayers, however, I tended to pitch my case to God like some broker peddling tax-deferred annuities. Unlike Dev, I lacked gratitude. My mind instead seized on whatever was broken or absent in my life—balding tires, ungraded papers, my mother's failing health. My comforts and good fortune never got a nod. Or so I began to notice.

I sought an unlikely Buddha (or rabbi or confessor, as you'll have it) for help with this. Jane works at a halfway house in Boston. Before she took up with God, she'd been a heroin addict. This led to a failed career holding up pharmaceutical warehouses. Ten years clean, she was possessed of that Roman quality the poet and monk Thomas Merton aspired to: *hilaritas*. She lit up any room she entered, but she was the least sentimental human I knew. Jail time had drained her of pathos. Yet I knew her faith in God was deep.

It was that faith I lacked, I told her. "Faith isn't a feeling," she said. "It's a set of actions. Get off your ass and pray every day. On your knees. Morning and night." She gave me a copy of the Saint Francis prayer: "Lord, make me an instrument of thy peace. Where there is hatred, let me sow love; where there is conflict, pardon. . . ." These sentiments were impossible to argue with. Still, I balked at kneeling. What kind of God required me to grovel that way? "You don't do it for God," she said.

A week later, a student invited me to a Zen meditation service designed to still a scampering mind like mine, and I went. Alone. The fact that I went without Dev, who couldn't endure a two-hour "sit," forced me to admit—for the first time, really—that I'd become a searcher in my own right.

My enemy in this search, however, was my own head. I'd begun to notice as I tried praying that my head prattled more or less constantly, and most of the urgent truths it issued were, in fact, solely made up by it. Mostly my head liked to warn me—volubly and in great detail—against plots and disasters it saw hurtling my way (that bruise is bone cancer; a late-night hang up on the phone is a mad stalker).

The Buddhists find in silence a cure for this. Their service starts with chanting the names of bodhisattvas in Sino-Japanese for five minutes or so. You could be saying jump-rope rhymes, the monk informed me before the service. The breathing of the chants, however, relaxes you into the posture you're asked to maintain for two hours. Supposedly, you were counting each breath up to ten, then starting over. Me, I rarely got to three before my head started planning new tax strategies and composing oratorios.

A few times I broke through into peace, which was wholly foreign. My head shut up for some minutes. I indeed felt "empty" then, but vastly so, as if some internal ocean powered my breathing and I merely surfed along without care. The process of sitting had thrown the random skittering of my mind into stark relief. I felt something akin to peace, which is why I practice meditation at home every day and go back to that zendo a few times each month.

But I still wanted a fellowship or set of beliefs to fill the emptiness that the Buddhist practice had started to carve out. And I wanted it to involve Dev. When friends active in a somewhat renegade Catholic church invited us to Mass, I said yes, but with trepidation. I'm emphatically pro-choice, for one thing, and canon law calls abortion a mortal sin. Also, the church hierarchy I'd known in the past was punishing, exclusive, doctrinaire—everything I wanted to avoid.

The feeling in this church, which I now attend regularly, counters all that. Toddlers zigzag down the aisles, and babies squeak and yell, which adds a comic element, a sign of life that opposes the sterility of many other parishes we passed through. One Sunday close to Halloween, kids costumed as various saints took turns at the altar, each telling a brief (and somewhat sanitized) story of a martyrdom. The tiny boy Saint George—visor askew, plastic breastplate listing—came last, announcing, "You can be a saint, too!" Which brought down the house.

A few Sundays, the ritual brought me to tears, the result of my own yearning for certainty, perhaps, or familiarity from childhood when neighbors would drag me to Mass. Much of Catholicism has changed since then, of course. Latin's gone. There's a regular gay-and-lesbian service. The priest also spoke of Jesus as a Jew whose teachings aligned with the Torah. Most surprising, though, was how laypeople—including women—had taken over his duties, handling all aspects of the service but the liturgy.

The Eucharist particularly moved me the time Dev illegally received it. While I was thumbing the missal, he got lured into the Communion line by his pal Osiris. Osiris beckoned, and Dev shot out of the pew, which horrified me. Surely someone would know Dev was unchristened and would pull him aside for a scolding. I leaned forward to pinch his sleeve. He jerked loose. The line edged forward a few notches. I hissed at him to sit down, and he ignored me. People turned my way with tolerant smiles. Once the line curved, I lost sight of both boys till they popped up near the altar.

Before the priest, Dev stood reed-slim and somber. His expression flooded me with sweetness. I thought how his ancestors on all sides had found comfort in this Eucharist, which is painfully actual once you think of it. The body of the god is taken into the human body to nourish the spirit; a wafer of light is laid on the very meat of the human tongue. Dev's mouth opened like a baby bird's to receive it.

Afterward, the boys plopped down beside me whispering, their hands busy before them. What obscene gestures, I wondered, were they practicing? But I craned over to catch them in the midst of that old hand game: "Here's the church. Here's the steeple. Open the door"—you wiggle your interlocked fingers at this point—"and see all the people." The game had been passed down for decades, no doubt, one kid teaching another how to bear long, adult-prescribed intervals when play was forbidden.

Here was a lineage I belonged to. Everybody did, really. That's how comfort is passed down, hand to hand. Then some window in my head flew open, and the light poured in: Church worked the same magic, or was supposed to.

While the priest spoke and responses were given, I began to feel myself as an animal herded among similar animals. Strangely, I thought of my uncle's cows, how during cold spells they huddled together for warmth. In order to speak the liturgical responses, I had to breathe in the same pattern as these other people did. Our bodies bent at the same angles to kneel. We had hair in most of the same places. At one point individuals in the pews took turns calling out their intentions, people for whom they wanted prayers said: "My son, whose tumor has metastasized"; "My mother, who suffers from Alzheimer's"; "The refugees from Bosnia and Rwanda." Here was the acknowledgment of suffering that I'd missed in the superliberal parishes. Here was a place to give voice to your worst fears among others likewise scared.

Is this a conversion story for me? I don't know. I've yet to take instruction or Communion in that church, but Dev and I go most Sundays. The Buddhist meditations help to empty my head of its incessant worry; the Catholic Church somehow fills that emptiness with unexpected light. Kneeling in Mass, I partake of both human suffering and an ancient human hope. Something warm has started to unfold in my chest, I swear. It's still unfolding.

Grandfather's Heaven

My grandfather told me I had a choice.
Up or down, he said. Up or down.
He never mentioned east or west.

Grandpa stacked newspapers on his bed
and read them years after the news was relevant.
He even checked the weather reports.

Grandma was afraid of Grandpa
for some reason I never understood.
She tiptoed while he snored, rarely disagreed.

I liked Grandma because she gave me cookies
and let me listen to the ocean in her shell.
Grandma liked me even though my daddy was a Moslem.

I think Grandpa liked me too
though he wasn't sure what to do with it.
Just before he died, he wrote me a letter.

"I hear you're studying religion," he said.
"That's how people get confused.
Keep it simple. Down or up."

Claudia Sternbach

Cradled in the Hand of God

Little Bear needed a new outfit. My daughter Kira is ten years old and has been sleeping with Little Bear since she was an infant. My husband Michael and I bought Little Bear when I was hugely pregnant; he has lived his life with Kira, stuffed in backpacks for overnights, made up in the bed, causing an unexpected lump, tossed around in the washer and dryer after being thrown up on. His soft yellow fur is matted and worn. And Kira loves him.

For days Kira has been asking me to take her shopping for fabric and sewing supplies. She wants to make a nightshirt for Little Bear. And possibly some overalls. A shirt and shorts would be nice too. I mean you never know where Little Bear might want to go. Or where he'll be taken.

So here we were, on a Thursday afternoon in late October, surrounded by bolts of fabric. I wasn't wearing my glasses and the colors and patterns scrambled in the distance.

A plaid flannel was chosen for the nightshirt, tie-dyed cotton for overalls. And then my daughter headed to the far corner of the building. The blur of blacks and oranges soon emerged as witches and pumpkins. We were in the holiday section of the store. Up front were the Halloween bolts of material. To the right of them were the more traditional fall fabrics, appropriate for Thanksgiving tablecloths, place mats, napkins. Just beyond these were the

28

Christmas reds and greens. Even Chanukah was accounted for with some shimmery blue and silver star-covered fabric.

I love the holidays. All of them. Every year I listen to people complain as the stores fill up with holiday goods earlier and earlier. I try to join in. But my heart isn't in it. At the first sight of it all a small seed is planted in my chest. And it grows daily, filling me with a sense of wonder. As if I were a child again and anything were possible. Nothing bad could ever happen. Dreams would come true.

Even now, as early as it is, there is a large suitcase at home sitting on the floor by my desk. Warm winter sweaters are stacked inside. The garment bag is hung from the bedroom door. A list of things to remember is stuck to the refrigerator with a Donald Duck magnet. We are getting ready to make our annual trek back east for the beginning of the holiday season.

We make this trip every year to my husband's parents' house in New Jersey.

Once we arrive we gaze anxiously out the windows, watching for snow, while consuming large amounts of turkey on Thanksgiving.

We draw names to see who will be buying whom Chanukah gifts. The smell of potato latkes fills the kitchen. Children seem to occupy every corner of the house. A lot of catching up is done between family members who haven't seen each other for months. The candles are lit. The ancient prayers are said.

This year we are adding a Bar Mitzvah to our busy schedule. The first of many as my nieces and nephew start approaching young adulthood.

And then we return home for Christmas.

I grew up in a Lutheran household. From the moment the Thanksgiving turkey had been turned into soup, we started thinking about Christmas. It wasn't just the presents, it was about the winter light. How gentle it was, how it complemented the candles in the windows. The lights hung in the eaves. It was about the smells of baking coming from the neighbor's house, a sure sign of a cookie delivery to be made later in the day. It was about keeping secrets.

Every Christmas Eve my mother would set out our finest dresses and warmest coats and coax us to midnight services at church. I remember being given a candle to hold. A cardboard collar at its base to catch the dripping wax. Once everyone in the congregation had theirs, the lights would be turned off and Christmas carols would be sung in golden splendor. "O Come, All Ye Faithful," "Holy Night." I recall the sleepy ride home, warmed not only by the heater in our old Chevy but by some unnamed feeling inside.

And the magic didn't end with childhood.

The first year Michael and I were married, we stayed at his parents' house longer than we had anticipated. We stayed through Christmas.

I really thought it would be no big deal. I had celebrated Christmas for over thirty years; skipping a year wouldn't be a problem. After all, Michael had never celebrated Christmas, and it hadn't hurt him.

So I thought I'd be fine, really.

And then Christmas Eve arrived. Michael and I met some friends and went to a movie. About midnight I remember standing out in the theater parking lot, looking up at the sky. The feel of snow was in the air. No stars to be found. Just the hint of a moon. And something was missing for me.

We piled into the car and turned on the heater. Halfway down the block, Michael slowed the car. Turning into another parking lot, he parked next to a high cyclone fence. A few end-of-the-season Christmas trees were leaning against the wire mesh.

He didn't even turn off the engine, just set the brake and

got out of the car. There was still an attendant on duty. Michael slipped him a few dollars and came back to the car with a tiny evergreen, maybe two feet tall.

He put it in the trunk.

"My parents have never had a Christmas tree in the house before," he told me. "Better start small."

I hoped that they didn't hear us as we crept quietly up the stairs to Michael's old room. I cleared a place on the dresser and Michael set the tree on top, right where I could see it first thing in the morning. Until that moment I hadn't realized how much celebrating Christmas meant to me. Traditions are difficult to give up.

But what would Michael's parents thing of it all? Not only was their newest daughter-in-law not Jewish, she also seems to have come with a tree.

I curled up next to Michael and fell asleep in the evergreen-scented room.

The next morning we woke up early, trying to think of a way to explain our actions to Michael's mom and dad. The sun was shining through the blinds on the window, making golden strips of light dance among the branches of the tree, picking up the blue sheen on the ribbon wrapped around the narrow white box under the tree.

Santa, it seemed, had actually stopped by.

Attached to the ribbon was a tag. Written on the tag, in my mother-in-law's handwriting, was "Merry Christmas, love Mom and Dad."

Last year, two days before Christmas, I was diagnosed with breast cancer.

One week before Christmas, after returning from dinner at my sister's house, I found a lump in my right breast. Michael and I were stretched out in bed watching a Woody Allen movie. I was doing one of those sort of absentminded kind of breast exams when I felt something unusual. I tend to get lumps, but right away I knew this one was different. I asked Michael to feel it. All he could really do was confirm that it was there. I made a mental note to call my doctor in the morning.

Expecting to be told it was nothing, I took Kira with me. No big deal, I told her. We'll just be a few minutes.

I was wrong. By the time I had been sent for a mammogram and an ultrasound, I knew I was in trouble. Or at least this wasn't going to be fixed today. I called a friend and had her come and pick Kira up and take her home.

That was on a Monday.

Tuesday I was in surgery having the lump removed. That night I sat on my front porch swing as Christmas carolers sang under the moonlit winter sky. I wrapped myself in one of my grandmother's old quilts. I still felt safe. Christmas was coming. My friends were here. Everything would be all right. The doctor would call with the results.

Wednesday I sat by the phone.

Thursday I waited.

Friday the results were in.

As I sat on the couch and watched Kira and her friend Erica practicing "cat's cradle," I held the phone to my ear and listened to my doctor tell me I had cancer.

As he explained what had to be done next, I gazed at the large evergreen standing against the living room wall. Well-wrapped packages were stashed underneath, waiting to be ripped into. Handmade ornaments nestled with store-bought among the branches. The angel that no one but me likes perched where she has for twelve years, right on top.

And the tendons in my throat tightened as I tried not to cry.

Sitting my daughter down to tell her I had cancer was unbearable. In the glow of Christmas tree lights it became obscene.

We have a small nativity scene that is kept on the coffee table during the Christmas season. It is carved out of stone. The pieces are polished smooth. I picked up the baby Jesus and rotated it in the palm of my hand as I spoke, cradling Him. I told her that no matter what, everything would be all right. I had to tell her that. I had to calm her fears. I am the mother. She is the child.

But did I believe what I was saying?

Everything began to move very quickly. Decisions had to be made. Appointments were set up with unfamiliar doctors, long lists of words were added to my vocabulary. I took notes. Looked things up when I got home.

Every evening the phone rang and rang. I found myself repeating the story again and again. Answering the same questions over and over. I became accustomed to wandering the house in the middle of the night, rooms lit only by the rising moon.

And when I did sleep, I woke tangled in the sheets, exhausted by my dreams.

The first few days seemed to fly by. We made it through the holidays. I wanted everything to be as normal as possible. I wanted to prove to Kira, to Michael, to myself, that a woman with cancer could still hang Christmas stockings. Attend parties. Not miss a beat.

Then my second surgery was booked.

Christmas was over. The weather was rainy. Needles were dropping off the tree and being ground into the carpet. There were no packages left to open. No holiday surprises to look forward to. No more distractions. Once the tree was hauled out into the backyard, the house, which should have seemed empty, didn't. Cancer had moved in and we now felt its gray clammy presence in every room.

The day before my second surgery, Kira asked me if I was going to die.

She sat with me on the couch as we watched the rain in the backyard beating down on the now dead Christmas tree. Both of us were nestled under one of my favorite old quilts.

I told her that I didn't think so. But that I couldn't know for sure.

If I did die, she wanted to know, did I think I would go to heaven? Did I believe there was such a place?

I had to think. I didn't want to give her some pat answer, some quick fix.

What did I really believe?

I shifted my weight and put my left arm around her. Under the blanket, our legs twisted around each other.

I do believe in heaven, I told her. But I don't think of it as a place. I think it is everywhere around us. Heaven, to me, is being with you. With your dad. With friends and family whom you love.

As I sat there, I began to feel calm. This calmness spread over me like a second blanket.

I had been too busy to stop and think about what I believed. But now, with Kira asking the questions, I was beginning to sort it out.

Even if I die, I told her, I'll still be here.

As I spoke these words, I felt such a certainty. For me, this was the truth. My physical self might break down. But what makes me, me, will go on. I am a spiritual being, living in a less than perfect human body. But when my body is finished, I won't be.

I swear, I told her, even if you can't see me, I will kiss you every night. I will be with you in the yard at school. I will be in the car with you as you learn to drive. When you fall in love, I'll be there. I will know my grandchildren. And when your time is finished here, I'll take your hand and guide you to me. And we will go on together.

And as I told her this, I found I believed it completely.

I sailed through my next surgery. My lymph nodes were clear. I went through two months of radiation therapy. I am doing everything I am told to do by my doctors. I am not ready to die.

The holidays are approaching.

As Kira and I stood in the fabric store, surrounded by

bolts of brightly colored fabrics, I wondered what this Christmas would hold for us. As the first anniversary of my cancer diagnosis approaches, I can't help feeling frightened.

So there we were, our arms loaded down with fabric and trims. I gazed at the bolts of holiday prints. I tried to envision new pillows for the couch. Or a tablecloth for the dining room table.

As we left the store I could feel tears forming. Kira took my hand and our fingers linked. The late afternoon sun was warm on my back.

After arriving home, we stacked our bundles on the dining room table. I stood there looking around our living room. Our menorah is up on the shelf, waiting to be lit. The desk in the corner will have to be moved to make room for the Christmas tree. Our Chanukah gifts still need to be wrapped. My daughter has a new dress for her cousin's Bar Mitzvah. It's hanging on the door. Her Hebrew school homework sits on the table. We have joined the temple and she too has started that long journey toward her own Bat Mitzvah. And it all works for us. The warmth I feel while watching my daughter light the candles of the menorah and sing the prayers is the same as when I was a child lighting my own candles in our small Lutheran church.

I realize that cancer has given me something. It has sharpened my recollection of holidays past. It has removed the gauzy haze that surrounded those long-ago winter days. It has shown me the beauty that has been my life. And it isn't over. I get more.

The late afternoon sun is shining through the kitchen window. Dust is dancing on the rays. I decide to head down to the beach for an end-of-the-season swim. Kira's content to stay behind, fabric unfolded on the floor in front of her. In her mind, the nightshirt for Little Bear is already taking shape.

I know the beach will be almost empty. I park in the shade of the eucalyptus trees. The woodsy smell mingles with the sting of the salt air. Heading down the stairs to the beach, I notice dots of color on the sand. Umbrellas, towels, children in pink and yellow. Blue and green. I am not the only fall swimmer.

Reaching the beach, I leave my towel and sweatshirt on the dry, warm sand, and kick off my sandals.

The water is cold as it hits my thighs. It laps over my stomach. My breasts. My toes curl around the pebbles that have settled on the bottom. I dive under and open my eyes. Dark green is all around me.

I swim out past the wave-break. Pelicans are circling overhead. Rolling over, I stretch out my arms and close my eyes. I am weightless. The sun makes a pattern of golden flecks on the back of my eyelids. I am rocking. Gently rocking.

For the moment, at peace.

Cradled in the hand of God.

Sarah Rabkin

Saltshakers and Parachutes

> Responsible work is an embodiment of love, and love is the only discipline that . . . makes the mind whole and constant for a lifetime of effort.
>
> —THEODORE ROSZAK

> Ask yourself, and yourself alone, one question. Does this path have a heart? If it does, the path is good; if it doesn't, the path is of no use.
>
> —CARLOS CASTANEDA

My friend Jenny Keller, who teaches natural science illustration at the University of California at Santa Cruz, often leads her classes on field-sketching trips to the Monterey Bay Aquarium. On one trip a few years ago, after the hour-long drive down the coast from Santa Cruz, the students dispersed as usual to draw the bright life in the pools and tanks, while Jenny detoured to the aquarium café to set up makeshift office hours. As she sat down at a table, her gaze lit on the saltshaker. It was the ordinary restaurant variety, a clear jar with a perforated metal screw-cap. Sunlight poured through the café windows, glinting on the white grains encased in glass and steel. Jenny reached for her sketchbook.

She became so absorbed in her work that she barely noticed the student who stopped by her table to stare. "Why are you drawing a saltshaker?" he asked. Jenny guessed what he was thinking: why would she choose a mass-produced object, just like dozens she could have found a few blocks from home? After all, the class had traveled fifty miles to sketch the neon-hued sea slugs, the shorebirds scuttling over sand, the levitating nautiluses in their painted shells. But none of that mattered to Jenny at the moment. The saltshaker had called out to her, that particular saltshaker in that specific shaft of light, and no other drawing she might have attempted just then could have proved more fruitful.

In our conversations now, Jenny and I often return to the saltshaker story. It has become a touchstone for us, a shorthand code for the way she and I tend to approach watershed decisions. When one or the other of us finds herself at a crossroads, torn about which way to go, we listen for the voice that guided Jenny that day in the aquarium. Often difficult to hear, even harder to heed, this is the voice of our deepest insight. It can help guide us to good work, turning our gaze toward beams of light that illuminate our calling—beams that sometimes shine from unexpected sources. Yet in order to attend to this voice, we often have to defy others' assumptions, and sometimes our own.

Buddhists talk about the practice of "right livelihood," by which they mean, among other things, living mindfully, doing work that serves the world and causes no harm. Since I am not very familiar with Buddhist thought, I don't presume to understand or embrace the concept of right livelihood in all its subtlety. But I like the term, and in my mind I have respectfully extended it to apply to my own quest for what I might call a sacred vocation.

In this spirit, I take "right livelihood" to imply not an injunction against some corollary "wrong" way of life, but rather encouragement to cultivate spiritually satisfying work that arises out of passion, offers ample space to learn and grow, serves others, and suits a person's unique nature. I can think of few things that matter more. A girl-friend of mine used to say that the two keys to happiness were True Love and High Adventure. Add right livelihood, and you'd have a powerful recipe for a joyful life. Sadly, many people are so tied up in the struggle for a mere living that this ideal may seem a luxury impossibly out of reach. But in a truly sound society, everyone would feel entitled to genuinely useful, gratifying work. We all need the experience of giving our best energies to the world, just as acutely as we need freedom, kindness, and love.

Some gifted souls seem to slide effortlessly at an early age into their unique calling, into the passions and purposes of a lifetime. I turn wistful when I meet or read about such people: the professional naturalist who terrorized his parents with his bedroom bug collection when he was three; the prolific writer who drafted her first novel at twelve. I envy Jenny, who grew up with an artist mother, grandmother, and sister, and who can't remember a time when she didn't draw.

My path has been more circuitous. No shining highway ever seemed to rise up before me. Instead, as my mother once pointed out after observing my meanderings from environmental advocacy to high school science teaching to medical reporting, I have "made myself up"—an enterprise that has its joys and its drawbacks. I take comfort in the wisdom of songwriter Kate Wolf: "The shortest road ain't always the best," she sang; "sometime, let a back road take you home." Along my personal back roads, I have learned a valuable lesson or two: for example, that careful analysis and cogitation only get one so far in matters of right livelihood. Faced with a difficult decision about the next step in my work life, I have always, ultimately, listened to the saltshaker voice. To put it another way, I have followed my heart. And while I have grieved the losses incurred in many of those heartfelt decisions, I have never regretted a one.

But what does it really mean, to "follow your heart"? For those of us who seem destined to struggle rather than soar into a life of good work, what useful truths can we discern beneath the surface of that facile phrase? And as women who seek to give the best of ourselves to a world that we both lament and love, what obstacles are we likely to meet along the path? One way to learn more is to share the stories of our diverse journeys. In hopes of feeding the greater lake of our collective wisdom, I offer the following tale from the wellspring of my own quest.

Several summers ago, I read Barbara Kingsolver's novel *Animal Dreams*. Like countless other readers, I was bowled over by this story of a search for joy and meaning in a difficult world. I recommended it to anyone who would listen. But even as I heard myself exclaiming that this was the most life-affirming novel I had encountered in years, I felt gnawing at me a hollow, troubled ache.

The following autumn, I attended a writers' workshop in southern Utah, where I studied with desert ethnobiologist Gary Nabhan. On the first night of the workshop, three dozen of us gathered after dinner in the cozy lodge at Pack Creek Ranch to hear the faculty introduce themselves. A litter of half-wild ranch kittens played just outside the window in the chilly fall dusk; inside the living room, bathed in warm lampglow, we sat nursing hot mugs of coffee and cocoa. When Gary spoke, he summed up his purpose as scientist, activist, and writer in a single sentence that burned itself into my neurons. ''I try to help people cultivate sustainable relationships with the land,'' he said, ''in the places where we work and live; in the places that we love.''

His words broke through the vague unease that had haunted me ever since I had read *Animal Dreams*. Sitting there in the crowded lodge, tears edging down my face, I began to understand why the novel had upset me so. The quest of Kingsolver's heroine, it seemed to me, was to find her proper home: not only geographically but emotionally, culturally, politically, spiritually. Codi Noline dared to look for True Love, High Adventure, *and* Right Livelihood, all in one place—Grace, Arizona, the home of her childhood. And even though things only came together for Codi at the eleventh hour, she never settled along the way for anything less than a true homecoming.

This, I realized, was not my story. I had, in fact, settled. My teaching job and freelance writing brought me stimulation and some sense of usefulness; the Santa Cruz landscape embraced me; my circle of friends nourished me. And yet that evening at Pack Creek, my heavy heart forced me to admit that I had given up on something essential.

As a teenager, despite the haziness of my vocational vision, I had imagined that the work I eventually found would help repair the heartbreaking rifts I saw everywhere around me: among people; between people and the sacred places we were destroying. I had harbored vague yet sincere dreams of helping save my beloved coastal California homeland from the forces that were tearing it apart. But as an adult, sampling various disciplines and mastering none, I seemed to be skirting the edges of that adolescent hope. *Animal Dreams* had awakened me to a sobering truth: out of a lack of faith in myself, I had abandoned my own tentative vision of a deeply purposeful life. Now here was Gary, a great and brilliant soul, who not only dreamed his vision but lived it. My admiration was matched by a fierce yearning to do the same.

During the course of the four-day writing workshop, I reached a decision. Whatever it took, I would arrange for time off from my job, find the money to go back to school, and learn the naturalist's skills that would help me to become an effective champion of the lands I loved.

On my last night in Utah, I stayed at the home of an acquaintance in Moab. Casting about the living room for something to read before I dozed off on her sofa bed, I found a small, spiral-bound collection of quotations published by the Hurricane Island Outward Bound School. Penciled onto the flyleaf was a quotation from *Animal Dreams:* "The very least you can do in your life," it said, "is to figure out what you hope for. And then the most you can do is live inside that hope. Not admire it from a distance but live right in it, under its roof." This time,

Kingsolver's words brought solace in place of despair. With tenuous faith but mounting determination, I found myself peering down the road toward the house of my hope, making plans to move in.

A year and a half later, I stood in an April snowstorm in Vermont, gazing toward New York State across twelve frozen miles of Lake Champlain. I had joined several graduate students on a birding trip. This was part of my three-day interview for a master's degree program for field naturalists, the most alluring option my search had turned up. Two years of intensive classroom work, interspersed with frequent day trips, followed by long weeks of field time in New England, Alaska, Costa Rica—a dream come true. The program accepted only five new students each year, providing full scholarships and stipends. The aim was to teach people to be old-fashioned naturalists with contemporary knowledge—latter-day John Muir types—who could look at a landscape and understand the forces and interactions that had created it. The program's faculty intended their graduates to interpret the land for the benefit of its human inhabitants, to midwife sustainable relationships between the two.

The school accepted me; I was ecstatic. By late spring, I was on my way, mentally, to Burlington, Vermont. I sent notices for a friend to post in the local food co-op, advertising for a place to live. I heard from an art professor who was interested in sharing her home with me. She lived in a two-bedroom house with a garden on an island on the lake, a twenty-minutes drive from campus. We hit it off over the phone. I would live with her in the fall, and when she went on sabbatical in the spring, I would have the house to myself for the same low rent. In my mid-thirties, I hoped a real home with another grown-up might offset the jarring transition from professional life to the potentially infantilizing role of graduate student. A small house in the country with another woman and lots of privacy seemed exactly right.

But when I called four or five future teachers and senior classmates with this news, they were skeptical. Not a good idea, they warned. Forget the house on the island. You will be so busy in this program, you will want an apartment next door to campus, where you can crash for the odd twenty minutes between commitments. You will be heading into the field at six in the morning, back in the late afternoon for classes, up late for evening lectures, library work, paper writing, number crunching. You will be lucky to get a decent night's sleep, to remember to eat, to find time for anything other than schoolwork. And if you really care about having a garden, this is probably not the right program for you.

One student whom I especially liked poured out her frustration over the phone. Describing a typical field trip, she said, "There we'd be on the shoulder of a mountain on a gorgeous New England fall day, the air crisp and the trees aflame with color—and we'd be totally stressing ourselves out. We'd be so hurried and uptight about collecting our data, doing it right, making sense out of it, that it seemed to me we would forget what had brought us into the field in the first place. I got branded as the token touchy-feely flake because I was always the one to ask, 'Doesn't anybody want to stop for fifteen minutes and just see where we are on this mountain?' Nobody seemed to get what I was talking about."

As soon as I hung up, I burst into tears. To stop and see where we were on the mountain was what I wanted more than anything else. For all its gifts, this graduate program suddenly seemed to have come at the wrong time in my life. Certainly it could teach me a great deal, and much that I wanted desperately to learn. Yet I balked at the hoops I would have to jump through on the way. I was willing to work hard, but I didn't have it in me to turn myself into a caffeinated wreck or repress my aesthetic responses to landscape, in order to become a better naturalist.

Turning down this opportunity seemed an enormous risk: in doing so, I might make the mistake of a lifetime. When I sought help with my dilemma from friends and colleagues, some reinforced my fears, responding as if I had announced my intention to draw a saltshaker at the aquarium. They reminded me of the practical benefits of a master's degree and urged me to put up with the program's frenetic demands for two years in order to reap its rich benefits. Although their advice made logical sense, it failed to pacify my troubled spirit.

When resolution finally dawned, it began with a series of dreams about a female mountain lion. This mama cat appeared to me on several nights, emanating wisdom and strength. In each dream, she seemed to tell me that I should trust my own instincts. A month later, still wrestling with my decision, I was back in Utah—this time to teach a writing-and-drawing workshop with Jenny. Perusing the bookshelves at the field school sponsoring our class, I picked up a book of Native American wisdom about animal totems. I flipped through it and found the following passage: "If Mountain Lion has come to you in dreams, it is a time to stand on your convictions and lead yourself where your heart takes you."

I returned to California and withdrew from the graduate program. I chose instead to take an independent year, live off my savings and income from freelance writing, and explore my own home territory with my journal. I walked around my neighborhood, took note of what lived and grew there, watched otters play and pelicans dive in the nearby harbor, attended to subtle changes in the seasons and in my own state of mind. I wrote nearly every day. I traveled and taught outdoor-writing workshops. I took a sketching class from Jenny and learned to make visual as well as verbal records of my experiences in the field. In this fashion, I did acquire a bit of natural history knowledge:

not through disciplined or systematic study, but by observing closely and teaching myself to ask questions about
what I noticed.

*   *   *

Did I make the better choice? On the one hand, I can't honestly say that I have fully resolved the longings that
emerged at the Pack Creek writing workshop. I still hope
to tap my own capacities more deeply than I have managed to do so far. But on the other hand, there is great
power in having followed my inner compass. While I
grieved over what I gave up in turning down the graduate
program, I honestly do not regret the decision. I no longer
suffer nearly as much as I once did from a sense of inadequacy, of not being or doing enough. I felt increasingly expansive and joyful over the course of my independent year.
Somehow, even though I haven't become the skilled naturalist I so hoped to be by now, I do feel that my work is
edging closer to fulfilling the longings that surfaced at Pack
Creek.

In the years since the decision, I have begun to see with
more forgiving eyes the crazy quilt of abilities that make
up my vocational history. I have noticed that in comparing
my peripatetic work life to the careers of admired colleagues and mentors, I usually find it far easier to discern
an essential pattern and purpose in their endeavors than in
my own. Yet perhaps I don't truly lack focus; maybe I simply find it more difficult to recognize the patterns that
emerge in my own unfolding life.

Can I say that I now can give more to the world because
of my soul-searching year—my year "on," as I came to
call it? I don't know for certain. But I am soothed by Mary
Oliver's poem "Wild Geese," in which she writes that "you
do not have to be good. . . . You only have to let the soft
animal of your body love what it loves." Perhaps, for reasonably compassionate people, to do what we love most *is*
to do well by the world. Maybe it helps not to worry so

much about whether we are doing the exact right thing, the best most responsible most impressive thing, and instead to trust more that if we are doing the joyful thing, we will land right.

I don't mean we should sell ourselves short, should be cavalier about our potential or our responsibilities. But I do think that sometimes, misled by self-critical and self-punishing voices from difficult childhoods and a harsh world, we may misconstrue our calling. In thinking we need to Change the World, we may miss opportunities to perform the small yet profound acts of which we are capable.

This is not as easy as it sounds. In particular, I believe that the effort to create a sacred vocation involves a special edge, a unique element of challenge, for women. Certainly, men in this society have their own struggles in the search for meaningful work—struggles rooted in society's expectation that men should equip themselves to act as providers before considering their own creative passions. Yet the accomplished men I admire—at least those who grew up with some resources and encouragement—seem nevertheless to proceed from a strong sense of entitlement to right livelihood. They tend to plunge in with relatively little ambivalence, trusting their enthusiasms. On the other hand, many women I know—including those who are unquestionably talented and seem self-assured at first glance—battle an insidious lack of confidence in their own talents and inclinations.

Perhaps this is partly because women have taken to heart a set of cultural messages about the prime importance of winning and bestowing love, which we may have been misled to think means putting others' comfort before our own creative drives. For women like me, who have been privileged to grow up in loving, middle-class families and to receive university educations, these voices are oddly mingled with encouragement to do well and make a difference in the world of work. The result, when we set out to do our work, is a push-me-pull-you tussle between accel-

erator and brake, and an attenuated trust in our own instincts.

Even as I write this essay, for example, I hear an imagined reader dismissing it as self-indulgent, irrelevant, bor-
ing. Why do I waste column inches agonizing on paper,
nags this critical voice inside me, when I could and should
just be *out* there, like dozens of male scientist-writers,
doing the work, writing about What Matters, saving the
world?

But for me, this *is* the work, even if it's only a saltshaker. If it calls, there's something in it of value that I
must attend to. As a writer, I have to remind myself of
this. I keep a scrap from Annie Dillard's *The Writing Life*
plastered to the wall beside my desk: "Why do you never
find anything written about that idiosyncratic thought
you avert to, about your fascination with something no
one else understands? Because it is up to you." If self-doubt
is part of my internal landscape, then rather than despairing over comparisons with others and inwardly competing
with their accomplishments, I must acknowledge my particular struggle, use it, tell its stories—even as I attempt to
move through and past my limitations. I have to hope
that, rendered skillfully, honest words about my own
hard-won lessons constitute not solipsism, but an offering
that may benefit somebody else.

It is important to remember, too, that in the midst
of our striving, we cannot ever fully know the impact
of our acts on those around us. I have a Yosemite ranger-
naturalist friend, Ginger, who leads snowshoe walks at
Badger Pass each winter and works in Tuolumne Meadows
in the summer. One summer season, jogging out of uniform on her afternoon off, she heard someone call her
name and turned to see a woman she didn't recognize. It
turned out that this woman had participated in one of Ginger's snowshoe walks several years earlier. To Ginger's
utter surprise, the woman recognized her without any difficulty, and insisted on thanking her for the long-ago walk.

"I was never a very outdoorsy person," said the woman. "I was always kind of scared of nature. When you were introducing that snowshoe walk near the Badger Pass lodge, it started to snow. I watched the flakes begin to accumulate on your Smokey-the-Bear hat, and I thought for sure you were going to cancel the walk. I was amazed when you seemed to think nothing of the weather, and turned to lead us off into the woods. That moment changed me somehow. I realized, watching you take that snowstorm completely in stride, even enjoy it, that maybe I didn't have to be so afraid."

All Ginger had done was to be herself and do her job, yet that alone had provided an epiphany for someone. At the time, Ginger had no idea of her effect—just as Gary couldn't have known how his public words would serve as the catalyst for a change in my life, and Barbara Kingsolver couldn't have realized that her novel would help push this particular reader out of a period of quiet desperation. Ginger's story reminds me that we often serve others well simply by doing our loving best in any given moment.

Finding Castaneda's path with "heart" is both a solitary and a social process. As he says, you do ultimately have to ask "yourself, and yourself alone," which way to go. But that's not the whole story, for we often play an essential role in each other's journeys. I cannot recall any of the watershed decisions in my life without remembering the books that inspired me, the friends and colleagues who helped by listening, reflecting me back to myself, offering their wisdom, and showing me their trust in my choices. Jenny and I arrived at the notion of the saltshaker voice together, and together we reinforce each other's faith in it, especially when following it means swimming upstream.

Moreover, sacred vocation itself depends upon the existence of a community. Even the maverick artists among us create meaningful work in a social context. I remember the parachute we played with in sixth-grade gym class. The P.E. and dance teacher helped us spread the white nylon over the blond wood floor of our high-ceilinged auditorium, then had us squat around it—a couple of dozen kids spaced evenly in a circle, each holding the edge of that great gossamer cloth. At her signal, we'd rise quickly to stand, clutching the edge of the chute in our hands while we raised our arms in unison. The air would rush in underneath and the chute would billow up over our heads, an exultant dome. Briefly it seemed that the upward momentum would continue pulling the chute toward the ceiling, taking us with it. Then the tension on our upstretched arms would ease, the chute would gradually collapse and float to the floor, and we would stoop to begin again.

My young classmates and I at Columbus School relied on a circle of comrades in order to give shape to our parachute. We were rooted in place, yet in motion together. In order to take flight, a life of good work requires not only the air to buoy it but the hands to hold it in place. "No strings, no flight," mused the writer William Least Heat Moon as he passed a couple of boys flying kites along one of the blue highways of North America. Making ourselves up requires a skillful combination of independence and connection.

The other day I watched my artist friend Jenny teach my writing students. They were studying the theory and practice of keeping journals, and I had invited her to show them how writing complements the drawings in her own stunningly beautiful notebooks. As I observed Jenny's animated body language and listened to her lively voice, I sensed the care and love that she had invested in preparing this class. I saw my students enthralled. In the light shining from Jenny's eyes, I picked up reflections from the aquarium saltshaker of several years ago. I knew that Jenny has become a gifted teacher not so much by straining outward to attain what she thinks she ought to be, but by following her heart: by keeping her eyes open while tapping into the world of wisdom and vision that is already within her. In my own quest for a life of good work, I return to this lesson again and again.

Judith Harris

Wherever in the Language of Jewish Women a Garden Grows

It is no superstition that a woman has many lives. For a woman has always lived by the moon, shuddering and waning. I am a Jew, and a woman who wants to write about Jewish women, a paradox. Opening to the bold-faced illustrations in my Hebrew book, as a child, I recall myself there, floating above the *alephs* and *hays*, barefoot and veiled, tied to a mother or daughter, carrying a basket of berries or figs in a huddled cadre of goats. Or I am that girl in a steamy stock car, in 1944, shoved in a corner, hiccuping the way hounds do before dawn, watching women with eyes like burst corks beating their breasts and pulling out their hair. A hand comes in through the peephole, a small rectangle barred for breath like a dogcatcher's wagon, or priest's confession box. What wild hair, yellow and red and black and gray, in a heap of smoke and twilight, flickering in the ashes of a woman's shining pride or single beauty. Although we ride standing up like cattle to the slaughter, we are not beasts, we are not.

Unable to sleep, I decide to read something short, something for pleasure, and choose Singer's "Yentl" from the *Collected Works*. Tomorrow I teach my course in American literature. The students will rattle their tissue-thin pages penning little scrawls like chicken scratches on the anthology's page, numbered 1059. In sheepish orchestra some will stretch and yawn or look out the windows, having left their weighty books at home. At any prod of the wind, the venetian blinds will bang against the crank as if to challenge or applaud my points. Some of the students will be distracted by the banter and music on the fraternity lawn that faces my classroom. Only one or two students will answer the questions, and two or more will question those answers before our time is up. On my way home, in the world without language, without prescriptive morality or amplification, I will see trees shake off their leaves like a cat cleaning its fur. Ideas will be simple again.

Yentl did not want to be a woman because she could not study the Torah, so on Sabbath nights she transformed herself by dressing up in trousers, fringed ritual garment, and skullcap, and covering her hair. In a man's place, Yentl's soul thirsted for knowledge, but it was the weakness of her woman-side that brought her down. In the end, she is forced to wander alone, cast out like a traitor to *both* men and women. The Talmud states: *Women are temperamentally light-headed* (Shabbat 33b).

Singer wants us to know that the sexes are incompatible, and that the knowledge that Yentl gains as a male yeshiva student is wasted on the woman who becomes infatuated with the flesh. The impossibility of consummating such a love that Yentl has for Avigdor leads her to Hadassah, who is faithful, blind, and stupid. Hadassah is just another side of Yentl, a mirror grazing the real.

I do not blame Singer for making Yentl a villain, for poking fun at Hadassah's gullibility. Knowledge is not wisdom. To Singer, learned women are masquerading, and will abuse the best of what is offered to them, although they have lived as many lives as there are layers of skin. Now, with my thoughts, I walk through generations of women's gardens, some scanty, some rich, a ghost among ghosts.

Say I am wanting to be a scholar, a woman, who blindly digs *under* the words, looking for old roots to pull up like

potent radishes, something to hoard in the cellar. Say I am
again that Jew, at the foot of Sinai's mount, waiting for a
sign from man or God, or say I am a woman denied access
to the law, although I've been taught to obey. *Here is a
proposition:* If I am the one I have always been, inside the
seed of mother and grandmother and great-grandmother,
stirring the pot, plowing my body for the crop of sons,
then I don't need words but *things*—the barn, the garden
toppled with cabbages that loll slantwise like the globe, the
earth divided like so many puzzles.

Because these hours are mine while others are asleep in
the house, I try to imagine that I am the girl I once saw
years ago in an old sepia photograph framed in nickel silver, a girl in black stockings and high-button shoes, two
stiff braids, and a muslin smock, holding what appears to
have been a small violin. It is because of Singer that I am
retracing her footsteps. The year is 1899, the place is a village in the hills of a country that keeps changing its name
and its borders. Perhaps Austria, perhaps Poland, perhaps
Hungary. The photographer comes up from under his
black sorcerer's cape and smoke puffs with the shock of
the shutter.

Back in the small shack, I am hiding the sugar on the
top shelf of the pantry, avoiding the pond where women
wash their Sabbath cloths because it is yellowed with ty-
phoid. In the road, I am watching the grass widow kicked
by a soldier's boot, hurrying home to my mother who is
outside tossing kernels to the geese. It is the day before
Sabbath in the shtetl, and my mother has wrung the chick-
en's neck, plucking the wispy feathers and letting them
flutter over the floor like an angel's wings. She washes the
silver, polishes the candlesticks, takes a knife under my
nails. Twisted challah frowns black in the oven. Lighting
the candles, she spooks me. Her blood is magical but evil;
a woman's blood is different from a lamb's or cow's because it does not splatter or gush from the ax, but runs like
a tear.

I have been thinking about God again. I imagine him constantly watching over me and talk to Him whenever I think. My Sunday school teacher says God does not have a long beard, nor does He carry a staff. God is only mist, like the smoke that seems to rise from the tar wood path after a storm in the white summer.

I have studied over this, although studying is prohibited for girls, but in my own way I have searched in every cratered rock, every climbing tree, for proof of this God who enters sorrow like the throb of a frog. I think of God constantly, and sometimes curse Him, although I know it is a sin—He has not yet struck me down for it.

What do the men know as they unwind the Torah scroll the way we unwind our braids at night in secret? I have thought about the text, the holy tongues of men who lack any pleasure of harmony. Do they rise as we do, to the attics, and lower to the slops of the yards? What if each of our chores, our duties, was recorded like history? How many sentences we would have, how many conversations, writing over and over the walls with our lye sponges. Men walk home in their black hats, and supper becomes round with serving and passing and washing and drying and the moon is a full cup in the kitchen window, a fire by which we dip and light the stars.

A Jewish girl is not taught, but has stooped to clean the droppings of gold and black animals. At night, I read my body for the first letters of blood, monthly. And what is the female body inside but yeast, and trapped wind that mixes with the blizzards of flour and the milk? Inside my body is already a child, a name, a bubble, an egg, a crinkle in the well.

I take up Singer, and the little girl disappears in the funnel of lamplight, like the empty space inside the circle of a telescope, or a bolt of fabric. I'm an academic. In the smaller room, my own daughter dreams of trivial things like wearing a red satin dress to sleep. What will I tell her about where she comes from? Good or bad, she will see no open trunks of candlesticks nor sniff the odors of the strange cooking things. She won't have to try and decipher the irritability of Yiddish as a clan gathers for gin rummy with foreign currency. What I know is that my grandmother was once a chambermaid and her day was from spigot to spigot as if water were a single rope that wrapped from pot to bowl to trough, that spilled a little trail behind her.

Before she died, she opened her trunk and gave my mother the cinnamon-colored photograph edged and burnished under a dull silver frame, dated with a quill pen: 1899. "Here is the picture of your grandparents and your aunt and myself in the old country," she said. There, seated, was a hollow-eyed woman on a rickety chair, her hair covered by a kerchief. In her black lap, she held her hands over a book that appeared to be the Bible. Next to her, a man stood with an ill-fitting black jacket that was too short at the wrists, and tugged to button. Next to him, a fashionable young woman wore a hat and fur muff, her hair gathered in a Gibson bun and ringlets, as she clasped a straw suitcase. And next to her was the girl, the little girl in the muslin smock who dragged the small violin, the one who had entered my thoughts as I read "Yentl," the one that vanished as I turned the last page.

The photograph stands now in a hutch in my mother's bedroom. I remember that the backdrop was a painting of a Bavarian castle with a moat and fading rocky cliff. When I asked if the woman could read the book in her lap, or if the pretty aunt was boarding a train, or if the child could play, my mother explained that the objects in the picture were photographer's props, a part of the illusion. No one was really reading, or traveling in high boots or fake ermine, or owned a black supper jacket, or could play a violin that was broken and missing its strings.

My great-grandmother had already buried two stillborn infants when my grandmother was born. She paid a nun to perform an exorcism with a cross and water over the wailing baby girl to break the spell. It worked: She prospered, had sons, and thought God was now pleased. The girl was sent away to work in the hotel where convalescents came to bathe in salty springs. My grandmother is the little girl who stares straight ahead in the picture with her schoolroom costume and useless instrument.

To avoid an arranged marriage, my grandmother escaped to America and went to work. My grandfather chanted the Talmud, but could find no real labor that suited him—although he tried being a broom maker, a pelt tailor, a shoveler of coal. He was too dreamy and spoiled; he had not known the labor of chipping the ice that peeled away the reaps of the garden, and how to blend a few chives, a chicken wing, and a half potato into a supper that would last for a week.

This grandmother worked in a dress shop, beading material for bonnets and hats, trundling a pushcart. She was a gruff, unbearable woman, who grew fat under the whalebone ribs of her corset. At fourteen, my mother was sent to work sewing buttons on leather shoes, and all through high school she sat on a hard stool in the lunchroom, ringing the register, while the others balanced their liverwurst sandwiches and custards on their trays. She became a secretary/bookkeeper to help put her brothers through college and dropped out of school.

My parents did not carry with them the traditions and obligations of their parents, and we received little formal training in Judaism. In the 1950s, Jews were assimilating; we went to Hebrew school and to synagogue on high holidays. We didn't light Sabbath candles, but I said the "Sh'ma" each night, the way some count sheep. My parents put away their brittle prayerbooks and replaced them with authoritative titles on child rearing and modern Judaism. At school, I was excused, by note, from kneeling, or saying grace. While other children coiled ornaments around a real Christmas tree, I was given loose paper and

a pencil to draw a menorah crested by an exotic, six-point
star.

   Occasionally, one of my classmates would try to convert me in our finished basement, explaining all about the
crucifixes hanging in their living rooms. I hated to see the
excruciating pain on Christ's face—his porcelain, wooden,
or plastic arms and chest stabbed with tiny streaks of red
paint, like Maybelline polish, and think it was, as my
friend said, the Jews' fault. My mother sewed, and tried to
bake, and tried to carry out her duties as a Jewish wife and
mother, as she'd been taught to. But soon she went back
to work, taking the bus back and forth, even on Fridays
and after sunset.

I am thinking now of the women, the heroines of the Bible
we colored in Old Testament coloring books. Sarah, who
laughed out loud when the angels came to tell her she
would, at ninety, bear a son. She was baking when they
arrived, and probably offered them a roll or sweetcake. I
can see her rocking, her bones had already dried and shriveled, laughter splitting her sides, laughter breaking her in
two. Sarah is patience, piety. The rock of mother into
which the moss digs and grows, opening tiny thistles and
flowers. Rachel, the one who was kind at the well, the ewe,
the chasm in the earth, the veil. She is all heart, resonance.
Last, there is Ruth, who lay at the feet of Boaz, and who
followed Naomi and became her guardian. Ruth threshed
and bundled the wheat and carried it for the old woman,
who could walk only with a tremor and cane. Ruth is pro-
vision, fidelity. These are the women I remember even before Esther, crayoning their robes, and naked shoulders
and feet. I gave them their own alphabet of blue skies, a
punctuation of birds, lips the shade of persimmons.

When I was ten, I dreamt that God was a woman. She was
seated in a throne like Lincoln's memorial. Her hair was a
widow's peak and a bun at the back. Unlike the God I

knew, she spoke like any woman. I was a tiny mote at her thonged marble feet, a sightseer. Unlike the frozen God of Abraham or Moses, she made no commandments, injunctions, or demonstrations of wrath. Instead she *was* her throne, the stone, the tablet. A Jewish woman in this God's form has always been slate, the unspoken upon which the law is written, the signs of *what shalt not be*, the part of the hardest mountain that neither bleeds nor weeps. And she is not the thunderous word but the soul of the word, what is etched into the earth or rubbed into the scroll.

Meanwhile, the flowers grow taller like children. The minutes touch our faces. It is almost dawn, and I decide to make lists of things to do or get and of the things my daughter has asked for. She wants a Cinderella dress and glass slippers and beads and a fairy godmother she can call upon anytime for a whim. I remember my own Cinderella doll and twirling it like a baton on the long Passover trips we took to my grandparents' Brooklyn apartment. When I was seven, I practiced the Four Questions all the way from Washington to the Jersey Turnpike. My time as the youngest in company was short-lived. A boy cousin came, and then another, and finally a girl. My grandfather never acknowledged my sister and me at the long white-draped table—only the boys who sat closer, raising our suspicions when they recovered the *afikomen* each and every time.

I have already started to write. I use man's language, I have studied it, and spoken it, and written it for the acceptance of men. I have given it authority. I have read it in prose, in poetry, philosophy, and a little science. I have climbed down in the footsteps of women, dreading the height of the cliff. That is the secret: the secret in the book, the crack in the tablet, why the sky is shut, and the stars fade back like metal. As women and as Jews, we climb down, with our rough stones. Below, our shadows lie flat as the grave. And God, in whom we believe and do not believe, who would not abandon a fly, sleeps like a feather in His name.

Mythology

You read us the words
you have written about
Demeter, Hecate, Diana.
When we no longer want to listen
you say—
But your people have myths of their own.
Why don't you find them out?
Why don't you write them down?
Why don't you bring them
for us to read?

Yes, we know that
our great-great-grandmothers
remembered many truths.
We also know
how those ancestors were
separated and sold
severed by the middle passage
disease, death
and design
so no two
women who spoke the same language
came to the same place.

To talk in the old tongues
was forbidden.

To learn to write
forbidden.
To sing the old stories
forbidden,
forbidden even
to speak secrets in
the sacred voice of the drum.

We live out our lives
in languages with no names
for the Goddesses
of our great-grandmothers,
no characters in which to inscribe
their wisdom,
no verbs that encompass
their power,
no constructions that can contain
their rage.

Yes, we will find them out.
As we uncover and claim those words
we may never choose to write them down.
We will not be bringing them
to you.

Robin Podolsky

The Goddess Surfaces

I don't believe in a great plan at work in human affairs. I can't use a worldview that I'd be embarrassed to share with a nine-year-old burn survivor or a twenty-year-old single mother whose job just moved overseas.

I believe that the child had an accident she didn't deserve and the mother is paying the consequences of decisions not her own. I believe that while I'm not the dealer, I am responsible for how I play my hand. The notion that everything is happening exactly as it should strikes me as an insult to the punishing effort it costs too many decent people to survive. And the idea of the Divine as a conscious, omnipotent personality has always, given the state of things, been too terrifying to consider.

Nevertheless, I work with altars and ritual, marking desires and questions with candles, incense, flowers and oil. I attend synagogue. I've learned fragments of traditions, some that could reasonably be considered my birthright, some that come from times and places I've never seen. I've invented some practices and learned others from teachers and friends.

About six or seven years ago, I was suddenly beset, in an apartment where I'd always felt comfortable, by a persistent apprehension that I was not alone in rooms that were empty of other people. My body did all the things it does to warn me that I have company: my inner ear set up a jangle, my neck twitched, my heart revved up in my throat.

Theology aside, I always thought that the entire body of experience assigned to the area of "psychic phenomena" can't be all fantasy and hysteria. I also don't believe that, hypothesizing a field of psychic energy as real as electromagnetism, everything that runs around in such a medium is necessarily benevolent by my standards or moved by any set of purposes I could recognize. So the prospect of visitors from some unknown corner of reality—or from my own mind—made me nervous.

Eventually, I began to relax some inner muscle. And I started to have certain dreams. The dreams sometimes ended in a blood-red haze—one that persisted for a while after I woke up. (Yes, I consulted a therapist, hoping that she could tell me what was wrong with my mind—or my optic nerve. "Spirit guides come in colors," she said, not troubling to explain further.)

At the time, I was furtively contemptuous of feminists who prayed to "the Goddess," who was always presumed to personify the receptive, fecund, gentle, flowing, giving, nurturing side of things. She was linked with essentialized notions of gender that reflected political despair. There seemed to be little hope, in the Reagan years, of attaining quality child care or equal wages or of teaching heterosexual men to clean up whenever they mess up. In some feminist circles, the focus began to shift from leveling the playing field to garnering "respect" (not necessarily compensation) for "women's work"—i.e., emotional and physical housekeeping. Women, it seemed, would always be Demeter—compulsively offering a breast to the world— when they grew up; men would always want to rape Persephone, the eternal victim.

Then, one night, I went to hear the poet Judy Grahn read from her play *The Queen of Swords*.

"I of the snarled hair," Judy chanted, "the one earring/

the brassy metallic nail polish/I am your wild cherry sister. . . ." How weird. Judy was describing me, down to the red and black motif of my favorite costume, the one I was wearing that night. . . . No. Of course she wasn't. She was reading a poem about Erishkegal, Lady of the Great Below, the terrible mother of birth and death, translating into modern terms elements of description that originated in Sumeria more than five thousand years ago.

The Queen of Swords retells an epic quest, that of Erishkegal's sister, Inanna, Queen of Heaven and Earth, who descends to the underworld, which in Judy's play is a contemporary lesbian bar. Inanna, in ancient Sumeria, was the deity most active in human affairs: ruler of love and war, of the storehouse grain and of urban smithcraft, of poetry, of the erotic. Erishkegal (the play's saucy bartender) was an elemental power, the primal creative—and destructive—force through which Inanna can work.

The Queen of Heaven encounters seven gates to the underworld. At each, she must give up some symbol of her high station: her jewels of power, her clothes. Naked, she meets her sister, who reminds her that she entered the underworld uninvited of her own free will. Erishkegal flays Inanna until she drops, and hangs her body on a peg for three days to rot.

Then Erishkegal undergoes her own trial. She goes into labor and Inanna, the Queen of Heaven, is reborn to ascend to her proper realm. The world moves from winter to spring. When Inanna returns to her throne, she finds that her human consort, Demuzi, has usurped it. Remembering a promise to Erishkegal that she would send someone to the underworld in her place, Inanna casts down Demuzi for his presumption. When his sister, Geshtinanna, pleads for clemency, Inanna allows her to take Demuzi's place in the underworld for half of every year. Prior to the story of Persephone's rape and seasonal return was a story of female chivalry and willing sacrifice.

It's worth noting that Inanna has a sidekick, the butch

demi-Goddess Ninshuber, who, in another of the Sumerian myths, battles sea monsters and the like for her Lady's sake. Here, then, before Gilgamesh, the complex possibilities of the heroic persona are split between two females. Inanna's role is shamanic—she models an ordeal for humanity's benefit—while Ninshuber is a martial hero, the ideal warrior.

And between them, Inanna and Erishkegal personify an enormous range of human and divine attributes. Inanna stands for human enterprise: intellect, initiative, the transformation of the world through artifact (the sword *and* the plowshare)—and for the complexities of human desire and emotion as well. Erishkegal, despite evolutional and seasonal changes aboveground, remains what she has always been. Everything comes from her wet, bloody darkness, and everything will return to it. She is the abysmal heart of life's mysteries, the side of nature that is without pity. But she is also infinitely compassionate. She kills her children so that the next generation will have room to live.

This vision of the Goddess—one of the oldest ever written—electrified me. That one of the first complex urban civilizations had among its primary deities two female figures who were central, powerful and *complex*, a far cry from "fertility figures" and "flower spirits," gave the lie to those who would say that female equals "feminine" equals soft. Here, in Inanna's descent, was a quest story with a hero that did not exclude my identification. Here were images of the Divine that I could respect and, yes, worship.

It excited me also that I could connect such a vision to my own ethnic heritage. This was in the days when most women who referred to "the Goddess" tended to rely on Hellenic figures, such as Aphrodite and Athena. Some women were rediscovering the Old Religion of Western Europe, witchcraft or Wicca. While I have enormous respect for the craft, I could not embrace an identification with "women-centered" spirituality if it meant discarding my identification as a Jew. But Erishkegal and Inanna were born in the fertile crescent, the birthplace of Sarah, considered the mother of the Jewish people. It was a Semitic priestess, Enheduanna (the daughter, admittedly, of a very warlike king), who first had the hymns of Inanna put into writing—fierce hymns to a great and terrible judge, not unlike the Yahweh of later years, sexy hymns to an adored collective lover who survives in the Hebrew Bible as an abomination to whom the people kept returning. Before the ancient Hebrews became Israelites, they knew a spirituality that offered very different views of gender and sexuality from those that are dominant today.

Power, in this ancient story, is not "male-identified." Neither is it devoid of tenderness or carnality. Inanna wields power; Erishkegal *is* power. Yin and yang, butch and femme; these girls have it all.

During the night after I heard Judy read her play, I woke up with the red mist all around me, and I wasn't afraid anymore. My cat, who is sensitive to intrusion, was sleeping on my neck, happily sawing logs. In my dream, I'd been told, "The colors of the Goddess are red and black and white." I wondered about the white for a while (having just learned that Erishkegal's colors are red and black) and then forgot about it. Years later, I learned that, for Wiccans, the Goddess's colors are white, red and black for Maiden, Mother and Crone. (Inanna is also associated with white.)

I can't tell you how much I *wasn't* looking for experiences like these. To descend into belief—to narrow the immanent presence of everything in the world to a named personage, to impart Agency to the chaotic world of indifferent phenomena—had always seemed like an intellectual capitulation to psychological need. I prided myself on living ethically without the sop of a deity to reward me or to punish me if I screwed up.

But something was happening to me that I had no method of categorizing. I had not generated the Erishkegal myth out of my own subjectivity. So why was I modeling her attributes before I knew who she was? No, I don't believe myself to be the avatar of a goddess. But something in an ancient power, named by the ancestors of my own Jewish people before they left Mesopotamia for Canaan, speaks to much of what, by nature or nurture, I live by and respect.

It's easy to say that what we believe in is "real" for us. We're quite comfortable talking about metaphor and paradigm as social forces. But how can metaphors tap people who've never heard of them on the shoulder—in their dreams, for instance? There are webs of causality that we don't understand.

Soon after that vision, I lost my way. I didn't trust my dreams enough, or I didn't trust myself to work with them without a guide, and I trusted no one in my world to help me. Be careful—if you send those dreams away, they go. If you welcome them back, there's still hope. But, for me, it's never been that easy again. I remember those dreams with a sweet pang, like recalling a first love I never had the nerve to give my cherry to.

Meanwhile, like a lot of self-educated intellectuals of my generation, I was trying to see what could be salvaged from Marxism and existentialism. I couldn't accept a world where people who work hard all their lives are neither secure materially nor in control of the institutions that shape their situation, and I wanted to spend my life doing something about it. (I still do.) I believed, like the postwar existentialists did, that to find a moral authority outside of one universal Authority, one could look only to the shifting, unstable world of human consequence. (I still do.)

But modern Marxism just wasn't working out, to a great extent because Leninism, the only apparently effectual Marxist strain, had committed gross failures with regard to democracy. I had to admit that while many people's lives did seem to improve materially in countries that called themselves socialist, power was still concentrated in a few hands and the results were nothing I wanted to live with. (And the Scandinavian social democracies have immigration policies that would please Jesse Helms.) I had to admit that I am, after all, an American girl and I cede a lot of authority to the individual conscience.

Then along came deconstructionism to remind me of an insight that had led me to respect Marxism in the first place: the individual conscience is generated from transitory webs of social conditions and assumptions that we neither create nor control. Of course, as the existentialists remind us, that in no way obviates the individual's responsibility for the effects of any action or inaction one commits.

What a turmoil. The more it became clear to me that, in an increasingly out-of-control world, what I wanted at the very least was to be a good person, the less I understood about what such a thing might mean. The competitive, wasteful world of capitalism still made no sense to me, but what might replace it seemed less and less evident. The social movement to which I had devoted the first decade of my adulthood was in disarray. In addition, with the rediscovery of my individual conscience came the acknowledgment of huge, repressed individual ambitions.

Every idea I'd ever held was up for grabs. I needed a whole new intellectual and moral apparatus. And then, to top it all off, came this weird stuff that started with dreams and appeared to be leading me toward spiritual practices that, I had once thought, were silly, naïve and reeked of *bad faith*.

It finally occurred to me that I didn't know enough about anything to abandon any one of those investigations. So, several years ago, I decided to study Wicca. To work, with the utmost seriousness and respect, with people who deal in correspondences and relationships that no Western science has a vocabulary for. To spend at least a year and a day complying with the rituals and premises of an organized religion; moreover, a religion that tends toward pacifism, nurturing, ritual costume, arts and crafts, incantations, earthy images of the Mother and a fondness for agricultural metaphors—everything at which I'd turned up my pert little intellectual nose.

I have learned that there are reasons to take ritual seriously. And I have learned that while all paths *may* lead to the same source, the path itself—the journey's character—matters a lot.

Ancient words and gestures have weight, meaning and power, because when we perform them with care, we're linked to everyone who ever walked that path before us. Perhaps those rites which are performed often by large numbers of people with a shared purpose acquire a peculiar tang through the accretions of collective intentions and attitudes. Perhaps they become a kind of magic neuronic pathway, shunting practitioners along their course. When we enter those paths, we change them, just a little, and they change us.

When a witch invokes the power of "three times three" and says, "As I will it, so mote it be," she enters a world where the intention and spirit of her amplified desires are a force in her life and what she puts out will come back to her, three times over. That's why, contrary to stereotype, Wiccans rarely curse anyone or anything. When I see the meanness of a Jesse Helms or a Pat Buchanan, I'm careful not to put intent behind wishing them any specific ill—although often enough I find myself muttering, "May it all come back to you. All the harm you've ever done. Without exception. And soon." And then I wonder why luck becomes unforgiving of even my smallest failings, why the world doesn't seem to be cutting me any slack.

So I'm confronted with an interesting question. If a Goddess of my mothers can detach herself from the ecumenical dance of quantum connectedness and have actuality and personage, what about the God of my fathers?

*   *   *

Being a Jew used to be a cultural imperative only. Now I have to acknowledge that my love of books, and avid debate, the smart mouth that gets me in trouble, and my nagging need to repair the world amount to a spiritual condition.

There is a tradition of scholarship which is worship, a five-thousand-year-old evolving, breathing text that is my birthright. There are words of power that accompany that tradition. If I'm willing to study a Western European religion like Wicca, then what about the faith in which I grew up? Raphael Patai has suggested, after all, that Inanna survives in the Zohar as the Shekinah, the female aspect of the Divine. It's not always so easy to reconcile the Goddess with a jealous God. But what if we're talking about the variety of human metaphor for something so vast that all our names and pictures are incomplete?

On a more familiar hand, many people I respect believe that hunger for guaranteed meaning is the root of all evil and that "divine" inspiration has mostly served to put a gloss on acts of tyranny. That if we had to accept responsibility for our own behavior and acknowledge our true stake in the social choices we make, if we could learn to live with ambiguity and not knowing, the world would, paradoxically, be a safer place.

Actually, I believe that myself.

Can I simultaneously believe in randomness and that the meanings people give to those conventions we call self-evident (family, work, love, murder) are so violently disparate as to render universalism impossible—and that there are causal strands that extend to our species' beginnings and perhaps before?

Can I believe that gender, romantic love and social management of reproduction are human artifacts, specific to culture, time and place—and, simultaneously, claim queer ancestry from Inanna's ancient hymn: "The people of Sumer parade before you. The women adorn their right side with men's clothing. . . . The men adorn their left side with women's clothing. . . . The coiffured priestesses walk before you. They carry the sword and the double-edged axe. The ascending *kurgarra* [androgyne] priests raise their swords before you."*

How, in the same world, do antibiotics cure some people while others respond to the *huevo negro?* How can light be both a particle and a wave? And how come I still lose my car keys?

What if the Western intellectual's refusal to categorize—and therefore perceive—anything to do with what we call psychic or spiritual is as culturally specific as any other mode of perception? What do *you* call that part of flirting when you stare at somebody and they suddenly turn around?

It's been said, referring to language and other logical systems, that the map is not the territory. It's useful to think of paradigms as road maps; they have to be internally consistent and solve certain problems. And while several kinds of maps may be necessary to plot a journey, none of them are the quest itself.

I am no smarter than I was before I began this voyage. I don't know any more than I did about what happens after we die. I am no nicer, or more possessed of a talent for effectively kind behavior. Perhaps I've become more deliberate in my actions than I was, less inclined to compartmentalize my ethics. I still can't trace my ideas and impulses to anything more reliable than my fallible and limited perspective. I'm as committed, nevertheless, as I was before, to an engaged and implicated life.

I *can* tell you that when I enter into spiritual investigations, allowing myself to comply with methods and practices that address the immanent world as Goddess/God,

*Inanna, Queen of Heaven and Earth, by Diane Wolkstein and Samuel Noah Kramer (New York: Harper and Row, 1983).

things happen. Groups can raise energy, which is no news to anyone who has ever participated in a protest march. In ritual, groups can make energy palpable, make it hot or cold, can make a perfumed weight of grief or sexual excitement and wield it.

In the solitary practice of meditation, prayer and ritual, invented or inherited, I learn things about myself: what I'm really angry about, afraid of or hopeful for. Things that conscious introspection won't reveal. When I pray about a problem and let go of my expectations for the outcome, what happens next can be so much more constructive and wondrous than anything my puny imagination might have come up with. When dance, drumming, the Kol Nidre, sitting meditation or sacred sex leads me to surrender to that which is larger than myself, my body learns to feel what my mind knows: that everything is connected to everything else, that everything is dying and becoming something else, that there is no guaranteed result to anything I do, but that everything I do—and refrain from doing—has consequences.

Mostly, I grope along, aware that the traditions I draw from evolved generations ago, from sets of imperatives that I can only guess at. (How would I know what Inanna's priestesses or the early Kabbalists really thought or how they lived?) Often I feel like some cavewoman in a postnuclear science-fiction movie who wanders the ruins of our cities, talking back to tape recordings and ignoring cans of food. And sometimes I feel like a dancing particle in a huge pageant of processes, transforming the world as minutely and inexorably as rust.

Litany to the Dark Goddess

Coatlicue, Mother of All Gods,
Coatlicue, She of the Serpent Skirt,
Coatlicue, Goddess of Earth, Life, Death,
Coatlicue of Coatepec,
Teteoian, Mother of the Gods, Mother of Four Hundred
    Thousand,
Tlaliyolo, Heart of the Earth, Blood Giver and Blood Taker,
Tititl, Stomach Where We Were Born,
Omecihuatl, Lady of Duality,
Cihuocoatl, Woman Serpent, She of the Windowless
    Temple,
Yoalticitl, Goddess of Cradles, Protector of Children,
Cuaucihuatl, Eagle Woman, Woman of Claws,
Yaocihuatl, Warrior Woman, Woman of Unflinching Gaze,
Quilaztli, Sorceress, Transformer into Animals,
Toci, Our Grandmother, Woman of Wrinkled Uterus,
Teotenantzin, Beloved Mother of the Gods,
Tzizimicihuatl, Infernal Mother,
Tonantzin, Our Venerated Mother,
Tonantzin of Tepeyac, Patroness of Midwives and Healers,
Virgin
Virgin of Tepeyac, Virgin of Guadalupe,
Virgin of Roses the Color of Blood,
Goddess Who Fears No Serpent,
Goddess Who Floats on the Moon,
Goddess of Folded Hands, Goddess of Folded Body,

71

Hidden Goddess,
Dark Goddess of Duality,
Coatlicue, Tonantzin, Guadalupe,
Silent Pedestal Goddess,
Colonized Goddess,
Goddess of Downcast Eyes,
María full of sorrows,
Santa María llena de gracia,
Virgin of Virgins,
Mother Most Pure,
Intact Mother,
Spotless Mother,
Santísima virgen,
Spiritual Vessel,
Tower of Marble,
Rosa mística,
House of Gold,
Morning Star,
Dulce madre,
Mother of Mothers,
Mother of Hope,
María de miel,
Despierta,
Dreamer of your Many Manifestations,
Despierta.
Dreamer of Fierce Origins,
Despierta. Oyenos.
Claw through their babble,
we're straining to hear.

HEART OF COMPASSION

*May my body
be a prayerstick
for the world.*

—JOAN HALIFAX

The Medicine Woman's Daughter
A charm to keep you part of the whole

May the white bark be nine times your mother
May my burnished cheeks be twice sun-daughters
May the apple that divides seeds into simple stars
   be the multiple of your life
May my breasts be the marigolds in your night garden
May the dark broom that is your shadow be a memorial
   to your father
May you live between my thighs and in my heart
May lapwings rise at your feet from every crossroad
May I be in between your two hands the way sky is
   the center of beech dreams
May our love be the mystery of wind and the soul's
   duration
May your life be as charmed, as strong, as the single
   white rose blooming in snowy circles

Joanna Macy

Three Lessons in Compassion

I thought I knew what compassion was—it is a familiar concept, common to all religions. But in that first summer I spent with the Tibetans, it appeared in dimensions new to my experience.

I wasn't a student of Buddhism then, when I lived in India with my husband and children, and when in January 1965 I encountered Tibetan refugees in the foothills of the Himalayas. Nor was it, I thought, interest in the Dharma that drew me back to them the following summer—back to that ragtag collection of monks and lamas and laypeople who, with their leader Khamtul Rinpoche, had come out from Kham in eastern Tibet. I simply wanted to be around them. I felt a kind of wild gladness in their company, and imagined I could be of some use.

Despite their colorful, stirring ceremonies, they were in difficult straits. Prey to diseases unknown in Tibet, they were living hand to mouth, crowded into rented, derelict bungalows in the hill station of Dalhousie. With no remunerative livelihood or land of their own, they were fearful of being separated from each other and shipped off by Indian government authorities to different work projects, road gangs, camps, schools, orphanages, and other institutions being set up for the thousands of refugees from Chinese repression in Tibet. So, along with an American Peace Corps volunteer, I worked to help them develop an economic base that would enable them to stay together as a community. When my children were free from school in Delhi, we moved up to Dalhousie for the summer.

Our goal was to help the refugees draw on their rich artistic heritage to produce crafts for sale, and to set up a cooperative marketing scheme. In the process, friendships took root that would change my life.

It was clear that the Rinpoches, or venerable incarnate lamas of the community, were great masters of Tibetan Buddhism, but I did not ask for teachings. Given the conditions with which they were coping, and the demands on their attention and health, that seemed presumptuous. I wanted to ease their burdens, not add to them. The precious hours when we were free to be together were devoted to concocting plans for the community, applying for government rations, or choosing wools, dyes, and designs for carpet production. Walking between my rented cottage with four children above Dalhousie's upper circle road and the Khampa community on a lower ridge a mile below, there was not time anyway for reading scriptures or learning meditation. But the teachings came anyway. They came in simple, unexpected ways. Three incidents live vividly in my memory.

One day, after my morning time with the children, I was walking down the mountain to meet again with my Khampa friends. On the way I had accompanied my oldest, my eleven-year-old son, to a Dharma class for Westerners at a school for young Tibetan lamas. The English-speaking nun in charge was teaching and she said, "So countless are all sentient beings, and so many their births throughout time, that each at some point was your mother." She then explained a practice for developing compassion: it consisted of viewing each person as your mother in a former life.

I played with the idea as I walked on down the mountain, following a narrow, winding road between cedars and rhododendron trees. The astronomical number of lifetimes that the nun's words evoked boggled my mind—yet the intent of this quaint practice, for all of its far-fetched fantasy, was touching. What a pity, I thought, that this was not a practice I could use, since reincarnation hardly featured as part of my belief system. Then I paused on the path as the figure of a coolie approached.

Coolies, or load-bearing laborers, were a familiar sight on the roads of Dalhousie, and the most heavily laden of all were those who struggled up the mountain with mammoth logs on their backs. They were low-caste mountain folk whose bent, gaunt forms were dwarfed by their burdens, many meters long. I had become accustomed to the sight of them, and accustomed as well to the sense of consternation that it triggered in me. I would usually look away in discomfort, and pass by with internally muttered judgments about the kind of social and economic system that would so exploit its own population.

This afternoon I stood stock-still. I watched the slight, bandy-legged figure move slowly uphill toward me, negotiating its burden—which looked like the trunk of a cedar—around the bend. Backing up to prop the rear of the log against the bank and ease the weight of it, the coolie paused to catch his breath. "Namasté," I said softly, and stepped hesitantly toward him.

I wanted to see his face. But he was still strapped under his log, and I would have had to crouch down under it to look up at his features—which I ached now to see. What face did she now wear, this dear one who had long ago mothered me? My heart trembled with gladness and distress. I wanted to touch that dark, half-glimpsed cheek and meet those lidded eyes bent to the ground. I wanted to undo and rearrange the straps that I might share her burden up the mountain. Whether out of respect or embarrassment, I did not do that. I simply stood five feet away and drank in every feature of that form—the grizzled chin, the rag turban, the gnarled hands grasping the forward overhang of log.

The customary comments of my internal social scientist

evaporated. What appeared now before me was not an oppressed class or an indictment of an economic system, so
much as a distinct, irreplaceable, and incomparably precious being. My mother. My child. A thousand questions
arose urgently in my mind. Where was he headed? When
would he reach home? Would there be loved ones to greet
him and a good meal to eat? Was there rest in store, and
songs, and embraces?

When the coolie heaved the log off the bank to balance
its weight on his back again and proceed uphill, I headed
on down the mountain path. I had done nothing to change
his life, or betray my discovery of our relationship. But
the Dalhousie mountainside shone in a different light; the
furnishings of my mind had been rearranged, my heart
broken open. How odd, I thought, that I did not need to
believe in reincarnation for that to happen.

The second incident occurred soon after, on a similar
summer Dalhousie afternoon. It was one of the many tea-
times with Khamtul Rinpoche, the head of the refugee
community from Kham, where with two younger tulkus
or incarnate lamas we were devising plans for their craft
production center. As usual, Khamtul Rinpoche had a
stretched canvas propped at his side on which, with his
customary, affable equanimity, he would be painting as we
drank our tea and talked. His huge, round face exuded a
serene confidence that our deliberations would bear fruit,
just as the Buddha forms on his canvas would take form
under the fine, sable brush in his hands.

I, as usual, was seized by more urgency in pushing
through plans for the craft cooperative and requests for
grants. I could not know then that this work would even-
tuate in the monastic settlement of Tashi Jong, where in a
few years, on land acquired up Kangra Valley in the Hima-
layan foothills, the four-hundred-member community of
Khampa monks and laypeople would sink their roots in
exile.

On this particular afternoon a fly fell into my tea. This

was, of course, a minor occurrence. After a year in India I considered myself to be unperturbed by insects—by ants in the sugar bin, spiders in the cupboard, and even scorpions in my shoes in the morning. Still, as I lifted my cup, I must have registered, by my facial expression or a small grunt, the presence of the fly. Choegyal Rinpoche, the eighteen-year-old tulku who was already becoming my friend for life, leaned forward in sympathy and consternation. "What is the matter?"

"Oh, nothing," I said. "It's nothing—just a fly in my tea." I laughed lightly to convey my acceptance and composure. I did not want him to suppose that mere insects were a problem for me; after all, I was a seasoned India-wallah, relatively free of Western phobias and attachments to modern sanitation.

Choegyal crooned softly, in apparent commiseration with my plight, "Oh, oh, a fly in the tea."

"It's no problem," I reiterated, smiling at him reassuringly. But he continued to focus great concern on my cup. Rising from his chair, he leaned over and inserted his finger into my tea. With great care he lifted out the offending fly—and then exited from the room. The conversation at the table resumed. I was eager to secure Khamtul Rinpoche's agreement on plans to secure the high-altitude wool he desired for the carpet production.

When Choegyal Rinpoche reentered the cottage he was beaming. "He is going to be all right," he told me quietly. He explained how he had placed the fly on the leaf of a branch of a bush by the door, where his wings could dry. And the fly was still alive, because he began fanning his wings, and we could confidently expect him to take flight soon. . . .

That is what I remember of that afternoon—not the agreements we reached or plans we devised, but Choegyal's report that the fly would live. And I recall, too, the laughter in my heart. I could not, truth to tell, share Choegyal's dimensions of compassion, but the pleasure in his face revealed how much I was missing by not extending my self-concern to *all* beings, even to flies. Yet the very notion that it was possible gave me boundless delight.

My third lesson that summer also occurred casually, in passing. In order to help the Tibetans I wanted to tell their story to the world—a story I was just beginning to discover. I had stunning photos of the Tibetans in exile, of their faces and crafts, and the majestic lama dances of their lineage. I envisaged an illustrated article for a popular periodical, like the *National Geographic;* but to hook Western sympathies and enlist Western support, such an article, I figured, should include the horrors from which these refugees had escaped. Stories of appalling inhumanity and torture on the part of the Chinese occupation had come to me only peripherally, in snatches, from laypeople and other Westerners. The Rinpoches themselves were reluctant to describe or discuss them.

I presented my argument to Choegyal Rinpoche, the most accessible and confiding of the tulkus. He had been a mature thirteen-year-old when the Chinese invaded his monastery, and he had his own memories to tap of what they had done to his monks and lamas. I suspected a voyeuristic element in my eagerness to hear the ghastly tales—a voyeurism bred by the yellow journalism of Sunday supplements in my New York childhood, and by horror movies of arcane Chinese torture; still, I knew that such tales would arrest the attention of Western readers and rally support for the Tibetan cause.

Only when I convinced Choegyal that sharing these memories with the Western public would aid the plight of Tibetan refugees did he begin to disclose some of the details of what he had seen and suffered at the hands of the Chinese before his flight from Tibet. The stories came in snatches of conversations, as we paused outside the new craft production center or walked over to the monastery in its temporary, rented quarters. Only then did he divulge some elements of what had occurred. Many of these elements, the forms of intimidation, coercion, and torture employed, have become by now, over a quarter of a century later, public knowledge. Reports now available through agencies like Amnesty International and the International Council of Jurists may not have the poignant immediacy of Choegyal's words, but they give the gist.

The lesson I learned, however, and that will stay with me forever, is not about the human capacity for cruelty. I was standing with Choegyal under a rhododendron tree, the sunlight flickering on his face through the leaves and the blossoms the color of his robes. He had just divulged what perhaps was the most painful of his memories— what the Chinese military had done to his monks in the great prayer hall, as his teachers hid him on the mountainside above the monastery. I gasped with shock, and breathed hard to contain the grief and anger that arose in me. Then I was stilled by the look he turned on me, with eyes that shone with unshed tears.

"Poor Chinese," he murmured.

With a shudder of acknowledgment, I realized that the tears in his eyes were not for himself or for his monks or for his once great monastery of Dugu in the land of Kham in eastern Tibet. Those tears were for the destroyers themselves.

"Poor Chinese," he said. "They make such bad karma for themselves."

I cannot emulate that reach of compassion, but I have seen it. I have recognized it. I know now that it is within our human capacity. And that changes for me the face of life.

Brenda Miller

A Thousand Buddhas

My hand's the universe,
it can do anything.
—SHINKICHI TAKAHASHI

I.

I could tell you I once received a massage from a blind person, but that would be a lie. I've never been touched by someone blind, but I can imagine what it would be like. She would read me like Braille, her fingertips hovering on the raised points of my flesh. She might peel back the sheets of my skin, lay one finger on my quivering heart. We could beat like that, two hummingbirds, and become very still. Her hands might move across my abdomen, flick the scar below my belly button. My eyelids would flutter at her touch, and my skin dissolve into hot pools of tears.

I have never been touched by someone blind, but I have given whole massages with my eyes halfway closed, and the bodies I touched became something else. Their edges dissolved, and they spread out on the table—masses of flesh, all the borders gone. I touched them in tender places: under the cheekbones, between the toes, along the high, arching curves of their feet. When I opened my eyes they coalesced into something human, but I walked outside and slipped into the pool, feeling like a primordial fish, all my substance gone. I'd see them afterward, and they leaned toward me, their mouths open, but they hardly spoke. My

83

arms opened and they fell against me; I held my hands on the middle of their backs, holding their hearts in place.

Sometimes they cried. I was too professional, then, to cry, knew that I had to keep some distance in order to make it work. If I had cried, then we might have been lovers, and that would make it wrong somehow when they handed me the check for thirty dollars. Sometimes they pressed it into my hands and looked away, saying, *I can't even tell you.* I nudged them in the direction of the baths, and they went like obedient children, their naked bodies swaying under their towels as they shuffled across the old, wooden bridge.

II.

I have a picture from that time—of myself in the hot tub at Orr Hot Springs. At least, some people claim it is me, pointing out the slope of my breasts, the flare of my hips, the circumference of my thighs. Positive identification is impossible since the woman in the picture cradles her face in her hands.

Light streams through a doorway into the gazebo, and this young woman leans her back against the deck. The sunlight zeroes into a circle on her belly. Jasmine bush and bamboo are reflected in the glass. The woman bends her head and covers her eyes as if she were about to weep. Steam rises in flurries and beads on the glass, obscuring detail and memory.

The woman is not weeping. She is scooping up the water from the tub and splashing it on her face. If this woman is me, she is mumbling some kind of grateful prayer, alchemizing the water into a potion that will heal.

It's easy to know what you're doing, once we're not doing it anymore.

III.

Before I lived at Orr Hot Springs, I spent a summer baking bread for fifty children on a farm outside Willits. I

didn't know I was in training to become a massage therapist, but I knew I was mending wounds buried deep inside
me as I handled the huge mounds of dough.

The repetitive motions of my hands—the grasping and
pushing, the bend of my waist, the slow ache in my shoulder—before long, I became automatic and blank. I kept my
hands covered in flour and thought continually of food, of
nourishment.

Children swarmed around me, tugged at my apron,
took little balls of dough, and rolled them lightly between
their teeth. The bread rose and came out of the oven, broke
into tender crumbs, tasted good. I watched the children
and gave them small lumps of dough to press. I touched
their miniature shoulders and smiled, but said very little.
At the midsummer dance, they braided flowers into my
hair and held my hands, as if I were an old person conva-
lescing from a long, wasting illness.

IV.

Today I look at my hands. I remember the bodies I
touched, the lives that came through them. I look at my
hands sometimes and trace the edges of my fingers, like
children do in kindergarten on newsprint with green tem-
pera paint. Hands become what they have held; our hands
shape themselves around what they hold most dear, or
what has made an impression, or what we press on others.

My friend Dana once grabbed my hand off the stick
shift as I drove through L.A. "These," he said, running a
fingertip around my palm, "are healing hands."

I drove with my left hand on the wheel while he examined every finger of my right. I swerved to avoid a dog.

"They're like a sculptor's hands," he said dreamily,
dropping my hand and gripping his own.

Dana is a sculptor, with a propensity for twisted nude
forms, estranged limbs, fingers in a bowl. Once, he left for
Ecuador and painted all his walls, the appliances, even his

books, a startling white; a "blank canvas," he said, for his friends to spill upon. And we did, troweling up purples and reds, oranges and blues, a cacophony of personalities rolling across his walls.

I pressed my hands in blue paint and hand-walked an awkward bridge above his couch.

V.

What follows may, or may not, be true:

"It's been too long," the man said.

My old lover Jon stepped inside and closed the door, settled himself carefully on the edge of my massage table. "I just came to soak in the baths, decided to get a massage on the spur of the moment," he said. "I didn't know it was you."

We stared at each other. I don't know what he saw in my face, a barrier perhaps, a careful retreat, but in his face I saw a deep sorrow. My eyes involuntarily shifted into professional gear, and they flitted over his body, making notes: a slump in the left shoulder, a grim tightness in the left arm and fist, chest slightly concave, breathing shallow.

In massage school, before we were lovers, Jon and I had been partners. The teacher insisted on partner rotation, but somehow Jon and I ended up together more times than not. We learned well on each other. We breathed freely; we allowed each other's hands to cup the muscles and slide so slowly down the length of connecting fibers and tissue; we allowed thumbs to probe deep into unyielding spots. It was like a dance, the way our teacher said it always should be, an effortless give-and-take, back and forth, with the breath as well as the body. Communication—transcendent and absolute.

"Listen," Jon was saying. "I understand if you don't want to do this." His body leaned toward me, and my spine tipped forward in response. A massage room is a very close environment. Intimacy is immediate; truth prevails.

I glanced away from him and gazed at the far wall, at the painting of *A Thousand Buddhas* Jon had given me as a graduation present. For the last year, I had looked at that picture every day, and every day it reminded me of Jon less and less. A process of pain, moving ahead on its own momentum. The primary Buddha sat in the center, immovable, surrounded by a helix of Buddhas that spun around and around.

My palms relaxed, a good sign. "It might be awkward," I said, "but I'll try." I took a deep breath and whatever had been prickling at my throat subsided.

What did my body feel when I placed my hands on Jon's back? My palms curved instinctively to the crook of his shoulders; my own shoulders softened and I asked Jon to breathe, and he did, and I inhaled with him, stretching my lungs, and on the exhale my hands slid down his back, kneading the muscles on the downward slide, pulling up along the lats, crossing over his spine, and again, and again, until he seemed to flatten, and there was no distinction between the flesh of his back or the bones in his arms or the curve of his buttocks, no distinction in fact between his breath and mine. I felt a small opening in my heart, a valve releasing, and an old love, a love aged and smooth as wine, flowed down my arms and into Jon's skin. I knew then that sometime in the night I would remember this gushing, and I would be shattered by a sense of tremendous loss, a grasping ache in my palms, and I would cry, but even this certainty could not stop my hands in their circular route through Jon's familiar and beautiful body. He inhaled and began to sob. The tears shuddered through his back, his arms, his legs, and I felt them empty from him in one bountiful wave. My right hand floated to rest on his sacrum. My left hand brushed the air above his head in long, sweeping arcs.

There is a powder that covers the heart, a sifting of particles fine as talc. It is protection—gauzy and insubstantial, but protection nonetheless. Occasionally, a hand rubs against you and wipes a patch clear.

That's when the heart bulges, beating with a raw and healthy ferocity.

VI.

There is another picture, one that is hidden in a drawer. It is me, before I moved to Orr Springs; me, before I even knew such places existed. I am young, young, young.

I am standing barefoot on the porch of a Forest Service cabin in Prairie Creek State Park on the north coast of California. It is late summer. I am wearing a purple tank top, tight Levi's, and a forest ranger's hat. The morning sun is full in my face, and I am smiling a goofy, lopsided grin, my hands at my sides, my feet planted solidly on the wooden planks.

I am pregnant.

I am about three weeks along, and the embryo is curled tightly in the fallopian tube. The pregnancy will end one week later in a long, terrifying miscarriage, but in the picture I don't know this. I don't even know I am pregnant. I'm twenty-one years old and healthy from a long summer in Wyoming. It is a beautiful morning, and I am happy to be back in California. My world has not yet shifted to include the smell of bandages steeped in antiseptics and blood. I don't know about the indifferent hands of nurses, the blind lights of an operating dome.

Look carefully at the belly for some sign of the child, at the face for some indication of motherhood. There is none; the snapshot is flat and ordinary: a young woman on vacation, nothing more. But I look at this photo, and I sense a swelling in my pelvis, a fullness in my breasts. I feel my skin inviolate and smooth, the substance of everything I've lost and meant to regain.

VII.

Someone called them midwife's hands. A midwife's hands cradle and protect, hold a life between them. The classic posture for the hands in photographs you see: one hand cupped under the baby's emerging head, the other lightly curled on the baby's crown.

There is a polarity position like this: at the client's head, cradling, not pulling but imparting the sense of emergence just the same. If you stay long enough, motionless, the head appears to become larger; it grows and trembles. Sometimes I have touched the top of my head to the top of my client's head, and we are plugged in; we take big breaths, heave long, important sighs.

VIII.

Sean was born. Not from my body. From Rhea's. I held the mirror at an angle so she could see the crown of his head as it split her body in two.

The midwife placed one hand on the skull and rotated it so the face pointed toward heaven. The eyes were open, glazed with an unearthly shine.

Rhea screamed. The world paused and listened. His body followed, sheathed in cream and wax.

IX.

What does the body hold? And how do the hands release it? In the late seventies, "hug clinics" opened on college campuses in California. Distraught people were invited to drop in if they needed to be held in place by a pair of strong, encircling arms.

One of the most powerful massage holds I've used has the client on his side, curled in a fetal position. I cupped one hand to the base of the spine, the other lay flat on the back between the shoulder blades. These are the two places our mothers' hands fell when holding us as babies.

Some people cried with little shoulder-shaking sobs. Others promptly fell asleep. Most of them believed my hands were still on them long after I'd walked away.

X.

In the hospital, the nurse stuck an IV needle into the back of my hand, over and over. I squinted and clenched my teeth.

"Does that hurt?" the nurse said, looking up, scowling. I nodded.

"It's not supposed to hurt," she said, and set the needle aside, tried again.

When she was done, I lay on top of the covers, shivering, my eyes halfway closed, my palm flat on the bed. The IV fluid ticked into my blood. Already I could feel myself forgetting everything.

My body was a container of pain. And then it contained nothing. An absence so absolute I couldn't even cry.

XI.

The hand is shaped to touch the different parts of the world. We hurt, and the hand reaches to the chest. A newborn's head fits snugly into the center of your palm.

The midwife had fingers so long I almost asked her if she played the piano. The words were nearly out of my mouth, but then she handed Sean to me, and I forgot about pianos, about that kind of music.

I held him while the midwife and Rhea struggled with the afterbirth. I held him against my shoulder. His eyes were open; he blinked slowly and rarely, like a baby owl. The light in the room was gold, the color of honey.

I thought I saw something in his eyes, but I can't be sure. I thought I saw a nod of acceptance, a little man bowing to me, his hands pressed together in an attitude of prayer.

XII.

They came to me hot and pink from the baths, most of my work already done. They came naked and slick and gorgeous.

What did I give them? Nothing but myself, and not even that, but the benefit of my whole attention, the focus of my hands on them, the focus of my heart. I don't know how long the change lasted. They left the room and lingered in the baths, got out, got dressed, and drove the two and a half hours home. I waved good-bye and walked up the steps to my cabin, looked out my window to the luscious woods, and thought about these people more than I probably should have. When the time approached for me to leave Orr Springs, I thought about them with a frantic longing for a life that could be balanced and whole.

I wanted to massage myself before I left; I wanted to send myself off with a stroke of my fingers, a hand along my spine, an affirmation of abundance. A momentary release from every memory that weighed me down. I thought it might help, if only for the drive out on the rutted and dusty road.

XIII.

Years after I left Orr Springs, I worked for the Human Resource Council in Missoula, Montana. I didn't massage people anymore. I tried, but I zipped through the parts of the body as if I were taking inventory. I chattered like a barber giving a haircut. I thought about dinner, gas mileage, bills to be paid.

In my job, I interviewed clients and determined their eligibility for a heating-assistance program. Many of the people I saw were elderly and disabled; all of them had stories to tell, stories that could take a lifetime. I had only twenty minutes to spend with each one. I found that when I gave them my whole and complete attention for even five minutes, that was enough. I looked them in the eyes and smiled, laughed with them, murmured consolations. They looked back and told me what they knew. My hands kept very still on my desk.

One seventy-six-year-old woman spoke to me in short, disjointed sentences, her head nodding emphatically with each word, spittle forming at the corners of her mouth. She smelled of cigarettes and bitter lemons. As I walked her to the door of my office, she swirled about and grabbed me by the waist. She was only as tall as my chest, and I settled my arms onto her shoulders. We stood like that for a few seconds under the flourescent lights, the computers humming around us. I slid one hand down her back and held her there; my hand quivered, near as it was to her old and fragile heart.

XIV.

I'm lying on my massage table. It's for sale. I'm lying on it, and I feel utterly relaxed. My breath swirls through my body in a contented daze.

I'm lying on my back. I open my eyes, and I see my face. I see me leaning over the table. My right hand comes to rest on my womb; my left hand hovers over my throat.

Forgive Me. Those are the words that pass between us.

Lisa Vice

What Faith Is

On Tuesday morning, my cat Tommy woke up, blinked his eyes in his slow, deliberate way, but could not get down off the bed where he always sleeps, curled at my feet. When I lifted him to the floor, he stumbled lopsidedly like a drunk before he fell to his side, panting.

"It could be a brain tumor," the vet said, looking over my shoulder, as if he were addressing a ghost. "We see that sometimes in the old ones." Tommy lay in a heap on the table, crying pitifully, a terrified look in his eyes. With my hands on his thick orange fur, I felt him tremble and shake. I wanted to take him home, where I could press my face to his fur and talk to him properly. But the vet was saying something about tests, a chance of saving him, so I agreed to leave him overnight.

The next morning, the vet called to say he'd lost the cat. At first I took him literally, as if Tommy had gotten out of his cage, slipped out the door, and was on my doorstep right now, waiting for me to let him in.

"We can have him cremated," he was saying. Then I understood.

Every Wednesday, I have lunch with Doreen at the Monarch. Over egg salad sandwiches and iced tea, I tell her about the cat.

"From one day to the next, gone. Just like that." I have the sensation I am watching myself from a great distance.

The sun is bright, shining directly into my face through the half-open slats of the blinds and I am glad of this. It gives me an excuse to squint and rub my eyes.

"Jean," Doreen says. "You can get another cat."

"I don't want another cat. I want Tommy. He wasn't just any cat."

"Maybe he was your child," Doreen says. "In a past life." Since Doreen went to that psychic fair at the community college, she's been talking this way, convinced she remembers sixteen of her past lives.

"Maybe," I say. Not that I agree, I just don't know what to say. Then I tell her something she wants to hear. "I have an interview."

Doreen's whole face lights up like a three-way bulb being flicked on, and the skin around her eyes crinkles into hundreds of folds. She squeezes my hand. I haven't worked in years, but I've been looking for a job since that day Doreen dropped by and found me in my pj's at three o'clock in the afternoon. She ran around pulling up the shades, saying, "You have to get a job or something. You need structure in your life."

So every morning, I take a shower, comb my hair, then sit with the *Herald* folded open on my lap, circling possibilities: Front Desk Clerk. Bakery Sales. Receptionist. Cook.

"What's it for?" Doreen asks. My last interview was for an office worker/chimney sweep. I could see myself answering phones, swiveling in my chair to do some filing, then rushing off with a top hat on, climbing ladders, perched on a roof. Even though we both knew I was much too old to do such a thing, the young man who interviewed me had been very kind.

"A part-time innkeeper. Some kind of fancy bed-and-breakfast. But maybe I should cancel. I've got to do something with the cat."

"Do?" Doreen says. "Do? What are you talking about?"

"They said they'd cremate him. But I was reading in the

paper how when they cremate your pet and give you a Baggy of ashes, it could be anybody's ashes. A Great Dane or a poodle or a Siamese. They just shove them all in together like it doesn't matter.''

"What's all the fuss? The body's just a shell." Making comments like this is part of Doreen's psychic awakening. "It's like a chrysalis we crawl out of when our time comes.'' She waves up toward the ceiling where paper monarch butterflies dangle, decorating the restaurant.

Every year around this time, after traveling thousands of miles, the monarch butterflies make their way across the bay to rest in the pine and eucalyptus groves of our town. They fly slowly between the houses, exhausted from their journey. When I first moved here, I thought they would arrive in droves, the sky would darken, the air would fill with the sound of thousands of powdery wings fluttering by. But the butterflies actually drift along, alone or in pairs, buoyed by the autumn breeze.

"You and Nila were like husband and wife, Tommy's parents,'' Doreen is saying, dabbing at her lips with her napkin.

I choke a little on my tea. My heart thumps so loudly I'm sure Doreen can hear it. "Then you know?" I almost blurt out, thinking maybe she really is psychic after all. "Did you always know?'' I want to ask.

When Nila was alive, I used to tell her people loved us, they wouldn't turn their backs on us if they knew the truth. But she never wanted to risk it. "I'm not ashamed,'' she insisted. "I just like having our secret from the world.''

"Of course, you were roommates this time around.'' Doreen sucks the last of her tea through her straw. "But you acted just like an old married couple. Who knows? Maybe you were a king and queen on the Ivory Coast. Or an ordinary frumpy couple in Queen Victoria's England. A married couple, I'm sure of it. I wonder how I knew you then?''

* * *

My car is out front, and after Doreen leaves I get in it and drive toward Lighthouse Avenue. I took a special course for older drivers a few months ago. Not so much for the better insurance rates, but because I was having trouble. I'd make it to a stop sign, then not know what to do. I couldn't remember where I was headed or who had the right of way. Once, I pulled in front of a police car, and he asked to see my license. Now I look ahead, watching for pedestrians, careful of the cars backing out of parking spaces in front of the bank and bookstore. Always ready to yield to the drivers inching forward from the blind intersections.

When I get home, I tell myself that Tommy is not going to rush to the window to greet me. But still, as I unlock the door, I expect him to be there, rolling at my feet, offering his furry white belly. I look in the Yellow Pages and find that the only pet cemetery is in Watsonville. I wonder what it involves to have a cat buried there. I wonder if there are headstones shaped like the pets buried under them. I can't imagine making the call. What would I say first? I sit on the sofa and stare at the ads on the page: Thor's Termite Control. Fleabusters. The Golden Dolphin Pet Shop. I read every word like it really matters to me.

I can hear the tick of the second hand on my watch. I have another hour before my interview and my clothes are ready, so I lie back on the sofa. I keep thinking I see Tommy out of the corner of my eye, heading toward me. I have to restrain myself from calling out to him. Tommy would always come to me when I lay down. And when I wept he would creep slowly up my body until he rested on my chest, just under my chin.

"Tell me about yourself while I read over your application," the owner of the inn says. I feel he has already dismissed me. I stare at my hands in my lap, the speech I prepared already fading. All I can think of is how I'm old enough to be his mother. I can hear Doreen in the back of my mind, urging me on, so I smile and speak as best I can.

"We do everything for our guests except polish their shoes," he tells me at one point. "Would you have trouble carrying a tray with champagne and an ice bucket upstairs? There are a lot of steps." Most of his questions begin with, "How would you rate yourself on a scale of one to ten, ten being the highest . . . ?" Anything with numbers makes me panic, but I take a deep breath. When he asks about my ability to make decisions, I announce in a loud voice, "Definitely a ten."

What must I have been thinking? Just trying to choose between spearmint gum and peppermint can leave me standing at the candy counter at Sprouse long enough for a line to form. But I have nothing to lose.

When I am leaving, a young girl rushes up the stone steps, her sandals scraping the walk, her nipples pressing her thin white cotton blouse. I have an urge to place my palms over them. I am that hungry to touch. To be touched. I think of Nila murmuring into my hair, kissing my neck, her hands moving down my body, familiar as music. Would I really never feel this again? The thought takes my breath away. I lean against the stone wall watching the waves crash on the shore. A huge clipper ship, all the sails unfurled, glides like a mirage toward the harbor.

On the way home, I stop at the vet's. I'm still not sure what I'm going to do with Tommy. He is wrapped in a black garbage bag stuffed into the beige plastic cat carrier. It is unusually light as the boy hands it to me. Tommy was Nila's cat first, but I loved him too. I wonder what Nila would do now. I wonder what she would think if she could see me with a dead cat beside me on the front seat.

"Maybe I should have a Jewish funeral," Nila announced one night. She was driving us home from the Indian restaurant. I remember how it felt to sit in the dark car, to drive past the houses all lit up. I have no idea what prompted the discussion. Lord knows we were both old enough to be making such plans. But we'd never discussed it before. "I hate the idea of a stranger messing with my body after I'm dead," Nila said.

By the time we pulled up in front of the house, we'd both decided on cremation. It was fast, easy, and cheap. "Unless you buy a fancy urn," Nila said. I have often wondered if Nila had a premonition. Like Doreen did when she dreamt of buildings crumbling the night before the Loma Prieta quake destroyed downtown Santa Cruz. Had she had a premonition? Or had she known all along and only pretended to be healthy? Pretended to be heading toward the future with me by her side?

When I get home, I take the cat out of his box. His body feels like an overripe tomato. I want to open the bag, but not right now. What I do is I clear out the bottom of the refrigerator and I put him inside. It's such a strange thing to do it actually cheers me up a little, and I take out a beer to help me think. Out the window three wild parrots fly by, their feathers bright green against the blue sky. They scream raucously, as if to tease the neighbor's parrot, who screams back from the safety of its cage hanging beside the back door. I read somewhere how parrots outlive their owners. I wonder if this is how these three ended up swooping around town, resting on phone wires, calling from trees.

Nila had just celebrated her seventieth birthday. Seventy might seem old to some people, but it all depends on where you stand in relation to it. It seems young to me. But that's because I'm fifty-nine. Old? Ninety's old. But seventy? Nila was active right up to the end, riding her bike on the trail, hiking up Snively Ridge ahead of me.

When we first fell in love, Nila worried that if anyone found out what our relationship really was, she would lose her job. She was a children's librarian, after all. Imagine the scandal, she would say. So we let people think what they wanted all those years, never setting them straight.

But when Nila died, nobody knew how to comfort me. They were surprised by the extent of my grief. "The money will be a big help," everybody said when they learned I was her beneficiary. "You can do whatever you want." As if this was what mattered. It's not money I want. I want Nila. I want to wrap my arms around her soft waist and pull her close. I want to come home and find her on the sofa reading a book and lean over to kiss her. I want to walk down Pico Avenue, our shoulders brushing, our legs in rhythm, as we make our way to the sea.

The next morning, I am sure I feel a warm place by my feet where Tommy always lay. I imagine I hear the murmur of his purr. I get up quickly and go out to the kitchen. Even though there is the black plastic bag at the bottom of the refrigerator, I still reach for the can of cat food. Before I realize what I am doing, I have already filled his bowl. It sits on the counter while I sip my coffee. Outside, the wind rattles the eucalyptus leaves. The sky seems to be clearing, the thick fog dispersing like wisps of smoke blowing out to sea.

I take the bag out of the refrigerator and untie the knot, pulling it open to look inside. And there he is. The familiar orange coat, the dark markings I loved to trace. I feel as if I'm unwrapping a fragile gift. There's my good boy. My Tommy, curled at the bottom as if asleep.

"Tommy," I say, and pet the cold fur, convinced that if anyone saw me now they would never understand. They would think it morbid or even perverse. There is probably a law against it, but let them arrest me if they must. I've decided to bury Tommy out back. I put on my sneakers, get the shovel, and begin to dig in the far corner of the lot where Nila used to plant squash. The yard, always Nila's domain, is overgrown, a tangle of oxalis and marguerites choking the lavender and thyme. But the morning glories still climb up to the top of the porch like they have from the first year we bought the house and Nila planted them, fastening a trellis to the railing before the plants had more than two leaves.

"This is what faith is," she had said, laughing. It surprised us both when the flowers came back, year after year, planting themselves from the thick seed pods that fell to the ground, the vines reaching to the top of the steps, the bright blue blossoms cascading like a waterfall.

As I dig, I have this picture in my mind, as clearly as if I'm watching it projected on a screen. There is Nila in her nightgown, so small, her face deathly pale. I am beside her wishing she would say something, wishing she would open her eyes, give my hand an answering squeeze. One morning she sat up in bed, coughed, and her hand filled with blood. In a week her skin was as translucent as rice paper.

How I wish Nila were with me now, sitting in the red chair, watching me scoop the dark soil into a pile. I pry out a large stone and continue digging, moving rhythmically, as if to the steps of a dance, until the hole is deep enough so that years later, when someone else lives in our house, they won't unearth the bones.

There's a box under the house, just the right size. But first I wrap Tommy in his favorite blanket. Doreen has told me how in one of her past lives she was Egyptian. She was entombed with all her favorite possessions for her journey to the other side. I think of this now as I put in a fur mouse and a crocheted ball, along with a handful of treats, heart-shaped nuggets Tommy loved so much he would stand on his hind legs for one. I fit the box into the hole and scatter soil onto it. The soil makes a thumping sound, then it's just soil on soil, and I pack it down, push it down tight, not wanting the raccoons to come nosing around.

"Dust to dust." The words of the funeral come back to me. It's not an end but a beginning. The voices singing, "Holy, holy, holy." I remember how Nila and I used to stand in that church, Sunday after Sunday, year after year, side by side, never touching, afraid of offending someone. But in private we wrapped our arms around each other.

My body is unused to the work I have done. My back aches and my fingernails are crusted and black, but I feel good as I sit on the back steps. I pray, as I have so many times, that Nila will forgive me. She died believing we were the only ones who knew. But the nurse at the hospital had understood. This I am sure of. She never thought for a moment that we were sisters or roommates. She always pulled the curtain to give us privacy and never came around it without stopping first to say a few words to the Italian lady who lay complaining in the other bed. She spoke loudly, as if warning us she was on her way.

When Nila died, I crawled onto the bed, pulling her into my arms. The nurse left me this way for a long time, even wheeled Mrs. Manetti down to the solarium where the TV blared. When she came back, she put her hands on my shoulders. She was a big woman who stood tall in her white pants suit. She patted my back, murmuring, "I know. I know."

Then she brought towels and a washbasin of steaming water and left me alone. She'd understood, without saying anything, without asking, the way nurses understand the need for mothers of newborns to unwrap the swaddled babies and check every inch. I washed the familiar fingers, the scar on Nila's left palm where she'd cut herself on a broken glass, reaching into the dishpan. The bit of stone embedded in her knee that her mother had said would eventually work its way out. But skin had grown over it instead. I ran the warm cloth across the knobs of her spine, the smooth bones of her ribs, around the mole on her left shoulder and up the back of her neck, my hands sweeping her thick white hair aside. I washed her feet. Monkey feet I called them, and Nila would laugh and use her toes to turn on the radio, to pick pens up off the floor. I washed her breasts, the skin soft as crepe, and remembered the first time I kissed them. It felt like coming home.

On the other side of the fence, my neighbor begins to rake his yard. His parrot, excited to have company, reaches its beak through the cage for a kiss. "What kind of bird are you?" the man asks. "What kind of bird are you?"

"I'm a lucky dog. Lucky dog," the parrot squawks. "Where's the cat? Here kitty kitty." Then it does an imitation of a police siren and begins its litany again.

I sit on the steps and think to myself: I loved a woman. And I am glad of this. I try not to regret all the times I never touched her in public. Not even when we were so old it didn't matter. Two old women hand in hand, what's the big deal?

Down in the weeds I see something move. It's a monarch butterfly struggling to fly. I think maybe it's injured and I should try to help, but as I watch, it spreads its wings. They are bright as stained glass, soft as velvet. I watch it lift itself up with great effort, and then I see, clutched in its tiny legs, another butterfly, its wings folded like hands in prayer, hanging beneath as they glide up over the fence.

Doreen would say it is a sign and I suppose it is, but I don't want to think about what it means. Instead I think how in a few minutes I will go inside and sit on the sofa with the newspaper. I will circle all the ads for jobs I will not get. I will not be a baby-sitter. Will not earn four hundred dollars a month delivering newspapers in my spare time. Will never fix anyone's car or drive a school bus. The idea of all this makes me feel light-headed, almost giddy, as I go back inside.

Sally Miller Gearhart

The Pit Bull Opportunity

On that day in January of 1991 as I drove to Safeway from my cabin, I was confident of two things. First, despite the New Age psychobabble surrounding me, particularly The Seth Stuff, I was not going to fall victim to its Pollyanna-past-life-blame-the-victim mentality. Second, I would never have a dog companion. Within the next month both of those convictions would be dust.

In the mid-seventies a colleague lent me a copy of Jane Roberts's *The Nature of Personal Reality*. I dutifully read it and was untouched by any part of its message—I was busy being a lesbian-feminist-Maoist-Marxist-anti-racist-peace-jobs-and-justice activist. I returned it to her with a two-page single-spaced typewritten analysis of the book's flawed antimaterialist thesis and its total lack of social consciousness.

In the mid-eighties, other friends gave me a copy of the same book. I dutifully read it again, cover to cover, rolling my eyes heavenward, shaking my head, and sighing. I was busy being a fundamentalist-fearing gay rights activist, a worker for Central American Solidarity, and a crusader for animal rights. Create my own reality? Give me a break. The world was burning, Ronald Reagan was destroying not only the hemisphere but the Bill of Rights, and the pain of the earth, particularly that of its nonhuman animals, overwhelmed me. I refused to take responsibility for the creation of such disrespect, injustice, and violence.

103

Most enraging about the book was the suggestion that the personality endures after death. That idea to my mind had always been a sop for the weak-spirited, an easy way out of social responsibility, and a supreme denial of the fact of death. It was clear to me and to any other rational individual that such a division between body and spirit is precisely the problem with the world. I would point to my flesh and say, "See? *This* is my soul, this is my spirit—my body and spirit, one and the same! When we die, our bodies, which are also our spirits, simply rejoin the nitrogen cycle, and that's that."

As for the matter of A Dog in My Life: I had, over the years, placed scores of "unwanted" dogs in good homes. My rage at people who mistreated or neglected their dogs was unquenchable. "A dog is *not* for Christmas," I'd say. "A dog is for life. It's a twelve-to-twenty-year commitment."

But dogs, however wonderful, were too dependent. They followed you around with big eyes and waited for a pat on the head or a dish of food. Or you had to put them outside on a lonely chain or imprison them in a pen. And, god forbid, you had to take them for *walks* because they needed exercise and didn't use a litter box. And when you wanted to travel? What a hassle to arrange for their care! Your freedom was absolutely curtailed by a dog. With my busy life, I could never provide a proper home for one.

Besides, I had become A Cat Person. Cats struck that perfect balance of independence and affection that I needed. The two felines who lived with me would undoubtedly greet a dog with hostile acts of aggression or withdrawal. Furthermore, I had a wonderful lover and an incredible family of friends. I did not lack companionship. I did not want a dog.

So on that January day I cherished my two unconscious convictions and tried to figure, as I pulled into the Safeway parking lot, how I could possibly get my preparation done for the classes I was to teach in three weeks when

I returned to San Francisco State for the spring semester, let alone deal with the fact that Bush was about to catapult us into a machismo war in the Persian Gulf.

At the north door of Safeway sat a fairly large brindle-colored pit bull, collared by a fierce chain. The man beside her informed me that she was free to anyone who would take her. She smelled my open hand, licked it, and looked up at me with soft brown eyes. I refurbished my inner defenses and turned my attention to the man. He said the dog had been a breeder for fighter pit bulls and, as I could see from her drooping tits, had just had a litter. Yes, he did understand that it would be very hard to place a pit bull because they were the most feared (and, I knew, the most misunderstood) of dogs, but he had to leave for Europe. "Get away from this one quick," my inner voices prompted. "You'll never be able to place her." People would want her only to fight her or to breed her.

I tightened my resolve, gave the dog a last stroke (carefully avoiding those eyes), told the man that there were worse things than death and where he could take her for gentle euthanasia, wished him luck, and sprinted for the door to Safeway. Down the detergent aisle I thought of the more than two thousand dogs and cats that *every hour* of every day are put to death in this country, usually very painfully, because we do not spay and neuter our animals, because we continue even to breed them. All along the produce I thought of The Pit Bull Issue, on which I had reluctantly taken the public stand that sanctioned their being bred out of existence. At the checkout counter I resolved not to tempt myself again. I would avoid the immediate problem by leaving the store by the other door, the one to the south.

To my dismay, the man and the pit bull had also changed doors. There were those eyes again, patiently asking, that one white forepaw still extended. I spoke with the dog again, urged the man to get her spayed, and ran to my car feeling like Peter who had denied Christ. Twice. Well, at least there would not be a third temptation. So I thought.

A week later, having finally managed to convince myself that the dog *could* have found a good home, I was driving the country road from town when from the field to the left, as if she had been awaiting me, the white-pawed, brindle-colored pit bull, now collarless but with her tits still hanging, darted in front of my car. I slowed, and thankfully so did the approaching pickup truck that the dog was paying absolutely no attention to. I got off the road and turned to see her almost crawling toward me, cowed by her fear, yet still hopeful. "I can at least get her spayed," thought I, opening the car door and pulling the front seat forward. The pit bull looked, peed, leapt gratefully into the back seat. And has essentially been there ever since.

Now, I've been graced by profound friendships with both women and men, and with some very special nonhuman animals. The women who have been my lovers have introduced me to depths of intimacy and growth that have been sources of increasing amazement to me. And Bryndall Whitefoot, seventy-five-pound pit bull, has become the agent of yet another cycle of profound, amazing, and joyful lessons in this incredible life of mine. In her presence, by her guidance, and with her devotion, I have learned about impulses and acknowledgment, discovered stunning channels of communication, and glimpsed the heart of a transfiguring love.

Instead of preparing for classes that January, I tried in vain to place The Pit Bull. A badly abused pit bull, I soon discovered, for she had BB's lodged in her chest, needed immediate treatment for advanced heartworm disease, went wild at any attempt to touch her paws, and—as advertised—followed me around the cabin, never letting me out of her sight. On our walks she felt obliged to fight with every dog we encountered and to chase and kill any wildlife her sharp nose detected. If I left her alone in the cabin, she went into a frenzy of fear and wrecked the place with her attempts to get out; I began taking her with me wherever I went, leaving her in the car, where she snored peacefully, while I went to long meetings and peace demonstrations.

Desert Shield became Desert Storm, my class preparations were still undone, and I was faced with the prospect of either having The Pit Bull put to death or continuing my efforts to place her when I returned to San Francisco—meanwhile handling two cats AND a large dog in my tiny city apartment—though, truth to tell, both cats had informed me that *they* were handling her big presence just fine. Meanwhile, too, The Pit Bull and I would have to get some training and I'd have to take her for the daily walks she so loved. I would have to spend huge stretches of time with this dog, time I did not have. I would very soon resent her intrusion into my life.

"Well, honey, do you resent her now?" asked Morgaine, my lover in the city, during one of my desperate phone conversations with her.

I had to think. "Well, no—" I admitted, "but she even wants to get in bed with me. I know if I once let her do that then it's Katy-bar-the-door."

"Look," said Morgaine, who is one smart lady, "why don't you just let yourself love her? What have you got to lose?"

I wanted to scream, "My freedom! My time! My life!" but I just sat dumbfounded by the realization that *already* I was giving over my freedom-time-life to this canine being and actually enjoying doing so.

I muttered some vague words of gratitude to Morgaine and we hung up. That night, lying in bed, I watched The Pit Bull watching me from her blanket by the door. She always tried to be inconspicuous, curling up tight so as to occupy the least possible space with that mass of muscle. I sighed. "O.K.," I said, aware that my life was about to take another dramatic turn, "let's just try it for one night."

She understood immediately. The bed rocked with her leap. My face was covered with her kisses. When I bade her lie down she collapsed onto her side, fitted her body into mine, spoon fashion, her head just under my chin, and fell immediately into happy sleep. I lay there holding her, soothed by her rough snores, comforted by the heavy "there-ness" of her body.

"I have a dog," I said, to no one in particular. I was crying.

Now I'd always had some confidence in the importance of "attitude" in making my life happy. My mother had, after all, loved Peale's *The Power of Positive Thinking*, and I certainly had enough New Age friends who urged me toward joy. But child of Protestantism that I was, I'd always tried to change things by sheer willpower. Squinch the eyes together, screw up the face, and repeat, "Iamnotsick, Iamnotsick." Usually when I opened my eyes I at least knew that the exercise would carry me through the next hour or two.

Now I know that it's not willpower (or denial) that brings my changes, but a letting go and a yielding to impulses, to spontaneous desires and intuitions—in short, *letting myself do what I want to do*, and then *observing what is happening*. In my agonies about Bryndall I had clearly been doing what I wanted to do. She was *already* my companion. I had in fact been acting on feelings I was barely aware of. "Aha!" I said to myself that night, with a new twelve-to-twenty-year commitment cuddled beside me, "It's not that I have to *make* the reality; it's that I have to *acknowledge* that it's *already happening!*" Sure enough, as I paid attention to those small changes, affirmed them, expanded them in fantasy, and rejoiced in them, they became more and more material, more and more "the case," more and more what *was*.

In the following semester, as our government congratulated itself on winning a war, and as I miraculously managed not only to live with Bryndall but to teach my classes,

I also practiced *going with my impulses*. Insofar as the law would let me, I followed every crazy notion that occurred to me, every new path, every outrageous desire, every unmapped opportunity, every moonbeam. I practiced random kindness and senseless acts of beauty. Sometimes when I felt blocked or puzzled, I lay down beside her big brown body and breathed with my pit bull. As she helped me touch my deeper levels, I often "got" answers.

I began noticing how happy I was, in spite of tremendous overwork, how frequently I seemed to be walking six inches off the ground, almost ecstatic, certainly in a state of grace. I noticed and affirmed, noticed and rejoiced. I was changing, my life was changing, my relationships were changing—maybe even the world was changing. When I then read *The Nature of Personal Reality* for the third time, every line was an explosion, every page was heavy with meaning, so much so that I was months getting through it. I didn't try to understand what was happening to me. I just acknowledged it.

One day Bryndall and I were lying together in the park. The sky was blue, the grass was green, I had two hours before my next class, and in my mind I played out a fantasy. What if Bryndall and I had agreed in Framework Two (as Seth calls the dreamworld) that we would be boon companions in this life, learning from and caring for each other? What if we had carefully planned there on that Other Plane that she would be a dolphin and I would be a communications scholar studying the speech of dolphins? What if, when I declined the work with dolphins in Framework One (this reality)—as in fact I did—Bryndall had been so desperate to connect with me that she had then chosen to take on the form of a pit bull, knowing that we would meet and that I would keep her because a pit bull was the one dog I could never find a home for?

I was suddenly aware that the body next to mine was throbbing with excitement, that the trail by my outflung hand was in an apoplexy of ground-beating. "Yes, yes,

yes!" I distinctly heard from the seventy-five pounds of massive muscle beside me. I mustered a faint shred of reason and admonished myself, "Gearhart, stop this foolishness. It is only your imagination!" To my astonishment, Bryndall Whitefoot heaved to her feet and began ecstatically licking my face. "Yes," she seemed to be shouting, "yes, it *is* your imagination! And yes, it *is* the truth!"

A whole scenario filled my head. This dear and vivacious spirit whom I had known in another "where" had been ecstatic about the idea of becoming a dolphin, of speeding untamed through cold Northern California ocean waters with me, her human, swimming by her side. How we would swoop downward together and then surface on the bright sunlit waters, full of joy and discovery! How we would convince other researchers that dolphin-human communication could be accomplished only if both dolphin and human were free, not imprisoned!

I was struck by the full impact of her frustration at being confined instead to a bulky, landbound body, at the discipline she had endured in order to transform her hopes for the speed and grace of a dolphin into her acceptance of the sturdy galumphing of a devoted and well-trained pit bull. I relived my own decision not to move my career into dolphin research and suffered momentary guilt for having thrown a monkey wrench into our Framework Two plans.

In the next moment I was aware only that both Bryndall and I were rolling on the grass in a frenzy of laughter and delight. The only distinction between us seemed to be that her cheeks were perfectly dry while mine were covered with tears.

Now, I've been told a lot about love—what it is, where it comes from, why it happens, how it feels, how to do it, how to get it, how to keep it, how to let it go—and I'm convinced I've tried it all, particularly the romantic kind, which usually terminates with why-forgive-and-forget-when-you-can-remember-and-blame. I think I know, too, what it is to give and to receive that very precious thing we call unconditional love—wherein neither party could ever do anything that would make the love "stop." But I'm puzzled by the notion of unconditional love because I still suspect that "evil" exists. I'd like to be able, for instance, to love dictators, experimenters on animals, unfeeling people, anyone who exploits others.

My experience with Bryndall is probably one of unconditional love, but I'm puzzled here, too. During our first year together, in a loud, bloody, vicious, half-hour struggle, Bryndall killed a raccoon. Even through my pain I knew I (unconditionally) loved the raccoon killer, but I couldn't find that place inside me that loved her act of killing the raccoon.

Then, as I buried the raccoon, I glimpsed something that suggested how I might love that "evil" act as well as its doer, how in fact there might be no such thing as "evil." It wasn't that I suddenly understood Bryndall's genetic or acquired disposition to hunt, or the fact that Bryndall and the raccoon had simply acted out a prior agreement between them.

All that might have been true. But as I mused about the ugliness of the encounter, I stood for a moment in the big middle of an all-pervading love. In fact, I "was" love, the great "intransitive" love that had no specific object. I didn't "love X" or "Y." I just "loved."

In that remarkable second I heard again the words of the popular nineteenth-century transcendentalist message found in a Jamestown church. It began, "You are a child of the Universe. You have a right to be here." Somewhere in it was the assurance that "the Universe is unfolding as it should." It was that sense of "all right-ness" or well-being that I was being bathed in. Not just my well-being and all right-ness but that of Bryndall, the raccoon, the killing, the death of the laboratory rat, the bombings of Baghdad, every violent act—even the well-being and all rightness of every raped woman. *That* thought rattled me so profoundly that the moment was totally shattered and I've never recaptured it.

The thought is too radical for me even years later to embrace; that kind of love is still too incredible for me to contemplate receiving—or being. I'm no more ready for that dismissal of "evil" than I'm ready to suggest to some of my reason-based friends that they created their cancer.

But I vividly remember that moment. And I keep reading the Seth/Jane books, trying to act on impulses and paying close attention to the way I'm living my life. Someday I will understand this world as a place where no evil exists.

In the meantime, when Morgaine and I spend nights together—particularly cold ones—we will continue to argue about who gets to sleep next to the pit bull. And I'm tempted to put up a tiny monument in the Safeway parking lot saying "Shopper beware! On this sacred spot a whole life began its transformation!" For sure Bryndall Whitefoot will continue to lead me down miraculous pathways—and maybe even into exhilarating races in the California ocean. Daily, hourly, moment by moment, I am enthralled by that prospect and profoundly grateful for The Pit Bull Opportunity.

Charlotte Zöe Walker

The Virgin of the Rocks

I am in the lurching little bathroom as the train pulls into Victoria Station. I'm checking to see if I look O.K., if he'll think I'm too much older. I grab my things and jump off, and there he is, eyes rolled up to the high Victorian ceiling, with his funny sly-shy smile. His cheeks are English-rosy, and he's wearing a rainbow-striped sweater, another set of stripes in a stocking cap on his head, and nice pale blue jeans. Thin as ever. Not a bit older he looks. A little more colorful.

Oh, what a hug, a delicious hug. There's his whimsical voice again, always sexy, always witty, and pitched almost too low for my hearing. "Here you are," he says. "It's quite disconcerting—here you are after all that time." Well, that isn't witty, but it's said with a little leer, you see, and a bit of whimsy.

We're in his little green Mini now, pulling out into London traffic.

"Do you mind if we stop at a bottle bank?" he asks me.

"Of course not," I say. "What's a bottle bank?"

"It's a place to leave your empty bottles. I've boxes of them in back." I look in the back seat. All wine bottles.

At the first bottle bank, we climb out of the Mini and each carry a box of bottles, but there's no room to put them, it's all overflowed because last night was New Year's Eve, I forgot to tell you. A lot of broken glass lying around the bottle bank.

"Let's try another one, do you mind?" he says. He gives my knee a squeeze as we go swinging around a corner. "Ever so nice to see you," he says, raising his lovely, funny arched eyebrows. "I quite fancy you all over again."

"Well, I fancy you too," I say. After all it's what I came for. Our agreement was to be a bit cautious—no obligation to sleep together if the feeling isn't there after six years apart. But it was always there before, why not now? It's half my reason for coming here. Two years after my last love left me, I still haven't recovered. The thought of sleeping with Wendell is a last-ditch hope and consolation, a New Year's Eve flight into Auld Lang Syne.

"Here's another." We pull up to another collection of bottles on a curbside with a sort of shelter over it. This time at least there's not the broken glass in such abundance. We squeeze Wendell's boxes into the area, and off we go. "Awful thing to do to you when you have jet lag," he says.

"But now I'll drive you around a bit before we go home. I thought we could walk along the Thames a bit, now that the sun's come out."

It is simply sparkling, the Thames. There's a beautiful bridge, there are the houses of Parliament. There seem to be banners everywhere. Birds are flying. It's the first day of the new year. Wendell is smiling his funny arch smile at me, he's holding my hand, my cape is flying about behind me. Oh, what lovely energy, what a new, crisp, delightful, sensuous life.

Was it then that I threw my handbag into the air, credit cards, traveler's checks, identity and all? Oh, bright Thames, here take my identity! Wheeee! I'm going to make love again, it's going to be loveleeeee!

"Oh, dear," says Wendell. "You're so swathed in that cape, I never noticed you had a bag anyway. You always were a bit unreliable," he says. "But let's go back to the bottle banks, maybe it's there."

And so we drive all around London, back to the bottle banks, back to Victoria, no, it isn't anywhere.

"Never mind," I say.

"Never mind," he says. "You have no identity, you're in my power." Yes, his house is still next to the mental hospital, still next to the abandoned agricultural hall. But nicened up a bit all around. Just like last time, we race up the stairs together. What a fool. I have to make all those phone calls and feel such an idiot. And he does look annoyed and say in his soft voice worried things about me. "Oh, dear, you haven't changed, have you?" But then he kisses me on the bed a bit, and we begin to discover one another all over again, laughing and desiring all at once. He runs a bubble bath and both of us get in. Oh, porpoise-like, oh, porpoise in the Thames, how are you?

Wasn't I clever to come here, to have the nerve, the joie de vivre? My children have all gone away to college. My most recent attempt at love has ended in—once again!—my love's leaving me for a woman exactly ten years younger than me. Lonely, sad, and feeling restless, I answered a letter from Wendell, who has been my friend and lover off and on for a dozen years. We met as actors in a play at Williamstown years ago. We seemed to be so perfectly attuned to one another—a kind of instinctive harmony, I thought at the time. The relationship lasted throughout the next year, and I was just on the verge of thinking it might be important, and that maybe it was even mutual—when he told me one weekend that he'd just married another woman, someone he knew in England. "I don't know how it happened," he said apologetically. "It just came over us, somehow." We stayed friends, though, and I grew to like his wife quite well, even visited them in London a few years ago.

So when Wendell wrote to say that his marriage was over, I responded to the enticement of beautifully written, witty letters, which began crossing the Atlantic more and more frequently. At last I was the one to make the bold suggestion:

"Shall I come visit you in London during my winter break?" I wrote.

"That would be lovely!" came the postcard response.

But when I telephoned about the dates for my plane flights, a woman answered. "Oh, yes!" she said cordially. "I'll give him the message." When Wendell called back, I asked about the woman on the phone. "You're not living with someone, are you?" I asked carefully, holding my breath.

"Oh, no! Harriet and her little girl just rent a room from me. They needed a place in a hurry, and I took pity on them."

"Oh. Well, that's nice," I said. "She sounded very nice on the phone."

"Tell me about your lodger," I say now, over tea. "She really doesn't mind my being here?"

"Why should she?" he says. "We're careful of one another's feelings—but we have no agreement."

"What do you mean, careful of one another's feelings?"

"You see, normally I wouldn't bring someone home and she wouldn't either—but I've explained about you, and she understands."

I'm wishing I'd asked him more questions from the other side of the Atlantic. Perhaps I'd been afraid to. "So she *is* more than just a lodger?"

"There's no difficulty at all," he says. "She won't even be here for several days. She's on holiday."

Oh, well, then. Never mind, then.

"Come," he says, "woman with no identity. Come back to my boudoir."

"Before dinner?" I say. But I love the idea. It's the best, the very best way to deal with jet lag.

But there is another side to this story, one that doesn't seem to fit, that makes it all a paradox. I haven't come here just to see Wendell. My beloved friend Mira Bai is also in London. She is here with our yoga teacher, well, I might as well say it, our guru, a brilliant Indian physician who gave up his practice to teach yoga to a growing flock of disciples. Dr. Shanta had a stroke last year and has come to London for speech therapy at a famous clinic. Wendell, of course, has no interest in seeing Mira or Guruji, so we will have a nice separation in our days, as I leave him to his usual projects—scripts, rehearsals, negotiations—and make my way to Belsize Park, where Dr. Shanta and his entourage are staying.

So here I am in London, creating for myself exactly the same division I felt a dozen years ago, when I didn't marry Wendell. Well, not that I'm sure I would have, but I just didn't think of it at the time, and later he said that he'd just as soon have married me as Linda, the woman he married so suddenly that weekend. If only I had seemed to be interested, he said. Even with my children, he said. He quite liked them. For years afterward, I wished that I had known that. He probably didn't even mean it, but it haunted me sometimes—how much nicer our lives might have been, the children's and mine. Maybe his would have been harder, maybe he made the right choice. But we—we would have had his funny whimsical smile, his love of good cooking and country walks, his mild, clear boundaries between what he'd share with you and what he kept private. Anyway, it didn't happen.

And the same thing distracts me now that distracted me then—my spiritual connection. In those days it was much more intense than it is now, now that I'm older and have that something called perspective. Then, I was sure I had found the spiritual family, the ideology, that comforted me, gave meaning to my life, and if it was good for me, I was sure that meant it would be good for my children too. I would drag my children to the ashram on weekends and vacations, where we would spend the money we needed for shoes and school clothes, to be part of a community that didn't find us freakish (single mothers were that rare in our town in those days). Our dear friend Peg would be there too, happily urging us to use her new Sanskrit name, Mira Bai. I remember the first night we stayed over. There was joyous Sanskrit chanting, and Mira beaming with love for us, handing out rhythm instruments, tambourines, bells, and drums to us. The children seemed as enchanted as I, with the candlelight, the music, the lively, kindly dark face of Guruji at the center of it all.

With such inducements, such total embrace of our incomplete family, such a place to run to—how could I take mild and whimsical Wendell seriously? And yet no spiritual comfort would quite match the pleasure of being in bed with him. So I kept the two worlds separate—sleeping with Wendell when he showed up, flying kites, making jams with him and the children, imposing sprouts and salads, tofu and high-minded blessings on him. No wonder he was exasperated—the tofu and the blessings were especially not his style—and found someone else. I felt the loss, felt a little betrayed, but went back to the ashram for another weekend, immersed myself in spirituality, and found it fairly easy to let go.

Now, a dozen years later, he's single again, but there's a woman living in his house who is clearly more to him than he let on in our transatlantic phone calls. And my guru and Mira, my oldest friend, are living with a small group of devotees in a tiny apartment in Belsize Park. I have rushed across the Atlantic to find myself and, once again, I find myself split in two. When Wendell leaves for rehearsal in the morning, I get on the tube for Belsize Park, walk up the shabbily genteel high street, stopping at a little florist's shop to buy some freesias, and make my way past the Royal Free Hospital, where Guruji goes each day for post-stroke speech therapy, to the decaying corner building where they live—Guruji, Mira, and two young devotees. I bang on the door with my gloved fist. "Mittened on it manfully," I quote Dylan Thomas to myself. At first I pushed the doorbell buttons, but clearly they don't work. The door, though shabby with several peeling colors of paint, with a couple of empty holes where older locks used to be, is thick and sturdy. Though I pound and pound on it, nobody hears me. Just as I am halfway down the path to the street, looking for a phone booth to call them from, the door opens. A round old Indian man with a gray top-knot on his head and a big, gap-toothed grin lets me into the building.

"Thank you," I say. "I'm here to see Dr. Shanta."

"Yes, yes," he says, nodding happily. "Up there!"

I thank him again, and walk across the torn linoleum of the ground-floor hallway, then up the two flights to their floor.

I rap gently on the door, then push it open, for it isn't latched. Mira Bai looks up at me heavy-lidded, still deep in meditation. Her silver-gray hair curls in wisps and tendrils around her face, and is gathered in a barrette at the back of the neck. Her orange cotton sari curves and crumples around her softly, like clouds in a sunset. Her face, though etched with many lines, is like a sleepy angel's. I have seen her like this a hundred times or more. Always it is a little frightening to see how deep she goes, what tidal mysteries sweep her away again and again. She sits cross-legged in an armchair that is shoved up next to the kitchen door. Every bit of space in the room is taken up with some kind of bulky object. On the other side of the kitchen doorway is the chair where Guruji sits, and next to it a little table with an orange cloth over it. In front of his chair a small electric heater is buzzing away. Beneath the window, on a piece of wood over two cinder blocks, is a little altar, cluttered with pictures, flowers in various stages of freshness and decay, crystals and incense burners and beads, and a variety of odd mementos. At the other end of the room, there is a bed for one of the devotees, her own little altar, and a huge Bauhaus wardrobe in battered condition, which contains the clothing of all four of them who live here. Next to the entrance door, opposite the window wall, is another mattress covered in an Indian print spread, and yet another private altar, this one with dozens of pictures of Guruji on it. Among all these things are yet two more shabby armchairs, another end table, and an old leather hassock.

How much more crowded it must be when all of them are here! But I am lucky this morning, because the others are at the hospital for Guruji's speech therapy. Mira is alone in her meditation. I am gazing on her heavy eyes with pain and love.

"Why didn't you come sooner?" she says. "We could have had all this time alone for talking." Yet she can hardly talk.

"I was banging on the door for a good ten minutes," I say. "But nobody heard me."

"Ah," she says. "I wondered if I should go down and unlock it for you. Still, I was expecting you half an hour ago!"

"I know. I'm sorry. It took me longer than I thought to find my way."

"I'm so happy you're here," she says. "I want to show you all of London. I'm in love with the churches. We'll go to St. Martin-in-the-Fields, we'll go to St. Paul's."

"Churches?" I say, surprised.

"Sacred places are all the same," she says. "They all have that holy vibration. Besides, I have been very drawn to Christian images lately, to the Virgin especially. I'll tell you about it."

"Where shall we go today?" I ask her. "I haven't much money—I lost my purse in my first hour here! It's crazy, but I don't even worry about it, I feel so happy to be here!"

"It will be returned to you," she says decisively. "You'll see." She stands up a little unsteadily, giving her sari a little shake to uncrumple it, then looks up at me with a smile.

I laugh, reaching out my hand to steady her. "Well, I don't deserve it," I say.

"Yes, you do." She grins at me with that sweet old sparkle in her pale blue eyes, with the left pupil smaller than the right because of a car accident from long ago. She puts her arms around me in a great motherly hug, and I feel, as always, deeply comforted. But she is so thin, I feel that too. "Mira! You're not eating enough!"

"Oh, we're on a small budget here, the four of us," she says. "But we get along all right."

"But are you really eating your share?"

"Well, sometimes I can't eat right at the moment," she says, "and then there isn't anything left later on."

"They ought to save something for you," I say.

"Oh, they try," she laughs. "I do believe they try! It's hard, though, I admit it—hard to be cooped up with Lakshmi and Kamala in this tiny apartment."

I am looking around the cluttered, colorful space, trying to imagine how three more bodies could fit inside it, when we hear their footfalls on the stairs.

As the door opens, Lakshmi and Kamala, two devotees I know from the ashram, come in with Guruji. The two of them seem so much alike at first glance, both with long, uncombed blond hair, both in white saris. Lakshmi is first, holding the door open for Guruji, while Kamala is stooping at his side, helping him remove his black cotton Chinese slippers.

"Ohhhhhh!" says Guruji warmly, almost musically, as he sees me. His dark eyes are bright with welcome and surprise. He mumbles a bit, some effort at a welcoming phrase, but the words don't come out. He is a small man of stature, but his face is almost lionlike in its strength, its bristling brows, the dark gleam of his eyes—and yet full of kindness. Since his stroke he has not been able to shave, and has grown a dark gray beard that makes him seem more like an ancient swami, with his orange robes and the orange tam-o'-shanter on his head.

We are standing there in a kind of silent, dazzling greeting, as Kamala whisks his coat away and Lakshmi begins clucking about whether there will be enough food for lunch, then interrupts herself. "Oh, I don't mean to be rude," she says. "It's so nice to see you, Claudia. But I am just thinking, how will we make plans for lunch . . ."

"Oh, no," I say. "Mira and I are going out—aren't we, Mira?"

"If you don't mind, Guruji," she says, and he smiles and waves his hand as if to waft us immediately into a delightful adventure.

Suddenly I remember my freesias, still not in water, and quickly pick them up from Mira's prayer mat and hand them to Guruji. He breathes in their rich scent, saying "Ohhhhhh!" again, in that wonderful way.

"It's wonderful to see you, Guruji!" I say, as Mira pulls her coat from the big wardrobe and comes smiling toward us, ready to show me London.

In the evening, I say good-bye to Mira as she gets on the train to Belsize Park, and then head back to Wendell's house for dinner. His newly remodeled kitchen is in the basement, just as the original kitchen was a hundred years ago. Heavy beams above us, with an array of well-used pots and skillets hanging from them, a stained deal table in the center of the room, where I am cutting up tomatoes for the salad. He is cooking for me one of his Near Eastern specialties, a spicy couscous with eggplant and chickpeas. He smiles at me happily. "Isn't this lovely?" he says. "Like old times!"

The days and nights pass quickly this way, and I am ever dizzier and more divided, making love with Wendell, then wandering about with Mira Bai and meditating in Belsize Park. But now the lodger has come back, with her little girl. Did I tell you there's a little girl? We are in the old-fashioned basement kitchen where we have all just met. Heather, the child, is a spunky, modern little thing with a spiky, elfin haircut. "Where are you going to *sleep*?" she says in her clipped, perfect British child way.

"Oh, I don't know," I say. I look at Harriet, her mother, who is more beautiful than I feared. She is candid, lovely,

slim, and sparkling. Our eyes meet almost laughingly, then
skid away.

"But you must sleep somewhere," says Heather.
"Where will Wendell put you?"

Wendell's shoulders look a bit hunched as he turns
away, fiddles with a wine cork.

"Well, I expect he'll put you in the bathroom," Heather
says. "He often puts people there."

So that's settled. I'll sleep in the bathroom. Wendell
pours us some wine, and we all drink up. To the New Year.
"And to Claudia's luck," toasts Wendell. "Her entire handbag was returned to the embassy, can you imagine?"

"Lovely," says Harriet, and lifts her glass to me. "I'm
so glad."

I ask what it's like being a midwife.

"I love working with women," she says. "I love giving
them the support and the natural environment that doctors don't, and I love seeing babies into the world."

I tell her about my women playwrights class, promise
to send her my copy of an American feminist book about
midwives. Wendell relaxes. It's obvious we like each other.

The phone rings, and Wendell takes it in his study, leaving us alone for a while. We get on splendidly. We do like
each other, even more when he's out of the room. Given
time, we'd tell each other everything. After all, we're both
feminists and believe in sisterhood.

It's obvious that she loves him. Obvious he doesn't deserve it. But maybe I only imagine it.

"Do you think I only imagine it?" I ask Mira, as we sip tea
in the National Gallery's cafeteria—a respite, where we can
look not at the walls but at the people around us, sometimes dutiful, sometimes passionate, art-seeking people.
It's easy to spot the art students, clothed in black with dark
circles under their eyes, with their portfolios and folded
easels propped against their chairs. I watch them distract-
edly, thinking not of art but of love triangles, of passion,

or lust anyway, and betrayal, or at least deception. What a comfort to be here with Mira!

"It's been so long since I've been in that life," she laughs, chuckles really, in that funny, almost sensuous way of hers.

"But remember that time a million years ago," I say, leaning forward, wishing for that old Mira. "When you confessed to me how many lovers you'd had, and I confessed to you that I'd had no one but my ex-husband?"

"Oh, how we depressed ourselves that night," she says. "And really it was all the same thing, wasn't it? My dozen and your one, they gave us both such terrible sadness!"

"And I suppose you think that's all I'll find with Wendell now," I say.

"No, I only wonder why you bother with him at all! I wish there were room for you in our apartment, it's no place for you to be, that situation."

"You're right," I say. "You've always understood things when I was baffled. But how can I change things now? My return flight's just a few days away. I'll have to stick it out."

"If you need to borrow money for a hotel . . ." she begins, but I hush her, for I know she has even less money than I do.

"Let's go see some paintings," I urge.

"There's a special one I want to show you," she agrees.

We rush past masterpieces with hardly a glance, as she leads us to the painting.

"Here," she says finally. She sinks to the floor in front of it, gazing upward. The look on her face is profoundly devotional. I don't know what to do. Won't a guard make her stand up? But I sink to the floor beside her. "Leonardo da Vinci," she says softly, "The Virgin of the Rocks. Look!"

"How dark, how strange!" I exclaim. I have never seen such a Madonna. She is in a stark landscape, a bit of surf in the upper left corner, amid tall rock formations. The Virgin and child, with his cousin the infant Saint John and a serene, sisterly angel, sit in the foreground in a dark grotto, surrounded by great rocks, almost a Stonehenge by the sea. The Virgin's robe is darkest blue, and the only light is in their faces, the children's bodies, and a few small white flowers beneath them.

"That's my grandmother's brooch," Mira says. "I used to wear it all the time, remember?"

For the first time I notice the small black brooch that is fastened to the Madonna's cloak. "I'd forgotten it," I say.

"But you see the resemblance, don't you?" says Mira.

"To your grandmother's brooch?"

"To me," she says. "Don't you see it?" Her voice is different, not my bantering Mira's voice but something different that chills me. "I haven't told you this before, but an Indian psychic visited us last month—and he told me I am a reincarnation of Mary."

"But Mira, you didn't believe him?"

"Not at first," she says. "Guruji dismissed it, but I think it was a kind of jealousy on his part, for the psychic had a great spiritual power, and urged me to leave Guruji and follow him."

"Not at first . . ." I repeat.

"I don't expect you to understand right away," she says. "But I've been studying the Madonnas in churches, in paintings. The Pietà—it was the time my brother died, in that accident years ago, and I was holding him in my lap, waiting for the ambulance. I've lived the Pietà a thousand different ways, and Gary's dying was only the most recent."

"Oh, Mira, it's been too hard for you here, Guruji's stroke, and all the crowding in that little apartment."

"Just look at her," Mira says. "Look at the pain and mystery of all those rocks, look at the darkness. But I could always dive from rocks like that, dive right into the surf and swim like a seal!"

"But the Virgin doesn't look like a swimmer," I say.

"She was, though," Mira says. "I was always a great swimmer—and no one could beat me at high diving."

What must I do? Ask her to come home with me? Would she come? What can I do? But in my mind's eye, I am simply seeing Mira dive again, at a deep waterfall pool in the Catskills, skinny-dipping with her sisters and cousins. It was the first time I'd ever been skinny-dipping, and that was plunge enough for me. How I admired Mira, the perfect arc of her lean body plunging so surely past the waterfall, into the dark pool.

In the evening I join Mira and the others at a meditation in Belsize Park. The owner of their building, the elderly Indian who let me in the first day, has built a big temple in his basement, covered the floor in carpets and cushions for people to sit cross-legged in meditation, and built a huge stage full of statues in the front. I have never seen such a garish assortment of religious objects, brightly colored divinities of every description, four-armed goddesses with swords, Hanuman the monkey god, Ganesha with his elephant head—all made of plaster and vividly painted or clothed in actual fabrics. There are swags of Christmas tinsel and strings of colored lights, mingling with candles and incense. In the midst of all this sits Guruji, whose teaching attracted me because of its simplicity, its intelligence, its compassion: he seems out of place in this sideshow of colors and images. His small, brilliant-orange figure is seated on a blue cushion. His deep black eyes shine with life and humor and kindness, and it is a joy to be in the front row, even in this strange place, and find him smiling at me affectionately. Mira sits near him dreamily playing the harmonium for a woman from the Indian community, who is singing a devotional song, high-pitched, passionate, and complex.

What kind of spiritual ricochet bounced Mira from all this to the Virgin of the Rocks? Perhaps this cartoonish basement temple was just too big a shock, too big a change for her. Yet even here, the Indian goddesses are more appealing to strong women than the Virgin Mary, aren't they, with their four arms, their swords and conch shells and lotuses, their lions underfoot? For years, even before we began to study yoga, Mira was a kind of goddess to me. She was a divorced single mother ahead of me, and when my husband left me for one of his students, she helped me through the pain, she showed me that it was possible to carry on with dignity, and to find my own way just as she had. Strangely, I was the one who found yoga and introduced her to Guruji—but she was the one who dived in headfirst, gave up her career, gave her children to their father, so she could spend all her time as his disciple.

After the song, Guruji leads a meditation by chanting Ommmmm. And then one of his disciples plays a tape of an old meditation, from before the stroke that took away his power of speech. "Deeeeply relax your body," says the beloved voice from the past. "Ohhhcean of vibration. Feel it," the voice says with deep gentleness. "Deeeeeply relax. You are like the blue sky," he says sweetly, and I forget that it is only a tape, and that the Guruji in front of me can no longer speak. I forget that Mira thinks she is the Virgin Mary, and I forget the jumble of vivid statues behind them. My eyes are closed, and I am like the blue sky.

"How is your friend Mira?" asks Wendell, as we walk back to his house from the tube station late at night. The air is damp and misty, and the high street is a grayness, with pockets of harsh lighting and occasional neon. We have passed a group of rough young men with shaven heads, and heard the sound of bottles breaking, tossed against a wall for fun.

"I think she may be going crazy," I say. This is my world-self talking.

"But you've known that all along, haven't you?" he says. "Leading this odd mystical life for how many years now?"

"But that's only crazy the way I am," I say. "It's just a

more extreme case of—inspiration." Another round of the popping sound of bottles breaking a block or so behind us.

"Ah, so what is different now?" he says, smiling at me, striding along quite at home in his north London world.

"Oh. Nothing, I guess. It's just different."

"Maybe you're growing wiser," he says. But I know that isn't true, not the way he means it, not any way at all, in fact.

This morning, after intimacies that seemed to me both passionate and tender, Wendell goes to bathe in the big bathroom next to the room we sleep in, on the top floor. In a few minutes I hear Harriet's voice too. I hear the soft swirling sound as she slides into the bath with him. I hear their pleasant, intimate voices, endearments, kisses, and the sloshing of bathwater.

When she has gone downstairs and he is in the bedroom again, pulling on his pants, I protest. "It's rude, it's hurtful, it makes me feel terrible," I say. "You told me there was nothing between you."

"I didn't quite say that," says Wendell. "You may have misinterpreted a bit."

"I want to leave right now," I say.

"You mustn't leave," he says. "We'll have such a lovely time this weekend. I'm looking forward to it."

"She must be miserable having me here," I say. "If you're that close, then how must she feel, having me sleep up here with you?"

"We're not that close," he says. "We have an arrangement, we're both just alike that way, we have lots of friends."

"No, I can feel the tension when the three of us are together, and it's not just me. I know it's hard for her." Then I begin to feel angry at her too, for sharing that bath with Wendell. It was clever, though, it makes things clear. "But at least she doesn't have to hear us," I say. "*We* don't make love on the other side of her room, she doesn't have to listen to us. It was rude of you to do that just now!"

"So it all comes down to manners, does it? You sound quite British," he smiles. His clothes are all on now. None of mine are. I have been too hurt and angry to bother dressing. He sits down beside me. "I'm sorry," he says. "I didn't mean for it to be hard for anyone. I just really wanted to see you."

All the way to meet Mira at Victoria Station my thoughts are torn between that humiliation and the basement temple in Belsize Park. My life seems lost somewhere between them—and no hope of being miraculously returned, the way my handbag was. In the old days, Mira and I shared everything, told each other everything. But how can I tell a Leonardo Madonna about my shameful situation, the noises in the bath on the other side of the bedroom wall? No more than I can tell Wendell about Mira and the Virgin.

There she is, easy to find in the midst of the rush hour crowd. She stands tall, with an orange scarf over her soft gray hair, and her orange sari hanging beneath a battered car coat.

"You're late," she tells me. "We'll just barely catch the train!" As always, I run behind her, down the platform to the train for Cambridge. We laugh as we climb aboard, and find window seats facing each other.

"What fun!" I say, feeling suddenly happy, restored.

"I'm so glad you've come," she exclaims, an extra light in her pale blue eyes with the uneven pupils. "I haven't been to Cambridge in twenty years. My grandfather went there—Queen's College. I hope it hasn't changed too much!"

Soon we are walking across the lawn to Queen's College, the warm patina of the stone, the glitter of old windows in the wintry sun. The students are still away for the winter

break, and most of the doors are locked. Under a stone ar-
cade, we find a brightly lit office, and go in to ask for a key.

"My grandfather studied here," Mira explains. I realize
suddenly how odd she looks in her thick hiking boots,
bulky quilted-cotton car coat in dreary beige, and the orange sari hanging in folds beneath it. I am probably a little
odd myself by Cambridge standards, enfolded in my cape
of muted purples and greens. Mira's charm and education
never fail her, though. She is handed a big iron key, and we
are soon letting ourselves into the locked chapel.

"What a powerful energy here," she murmurs, closing
her eyes.

I begin to feel something too. I always feel a call to meditate when I'm with Mira. It's as if there is a presence
around her presence, a motherly aura that enfolds her and
takes me into its embrace also. I give myself to this feeling,
and everything else disappears—the dark wooden choir
stalls, the carved pulpit, the stained glass.

After a few minutes, I hear Mira's voice. "I feel myself
in all these figures," she says, looking at a large painting
of the Annunciation on the side wall. The Virgin, in volu-
minous blue draperies, is gazing in surprise and mystery
at the skinny angel, who is almost shyly holding out a lily
to her. "They have given me so many faces, so many
forms. But I find myself in all of them."

I am silent a moment. It is a beautiful idea, somehow. I
smile at her. "And I can't even find one self," I say.

But Mira is not paying any attention. She has stepped
down from the wooden stall and is kneeling on the marble
tile floor, gazing up at the painting. I shiver with fear, then
do the only thing that comes naturally to me at the moment. I join her kneeling in front of the Virgin in volumi-
nous folds of blue, who is just getting the news from that
frail angel holding out his lily. I lean forward, in a shiver
of ecstasy, and touch my head to the floor.

*   *   *

A day later, Friday afternoon, in the warm basement kitchen of Wendell's north London row house, Harriet and Wendell and I have been talking painfully. Harriet has just been crying. With rushed apologies, she and Wendell retreat into her little girl Heather's room to talk. Heather stays in the kitchen with me; in a burst of uncanny inspiration, this bright-eyed child with her short, modern haircut walks up to me with a paper sticker in her hand. She presses it onto my sweater, then goes off to her room.

"I want my room back!" she calls ahead of herself in warning.

I look down at the sticker—and find to my astonishment that it is a picture of a nun in a black habit. Where did she get such a thing? I quickly pull it off and crumple it into a tight little wad.

When Harriet and Wendell come back from Heather's room, all three of us sit down. An embarrassed Wendell makes tea while Harriet and I apologize to each other.

"I didn't know," I say. "I'm terribly sorry, I didn't know."

"Well—we didn't know either," says Harriet. "Or rather—we pretended not to."

"Still—Wendell should have told me. There was *something* he could have told me!"

"Yes—Wendell's been rather cowardly about it," says Harriet. "He's made it very hard for me—and for you too, I suspect."

Wendell hunches guiltily over the teakettle, like a found-out Dickensian villain, smiling up at us from his bent head, his loose blond hair hanging beside his arch brows, his embarrassed smile.

"I'll leave today," I say.

"Oh, no, you mustn't do that," says Harriet.

"We'll have our trip to Brighton, first," says Wendell. "I promised you that."

Afterward, I will always remember that I was desperate or greedy or confused enough to accept. That I allowed

Wendell to drive off to Brighton with me, leaving Harriet, who loved him, to work out her feelings alone with her child in London. Leaving Harriet, my fellow feminist, to sleep and think alone. And what about my own self-respect? Where had that fled to?

A bit embarrassed with each other, but bearing up brightly, Wendell and I drive through storybook villages to Brighton, past the disappointing pavilion with its tawdry onion towers, and find a charming little hotel, where our bodies bid each other farewell. It is such an old friendship, such a "funny glue," Wendell calls it, that draws us together even when we're saying good-bye.

"I'm sorry it's all turned out like this," says Wendell, as we sip coffee the next morning. "You see, I thought you'd be staying part of the time at Mira's, I didn't realize you'd be the whole time with me."

"I wish you'd told me," I say. "Because there wasn't room at Mira's, you know."

"I know," he says. "But if we'd discussed all that, you'd never have come, would you?"

I laugh. "Maybe not," I say.

"And are you so sorry that you did?" He smiles at me over his coffee cup, his eyebrows raised half-pleadingly, half-mockingly. We are in the hotel's tiny dining room, sitting at a small table near the lace-covered corner window.

I think, I search, I try to find the answer. "I'm sorry about the mess we made," I say. "I'm sorry to have hurt Harriet, and you know I'm not unscathed myself."

"Nor I," says Wendell.

"Not scathed enough," I say. "You seem to get off awfully easy somehow!"

"That remains to be seen," says Wendell.

"You mean, will Harriet forgive you?"

"Oh, I don't know, not that so much. Just—how I feel about things, I suppose. I do have a conscience of sorts, you know."

"But it comes into play so late, doesn't it, Wendell? I don't blame you, though," I say. "There were clues. I just didn't want to read them. I'll know better next time."

"I suppose you will," he smiles, gazing at me affectionately. "I suppose our funny old glue will have to dissolve sometime."

"I can't help being glad that I saw you somehow," I say, smiling back. "And ever so glad I saw Mira."

"No complications there," says Wendell.

"No, none there," I say, because I cannot tell him how changed Mira is, and how bewildered and worried I am.

"Come," he says, setting down his cup. "You must see Brighton Pier before we head back."

It's a chilly walk to the pier, the sky gray, the January wind blowing from the sea. Wendell leads us to the abandoned amusement pier, a strangely garish wooden structure over the water, full of boarded-up booths and painted signs, where almost everything is closed for the winter. Detached, companionable, we gaze out at the gray sea. Amid the shuttered booths, a glass case shelters a mechanical automaton "fat lady" who rocks back and forth with hands on knees. She sits draped in chipped and fading painted reds and blues, carnival threads with a Renaissance touch. Her pink-enamel cheeks bulge up against her merry eyes, as she laughs a ghastly, tinny laugh, inviting us to enter a show that has closed for the season. Hahahahaha! she cackles. The show is closed, but don't take it so seriously. Maybe you have new journeys to make, better discoveries than last season's sideshow! Hahahahaha! And the wind whips about, and the boards creak beneath our feet, and everything sways a bit, as we walk on Brighton Pier.

The next day Mira and Wendell meet for the first time in years, as they ride with me together on the train to Gatwick Airport. It is almost a party, the three of us so oddly together. They seem suddenly to like one another, in this festivity of my departure, trading witticisms and laughing at each other's jokes. I am laughing too, basking in the sweetness of this rare conjunction.

At the airport, I try to get them to pose for their pictures in one of the passport photo booths. "I don't have recent pictures of either of you," I urge.

"No, you give your picture to us," says Wendell.

"Yes, you must do it for us," says Mira.

"Only if you take your pictures after me," I say, and they hedge and demur, and push me into the shiny plastic booth. I smile at the face in the mirror. Fool that she is, she looks unscathed and smiles back at me brightly. She doesn't tell me what we have learned, though I know there is something. There are buzzes and clicks, and soon I have the strip in hand, three faces to divide between myself and my friends, with the help of Mira's nail file.

Next time I see Mira Bai, we are back in the United States, swimming in a pond where geese are nesting. Her speech has grown strangely halting, and her presence seems vague. "Do you see that lead goose?" she asks me, after we have pulled ourselves onto a little dock, and sit drying ourselves. "That's my Grandfather Morrow. He's come back as that goose to watch over me. Watch now, he'll lead them right to me." The goose indeed swims at the head of a flock of eight or nine, swimming in a V formation, right to the dock where we sit dangling our feet in the water. We have no bread to give them.

Soon after this we will learn that Mira has a cruel brain disease, one that leaves her memory but takes away her reason and finally all ability to function. It was probably in its early stages as we knelt together beneath Leonardo's Madonna. For a long time I am so devastated, so angry over this, that I blame Guruji, blame all religions and whatever is behind them, East or West—and I find ways to blame myself, as well. Finally, though, I accept that what betrayed her was not the spiritual life but something in her body's secret workings, something chromosomal, if the latest research is correct.

In the meantime, I have met the love who now brings hope and happiness to my life—a life that still seems to be expanding, while my beloved friend's diminishes so painfully. I thought of leaving this out of the story. Isn't it too big a stretch, to tell you my "happy ending"? Isn't it an afterthought, irrelevant? My love arrived in time to get to know Mira, while there was still enough of her left to know, before her jaunty voice, her laughter, her sweet meditations, are lost to a fading mind. But now Guruji has died, after years of illness borne with kindness and laughter, and Mira is too incapacitated, too near death herself, to speak; tears fall down the cheeks of her expressionless face when she is told of his death. When I go to pay my respects, chanting with others beside his body heaped with flowers, I wish that Mira could be with us; and I begin to hope again that maybe her years of meditation are somehow sustaining her beyond where I can know or see, like that glimpse of distant waters behind the rocks.

In a lagoon scattered with high, treacherous rocks, a smiling Virgin hands her child to the angel sitting near her, then climbs one of the highest rocks and stands there gazing down, that smile of rapture and adventure in her eyes. She unclasps the brooch that is a family heirloom, lets her cloak fall to her feet, and springs into a perfect dive, plunging in elegant form to the rough waters below. She swims like a seal.

The Vision

In my room, Kuan Yin guards my bed.
Goddess of Unmarried Women.
Goddess of Fertility.
Goddess of Mercy.
She stands on a throne of gold-tipped lotus,
holding a white horsetail duster
and metal rings to encircle
the heads of the disobedient.

Her black hair flows over her white veils,
and she smiles to me as her pink lotus flies
across the sky. Sometimes she carries
an infant in her arms,
but Kuan Yin is not the Virgin Mary.
The child she carries is not her own.

I have prayed to her since I was a child
before I knew what prayer meant,
when daily my mother slapped
the bamboo stick across my arms and legs,
and my prayers became the bridge across the pain.

My grandmother tells me to release my childhood,
remember only that Kuan Yin plucked me off
the wobbly junk of a boat gypsy
and flew me to her,
dark orphan, my skin rashed and peeling.

Today, walking through the streets of Chinatown
I buy images of her.
Sometimes pewter, sometimes bargain jade,
these small comforts
I collect like tokens
to buy my way across.

Helena María Viramontes

The Moths

I was fourteen years old when Abuelita requested my help. And it seemed only fair. Abuelita had pulled me through the rages of scarlet fever by placing, removing, and replacing potato slices on the temples of my forehead; she had seen me through several whippings, an arm broken by a dare jump off Tío Enrique's toolshed, puberty, and my first lie. Really, I told Amá, it was only fair.

Not that I was her favorite granddaughter or anything special. I wasn't even pretty or nice like my older sisters, and I just couldn't do the girl things they could do. My hands were too big to handle the fineries of crocheting or embroidery, and I always pricked my fingers or knotted my colored threads time and time again while my sisters laughed and called me bull hands with their cute waterlike voices. So I began keeping a piece of jagged brick in my sock to bash my sisters or anyone who called me bull hands. Once, while we all sat in the bedroom, I hit Teresa on the forehead, right above her eyebrow and she ran to Amá with her mouth open, her hand over her eye while blood seeped between her fingers. I was used to the whippings by then.

I wasn't respectful either. I even went so far as to doubt the power of Abuelita's slices, the slices she said absorbed my fever. "You're still alive, aren't you?" Abuelita snapped back, her pasty gray eye beaming at me and burning holes in my suspicions. Regretful that I had let secret questions drop out of my mouth, I couldn't look into her eyes. My hands began to fan out, grow like a liar's nose until they hung by my side like low weights. Abuelita made a balm out of dried moth wings and Vicks and rubbed my hands, shaped them back to size, and it was the strangest feeling. Like bones melting. Like sun shining through the darkness of your eyelids. I didn't mind helping Abuelita after that, so Amá would always send me over to her.

In the early afternoon, Amá would push her hair back, hand me my sweater and shoes, and tell me to go to Mama Luna's. This was to avoid another fight and another whipping, I knew. I would deliver one last direct shot on Marisela's arm and jump out of our house, the slam of the screen door burying her cries of anger, and I'd gladly go help Abuelita plant her wild lilies or jasmine or heliotrope or cilantro or hierbabuena in red Hills Brothers coffee cans. Abuelita would wait for me at the top step of her porch holding a hammer and nail and empty coffee cans. And although we hardly spoke, hardly looked at each other as we worked over root transplants, I always felt her gray eye on me. It made me feel, in a strange sort of way, safe and guarded and not alone. Like God was supposed to make you feel.

On Abuelita's porch, I would puncture holes in the bottom of the coffee cans with a nail and a precise hit of a hammer. This completed, my job was to fill them with red clay mud from beneath her rosebushes, packing it softly, then making a perfect hole, four fingers around, to nest a sprouting avocado pit, or the spidery sweet potatoes that Abuelita rooted in mayonnaise jars with toothpicks and daily water, or prickly chayotes that produced vines that twisted and wound all over her porch pillars, crawling to the roof, up and over the roof, and down the other side, making her small brick house look like it was cradled within the vines that grew pear-shaped squashes ready for the pick, ready to be steamed with onions and cheese and butter. The roots would burst out of the rusted coffee cans

and search for a place to connect. I would then feed the
seedlings with water.

But this was a different kind of help, Amá said, because
Abuelita was dying. Looking into her gray eye, then into
her brown one, the doctor said it was just a matter of days.
And so it seemed only fair that these hands she had melted
and formed found use in rubbing her caving body with
alcohol and marihuana, rubbing her arms and legs, turning her face to the window so that she could watch the
bird-of-paradise blooming or smell the scent of clove in the
air. I toweled her face frequently and held her hand for
hours. Her gray wiry hair hung over the mattress. Since I
could remember, she'd kept her long hair in braids. Her
mouth was vacant, and when she slept, her eyelids never
closed all the way. Up close, you could see her gray eye
beaming out the window, staring hard as if to remember
everything. I never kissed her. I left the window open when
I went to the market.

Across the street from Jay's Market there was a chapel.
I never knew its denomination, but I went in just the same
to search for candles. I sat down on one of the pews because there were none. After I cleaned my fingernails, I
looked up at the high ceiling. I had forgotten the vastness
of these places, the coolness of the marble pillars and the
frozen statues with blank eyes. I was alone. I knew why I
had never returned.

That was one of Apá's biggest complaints. He would
pound his hands on the table, rocking the sugar dish or
spilling a cup of coffee, and scream that if I didn't go to
Mass every Sunday to save my goddamn sinning soul,
then I had no reason to go out of the house, period. Punto
final. He would grab my arm and dig his nails into me to
make sure I understood the importance of catechism. Did
he make himself clear? Then he strategically directed his
anger at Amá for her lousy ways of bringing up daughters,
being disrespectful and unbelieving, and my older sisters
would pull me aside and tell me if I didn't get to Mass right

this minute, they were all going to kick the holy shit out of me. Why am I so selfish? Can't you see what it's doing to Amá, you idiot? So I would wash my feet and stuff them in my black Easter shoes that shone with Vaseline, grab a missal and veil, and wave good-bye to Amá.

I would walk slowly down Lorena to First to Evergreen, counting the cracks on the cement. On Evergreen I would turn left and walk to Abuelita's. I liked her porch because it was shielded by the vines of the chayotes and I could get a good look at the people and car traffic on Evergreen without them knowing. I would jump up the porch steps, knock on the screen door as I wiped my feet, and call Abuelita? Mi Abuelita? As I opened the door and stuck my head in, I would catch the gagging scent of toasting chile on the placa. When I entered the sala, she would greet me from the kitchen, wringing her hands in her apron. I'd sit at the corner of the table to keep from being in her way. The chiles made my eyes water. Am I crying? No, Mama Luna, I'm sure not crying. I don't like going to Mass, but my eyes watered anyway, the tears dropping on the tablecloth like candle wax. Abuelita lifted the burnt chiles from the fire and sprinkled water on them until the skins began to separate. Placing them in front of me, she turned to check the menudo. I peeled the skins off and put the flimsy, limp-looking green and yellow chiles in the molcajete and began to crush and crush and twist and crush the heart out of the tomato, the clove of garlic, the stupid chiles that made me cry, crushed them until they turned into liquid under my bull hand. With a wooden spoon, I scraped hard to destroy the guilt, and my tears were gone. I put the bowl of chile next to a vase filled with freshly cut roses. Abuelita touched my hand and pointed to the bowl of menudo that steamed in front of me. I spooned some chile into the menudo and rolled a corn tortilla thin with the palms of my hands. As I ate, a fine Sunday breeze entered the kitchen and a rose petal calmly feathered down to the table.

I left the chapel without blessing myself and walked to Jay's. Most of the time Jay didn't have much of anything. The tomatoes were always soft and the cans of Campbell's soups had rusted spots on them. There was dust on the tops of cereal boxes. I picked up what I needed: rubbing alcohol, five cans of chicken broth, a big bottle of Pine Sol. At first Jay got mad because I thought I had forgotten the money. But it was there all the time, in my back pocket.

When I returned from the market, I heard Amá crying in Abuelita's kitchen. She looked up at me with puffy eyes. I placed the bags of groceries on the table and began putting the cans of soup away. Amá sobbed quietly. I never kissed her. After a while, I patted her on the back for comfort. Finally: "¿Y mi Amá?" she asked in a whisper, then choked again and cried into her apron.

Abuelita fell off the bed twice yesterday, I said, knowing that I shouldn't have said it and wondering why I wanted to say it because it only made Amá cry harder. I guess I became angry and just so tired of the quarrels and beatings and unanswered prayers and my hands just there hanging helplessly by my side. Amá looked at me again, confused, angry, and her eyes were filled with sorrow. I went outside and sat on the porch swing and watched the people pass. I sat there until she left. I dozed off repeating the words to myself like rosary prayers: when do you stop giving when do you start giving when do you . . . and when my hands fell from my lap, I awoke to catch them. The sun was setting, an orange glow, and I knew Abuelita was hungry.

There comes a time when the sun is defiant. Just about the time when moods change, inevitable seasons of a day, transitions from one color to another, that hour or minute or second when the sun is finally defeated, finally sinks into the realization that it cannot with all its power to heal or burn, exist forever, there comes an illumination where the sun and earth meet, a final burst of burning red-orange fury reminding us that although endings are inevitable, they are necessary for rebirths, and when that time came, just when I switched on the light in the kitchen to open Abuelita's can of soup, it was probably then that she died.

The room smelled of Pine Sol and vomit and Abuelita had defecated the remains of her cancerous stomach. She had turned to the window and tried to speak, but her mouth remained open and speechless. I heard you, Abuelita, I said, stroking her cheek, I heard you. I opened the windows of the house and let the soup simmer and over-boil on the stove. I turned the stove off and poured the soup down the sink. From the cabinet I got a tin basin, filled it with lukewarm water, and carried it carefully to the room. I went to the linen closet and took out some modest bleached white towels. With the sacredness of a priest preparing his vestments, I unfolded the towels one by one on my shoulders. I removed the sheets and blankets from her bed and peeled off her thick flannel nightgown. I toweled her puzzled face, stretching out the wrinkles, removing the coils of her neck, toweled her shoulders and breasts. Then I changed the water. I returned to towel the creases of her stretch-marked stomach, her sporadic vaginal hairs, and her sagging thighs. I removed the lint from between her toes and noticed a mapped birthmark on the fold of her buttock. The scars on her back, which were as thin as the lifelines on the palms of her hands, made me realize how little I really knew of Abuelita. I covered her with a thin blanket and went into the bathroom. I washed my hands, and turned on the tub faucets and watched the water pour into the tub with vitality and steam. When it was full, I turned off the water and undressed. Then, I went to get Abuelita.

She was not as heavy as I thought, and when I carried her in my arms, her body fell into a V, and yet my legs were tired, shaky, and I felt as if the distance between the bedroom and bathroom was miles and years away. Amá, where are you?

I stepped into the bathtub one leg first, then the other. I bent my knees slowly to descend into the water slowly so

I wouldn't scald her skin. There, there, Abuelita, I said, cradling her, smoothing her as we descended, I heard you. Her hair fell back and spread across the water like eagle's wings. The water in the tub overflowed and poured onto the tile of the floor. Then the moths came. Small, gray ones that came from her soul and out through her mouth fluttering to light, circling the single dull lightbulb of the bathroom. Dying is lonely and I wanted to go to where the moths were, stay with her, and plant chayotes whose vines would crawl up her fingers and into the clouds; I wanted to rest my head on her chest with her stroking my hair, telling me about the moths that lay within the soul and slowly eat the spirit up; I wanted to return to the waters of the womb with her so that we would never be alone again. I wanted. I wanted my Amá. I removed a few strands of hair from Abuelita's face and held her small light head within the hollow of my neck. The bathroom was filled with moths, and for the first time in a long time I cried, rocking us, crying for her, for me, for Amá, the sobs emerging from the depths of anguish, the misery of feeling half born, sobbing until finally the sobs rippled into circles and circles of sadness and relief. There, there, I said to Abuelita, rocking us gently, there, there.

Nancy Mairs

From My House to Mary's House

"Charity" is a tricky concept. At its root, which it shares with "cherish," the word suggests no ordinary, indiscriminate affection but the love of something precious (costly, dear). Why then has it come to imply condescension? As with so many other ideas pertaining to relationships, our vast cultural passion for hierarchy must be at work. And where did that come from, I often wonder: out of the forest primeval, where if I perched in a tree while you skulked on the ground, I could more readily make you my lunch than you could make me yours? But that was quite a while ago. My mouth no longer waters when I glimpse you, even at lunchtime. Isn't it time we dismantled a structure that so poorly organizes human interactions? Not that this would be an easy task. Our language, and the consciousness it shapes, is permeated with figures of domination and subordination so thoroughly that if we tried to extricate them, the whole fabric might unravel and leave us gibbering, unable to construct a single coherent thought.

It's a risk we'll have to take, I think, if we are to survive as recognizably human(e) beings in a world of finite resources. Of course, nothing guarantees that we *are* to survive, and a good bit of recent evidence suggests that we aren't, but I think we ought to give survival a shot. I'm not talking about "hanging in there," I'm not talking about a few minor adjustments, or even a lot of major adjustments. I'm not talking about a new world order that permits Iraqi women and children to be bombed at the command of rich white men just as Vietnamese women and children were under the old world order, only more efficiently and with wider approval. I am talking about an upheaval so radical that it exalts every valley and makes the rough places a plain, not along the San Andreas Fault but in the human psyche, which will no longer choose (not desire—it may well still desire—but choose) to organize itself and its relationships with others in terms of power and rank.

We might begin where all things begin: with God. We need to revise the language we use to conceptualize God in relation to ourselves. No more "Lord" and "Master." No more "thrones" or "principalities." No more oracular pronouncements "from on high." God with (in, among, beside, around, not over and above) us. This is one of the reasons that I've trained myself (and I balked badly at first) to refer to God with the feminine pronoun. I don't think God is a woman, any more than I think she's a man, but we're stuck with a gendered language: God has got to be he, she, or it. As a woman, I now feel most comfortable with "she" because traditionally in my culture women have not occupied positions of political dominance, associations with which might corrupt my experience of the holy, and because I identify with her, thus becoming aware of her presence in me, more readily when I use the same pronoun generally used for me. For a long time I considered changing "God," trying out "Goddess," "Holy One," "Yahweh," and the like, but they always felt contrived. Sometimes repeating "God" instead of using any pronoun is effective, but frequent repetitions at short intervals, by calling attention to themselves, distract me. The shift to the feminine pronoun seems to do the trick.

The purpose in finding a comfortable mode of address is to become aware of God drawn "down" into the midst of us, by whatever means will work. If she abides there, then the love we feel both for her and for one another as we embody her moves laterally, not hierarchically, and charity can never be tainted by condescension. When I use the word, I never intend it to suggest the act of a "do-gooder" who gives a "handout" or a "hand-me-down" to someone "less fortunate" than himself; no matter what decency and goodwill both donor and recipient may feel, that "less" in the consciousness of one or both ineluctably skews their relationship. Charity is not a matter of degree. It is never nice. It wells up out of a sense of abundance, spilling indiscriminately outward. True, your abundance may complement someone else's lack, which you are moved to fill, but since your lacks are being similarly filled, perhaps by the same person, perhaps by another, reciprocity rather than domination frames the interchanges. Some people may be "more" fortunate and some "less," by whatever standard you choose. But absolutely everybody has abundances.

Of course, an abundance may not take a form you much like. I recall stopping, one blazing afternoon several years ago, at the Time Market for a carton of milk. Outside, I was approached by a man wearing few clothes and fewer teeth and a lot of sweat (life on the street in Tucson in midsummer is grueling), who asked me for a dollar. In those days, I didn't give money to people on the street because I knew they'd spend it on booze and I felt guilty assisting their addiction. Later, I was persuaded by the example of my beloved mentor Jerry Robinett that my task was to give what I was asked for, leaving responsibility for the use of my gift to its recipient. But on this day I still thought of myself as a moral guardian, so I shook my head. Inside, as was my habit when I'd been panhandled, I bought in addition to my milk a large apple and a granola bar (oh, the smugness of us virtuous types—why the hell not a red Popsicle and a Twinkie?).

When I offered these to the man outside, he snarled and turned his back. He'd been joined by a friend, who said to him quietly, "You know her. From the Casa. Go on and take them." He just shook his head, so I extended them to the friend, who took them and smiled. There was genuine grace in his gesture, his reluctance to hurt the feelings of a woman he'd seen at the soup kitchen, and I welcomed that gift from his abundance. But the other had an abundance, too—an abundance of resentment—from which he'd given just as freely. I was chastened by the gift, by his refusal to say "Thank you, kind lady," accepting my stupid health food when all he really wanted was a cold six-pack. If he'd done that, I'd never have found out that I'd offered him the wrong thing. I might have gone on believing that poor people were obliged to take what I gave them, consider themselves lucky to get it, and probably thank me politely in the bargain. I never said you had to *like* getting your lacks filled. I just said that someone, out of his abundance, would take care of the job.

Under ordinary circumstances, our abundances need letting off, like steam, and the family model chosen by contemporary middle-class society, wherein the whole huge human family is fragmented into clusters of only a few members each, which are packed separately and antiseptically, like cans of peas or jars of pickles, into houses and apartments and minivans, lacks adequate amplitude and ventilation. Accumulated, hoarded, our abundances build up an excruciating pressure that we seek to relieve in material acquisition, but the relief this measure brings is always only temporary, and eventually we find ourselves stopped up and sick with things.

I'm not preaching from a lofty perch here, looking down in pity on the rest of you poor fools gagging on your glut. I'm gasping claustrophobically under the weight of my own heap of possessions. Look! Down here! Under the three pairs of boots and the second television set! Admittedly, the boots are different colors to complement different articles in my wardrobe, and the television is a black-and-white portable with a five-inch screen: I'm a practical accumulator. But maybe color-coordination is

not a laudable end or even a reasonable goal; and no one
except my sports-crazy stepfather attempts to watch more
than one television at a time. What am I really doing with
all this stuff?

I know what I should do with it. I accept Jesus' admoni-
tion to the rich young man: "If you would be perfect, go,
sell what you possess and give to the poor, and you will
have treasure in heaven; and come, follow me" (Matthew
19:21). I know that such actions can be carried out, because I have friends who have done so. And I like to think
I have developed to the point that, if only I were healthy
and vigorous, I could do the same. If only. . . . Here's where
I get stuck. I am too debilitated now to hold a job or even
to care fully for myself. My husband has metastatic mela-
noma. When he dies, the modest resources we've accumulated may not even provide for my shelter and custodial
care. If I were to give them away, then I'd become a public
burden, worse than useless even to the poor I sought to
serve. Conserving them seems less like greed than like social responsibility. And so I get off lightly. I can indulge in
the fantasy that under different circumstances, I would be
"perfect" without ever having to put myself to the test: a
saint manqué.

Well, what I would do if I could we'll never know. I
must do what I can. Carrying out the injunction that closes
every Mass, to "go in peace to love and serve God and our
neighbor," takes the form of the works of mercy, seven of
which are "corporal": (1) to feed the hungry, (2) to give
drink to the thirsty, (3) to clothe the naked, (4) to visit the
imprisoned, (5) to shelter the homeless, (6) to visit the sick,
and (7) to bury the dead. Another seven are "spiritual": (1)
to admonish the sinner, (2) to instruct the ignorant, (3) to
counsel the doubtful, (4) to comfort the sorrowful, (5)
to bear wrongs patiently, (6) to forgive all injuries, and (7)
to pray for the living and the dead. "As far as I can tell, I'm
supposed to do all of these," I say to George, "but some of
the spiritual ones make me uneasy. They seem so pre-

sumptuous." He nods as I go on: "I'd rather just clothe the sinner"—we burst out laughing and say together—"and admonish the naked."

Seriously, at the risk of spiritual dereliction, I think I'll leave admonishment to someone with more of a flair for it and stick with bodies, their shelter and nurture and dispatch, for which a quarter of a century of mothering all creatures great and small has better fitted me. Let me feed the hungry. Let me clothe the naked (and sinners too). I won't do it well or often enough, I know from experience, but charity isn't a competition to be judged by the Big Examiner in the Sky, who'll knock off seven years of purgatory for every sack of groceries you drop off at the Community Food Bank. Nobody's looking. It's more like a game in which everyone gets a turn, or a dance for which everyone can choreograph a few steps. Even a woman too crippled to tie her own boots or drive a car can, at least if she has a partner who shares her sense of plenty, find a place in the vast web of transactions that binds and sustains the human family.

In such exchanges, no matter how equitable, the power of the giver to dispense or withhold some good is subtly privileged over the right of the receiver to accept or reject the offering by the fact of possession: you've got what I need. Even though I've long understood this distinction, only in recent years have I felt its force. What I need—repetitively, interminably—is help in performing even the most elementary tasks. I can't butter my own bread. Before long I may not even be able to use the toilet by myself. My dependency, in resembling that of a very young child, makes me feel demeaned, diminished, humiliated. This is a horrible situation, one that wracks me with grief and fury for which no socially acceptable outlet exists. What am I going to do if you offer to button my coat, after all—bite your fingers and then freeze to death? Of course not. I'm going to permit you to clothe the naked.

Horrible situations have their uses, however. Mine, in

depriving me of the status associated with personal control, has forced humility upon me. I cannot patronize the poor. I am one of the poor. Currently my poverty isn't economic, though it may one day be that as well, but its effects are similar. I must be not only the agent but the object of the works of mercy. I must discipline myself to accept and welcome others' care. I wish I could tell you that I'm doing a terrific job of it, that I'm just the sweetest, humblest little woman you've ever met, but I can't. All I can say is that, in learning to give care whenever I can and receive care whenever I must, I've grown more attentive to the personal dimension of the works of mercy.

So accustomed are most of us to thinking of human neediness not in personal but in economic terms that, asked for a charitable donation, we reflexively whip out our checkbooks and pens. Writing a check to a "charity" is not on the list of the works of mercy, however. It's a generous act, one that ought to be performed as frequently as the budget will bear, but it can't substitute spiritually for direct engagement with people in need. "Poverty" and "affliction" and "oppression" are abstractions whose remedy might seem to lie in the intangible transfer of a monetary amount from one account to another. Poor and afflicted and oppressed people have faces, and we are required to look squarely into them. We can't love what we won't experience. For this reason, George and I have always sought to make our charity concrete.

Although our most sustained and intimate charitable relationships have grown out of taking people into our home, not everyone has the physical plant or the emotional resources to make room for one more, and currently that includes us. Over the years, however, we've discovered other ways of developing caring relationships, making us, I suppose, one of those "thousand points of light" upon which conservative politicians have wished like stars in recent years. What speechwriter, I wonder, came up

152   *Nancy Mairs*

with an estimate so small in a country so vast, evoking brave scattered flickers of individual endeavor in the very heart of darkness?

Beneath such a metaphor lies a shift from public to private torchbearing which suggests that the government can just excuse itself from tending to messy human needs and get on with protecting oil supplies and national security and the "American" flag (as though ours were the only one) and capital gains and other things that matter. In this model, even when human beings enter the government's purview, they tend to do so as things, not people. The unborn child—as yet untouched, invisible—must have the government's protection, but the embraceable infant, demanding breast milk and then a warm snowsuit and later textbooks and finally a steady job, gets thrust into the arms of one of us blinking lights. Unless by acting up she converts herself back into a thing—goes on a murderous shooting spree and has to be put to death, say, or fails to pay her taxes—the government will scarcely concern itself with her again.

This model has served us badly, and will continue to serve us badly, because it draws a false distinction between private and public concerns and between personal and governmental responsibility for coping with them. No things matter, either publicly or privately, except as they preserve and enhance the intricate process that I would call God's creation. All actions, both public and private, have equal impact, for good or ill, on that process. And no one, not even a dim bulb like George Bush, is excused from equal participation in it. We all lead lives of public service, and at last count, there should have been about 250 million points of light in the United States alone, plenty for a conflagration.

Individually and collectively, we must take on the tasks at hand, imbuing them with the reciprocity that arises out of our various abilities and diverse requirements. Until a few years ago, for instance, I refused to hire help around the house because I couldn't stand the thought of making someone my "servant"; eventually, with George teaching in two programs and my physical condition deteriorating, I was forced to find a weekly housekeeper or suffocate under a drift of grease, desert dust, and corgi hair. At this point, the mistress/servant model no longer represented my reality. Because the need my housekeeper has for the money I pay her is no greater than my need for assistance, our dependence is mutual.

And our relative authority must be balanced accordingly. Since I cannot clean my own house, it has become to some extent no longer my *own* house. It has slipped from my control, a very good thing, since Celia takes far better care of it than I would have done even in the days when my arms and legs still worked. She cleans between all the buttons on the antiquated push-button stove so that our fingers no longer stick and release with a schloop every time we want to go from hot to warm. She keeps the sliding-glass door so clean that after my daughter walked through and shattered it, we had to paste a hedgehog decal onto the new one to ward off future incursions. But she does not know where things "belong," like the fish-shaped soup tureen on the sideboard; although this "should" be placed sideways, she invariably points its pouty face out into the room. At first I'd turn it back after she left; later, when I got too weak, I'd simply look at it and fret; at length, insight struck: *Whoa, wait a minute! Whose fish is this anyway?* It's mine, I know. When my friend Mollie left Tucson, she gave it to me to hold until her return, but she liked Seattle better and I've got the fish by default. But it's Celia's fish, too, she's the one who takes care of it, and apparently it "should" stare out at us broodily, even though I think it looks dopey that way.

To relinquish not merely control but the claim to control, permitting someone to do what she does best in the way she chooses to do it and viewing the outcome as collaborative rather than "right" or "wrong," balances a re-

lationship that might otherwise be skewed by issues of
ownership or prerogative. Celia and I have a hollow cream-
colored stoneware fish. If you want to help us with its up-
keep, you may have it, too. If no one drops it, it will outlast
both Celia and me. One day, however, it's bound to be
smashed, and then no one will have it anymore. Things
come to us, and we cherish them for a while, and then they
or we are gone. When Jesus says, "You cannot serve both
God and mammon," it is not the thinginess of our possessions he repudiates but our relationship to them: the way
that, instead of simply tending them and putting them to
use, we grasp them with knuckles turned white, clasp
them against our chests, invest them with the power to
represent our worth. Perhaps for this reason the early
Christians held their goods in common: so that they
wouldn't be tempted into controlling one another through
commodities.

As valuable as personal relationships like mine with Celia
are in transforming abstract works of mercy into concrete
expressions of love, in the end you cannot know every person you serve. Lacks are too great; energies are too limited;
and anyway, just as some donors prefer to remain anony-
mous, so do some recipients. To serve such needs on a large
scale requires a whole charitable community like Casa
María, which runs Our Lady of Guadalupe Chapel and Free
Kitchen. At the core of this community, which occupies
several small houses on Tucson's south side, are Brian
Flagg, voluble and hyperkinetic, and George Petit, soft-
spoken but equally fierce in his commitment, his wife, De-
bbie, and their baby, Catie, together with several veterans
of life on the streets: Lonnie, Lowell, Andy, Bill. These now
form our family, too. With them we celebrate marriages
and baptisms and birthdays, attend rallies and marches
and vigils, and get arrested for civil disobedience, to the
consternation of some of our less radical relatives.
      Although, in order to avoid the NIMBY syndrome that

has closed down similar projects around town, Casa María is a consecrated chapel, where Mass is said every Monday morning, one is required to pray for her or his supper. Holding fast to the thousand-points-of-light principle, the federal government no longer contributes surplus goods like cheese, and operating expenses have soared to about seven thousand dollars a month. The program subsists on donations of money, food, and time from all over Tucson and even beyond: The last time I was there I met several Mennonite grandmothers from the Midwest who spend three months in Tucson every winter; while they make and bag sandwiches, their husbands do home repairs for poor people. Established just over ten years ago for the explicit purpose of performing works of mercy, Casa María initially served one meal a day—soup, a couple of sandwiches, fruit, a sweet, coffee, and milk when available for the children—to a couple hundred people. On a recent Saturday the number was thirteen hundred. Although the number of single men has stayed stable for several years, more and more families have come as the realities of Reagan-Bush economics have taken hold even here in the supposedly recession-proof Southwest.

"All those people want is a free ride," a woman at an adult education conference told me over dinner a couple of years ago when I mentioned my involvement with Casa María. "I have to drive by that soup kitchen on my way to work, and I've seen them lined up three times a day waiting for their handouts."

"Odd," I said. "The soup kitchen serves only lunch."

"Well, whatever. I see them there, just hanging around. They don't even want to find work."

"That's true," I said. "Some of them don't. And some are too sick to work. But some of them do. They're all different. Why don't you stop on your way to work one day and ask them?" The question was rhetorical. I couldn't imagine why this woman drove by the soup kitchen, which is not on a main thoroughfare, but I could imagine how: locked tight in her car, as fast as she could get away with in a neighborhood heavily patrolled by the police and La Migra (Immigration and Naturalization Service). And who could blame her? Families there come and leave quickly. Most of the people hanging around the kitchen are men who, now that the old SRO (single room occupancy) hotels have been torn down to make room for luxury condominiums and motorways, live on the street. Unwashed, unshaven, in wardrobes chosen from the boxes of donated clothing Lonnie supervises, they look bad. (They can also smell bad, which is not a problem for this woman with her windows rolled up tight but is for me, afflicted with a hypersensitive nose, when I'm among them.) They tend to be grumpy, as you probably would be too if you sought your night's rest under the Murphy Overpass. A woman alone might well choose not to mingle in such company.

Her loss. I must sound supercilious, but I'm not. I mean she really has cheated herself of experience in the way we all do when we whiz past the world with the air conditioner pumping full blast and the *Goldberg Variations* trilling from the tape deck. She has lost the opportunity to know a little more about the world: "know," that is, not in the way she "knows" that the people queued up outside the soup kitchen are freeloaders but in the way she "knows" Paris, say, having spent a summer there between her junior and senior years in college. We know the world, as God knows the world, only by entering it. Photos in *Newsweek* or *National Geographic* won't do. Editorials in *The Nation* or *The New Republic* won't do. Sixty-second clips on the nightly news about unemployment, homelessness, substance abuse, mental illness, and serial murderers won't do. You gotta *be* there.

And if you're there with even half an eye open, you see that nothing so simple as freeloading is going on. To begin with, nothing's being given out that would seduce you away from a regular paycheck. Except maybe the soup, which is generally excellent, hot, and highly spiced. The sandwiches are most likely orange cheeselike food or peanut butter mixed with fruit cocktail on day-old bread. The apples and bananas are bruised. There might be a stale Ding Dong or a Snickers bar, but if your teeth have rotted to stumps, these furnish more pain than pleasure. You can squat on the ground and eat this stuff if you can fend off the damned pigeons long enough. If you need to take a crap, there are a couple of portable toilets in one corner of the yard. If the soles of your boots have holes, Lonnie might be able to find a pair not quite as worn and more or less your size.

The lap of luxury doesn't draw these people, then. Some are temporarily down-and-out, but many are chronically hungry and/or homeless. The family bags usually go to people in the neighborhood who can afford either rent or food but not both. Of the people on the street, most are men, a disproportionate number of them Vietnam vets. A lot have fevers, wracking coughs, ulcerated legs and feet, abscessed teeth. Some drink, smoke marijuana, do heroin or cocaine. A few are crazy as bedbugs, "freed" from state institutions in the early seventies to be turned over to a community-based mental health system that nobody ever got around to establishing. No amount of exhortation will make these people "better," to use the standard of my dinner companion, or "different," to use a less loaded word. Am I to say to the man who asks for a cigarette and, when I give it to him (a dubious charity, I'll admit), showers me with kisses and calls down the blessing of Cristo upon me: "Good God, man, pull up your socks and get right down to the Department of Economic Security for a job interview!?" Who the hell would want him around? I've had him around for at least five minutes now and I don't want him, I assure you.

At Casa María one learns, sooner or later depending upon one's resistances, that in spite of all our charitable efforts, some of the poor we will always have with us, just as Jesus warned, and our care for them can never cease.

I'm no defeatist. In the decade George taught adult education, we saw person after person on public assistance earn a GED, attend community college, find a job, and become (a point of pride) a taxpayer; and if the government would hand us illuminati out here more funds, instead of blowing them on bomb tests and the bad debts of persons in high places, such successes could mount exponentially. But there will always be a Frances, wearing my white wool tam-o'-shanter at a jaunty angle and leading on leashes her two pet chickens, invisible to the naked eye, around the encampment of homeless people at the county courthouse on Christmas Eve. Frances can't depend on herself; she can't even depend on the damned chickens, who disappear unpredictably even from her view. At the least, she ought to be able to depend on me.

Wholehearted commitment to people who are poor, afflicted, or oppressed, although it inevitably necessitates political choices and leads to shared political action, must first be rooted in personal conversion, described by the liberation theologist Leonardo Boff as follows: "The conversion demanded by Jesus is more than a mere change of conviction—a change in theory. It is also, and mainly, a change of attitude—a change bearing directly on practice. Nor is it a change only within a person—a change of heart. It is also a change in that person's living, functioning network of relationships." Not by chance, I think, was Dorothy Day, the founder of the Catholic Worker movement, a convert to Roman Catholicism. Every Frances necessitates a new and conscious conversion—a turning again to enter communion at each fresh encounter—for which Dorothy showed an extraordinary gift. One needn't be a Catholic, or even a Christian, in order to undergo such a change or carry out such action, of course, but one must by some means learn the habit of turning toward and taking in.

The charity that begins at home cannot rest there but draws one inexorably over the threshold and off the porch and down the street and so out and out and out and out into the world which becomes the home wherein charity begins until it becomes possible, in theory at least, to love the whole of creation with the same patience, affection, and amusement one first practiced, in between the pouts and tantrums, with parents, siblings, spouse, and children. Relationship: connection: kinship: family: love: the movement from an abstract and emotionless awareness that there are needy people out there to the give-and-take— tender, quarrelsome, jokey, impassioned—of siblings crowded together under the roof of Mary's House. The choice to name Casa María for La Virgen de Guadalupe is especially apt, not only because she is the patron saint of Mexico, only seventy miles from Tucson, but because she appeared to a poor man of questionable mental stability: the Queen of Heaven placed a rose in the hands of a bemused peasant. In charity distances dissolve. As a response to the gratuitous outpouring of God's love, charity demands that one turn one's face toward the face of another and confront there both oneself and God.

Lucille Clifton

brothers, part 6

"the silence of God is God."
—CAROLYN FORCHÉ

tell me, tell us why
in the confusion of a mountain
of babies stacked like cordwood,
of limbs walking away from each other,
of tongues bitten through
by the language of assault,
tell me, tell us why
You neither raised Your hand
nor turned away, tell us why
You watched the excommunication of
that world and You said nothing.

Sacred Place

*I took myself to prayer and in every lonely place
I found an altar.*

—OLD ELIZABETH

Laurine Ark

The Tappin

And it came about that when Jehovah was to take Elijah in a windstorm up to the heavens Elijah and Elisha proceeded to Gilgal. . . . And it came about that as soon as they had gone across Elijah himself said to Elisha: "Ask what I should do for you before I am taken from you." To this Elisha said: "Please, that two parts in your spirit may come to me." At this Elijah said: "You have asked a difficult thing. If you see me when I am taken from you, it will happen to you that way; but if you do not, it will not happen. (2 Kings 2:1, 9–10)

He werent my Father but he were like one. He noed my thots all most bafer I did. I never had ta tell him nuthin.

Folks round here raise there eyebrows and say it werent rite a young gerl like me spendin time with a old man who dint talk much but I werent purdy not evun at elevun. My skinny legs were to long. My hairs were all sunbleeched. My dresses were seckund hand. Old man and me holded hands sumtimes but we walked in silents mostly. I dint worry what nobudy sayed. I no most peepoles talkin dont meen nuthin.

Ever Sunday afer church Ma and Gracie Harper and a bunch a dem nosey ladys use ta gather in a cerkle in the shade a the buildin and start kluckin bout everbudys bizness. Sooner er later sumbudy all ways say: "Sumthins funny bout old man. He aint God feerin." Then Ma wood skweez my elbo and look at me. Dem eyes a hers sayin I telled yer so. But I dint care. I kicks the sand and lifts the hairs offa my neck. I here old man say wunce aint nuthin

163

ta feer bout sumthin sweet and luvin like God. Dem ladys talkin were all ways the same. Nobudy kud reckin how old man servived out in the deszert. Livin a lone. Eatin sand. Burnin in that heet.

But I noes so I just looks a way. I here him say wunce. It were the tappin.

We in Airyzoner then. I member sumbudy sayin wunce Airyzoner were an Indean werd meened spring. I laffed. All I ever seed were sand.

Most folks were fromed Texus. Movin west when the floodin comed. Ma sayed now that Pa were gone weed best be leavin to. She be to old ta fix the farm. So we selled it. We packed up what we kud in the big truck. We bringed Mas soin masheen and sum furnychur. And comes a Airyzoner. Wees been here a whyle. Folks still talked Texus tho.

Everybudys gots one a dem cemint kinda houses with reel winders. Guvamint er sumbudy builds um. Sum folks sayed they were to small but fer Ma and me it be ok. Sides I gots my own room and the cemint were kool. We gots chickens in the back and Ma gots a gardin. There be lotsa snakes and lizerds round. Ma were all ways makin me chase um. We gots our milk from the Harpers Bessy.

Only kid that talked ta me were a kinda peeyounee boy with a wet wheeze. Folks sayed he gots one a dem kunjennytall hart kundishuns. He gots black glasses and kurly hairs. His name were Lynn. Kids teezed him lots sayin Lynn were a gerl name. Ceptin me. I dont think Lynn were sissy. We looked Lynn up in one a dem books bout names. Book sayed Lynn meens lake. Pool. Klear water. That stuff.

I goed ta skool ever mornin. It were a long walk but I dint care. Gived me time fer thinkin and lookin. Skool room were all ways be to hot. Like it got no air. Sides it smell bad in there like boys afer recess er like Mista Harpers bull do in the fall when the she cows be comin in. So I walks slo so I can be late and set in the back. Winders in the back. Teecher say if I comes up frunt I be disterbin the others. I dint care. I like lookin outta the winder past the play yard. Starin at dem grains a sand. Sumtimes there be wind. Sumtimes wind be blowin sand up like it were goin to heavun.

Skoolin comed hard fer me. I werent smart. Never got good grades. Teecher sayed it was cuz I to restless. A day-dreemer lost in reverly er sum werd I dint no. Teecher keeped sendin notes home ta Ma bout me. They all say the same thin.

"When called on in class yer dauter say Sorry Mam what's the kwestshun? She dont study. She cant spell. She can hardly rite her name."

a sayed she were given up on me cuz I were ill literrat. To tall. Dumm. And I gots crooked eyes like Pa. I were only good fer werkin. I figgered she were rite. I noed Ma needed me cuz she were small. To daynty fer reel werk. So I warsh the dishes. Mops the floor. Hall the trash. Feed dem chickens. Sweepin sand outta the walkway that the stuped wind wood blo back bafer I kud get my broom put a way. I werk. I dint talk much.

All thins konsidered I nu I were kinda lucky. Longs I did dem chores and whatever Ma be leavin me a lone bout most thins. Ma were busy most mornins puttin thins by. In the afernoon she be mendin sum a my dresses er soin fer sum other folks. Sumtimes she cuts my hairs. I likes um short. Keeps me kool. At nite Ma be klutchin her roserry beeds ta her bosum. Her lips be mumblin dem Hayel Marys. Her mind sortin out nex days doins. How she gonna fix one a dem town ladys weddin dress. I all ways noed what Ma were thinkin. Old man sayed that were one a the reesons I kud lern tappin.

Now old man werked hard out in the middel of thins everyday. His skin were dark but evertime I kist his cheek it were soft. My lips sinked inda it like I were bitin whip cream. His hairs were whyrey and full. It were reel long and brown.

Everday afer skool I runned home evun if it were hot. My dress bloed up but I dint care. Runnin make wind on

my face and bloed the swet outta my hairs. Ma be takin a
brake from soin. Sippin warmed over koffee with Gracie er
snuzzin on a sofer all rapt up in a kwilt she maked with
her Ma when she were my age. Evun when it were 95 da-
grees Ma be rapt up tite. Reckin it make her feel luved er
sumthin.

I change my close and puts on my short pants with big
pockits. I do whatever Ma had me do as fast as I kud. I
hated dem chores. Soon as I were done I runned off. Out ta
dem fields like the folks called um but it were reely just the
deszert. Old man all ways be out in the fields. He were all
ways smilin. Tappin do that. Tappin make him smile. Tappin fix all folks problums. O I luv runnin ta old man tho
my feets be gettin toasted in that hot sand. My toes prickt
by dem stuped caktus flours and deszert brushs.

"Howdee!" I sayed when I gets ta old man. He still be
smilin. I take his hand. A sweet smellin swet be riverin
down his neck. I look up at his face. Sun wood get behind
him. Dem eyes a his be sparkelin like stars. Dark blue cerkle be round his head like a bubble er sumthin. Then I seed
the rays a the sun comin out from round that bubble. He
bend down and touch my forhead and kinda roll his eyes
back and my hole breath goed a way. We goed flyin up
over dem hills. I be feelin it. I never telled nobudy but I
never luved nuthin like I luv old man.

"Tell me sum more," I sayed ta him tuggin on his arm
afer we comed back. Old man telled storys. Best storys in
the countee.

He smile. He gots the only teef in a hunred miles werent
full a holes. Doc Phillips the teef doc evun sayed so. He take
my hand again. We walk outta dem fields but I never feeled
my feets on the ground. We gets up ta his place over by the
big dune. He call it his cave ceptin it were like a cabin made
outta white fur and Airyzoner cypruss. He say he halled it
down outta dem hills wunce afer he comed back from tappin. Wood were all grayed like Mas hairs and rinkled like
Gracies face but it were holdin up ok.

In old mans cabin be bolls cherrys peachs and nanners. Masen jars fulled with furn leafs and roses and daffydills were settin on the table and winder sills. Sumtimes there be this white bird like a swan settin on his roof.

Old man gots a big porch in frunt a his place. He set on the top step. I be on the bottum restin my legs kross his feets. Layin my cheek on his nee. Sumtimes that boy Lynn be there to restin his chin on old mans other nee. Sum other kids used ta come but they kwit. They laff say they is to growed up fer old mans crap. I dint care. I dint never think it were crap. Me and Lynn sets there fer hours lookin up at old mans big brown eyes. He be so purdy. He be dressed in an orange er blu cottin thin like a nitey but he were just a man.

"Tell me bout the place again," I begs him whenever he stops talkin.

Old man all ways gots a nu story. "This be my home I is tellin yall bout," he say and kinda shakes his voice. "The place I comed from."

I close my eyes and lissen. Sumtimes sumthin comed over me. I be skaweezin old mans nee and kissin it. "I wanna go there."

"Take the fastess root," he say. "Lern the tappin."

"Teech me the tappin." Me and Lynn say togedher. We jumps up.

Old man smile and touch our hairs. "May be in fall. May be yall be reedy by then." He stroke my head more. Shore make me feel bedder. I dont worry bout it.

Summer comed. Ma took ta inventin nu chores. I hartly evun seed old man.

"Werkins good fer ya," he say when I is abel ta get a way. "Do yer werkin. It be helpin. May be we do sum tappin come fall. Yall be good now."

I thot I die waitin on summer ta end. Ma findin more deszert brushs fer me ta kleer everday. Gardin were diein but she make me ho it just a same. One afernoon I were cryin. Thinkin bout old man. I looked out in the fields and

there he be walkin to me. I dropped my ho and runned ta
him. "Ya gotta teech me tappin." I cryed these big teers
and all. "I die if ya dont teech me now. Rite now."

"Gotta be payshent if ya gonna lern tappin. Tappins
spechell." Old man bended down and kist my face. "Gotta
werk hard lil one. Get yer werkin part outta the way. Con-
vinse um yous reddy ta lern. Tappin aint eezy."

But I noed evun then I kud do tappin. I be gonna lern it
from the master. I be goin home.

There be lots a thunderin that summer. Lynn sayed it
were the old man gettin reddy ta teech us tappin. "My
harts a poundin. Waitin on him," Lynn sayed grabbin his
chest like he were painin.

"I no!" I slaps at Lynn til he sets. "But we gotta lern ta
be still. Old man say wunce furst step in tappin is be in
still. Member?"

Come Septembur skool were startin. Ma goed with me
furst day. Teecher taked me and Ma a side and sayed I best
be whyzin up er I is gonna get kicked out. Ma sayed, "I
telled yer so! I doin all that prayin fer nuthin. Ya cant spell.
Ya cant rite. Ya askin stuped kwestshuns all the time." She
skweez my elbo hard.

Crap. I started chokin on teers and runned off. Nobudy
noed wair I goed ceptin Lynn. He no I go see old man.

Old man. He were standin on the steps. His hands on
his hips like he noed I were comin. Like he were waitin on
me.

"Pleez!" I begged old man. "I gots ta lern tappin." I
falled by his feets.

He looked at me fer a long time then he picked me up
and sayed, "OK. I teech yous both. Go back ta skool now
and get skool lernin reel kwik. I want ya ta lern ta rite lil
one. It be reel importent. Ya gonna be teechin others sum
day."

"Whats that meen?" I asked old man.

"I tells ya later." Old man just smile. "Ya tell Lynn he

can come ta lern tappin to. Member best time fer tappin be dawn er midnite er lunch er supper."

"Ok." I kist old man and thanked him.

"Now get! Folks and yer Ma be steamin if they no ya comed here." Old man shooed me off and smiled. I kist him again and runned back to skool.

At recess I taked Lynn a side wair nobudy can here.

"Oh, no!" Lynn started cryin when I telled him what old man sayed. Lynn be grabbin his hart. "I cant go. Granny makes me practiss readin ta her at nite."

"Ya gots ta think a sumthin," I telled him. "Bafer ya goes ta sleep, close yer eyes. Talk ta old man. He be tellin ya what ta do."

Nex day Lynn stopped me bafer we go in skool and sayed, "I thinked on it. Granny sleeps late. I all ways be gone a skool bafer she gets up. I can sneek off earlee lern tappin bafer skool." Lynn grinned. "Old man help me fig- ger it out."

Now I had ta think bout when I kud be gettin off ta lern tappin. I set in the back a the skool room and looked outta the winder. I thinked reel hard. I watched the wind bloin in dem fields. I gots mornin chores but at nite Ma be in her room mumblin feelin dem beeds. Her mind be shufflin on whats fer breakfass er sum nu soin job. I all ways kiss her at nite bafer she start. I kud sneek out lern tappin at nite. Anybudy ask I say I just takin a walk on a fine nite.

And a fine nite it be to. The nite I start lernin tappin.

I members it good. Gerl like me never fergets a time like that. My hart were poundin like Lynn say his do. Sneekin outs eezy cuz it be so hot all dem winders in our place all ways be opin. I walked reel eezy outta the yard then I runned like one a dem jack rabbits kross dem fields. All the time I keeped thinkin on old man and the tappin.

The tappin. The Tappin. I were gonna do the tappin.

Old man gots a lite in a winder so I seed my way. Aint no moon out that nite. Swet be riverin down my back. I gots troubel findin my breath. But I make it.

There he be. Old man rockin on the porch. Chair be skweekin.

"Howdee!" I howlered comin near ta his place. I ketch my breath. I putted my hands in my pockits actin like I were all redy kooled down.

Old man dont say nuthin. It be to dark ta see his face.

"Howdee!" I sayed again.

Old man still dont say nuthin.

"Hay there. Lets start the tappin." I runned up dem steps. I kist old man. His eyes be closed. His back kinda stiff. His skin were kool. "God! No!" I shaked old man. "Dont be dead old man. Dont be dead on me now. Old man!"

Nuthin.

"No!" Dem teers started riverin. I runned in the cabin and grabbed the lite from the winder. My foot dont no wair it be goin and I hitted the tabel with my leg. Dem bolls of fresh froot goed splottin on the floor. "Crap!" I dint stop ta pick it up. I runned back ta old man. I shined the lite on his face. He smilin but he were stiff like Pa when he died. "Old man," I cryed reel hard. I layed my head on his chest. Werds got cawt in my throat. "Old man, Ommm!" I thot it were all over. Then I feel old mans hand on my head. He stroke my hairs like bafer.

"Dont be cryin now lil deer one."

"Ya all rite?" I hugged his neck.

"Yes." He speek reel plane. "I were practissin the tappin."

"The tappin." I setted at his feets. Huggin his nee. "This be the nite."

"Yes. We start now." Old man talk ta me fer hours bout goin home and his Ma.

I lissen. I luv ta lissen.

Nex nite I runned off same way. Old man on the porch. Stiff and eyes back. I thot he were dead again. I shaked him and started cryin on his sholder. Then I feeled his hand on me all warm and full a luv. "Why ya do that? Dont die on me."

"I aint diein." Old man smiled. His white teef be shinin. "I just reel still. It be part a tappin. Ya no soon enuf. If ya needs me just hum this lil song in my ear." Old man teech me a nu song. Sound kinda like hummin. I luv it. It sound like the wind. Like Gracie big sea shell. Like sumthin powerfilled. It must be strong I figger. It wake up old man.

Then he talk to me bout his Ma again. She be so sweet. He luvs the Ma. I do to. She be deevine.

Fer a year and a haff I lisstened at old mans feet. He were teechin me a lot of nu werds. About lots of purty thins. Sumthins inside me were growin. Changin. Ever since I started to lern about the tappin. Ma sayed it were cause I wuz a womun now cause I got my cykles. But it were different. It were more. Lynn sayed he were feelin it to. The kids wuznt teezin no more. He could talk easier. I didnt no. But it feelt good.

Grade skool were endin soon. There wuz a new hi skool built a cuple of miles from the south fields. Ma sayed it werent worth it for me to think about goin.

"You miss to many chores and basides you just aint smart enuff honny." Ma put her arm round me trying to make me feel bedder.

"Its ok." I didnt care. I just wanted to learn the tappin.

Then a funny thin happened. All the kids at school had to take a big figurin and ritin test to get reddy for hi school. Old man all ways sayed I should do my best so I tryed hard. Next day Teacher called me to the side. I was fearin her foot in my ass cause I did bad on those tests.

"I want to kungradulate you," Teacher sayed and smiled. She handed me my ritten papers. "Im given you a C on these. Your ritin is lots better. Most of your centenses were compleat with nouns and verbs. Your spellin is startin to impruve. You still need to do lots of work but your grammer is better. I think you should go to hi school."

I didnt no what to say. So I just smiled.

That nite I told Ma. She didnt beleave me till I showed her my papers.

"Prays be!" Ma clapped her hands togedher like she was prayin. "I got to tell Gracie."

Ma run off to Gracies. I run to old mans. He smiled.

"Good for you littel deer one. Im very proud of you. You are learnin. Your workin hard. Tonite we start practissin the tappin."

"You mean the talkin parts over?" I grabbed his arm.

"Therory must be put into practiss." He smiled again and we went into the dezert. He dropped down. I felled baside him. We closed our eyes. Everythin was dark. "Dig," he said. "Dig thru the darkness."

"With what?" I looked around for some tools.

"All you need for the tappin is yourself and a beleaf that you will suckseed."

I didnt understand. But I loved old man and I did everythin he told me.

Later Ma talked with Teacher. They decided I should try the hi school. Old man thot so to. So I said ok. Ma made over some of Gracies old dresses for me. The first day of school she surprised me with a brand new skirt and blouse she made from some xtra matereal. She kissed me. "Your lookin reel fine honny. You do a good job now." I tryed hard.

The next year I keept diggin. I had to learn the tappin. I had the first part down. Old man said that was workin hard. I had listened to his talkin about his home and his Ma. Now I was practissin every nite. Still it wasnt allways eazy.

"I like tryin to dig a hole in these sandy fields," I told old man one nite before we started. "Everytime I brush some away more falls and fills up the hole."

"Dive deeper."

I closed my eyes and tryed. After a few more weeks my

hands bleeded. Sand got in the cracks in my skin. The pain was bad. I thot I would die.

"Press on." The old man shook his head at my tears. "Dont be so concerned with the fizzycal sacrafices you make for the sake of learning the tappin."

"But all I see is darkness. Nothing. Just the black."

"Watch your breath. Relax. Control. Feel the forse of life within you." Then the old man would touch me and I would go on.

High school was hard but I did my best to pleaze the old man. Lynn was at the same school. I saw him there sometimes. Lynns fingers were toren too.

"Granny saw me sneak off once." Lynn bounced a little on his toes and pushed his glasses up on his nose. He told me he was very worried.

"I dont care if they catch me." I put my hands in my pockets. "But we better figure something out."

We didnt eat lunch that day. We went into the fields. We closed our eyes and talked to the old man. He showed us how to make it look like our bodies were still in bed when we practised. No one would ever know we were gone.

About a month after that the sores on our hands began to heal.

"Its cause were gettin better," Lynn said. He was feeling proud.

"I feel better Lynn," I told him as we studied the tiny scars on our fingers. "We are closer." We squeezed hands and sang the old man's song.

Two years of high school passed. One of my teachers attached a note to my report card. I saved the news until after dinner when my chores were done. Ma and I did our best talking in her room, sitting on her bed, after the sun set. This would be a big surprise.

I took a long bath in cool water. Ma's door was closed when I finished. I hesitated before knocking, lingering in the hallway, searching for just the right words, listening to the high-pitched buzzing of her sewing machine.

"Ma? Are you still working?" I asked, my fingers on the doorknob. "Come on in, honey." Her answer was muffled.

I took a deep breath and went inside. Ma was hunched over her machine. The racing squeal of the motor slowed to a gentle purr as she eased the pressure on the knee throttle and glanced up at me. There were dark circles of puffy skin under her eyes. Frailty replaced her daintiness. Her thin lips were pressed together, holding red- and yellow-headed straight pins.

"Hi, Ma. I came to kiss you good-night. It's almost ten o'clock." I smiled but held my report card behind my back. "You've done enough work for one day."

"Just a little more to do," Ma mumbled, holding her lips tight, and finished pinning a hem in the sleeve of the yellow shirt she was making.

"Save it." I came to her side. "I want to tell you, I got my grades today."

"You did?" Ma's eyes grew wide as I revealed my report card. "Well, I guess—" Ma's gaze darted from the paper in my hand to her supply box. She was fearing my failure. She reached for a spool of black thread. "I mean, if you—"

"Now, just listen, Ma." I patted her shoulder. "Put down that stuff, and let me read it to you."

"Oh yes." The spool spun on the wooden peg as she dropped it in its proper place in the box. She turned halfway toward me but stared at her work, picking at the frazzled threads of the raw edge of the sleeve.

"All right. Let me see here." I sat on the end of Ma's bed and read from the written evaluation section. "It says here, 'She'—that's me." I laughed and pointed to myself. The skin covering my cheekbones warmed. " 'She has shown unparalleled improvement in concentration, skill, and perseverance. Her work is done on time and with minimal error. Her effort is unmatched by any student.' "

"But, that's good, isn't it?" Ma peered up through her eyebrows without raising her head. Her brow wrinkled.

"*I* think so. Listen to my grades: C in Math; B in Biology; A in Home Arts—"

"An A in Home Arts!" Ma dropped the shirt on the head of the sewing machine and hurried over to the bed. She sat at my side. "An *A.*" She patted my leg.

"Yep." My grin cooled my face. "And look, a B in Typing, and an A- in English and Literature."

"You mean reading and writing?" Ma's hands trembled as she took the card.

"Yes, Ma, but it's more than that. I'm studying how people write. Oh, Ma, I want to learn how to be a great writer." I leaned closer to her, but I didn't explain the reason I was studying writing. "I'm learning how to put essays and stories together. Oh, I still make lots of mistakes, but I want to be good."

"But?" Ma flipped the report card over in her hands. "What is there to—"

"To learn?" I interrupted, swallowing the lump in my throat. "Well, there's paragraphing, how to choose the right word, how to write whole sentences instead of fragments." My voice sped up, as it always did when I spoke about writing.

"You're learning how to write stories?" There was a vertical crease between Ma's eyebrows, and her lips were pursed as she shook her head.

"It's just what I like to do, Ma." I took a deep breath to steady my voice. "Pa always said, 'A person's gotta do what they gotta do.' "

"Yes, but it's so, so different." Ma folded my report card in half, stood, and placed it on the spot where she had sat. She moved to the sewing machine and picked up the shirt. "I don't know if your father meant Big City kind of—" Her voice cracked, and she clutched the shirt to her breast. "It's just, just—"

"Don't worry, Ma." I put the card in my pants pocket

and went to her side. "My life won't change. Lots of authors live in the South and in the country. I won't be going anywhere." I thought of the old man. "It'll work out."

"I suppose." Ma rubbed her forehead. "I'm just tired, I guess."

"I know." I put my arm around her shoulder. "No more tonight." I took the shirt and set it in her box. "I'll turn off the machine. You get ready for bed."

Ma moved to the bed and drew her nightgown out from under the pillow. I watched her stare out the window for a moment before she began to undress. Then, closing her eyes, she slipped off her dress and pulled the gown over her head. She sat on the edge of the bed, folding her clothes. I unplugged the machine, taking a long time. Standing straight, I inhaled slowly and walked toward Ma.

"You're learning to write stories?" She cocked her head. "Well, your grades were very good."

"Thank you." I reached into the drawer of the end table beside her bed. Her rosary lay on top of an unhandseled Bible. My fingers skimmed across the worn pieces of carved wood as I scooped them up. They shone, polished by the accumulation of oil from Ma's hands. I gave her the beads.

"Thank you, honey." Her lips quivered as she got under the quilt.

"Good night." I kissed her on the forehead.

"Oh, honey. It feels warm there where you just kissed me." Ma touched her brow and closed her eyes. "Is it raining?" She glanced back to the window. "Is that lightning out there? Did I see a light as you touched me?"

"Could be." I nodded.

A gentle moan rolled off Ma's lips as she lay back on the pillow. "Praise Be!" she whispered.

I gazed down at her. I tucked the quilt around her sides. I felt older than I looked.

"What does it all mean?" Ma muttered, her fingertips caressing the beads. She began to think about going to Gracie's in the morning.

"I don't know, Ma." I smiled and shrugged and left the room.

But I knew. It was the tappin.

Another year passed. I never missed a night, even if it stormed. I run through the wind and the rain, free, un-afraid of the thunder. There he would be, like a promise. I could dig faster. He still smiled and touched me. I knew such peace, such bliss.

The third year of high school ended. I had studied very hard. My English teacher, Mrs. Chase, called me to her desk and returned my corrected final examination papers after the rest of the class had been dismissed.

"Nice work," she nodded, peering over the rims of her bifocals.

"Doesn't seem like it." I choked down a rising lump of frustration as I glanced at the pages stained by scribbled red lines. I had to perfect my writing.

"Oh, yes, it does." Mrs. Chase patted my arm after she made me sit down. "There are some errors here, but they're different. You're into a higher quality of mistakes now. Most of this is just suggestion anyway." Her long index finger traced across one of the critiques. "You've worked very hard. Soon, you're going to be flawless. You won't be needing me. You'll be *my* teacher."

I smiled, but I never told anyone about that.

That summer I had more free time to concentrate. One day in July the old man and I were together in the fields during late afternoon. Hours passed. Just when I thought I couldn't go on, I pushed myself harder. The darkness was split by two colliding stars. A million new stars were born, shooting out like comets, creating new colors, exploding in every corner of my mind.

"Oh!" I stood up, rushing about. "The stars, they're so beautiful!"

"I know." The old man made me sit again. "Go through

them. Don't spend time there. Pretty lights aren't your goal. That's not home."

My muscles tensed, aching at the thought I had failed. I began to cry.

"It will come, dear one." The old man touched me. "The tappin will come."

Our last year in high school Lynn was elected class president. He was still thin and wheezed when excited, but a new power was being expressed in his ability to lead others. I smiled more often and continued to study those things the old man told me would be important. But there was only one major force in my life, the drive to perfect the tappin. I loved the silence, the old man's humming song, the warmth of his presence I could carry with me. I thought then that Lynn would be a great leader, a benevolent forerunner to guide our times. And, for myself, I wanted the solitude, and a pen and paper. Something told me to document the old man's words. Stacks of notes were piled high in the closet and corners of my room.

Daily trials were solved with greater ease according to the depth of my contemplation. Ma hugged me sometimes. She said now that I was letting my hair grow it had more of a shine, like white gold, and my eyes seemed straighter and sparkled. Neighbors were paying Ma a good price for her sewing. She worked less and had more money. I could do my chores in half the time. Yet, I experienced a sense of constraint. There was still something holding me back, keeping me from a complete realization of the old man's concepts. Despite the slight separation, I went on. I knew it would come.

One month before commencement, late on a Saturday night, I had what I thought was the long awaited revelation. Alone, in the fields near the old man's cabin, I dug deeper than ever before. The bottom of the hole grew darker in color than the sides. First my hands felt cool, wet.

Deeper, deeper. My breath was slow, my heartbeat faint. My body seemed to be dispersing. Suddenly, trickles of water began to run down the sides of the hole and collected at the bottom in a muddy pool. I thought my heart would burst with joy, though I could not feel my body. Scrambling to find my feet, I ran to the old man.

"The tappin!" I hollered and tugged his arm, pulling him from the rocker to my place in the field. "Come, look! I've hit the source!" I pointed in wild gestures at the muddy wet sand. A golden shine emanated from the old man's head as I stared at him in the starlit night.

"This will never do." With kind but reproving eyes, the old man shook his head, assessing my progress. His long hair blew in the slight breeze of the desert.

"What?" I slouched, feeling as if a great weight had landed on my shoulders. "Why?" Disappointment creased my facial muscles.

"A puddle won't sustain life." The glow spread to the old man's robe while he explained in a whisper, "Go back inside. Find the *infinite* source."

Again I fought tears of discouragement. I swallowed the lump in my throat. But the old man touched me.

"Oh, my dearest one, you have done well. You never give up. You will reach it soon, very soon." He smiled and together we started over. In a while I was floating again. Then we listened to the humming song.

Spring was melted by the scorch of summer, yet I was filled with new determination and inspiration. School was almost over. All my teachers smiled with pleasure at my achievements. I could answer any of their questions. Lynn's eyes were clear pools, reflecting that which was invading my heart, expanding our minds.

The last week of school my guidance counselor, Mrs. Wysett, called my mother and me in for an appointment. I had been offered a scholarship to the University of New Mexico and one to a small fine arts college in the East. I folded my hands in my lap, my mother fingered a white handkerchief as we sat in Mrs. Wysett's modern, air-conditioned office.

"Your daughter has a special gift, a great talent that should be developed to the maximum of her potential." Mrs. Wysett went on to explain the opportunities, then added, "Good university training will offer her many advantages."

"Well, honey." My mother turned to me. Tiny drops of sweat on her forehead sparkled like diamonds under the fluorescent lights. "Mrs. Wysett says you have a special gift." Ma blotted the perspiration from her brow and remembered the three-day drive from Albuquerque to our town near the California border when we first moved from Texas to Arizona. "You have many things to think about, young lady." Her smile drooped at the corners of her mouth. She tugged on a bunch of loose threads in a worn corner of the damp hankie. "I a long way away."

That night I spoke of the meeting when I met with the old man. I sat on the porch steps at his feet. The rocker was still. The moonlight danced in his dark eyes. He listened in patient silence.

"I won't go from this place," I resolved, folding my arms across my chest. "This will be my life."

"You must leave," the old man said, and the rocker squeaked as he leaned back. "You will have a different life than the one here. Now you must go out; teach, write of these things you know."

"But I want to stay with you." I squeezed his knee and felt a stabbing in my heart. "What about Lynn?"

"I know about him. His work is in another place. Your path is your own. What you say will be accepted better when you have a formal education." The old man closed his eyes. "I'm going home soon," he whispered in a distant, slow voice.

"No, you can't! You mustn't." I clutched both of his

knees. "How will I know what to do?" In my anger I almost shook him.

"Be with me, dear one." His whisper grew fainter, like the vibration of a breeze. He stroked my hair as I lay my cheek on his leg. "Be with me when I leave." He gazed out into the fields. "Then you will always know."

Commencement came on the hottest day of the year. The setting of the sun brought no relief. Mr. and Mrs. Harper drove my mother and me to the ceremony in their station wagon with the wood panels on the sides. I sat in the back seat with my mother and listened as she breathed heated sighs and prayed for the winds she usually cursed. She had been busy that spring. Everyone wanted a new dress. I touched her hand and kissed her cheek.

"Thank you for everything," I said. "My present is gorgeous." Under my graduation gown I wore a creme-colored chiffon dress, an original design, with a lace bodice and a crocheted tie belt. We woke earlier than usual that morning to wash my hair and roll the ends in the small papers and pins that came in a do-at-home permanent wave kit. Now the gentle curls brushed on the top of my shoulder as I turned and stared out the window. A crowd was gathering in the high school parking lot.

"Starting a new life in a new place can be scary—" My mother paused, the crease in her forehead deepened as she realized she too would be alone. "But you'll do just fine, honey." She forced a smile and patted my knee. She blinked the moisture from her eyes and said, "You look beautiful."

"I love you," I whispered, and kissed her again.

As class president Lynn welcomed all to graduation. I was class valedictorian. I sat near the lectern, hands folded in my lap, legs crossed at the ankle, and waited for my turn to speak. Lynn talked of aiming toward one goal and developing the will to succeed. His Granny leaned forward in her seat, clapping at every natural pause in his speech, but Lynn's breath was quick, shallow, and his voice faded sometimes.

I looked out at the audience before me. My mother and the Harpers were in the first row, grinning and pointing up at the stage. The colorful rows blended like the pastels on an oil painting by Renoir. All the women were crowned by wide-brimmed straw hats with plastic sweet Williams or daisies in the headbands and garbed in flowered dresses with thin collars and midlength sleeves that belled out an inch above the elbow. Most of the men wore short-sleeved shirts, the neck buttons open. Yellow-edged sweat stains looked beige in the places where the material stuck to their skin. They sat with legs wide apart, every few moments reaching down, pulling out the folds in the knees of their pants. Half-naked children kneeled backward on the chairs, the ridges of their spines glistening with perspiration. Some women folded their programs lengthwise like Japanese fans, others were bent in the middle. All moved in a lazy rhythm. Right to left, left to right, anything to be cool.

Then came my turn to speak. Lynn grinned and winked as he returned to his seat. The principal called my name. As I rose the sweat that had pooled in the places where my knees touched streamed down my legs but evaporated before reaching my feet. I had taken a few note cards with me but left them in the side pocket of the graduation gown. I spoke extemporaneously on a theme from one of the old man's lessons. The words flowed from my lips almost as if I were nothing more than a channel for the expression of an infinite source of wisdom. I felt as I had never felt before, unaware of the uniqueness of my body, yet conscious of all physical existence.

As I glanced down at the rows, the audience began to appear distorted, uneven, like a reflection in the warped mirrors in the funhouse of a traveling carnival. Slowly the faces melted into a rippling wave of heat, the kind that rises up off the desert floor in the lethal noon sun. Then everything went black. I continued to speak. My darkness was my own.

A moment passed then a tiny five-pointed star flared in the center of my vision like a match struck on a starless, moonless night. A wind felt only by myself blew out the flaming star. Appearing before me were the big brown eyes of the old man. He was calling me. Blinded to all but his vision, deafened by inner yearning, I cried for his presence. I struggled to finish my speech.

"And so, in conclusion, as we embark upon this adventure we call Life, let us exemplify those qualities within each of us that are timeless; let us reflect the inner beauty of the soul; let us smile with the realization that all we need we carry within ourselves. In our consciousness is all that we need to be. Thank you."

I left the grandstand before the applause died down.

A light glistened in the smudged glass of the cabin window. The old man was in the rocker on the porch. All was still. The wooden steps, tired and dry, moaned and gave half an inch under the weight of my feet. The old man was silent as I approached. His eyes turned up. A smile of perfect peace graced his tender features. He was dressed in a fine silk robe that smelled fresh, never before worn. My fingertips slipped on the satiny surface. The old man's skin was cooling.

I hummed the song in his ear. There was nothing except the sound of my heart pounding. Again I hummed. Nothing.

Again. This time I knew there would be no response.

Oh God. I wasn't with him when he left.

I threw the cap and gown near the front door. I stumbled into the fields. An upcoming wind whirled sand, scratching at my face. I was alone. *Alone. Old man. Forgive me, come back. Don't be gone. I need to know.* I fell to my knees at the place the old man first started my lessons on the tappin.

I dug. Deep. Deeper. Past the cometing stars. Through the hole oozing murky mud. *Old man.* I did not cry. Then it came, bubbling, clear, full of life, boiling, yet cool water. Like a spring. I washed my hands in it. I splashed it on my face. A great gushing noise spewed forth, the roar of an ocean. The symphony of all sounds. I was jetted forward. Rays of light diffused into multifaceted patterns, geometric, exact, graphic. Colors unlabeled by language because they are not visible to the human eye burst forth in blends, splendid, iridescent, making the most dazzling of delicate rainbows seem gaudy. Tactile sensations, ever-present, yet too subtle to have experienced on the physical plane, delighted me. The slight tickle of the lightest feather would thereafter feel as heavy as a pounding by a cement ball. My mind opened like a thousand-petaled lotus, intuiting answers with the ease that breath flows into an athlete's lungs. Now mine were stilled.

On a new plane, I opened my eyes. Before me were acres of brown fertile soil. I moved on, my body was composed of fine light. I smiled. *The tappin.* In the distance an amber pasture of grain swayed in a slight breeze. Standing there among the wheat was the old man. Smiling, he raised a hand in benediction. The wind churned, lifting him up. His ochre cloak began to fall from his shoulders. I ran toward him. I lifted my gaze. The old man rose higher. The mantle tumbled down, covering my head like a veil, sealing me inside something like a warm bubble.

I remain there now, untouched, undisturbed.

Lynn followed the old man. Dr. Neumann signed the death certificates. She wrote "heart attack" in the boxes demanding cause of death.

It is all up to me now, the responsibility is mine.

I attended the small college. I still remember the morning I left Arizona. My mother clung to me and kissed me and said, "This is best, but I'll sure miss you a lot, honey." Fifteen years ago I earned a bachelor's degree. Over a decade has passed since my doctorate was accepted. I am older than I appear.

My mother wrote me letters while I was still at college. Investors came to Arizona. They bought out the Harpers and purchased some of our land. They built condominiums, a golf course, and a lake where the fields were. Northern tourists come and go, for the sun, they say.

I moved on, farther east. I see only one star now. People wait for what I write next. But it's always about the old man. I've gone back to using sentence fragments at times. Now that's called my style.

New students always come, for the lessons. I greet each one. They place titles in front of my name when they speak to me. Some stay on, they have clear eyes. We drink from the same cup. Most leave with tired, bloody hands they fear will be scarred forever.

Late in the night when others sleep, I go inside. I tap in. In the morning before dawn I come back. I breathe deeply. In the winter there are bowls of fresh fruit on my table.

I don't ask questions, there are only answers.

Inspired by Paramahansa Yogananda
Dedicated to Sri Daya Mata

Anita Wilkins

The Mystery of Things
Inextricably Bound

What someone gave me, years ago, without knowing
he did it, without intending to, was the earth again.
But now I've given it away—again. Silences in gullies
I can't listen to, the whisper of a turning leaf
that's not loud enough to reach me anymore.
Even the crash of the surf would not be loud enough.
Moon burns her hole in the monthly sky, and I see her,
but I don't see why she does it for me anymore. I don't
want it, that scorched sky leading down to whatever won't
let me pass, anyway, seeing me traitor and indifferent.
What happened to that wholeheartedness that wanted
earth in my arms, its trees, its grass, rocks, the high
shine of its rivers, the soft underglow of shadows
wherever they rested before they had to move on?
I mourned Chernobyl in the grapes of Greece we could
not eat that year and the beach stones we could not
touch. The sky, cursed, the stretched soul. Wherever
rain fell it was not kind anymore. It was like one more
loss in an avalanche of losses, and I learned to turn
away. I gave love elsewhere, even where nothing
came back to me, and I dropped my hands, time after time.
Because, it seemed, I had to stop learning. It seemed
I had to stop wanting. Trees drew the doors of their
branches closed. Water had no depth. Lizards became
rocks, their bright eyes closed against me. Earth, open

yourself for me. Rocks, breathe and blink, see me.
I don't know what to offer you from this emptiness.
I've forgotten what paths the soles of my feet made,
what calls of crows my ears understood, magpies' tongues.
Yet, like the owl's house,
something begins to build around me,
lining itself for my sake. And the mother's soft hootings
float down the hillsides with the last brushes of light.

Robin Drury

Mountain Spirit

Leaning across the tiny table, I brush the long hair from my eyes, tilt my chin toward my friend's proffered match, and inhale. Smoke curls around us, drifts from other tables, swirls slowly in the narrow beams focused on the musicians and lifts into the darkness. Dressed in black, from our turtleneck sweaters to our tights, we're nearly invisible. Having gotten in with a fake ID, I appreciate the illusion of invisibility. My college friends and I are "into" exploring the San Francisco "beatnik" scene, discovering what goes on in The City, in the coffeehouses of the Haight-Ashbury, in the little clubs like this one, in the side-alley entertainment spots—the Hungry I and the Purple Onion. Like everyone else our age, we're searching for the meaning of life.

Fifteen years earlier, I was reciting "Now I lay me down to sleep" for my Grandmother Rob. Soon after, I was sitting with other Sunday-best five-year-olds singing "Jesus Loves Me" in a circle of little green chairs. During visits to "real church" my mother produced pencil and paper to keep me from fidgeting during the sermons. But I was enthralled by the music—the rich, booming tones of the organ, whose double rows of pipes lined up across the back of the mahogany choir loft, and almost reached the high, peaked ceiling—and the hundreds of people in the congregation standing to join their voices in song. By high school I had joined the choir. The vibrations of the pipe organ thrilled through my chest every Sunday morning as I blended my voice with seventy-some others in the rich harmonies of Bach, Beethoven, Handel, and Mozart, backed by rolling chords that thundered through the sanctuary. On Easter we performed an arrangement of "Christ the Lord is Risen Today" whose variations of hallelujas and crescendos of organ chords shook the rafters and brought parishioners to tears.

Cynics might have thought that this exalted music was calculated to open their wallets for the building fund. For in a few years our red-stone, steepled Central Methodist Church at the edge of aging downtown Stockton was to be replaced by a modern edifice in a more "upscale" part of town. The futuristic modern design (some claimed it resembled a whale skeleton) would not accommodate, either aesthetically or architecturally, the big old organ and its thirty-foot-tall pipes. Learning that it would be replaced by an electronic substitute contributed to a growing disillusionment with my childhood faith; what held me were my youth-group friendships, and the moments of spiritual inspiration I experienced in the choir. The "day the music died" wasn't when Buddy Holly's plane crashed, but when they bulldozed my childhood church. For me, God was dead. I never lost my love for the music; I just stopped believing in what it stood for. My minstrels became the Kingston Trio; my hymns, folk songs. Count Basie's rhythms and harmonies, sweet blendings of strings and brass, replaced the rich, full sounds pumped out by old Kenneth on the pipe organ. Perhaps, all along, I had confused emotional response with religious experience.

I refused to attend the new church, and within a few years my younger brother, Dale, declared himself an atheist; it was my mother's turn to feel disillusioned. All those Sunday mornings of dressing us up for Sunday school, all those trips to choir practice, Sunday services and youth-group meetings. Hadn't they done everything right? What had happened to our spiritual lives, what would happen to our souls?

But it had been during summer trips to the Sierra and family picnics on Sunday afternoons, learning wildflower names from "Gram" Drury and wading in foothill creeks, that I had taken the first steps in my true spiritual journey. I remember my first visit to my uncle's just purchased cabin at Pinecrest when I was four. I stepped out of the car and stubbed my sandaled toe on a pinecone. But after "Grammy" Rob's application of first aid and comforting hugs, we admired the wild yellow iris, the red-orange Indian paintbrush, and soft gray-pink pussy-paws at our feet, and crooked our necks to the pines and firs towering overhead. Something was special here; the adults were quieter; even the air smelled different—spicy, tinged with woodsmoke—and refreshingly cool compared to the muggy San Joaquin Valley heat we had left behind only a few hours before. We took a short walk to the lake and back and collected small fallen branches for the woodstove. Then, while my aunt and uncle relaxed by the fireplace, Grammy drew me pictures by kerosene lamplight, of the robins we had watched together.

For the next twelve years, my family spent Dad's two-week summer vacation at the Pinecrest cabin. In a photograph from the forties, Dale and I, in wet, sagging underpants, play in the shallow ripples at the edge of a stream. Above us, a small stream of white water bounces down a jumble of granite into a bubbling pool. Looking at this picture, I imagine my father wrapping his limit of trout in mossy ferns, tucking them safely into his creel, and trading his rod and reel for his camera. There are snapshots, too, of my mother, posing gracefully on a boulder, waterfalls in the background. There are pictures of my father, of friends, grandparents, aunts, and uncles at the cabin, at the lakeshore. The faces are relaxed, even reverent. A feeling of peacefulness emanates from the pictures, and permeates my memories.

Vacation was a time when adults slept late, and in a reversal often irritating to our parents, kids got up early. Some days, though, the four of us rose with the sun, packed blanket, towels, and lunch into the Ford, and drove a few miles up the Sonora Pass Highway, turning off on some dusty, bumpy road—to Herring Creek, Middle Fork, or Clark Fork. While Dale trailed after my father, learning how to cast the deep green pools for rainbow trout, I jumped from boulder to boulder over foaming white bubbles. Wading barefoot in the icy shallows, I collected smooth, shiny orange, green, black, and purple stones to lay on the blanket next to Mom, who had found a comfortable, duff-softened spot under a fir tree and was catching up on the *Reader's Digest*. We lunched on sandwiches and potato chips, watched the jays and flickers, and laughed at the shy, quick chipmunks and squirrels. While my parents lingered after lunch, and Dale tried futilely to build a rock dam across the creek, I made little gardens of tiny pinecones, pebbles, and bits of stream-bank moss to take home. The mosses invariably died. That you can't take the mountains home with you was a lesson long in the learning.

I had relegated matters of the spirit to my childhood when, at twenty-two, in traditional white gown and veil, I walked down the aisle of the university chapel on my father's arm. Except to attend other weddings, my husband and I stayed out of churches. Nevertheless, my mother was appalled, when our first daughter was born six years later, that we weren't having her baptized. Mom had hoped that my lapse at seventeen had simply been adolescent rebellion, that I would return to the fold when I had children. She was convinced we were depriving Leslie of her soul; that I had lost my own was certain. When Courtney arrived four years later, and Mom didn't even mention baptism, I knew she had conceded that her own kids were doomed to be heathens. Myself, I wasn't sure, but I knew I found no solace in organized religion. Nor did my daughters, on the several occasions they went to Sunday service

with their grandparents. Our spiritual home was somewhere else.

The summer after I divorced their father, I traveled with
my girls—then seven and three—to Sonora Pass, that part
of the Sierra I had often visited as a child. The snow had
mostly melted, but we spotted a patch up on a distant,
barren hillside. We began clambering up what turned out
to be a much steeper slope than I expected, and stopped to
see how far we had come. Leslie looked back at the fractured cliffs across the narrow valley from where we stood,
at sunlit golden granite that seemed bonded like a movie
backdrop to the deep blue sky beyond, swung her arms out
wide as if to embrace it all, and exclaimed in an awed voice,
"WOW!" Something resonated for me, a recollection of
what I had felt as a child. I smiled and—past the lump that
had risen in my throat—said something affirming in response. The sense of wonder, nurtured in me, however un-
consciously, by my parents—was alive in my daughter.
But in that moment I didn't understand the connection between wonder at the natural world and our spiritual side,
or soul. That would take another lesson from my children.

A few years later, on a late afternoon in winter, not far
from Sonora Pass, the girls were playing in the snow along
the shore of drained Pinecrest Lake. As dusk began to
gather, Leslie came bursting into the cabin in a flurry of
excitement, exclaiming, "Have you ever seen the moon
rise?" Well, I thought I had, and I was reluctant to leave
the warmth of the fire and conversation with my friends.
To her uncharacteristically demanding "You've *got* to
come see," I replied, "I'll be out in a minute." It took five-
year-old Courtney running in with equal exuberance to
prompt me to pull on my boots and return with her to the
lakeshore. By then, I had missed the overture, the cre-
scendo, that surely had to have accompanied the rise of the
biggest, fullest, brightest moon I have (to this day) ever
seen. A magically glowing balloon, it had floated free of
the V-shaped canyon, perfectly centered, and was beaming

across the snow-covered lake bottom like a suspended searchlight. The hush was complete; not a bird peeped, not a twig snapped, not a person—and a number of children and adults had been out sledding—not one, spoke, or moved. After what seemed like forever, someone touched the dimmer switch, the glow spread and diminished as the moon rose higher, and a few quiet voices carried across the snow. It was minutes before I could find mine.

Since that December evening, seventeen years ago, I have chased full moons on winter nights. I long to recapture that moment, to experience moonrise over snow, to get the whole feeling my daughters were privileged to share. They still chide me for taking too long to join them. My fault; they're right. I have learned to take advantage of moments of wonder, light shows of brilliant pink sunrises and haze-painted crimson sunsets that dissolve into the indigo Pacific. When the autumn moon rises full and yellow-orange over the coastal hills, I stop and watch its glow spread out over Monterey Bay. The feeling of peace these moments bring keeps me open to the natural world, to the transcendence I reach in the mountains, but it doesn't equal the spiritual fullness I feel in the Sierra.

It's just that moments are not enough; one day at a time is not enough. I need sustained time in the mountains—time to let go, time to get in touch with the natural world and who I am in it. Time to revisit special places and to share them with family and friends, time to discover new paths, new streams, new waterfalls. My mother says, "You're always going, going, going. Don't you ever stay home?" Jokingly I explain that I get altitude sickness if I stay too long at sea level. The sense of peace I find in the Sierra, the solitude, the silence, that special music of the high mountains, I can't find anywhere else. I've tried to substitute the ocean, and the coastal hills; it doesn't work. Even though I learned as a child that their colors fade to drabness when they dry, I carry home smooth, shiny, river-polished bits of granite and quartz. They serve as reminders, like rosary beads, of the sacred. But they are only that. On a whim, I planted two *Sequoia gigantea*, the "big trees" of the Sierra, in my Santa Cruz backyard. They are growing full and tall, but this is not their natural home. Sometimes I wonder if it's mine, and dream about moving to the mountains. Then I remember, people don't live in cathedrals. No, I might live closer, but I can't live *there*. And I can't bring the mountains here. So I balance the practical realities of family and work with my need to sustain my spiritual connections with the Sierra, and go on collecting waterfalls.

For me, the uplift of mountains and of spirit are one. Give me the baptism of icy cold streams shuddering over granite boulders, leaping off of crags and ledges, tearing down glaciated canyons. Give me fragile stone-crop clinging to narrow cracks, and fringes of fern dripping with ricocheted spray. Give me the earthquake's tilt, brooks, and streams formed of a million years of uplift and erosion. Bluejay mornings and woodpecker afternoons, and the echoing silence of starlight. The thrill of immersion in spring-melt lakes, the balm of sun-warmed granite slabs, and the meditation of falling snow. I worship where clouds roll in on waves of thunder, where water falls from rock edge in a swirling dance of mist clouds, and spray bows play on sunny days and moonlit nights. Where my senses fill with the loft of lodgepole, the softness of firs, the tang of juniper, the butterscotch of Jeffrey pine, and the creek-side dampness of alders.

Leaning across the table in my parents' kitchen, I am showing them photographs from my recent backpacking trip in Yosemite. A picture of Tuolumne Meadows sparks a recollection, and Mom recalls a time in her twenties when she found herself standing by the river, just taking in the solitude. She says of it, "I felt God right there next to me. He really was right there. I felt so peaceful." She is eighty-four, and this is the first time I've heard her speak of experiencing nature in this way. Her voice quivers as she says, "It was just a beautiful feeling." "I know," I say, my throat tightening. "That's why I go to the mountains."

Melody Ermachild Chavis

Street Trees

I was drawn to my upstairs bedroom window by shouting in the street. The shouter was a middle-aged black man in shabby pants, and he strode, fast, right down the middle of the street. Storming across the intersection, the man beat the air with his fists and shouted into the sky. "Somalia!" he cried. "Somalia!"

Ours is a neighborhood where poverty and addiction have made misery for years, and this was when airlifts of food to the Horn of Africa were all over the nightly news. "I know what you mean," I thought. "Why there? Why feed them but not you?"

Then he walked up to the newly planted tree under my window, grabbed its skinny trunk with both hands, yanked it over sideways, and cracked it in half on his knee. He threw the tree's leafy top onto the sidewalk and stomped off, cursing. I pressed my palms to the glass as he disappeared up the sidewalk.

The tree was just a baby, one of the donated saplings our neighborhood association planted with help from the children on our block. Men from the public-works department had come and cut squares in the sidewalk for us, reaming out holes with a machine that looked like a big screw. The kids planted the trees, proudly wielding shovels, loving their hands in the dirt.

I had made name tags for each tree, with a poem printed on each one, and we asked the kids to give each tree a name. "Hi, my name's *Greenie*, I'm new and neat, just

195

like the children on our street." If we made the trees seem more like people, I thought, the kids would let them live.

Both trees and people around here are at risk of dying young. After our neighborhood was flooded with crack cocaine and cheap, strong alcohol, things got very rough. In the last five years, sixteen people have been murdered in our small police beat. Most of them were young black men, and most of them died on the sidewalks, where the trees witness everything: the children, the squealing tires and gunshots, the blood and sirens.

My neighbors and I did all we could think of to turn things around, including planting the trees.

But the dealers still hovered on the corners and the young trees had a hard time. Idle kids swung on them like playground poles and peeled off strips of bark with their nervous little fingers.

One of the saplings planted in front of my house had fallen victim to a car, and now the other one had been murdered by a man mad about Somalia.

Discouraged, I let the holes in the cement choke with crabgrass. In the center of each square, a pathetic stick of dead trunk stuck up.

When things are bad, I stand in my kitchen window and look into my own garden, a paradise completely hidden from the street outside. For fifteen years I've labored and rested in my garden, where roses clamber on bamboo trellises. There are red raspberries and rhubarb. Lemon, apricot, apple, and fig trees are sheltered by young redwoods and firs that hide the apartment house next door. I planted the apricot tree thirteen years ago, when it was a bare stick as tall as myself. Now I mark the seasons with its changes. In early spring the apricot blooms white, tinged with pink, and feeds the bees. When our chimney fell in the earthquake, I used the bricks to build a low circular wall I call my medicine wheel. Inside it I grow sage, lavender, rosemary, and oregano. A stone Buddha sits under fringed Tibetan prayer flags, contemplating a red rock.

Not far from my house is a place I'm convinced is a sacred site. Within one block are a large African-American Christian church, a Black Muslim community center, and a Hindu ashram. Someone put a Buddha in a vacant lot near there, too, and people built a shrine around it. All this is close to the place where the Ohlone people once had a village.

I dream of those who lived here before me—an Ohlone woman, members of the Peralta family whose hacienda this was, and a Japanese-American farmer who had a truck garden here until he lost it when he was interned during World War II.

I often feel I'm gardening with my dear old next-door neighbor Mrs. Wright. An African-American woman from Arkansas, Mrs. Wright came to work in the shipyards during the war. When she bought the house next door, this was the only neighborhood in town where black people were allowed to live. She was foster mother to many children, and she was sadly disapproving of the young people who used drugs when that started. Mrs. Wright farmed every inch of her lot, and had it all in food, mainly greens, like collards and kale. She gave most of the food away.

Her life exemplified the adage "We come from the earth, we return to the earth, and in between we garden." I miss her still, although she died six years ago, in her seventies, after living here nearly fifty years. I was almost glad she didn't live to see the night a young man was shot to death right in front of our houses.

A map of the neighborhood fifteen years ago, when my family came, would show community places that are gone now: bank, pharmacy, hardware and small, black-owned corner stores. There are a lot of vacancies now, jobs are gone, and people travel to malls to shop. Many families run out of food by the last days of the month.

On my map I can plot some of what killed this community's safety: the too-many liquor outlets—nine within four blocks of my house; the drug dealers who came with crack about 1985. Clustered near the drugs and alcohol are the sixteen murder sites: the fifteen men, the one woman.

"I want to get away from all this," I think often. But *really* getting away would mean selling our home and leaving, and so far my husband and I have been unwilling to give up, either on our neighbors or on our hopes for helping make things better.

But we do get away, to the mountains. We've been walking the John Muir Trail in sections the last few summers. I've never liked the way it feels good to go to the mountains and bad to come home. That's like only enjoying the weekends of your whole life.

According to my mail, "nature" is the wilderness, which I'm supposed to save. And I want to. But right here and now, if I go outside to pick up trash, I might have to fish a used syringe out of my hedge. That's saving nature too. The hard task is loving the earth, all of it.

The notes I stick on my refrigerator door remind me of the unity and sacredness of life. There's a quote from Martin Luther King, Jr., on "the inescapable network of mutuality." I know I can't take a vacation from any part of this world.

Still, the habit of my mind is dual. This I hate (the littered sidewalk); this I love (the alpine meadow). I could get into my car and drive to that meadow. But when I drive back, the sidewalk will still be dirty. Or, I could stay here, pick up a broom, and walk out my front door.

The sidewalk yields clues that people have passed this way, like trail markers in the mountains: candy wrappers the kids have dropped on their way back from the store; malt liquor cans and fortified-wine bottles inside brown bags. Sometimes there are clothes, or shoes, or car parts. I tackle it all in thick orange rubber gloves, wielding my broom and dustpan, dragging my garbage can along with me. I recycle what I can. "This is *all* sacred," I tell myself. "All of it."

There are bigger waste problems. But when I think about the ozone hole, I find that it helps me to clean up. Thinking globally without acting locally can spin me down into despair.

Or into anger. I know that other people somewhere else made decisions that turned our neighborhood, once a good place, into a bad one. Like the alcohol-industry executives who decided to aim expensive ad campaigns at African-American teens. I know decisions happen that way to the old-growth forests, too.

I went to a lecture at the Zen Center not far from my house, to hear the head gardener there. She talked about what is to be learned from ginkgo trees. I've always liked their fan-shaped leaves, bright gold in the fall, but I hadn't known they were ancient, evolved thousands of years ago. They exist nowhere in the wild, she said, but were fostered by monks in gardens in China and Japan. Somehow, ginkgos have adapted so that they thrive in cities, in polluted air. They remind me of the kids around here, full of life in spite of everything. I've seen teenage boys from my block, the kind called "at risk," "inner-city," sometimes even "thugs," on a field trip to an organic farm, patting seedlings into the earth like tender young fathers putting babies to bed.

The day after the lecture, I went to the nursery, ready to try planting trees again in the holes in the sidewalk. Now in front of my house are two tiny ginkgos, each inside a fortified cage of four strong metal posts and thick wire mesh. To weed them, I kneel on the sidewalk and reach in, trying not to scratch my wrist on the wire.

Kneeling there, I accept on faith that this little tree will do its best to grow according to its own plan. I also believe that every person wants a better life.

One evening last summer I lay flat out in a hot spring in the broad valley on the east side of the Sierra. I imagined one of the little street ginkgos growing upright from my left palm. Out of my right palm, an ancient bristlecone pine of the White Mountains. This is how the trees live on the earth, as out of one body. They are not separate. The roots of the city tree and the summit tree pass through my heart and tangle.

Terry Tempest Williams

Excerpt from
Long-Billed Curlews

There is something unnerving about my solitary travels around the northern stretches of Great Salt Lake. I am never entirely at ease because I am aware of its will. Its mood can change in minutes. The heat alone reflecting off the salt is enough to drive me mad, but it is the glare that immobilizes me. Without sunglasses, I am blinded. My eyes quickly burn on Salt Well Flats. It occurs to me that I will return home with my green irises bleached white. If I return at all.

The understanding that I could die on the salt flats is no great epiphany. I could die anywhere. It's just that in the forsaken corners of Great Salt Lake there is no illusion of being safe. You stand in the throbbing silence of the Great Basin, exposed and alone. On these occasions, I keep tight reins on my imagination. The pearl-handled pistol I carry in my car lends me no protection. Only the land's mercy and a calm mind can save my soul. And it is here I find grace.

It's strange how deserts turn us into believers. I believe in walking in a landscape of mirages, because you learn humility. I believe in living in a land of little water because life is drawn together. And I believe in the gathering of bones as a testament to spirits that have moved on.

If the desert is holy, it is because it is a forgotten place that allows us to remember the sacred. Perhaps that is why every pilgrimage to the desert is a pilgrimage to the self. There is no place to hide, and so we are found.

In the severity of a salt desert, I am brought down to my knees by its beauty. My imagination is fired. My heart opens and my skin burns in the passion of these moments. I will have no other gods before me.

Wilderness courts our souls. When I sat in church throughout my growing years, I listened to teachings about Christ in the wilderness for forty days and forty nights, reclaiming his strength, where he was able to say to Satan, "Get thee hence." When I imagined Joseph Smith kneeling in a grove of trees as he received his vision to create a new religion, I believed their sojourns into nature were sacred. Are ours any less?

There is a Mormon scripture, from the Doctrine and Covenants section 88:44–47, that I carry with me:

> The earth rolls upon her wings, and the sun giveth
>   his light by day, and the moon giveth her light
>   by night, and the stars also give their light, as
>   they roll upon their wings in their glory, in the
>   midst of the power of God.
> Unto what shall I liken these kingdoms that ye may
>   understand?
> Behold all these are kingdoms and any man who
>   hath seen any of the least of these hath seen God
>   moving in his majesty and power.

I pray to the birds.

I pray to the birds because I believe they will carry the messages of my heart upward. I pray to them because I believe in their existence, the way their songs begin and end each day—the invocations and benedictions of Earth. I pray to the birds because they remind me of what I love rather than what I fear. And at the end of my prayers, they teach me how to listen.

Tassajara

For Diane, Sally, Janice

Clear mountain streams converge; creek water eddies and pools in this place the Esselen Indians named, called home. Turtles rest on warmed rock. With their wings, cobalt-blue and burnt-orange dragonflies catch the sun.

Lynn and I collect red-gold stones, feathers, mineral water from the hot spring, for our walk to the shrine. Two years ago we journeyed to the dark heart of cancer. Nothing is as it was. We gather purple farewell-to-spring, blue foothill penstemon, golden yarrow, white yerba santa. Black-headed grosbeaks float sweet songs across the morning air. Hand in hand, we climb the narrow path, oak leaves slippery beneath our feet. From the mica-glistening rocks, heat radiates. Ahead, clear vistas of sky, last sliver of moon.

At the stupa, we place our offerings on the stone altar, light the white candle that someone has left, invoke the spirits of the Esselen Indians, the animals of this canyon: snake, bobcat, woodpecker, deer, owl, raccoon. In the distance we hear Sandy's drumming, the summons of the zendo bell. We burn the ceremonial Japanese incense, dark gold, fragrant with sandalwood, neroli, cedar; ask for blessings, for Diane, Sally, Janice—strong women in the middle of their lives, battling cancer for the third, fourth, fifth times. Wind carries the smoke up beyond the oaks. For the beauty that surrounds and gently holds us here we give thanks.

With my walking stick I draw a circle on the earth, mark three names in the dirt. From the base of the Suzuki Roshi Pagoda, riddled with woodpecker holes, Lynn takes a handful of redwood powder, scatters it over the circle. She anoints each name with the healing mineral water. The candle overflows, leaves a trail of white wax on the earth, first translucent, then opaque. Songs catch in my throat, rise up and out like winged prayers, the way a soul might leave the body.

We leave bread for the guardian lizard, who keeps a watchful eye on our every movement, scurrying from altar to circle to stone wall. Across the mountain two waterfalls plunge down a face of granite to the creek. Swallowtails flit from blossom to blossom across our path as we head back. Like votives, pale yellow yuccas light the canyon walls.

This small ritual is all that we know to do. Our faith is the mountain, now crisscrossed by shadow.

Kathleen Norris

My Monasticism

I was recently afforded the unusual privilege of joining a Benedictine community in North Dakota for its annual retreat. The community is a large one, over one hundred women, many of whom work outside the convent. They are nurses, social workers, chaplains, professors. Like many modern Benedictines, they try to strike a balance between the active and contemplative life, and once a year they make a retreat that returns them to the stillness at the heart of monasticism. One sister described it as drawing water from an inexhaustible well.

The retreat schedule was simple and livable, reflecting a moderation that is typically Benedictine. Morning prayer at 7:00, followed by breakfast; a conference or talk by the retreat director from 9:00 to 9:30; Eucharist at 11:00, followed by lunch; midday prayer at 1:00; coffee (optional) at 2:00; from 3:00 to 3:30 a second conference; vespers at 5:00, followed by dinner. Free time allowed for walks, reading, private prayer, naps, and assigned work, such as setting tables.

The most wonderful thing about all this is that it was conducted without any chitchat. I am a frequent guest at several monasteries on the Great Plains that follow silence at certain hours, but I had never before immersed myself in the kind of silence that sinks into your bones. I felt as if I were breathing deeply for the first time in years.

To live communally in silence is to admit a new power

into your life. In a sense, you are merely giving silence its due. But this silence is not passive, and soon you realize that it has the power to change you. I've gained a new respect for my more contemplative friends, Cistercians and Trappists; to live this kind of silence, day in, day out, must be an act of bravery.

During the retreat, even meals were held in silence, with the ancient monastic practice of table reading. As we ate, a sister read to us from an excellent essay on ecology. Meals in common were holy to Saint Benedict, and Benedictine life aims for continuity between church and dining hall, a continuity that silence tends to amplify. As we scraped and stacked our dishes, I noted that, as is usual with monastic people, very little food was wasted. You take what you need and eat what you take. The article reminded us that we all have a long way to go, but we could see that there was a connection between what we had been praying in church and practicing at our meal.

The meal also reflected the profound humility before nature evident in the earliest Christian monastics which has endured in religious life for over fifteen hundred years. Like mystics, monastic people have often been a counterweight in a religion that has often denigrated nature. Modern monastics are more fully grounded in the natural world than many who live in the rat race, measuring time in sound bites or thirty-second commercials. Even urban monasteries run on a rural rhythm, taking notice of sunrise and sunset with morning prayer and evensong.

As a writer I was intrigued by the conferences presented during the retreat, pithy talks on the life and ministry of Jesus given by a monk who teaches in a Benedictine seminary. I once heard him address a general audience on monastic history. But his retreat talks were not lectures; instead they were true to what Benedicta Ward has termed the essence of the ancient desert monks' spirituality, that which "was not taught but caught; it was a whole way of life." The retreat conferences were surroundings that could only have come from someone who has lived as a monk for many years, practicing *lectio divina*, the Benedictine term for meditative reading. Coming out of the depths of silence, these talks elicited a response that could only lead back to silence.

I've done many poetry readings in my life, and have attended countless more. I've also sat through sermons. Never had I experienced anything like this. The talks, preceded by ten or fifteen minutes of recollection, in which presenter and audience sat together in silence, were held in the church where we had Mass and common prayer. The space provided continuity and deepened our listening. Paying attention became a serious matter. "Listen" is the first word of Benedict's Rule, and of course it is silence that makes listening possible.

Ora et laboro, pray and work, is a Benedictine motto, and the monastic life aims to join the two. This perspective liberates prayer from God-talk; a well-tended garden, a well-made cabinet, a well-swept floor, can be a prayer. Benedict defined the liturgy of the hours as a monastery's most important work: it is, as the prioress explained it, "a sanctification of each day by common prayer at established times." Many people think it's foolish to spend so much time this way, but the experience of Benedictines over fifteen hundred years has taught them that doing anything else is unthinkable. It may be fashionable to assert that all is holy, but not many are willing to haul ass to church four or five times a day to sing about it. It's not for the faint of heart.

My monasticism is an odd one. It's not playacting, though I've wondered about that at times. It isn't even a case of what monks call "Benedictine-wannabe." No matter how much liturgy I attend with my monastic friends, I am not vowed to their communities, and that's what counts. But through the grace of Benedictine hospitality I have felt welcomed to church for the first time since I was a child. Theirs is in fact a childlike church, though it's anything but childish. Monks sing a good deal; they listen to stories without much interpretation; and despite (or perhaps because of) their disciplined lives, they seem more at ease with their faith than most other Christians I've met, tending to live it quietly rather than proselytize. What began as a strong attraction—the first time I visited a monastery, I dreamed about it every night for a week—has slowly developed into something deeper.

I come and go from the monastery, of course, and when I leave I try to carry with me some of its peace. As I often depart by Greyhound bus, I face an immediate challenge. One day in spring I left the monastery reluctantly. The winter had been hellish and I was exhausted. The last thing I wanted was a long bus ride to a conference where I'd have to be sociable. I hugged my monk friends good-bye, boarded the bus, and collapsed into a seat. Glancing across the aisle, I was greeted by an incarnation of Psalm 131, which we'd read aloud at vespers the night before: "Like a weaned child on its mother's breast, even so is my soul." A young woman, a poor young woman, to judge by her shabby clothes and traveling case, had dozed off with a small child asleep on her breast. Mother and child presented a perfect picture of peace.

Welcome to the world, I told myself; I hope I know a blessing when I see one. Later, when a young couple nearby began necking as I came across a passage from The Song of Songs in my breviary, I thought: how perfectly blessed we are. The bus sped on along the interstate, and I began to miss my husband, and as the couple's kisses gave way to a sleepy cuddling, the monk within me sang the praises of all the simple pleasures.

Sue Bender

The Emerging Ninepatch

When I set out to live with the Amish, my life had seemed like a crazy quilt—fragmented, with no overall order. I had wanted to get rid of my frenzied life because it was driving me crazy. I kept hoping another image would appear, but there was nothing I could willfully do to change it. For years I used the ninepatch as the basis for the Amish squares, but I never felt a personal connection to the pattern. Then one day, while I was talking to a friend about the squares, the image of the ninepatch suddenly became intensely personal in a way I couldn't yet put into words.

I knew I'd been given another important message.

But I was disappointed. If another pattern was going to replace the crazy quilt as the metaphor for my life, why couldn't it be one of those noble Lancaster County diamond quilts or the stoic, dignified bar pattern? How could the pattern for my life be so ordinary?

I had enough experience with the "it doesn't make sense" voice to know I shouldn't discount what it was saying. So I worked in the studio making more and more Amish squares and began thinking about the ninepatch.

Anything and everything could go into a crazy quilt. The ninepatch would force me to set limits. To simplify my life, I'd have to learn to say NO.

Before I could begin to simplify, I had to look at all the things that were filling up my life. Everything I was doing, everything I wanted to do, and everything I thought I had to do went into the symbolic pile—one large chaotic batch of desires crowding and bumping into each other.

The pile grew. The squares are storehouses of history, to be moved around, each one changing, responding to everything around it. I saw light in the dark squares and dark in the light ones. The patches, placed next to each other, formed a unity—a design for a life.

Those elegant, spare Lancaster patterns would never have worked for me. They work for the Amish because faith simplifies their lives. The ninepatch, which belongs to both the Amish and English worlds, is a halfway place between a crazy quilt and the plain, but for me too simple, truths of the Amish. What I needed for the purpose and unity of my life was contained within the everyday, ordinary elements of the ninepatch.

The world still comes to me in fragments, but I see now that the fragments themselves are not the enemy. If the pattern is strong enough, they will form a whole. It was a fragmented life that I didn't want.

My work began to change. I drew hundreds of individual ninepatches. Pencil. Ink. Paint. Material. One dark patch, one light patch, a tic-tac-toe grid, a checkerboard. The squares filled every corner of the studio. There was a lot of activity, but this time it wasn't frantic. Moving the actual squares around became a meditation.

I worked with no plan—letting the spirit of the Amish take over. Just as I was about to sew the individual nine pieces together, I saw that the squares didn't need sewing. Even that was too much control. If they were to succeed, they had to just be. The squares had a new freedom. I/we were on our own. When my ego got out of the way, the work had an inner light—something "beyond me," intangible and real. They were mine and not mine.

I no longer felt alone in this creative process. Now I wanted something from the viewer. I wanted to reach out and say, "Join me—now it's your turn to find what you need in the work." I wanted to create an empty space, a "fertile void," as the Chinese say. The Amish often leave a space, a seeming mistake in the midst of their well-thought-out plans, to serve as an opening to let the spirit come in.

I learned there is nothing simple about the ninepatch. The varieties, mutations, and possibilities are almost endless. Looking down at one as if for the first time, I saw the ninepatch with fresh eyes.

I saw a prehistoric marking, an icon, an ancient cross, and most clearly I saw a crossroads.

The Amish don't want their pictures taken. I have no photographs of them, but the following ninepatches are the "pictures" I brought back. As I worked the ninepatch in my studio, it became the metaphor for my life.

Each patch grew out of something I had seen or felt when I lived with the Amish. Each patch showed me a new way to look at something I had taken for granted. Each patch made me question my assumptions about what goes into the making of a good life.

Even if each of us picked a ninepatch for our life's design, no two would be alike. Each would emerge filled with the life, the subtlety, the contradictions, and the unity of the maker.

The patches are strong and fragile. BOTH. I'm not going to stitch them together. Nothing is fixed, and there is no right way for them to be. There are patches I'm still working on, not sure where they belong or if they belong. Some patches may clash, some may be missing entirely, and there are probably more than nine patches. Even so, raising the question "What really matters?" is important. Keeping that question *alive* is important.

PATCH #1
Valuing the Process/Valuing the Product
All work is important. All work is of value. The Amish honor what we would call the process *and* the product.

BOTH. What I saw among the Amish was the amazing amount of energy available to people who get pleasure from what they are doing and find meaning in the work itself. But they are practical people who want that can of beans at the end of the day and the sixty-six jars of relish. For them it's all connected.

PATCH #2
Living in Time
Since all work is honored, there is no need to rush to get one thing over so you can get on to something more important. The Amish understand that it's not rushing through tasks to achieve a series of goals that is satisfying; it's experiencing each moment along the way.

PATCH #3
Celebrating the Ordinary
"It's the everyday things that give life its stability and its framework." The Amish honor the daily practices; work, like objects cared for in a home, can turn into a shining thing. All of life is their practice.

PATCH #4
Home
Home is the focus for an Amish woman. The way she lives reflects her faith. With no special icons, her home glows in every corner with spiritual meaning. Home is as much an expression of who she is as any artwork, a place where she can practice what she believes.

PATCH #5
Community
Community life is a natural extension of home life for the Amish. Recreation and chores aren't rivals. Barn raisings, shared harvesting, quilting bees, communal singing mingled with feasting—times of celebrating. When the catastrophic happens, when lightning hits a barn, or crops are

destroyed by hail or a surprise flood, the Amish face the
unexpected with a measure of acceptance. They are not
alone to face these difficulties. Brotherly love is expressed
in practical ways. They share joy and hardship with others, their community.

PATCH #6
   Life as Art
Every Amish woman quilts and makes dolls for her children. There is no reason to single anyone out and label her
"artist." A doll or a quilt is no more special than a can of
green beans or a freshly baked cake.

   No deep search for self-expression goes into making the
doll, and the mother's ego doesn't have to compete with
the object. The beauty of the object, not the ego of the
maker, is important.

PATCH #7
   Limits as Freedom
When expectation and achievement match, a person is
content. The Amish standard of excellence is to do the best
you can. Their deeply felt religious principles set clearly
understood limits. As a result, they do not spend time
questioning who they are or where they belong. Accepting
who they are brings a different kind of freedom.

   Having limits, subtracting distractions, making a commitment to do what you do well, brings a new kind of
intensity.

PATCH #8
   Power of Contrast
It's the startling balance of one kind of energy coexisting
with a very different one that captured my imagination:
the austere simplicity of the freshly painted white house
with its thin black trim contrasted with the vitality of
Emma's garden exploding with unexpected luscious hot
colors.

The spartan geometric quilt designs softened by feathery, organic shapes of tiny dark quilting stitches make the whole surface come alive.

PATCH #9
Choice
Before I went to the Amish, I thought that the more choices I had, the luckier I'd be. But there is a big difference between having many choices and making a choice. Making a choice—declaring what is essential—creates a framework for a life that eliminates many choices but gives meaning to the things that remain. Satisfaction comes from giving up wishing I was somewhere else or doing something else.

Daa'iyah Taha

The Sacred Journey: The Gift of Hajj

It was 1993, during the month of Ramadan, the month of fasting, that I first knew I would be making Hajj, the Pilgrimage to Mecca. It is an act of love and devotion that every Muslim must make, at least once in their life. At that time, I had neither the money nor the means to even consider such a long and expensive journey. But through the days of prayer and contemplation that fasting had provided for me, I had come to realize that Hajj was no longer something that I could casually put off as a mere eventuality, deferring it to my previously laid plans, my lack of means, my fear of the unknown or anything else. I had become anxious, spiritually restless, knowing that something within me needed to change, needed to grow. I wanted to be closer to God. Something in my *soul* needed Hajj. So I prayed to God to allow me to visit His House.

In an effort to raise money for the trip, I spent the year marketing a self-published specialty book and selling women's clothing out of my home. I was working hard and saving what I could. But at the pace I was going, I realized that my efforts alone would not be enough to secure arrangements for me to make the Pilgrimage that year. Hajj was now only three months away. I had resolved to keep on working and saving, but reality was telling me that if I would make Hajj that year, it would be solely by the grace of God. And it was.

I was home one evening with my family, ready to settle

down with a snack and a good movie, when the phone rang.

"How you doin', baby?" I didn't recognize the voice on the other end of the line. I could tell it was an older African-American woman by the sweetness and the gentle tremor in her voice.

"I'm fine. Who is this?"

"This is Wincie."

My mind went into search mode. Wincie? Oh yes, Wincie, the hairdresser, my mother's old friend. She had known me since my childhood days of impatiently squirming in the beauty-shop chair, waiting for her to be done with my mother's hair. Over the years, we had seen each other only now and then at mosque functions, the last time being several years ago. Why was she calling me now? I listened curiously as she asked about the family and remembered everyone fondly. Then she remarked, "I saw an ad in the paper for your book. Can you mail me a copy?"

"Oh, yes," I replied, honored that she would even ask, thinking that I had discovered the reason for her unexpected call. I took down her address and promised to mail her a book right away. We chatted on a few minutes more, and then she said, "I'd like to ask you something."

"Yes?"

"Have you made Hajj yet?"

My heart began to race because I now knew exactly what this call was about. I answered slowly, "No, ma'am, I haven't."

"Good!" she said excitedly. " 'Cause I want to send you to Hajj! It was such a beautiful experience for me! I have been saving this money and trying to decide what to do with it. I'm so happy God blessed me to think of you. I just know you'll come back with so much that you can share in your writing."

I don't remember what we said next, or even hanging up the phone when we were through. I only remember the tears streaming down my face and the incredible feelings of both gratitude and unworthiness in my soul. This was the answer to my prayer. Through her generous gift, I was going to make Hajj!

I don't recall much of what transpired in the weeks before I left, except that my days were filled with hurry, each melting into the next, each bringing me closer to the moment when I would board that jumbo Saudia jet, headed for Hajj. And when I did finally lift off over the Atlantic, I remember a feeling of panic pushing up through my throat, making my body stiffen as the jet roared upward. I just could not believe that I was actually headed for Mecca, to Hajj, to the Holy Ka'bah, to see the sacred precincts toward which I had prayed every prayer for the last twenty years. I would be there in less than twelve hours.

I rested for most of the flight, waking periodically to the soft buzz of quiet conversation. And then the announcement came, about an hour before the plane touched down in Jedda. It was time for everyone to assume the ritual Hajj garment. For the men, two pieces of seamless white cloth, one draped over the shoulders, the other wrapped around the waist. For the women, any garment affording them modesty and comfort. Once in pilgrim garb, I began the ritual chant, "Here I am, O God! At your service! Here I am!" And the anticipation swelled within me as I realized that Mecca would soon be just a short bus ride away.

It was about three o'clock in the morning when we rolled into the Holy City. I peered into the darkness, through the bus window, looking for a sign that the Ka'bah was near. And then I heard it—this voice, ringing through the morning air like a sweet, melodious siren. It was the call to prayer, sounding out from the Sacred Mosque. I knew then that the Ka'bah was ever so near. At last, I would begin the rites of Hajj.

I stepped through the doors of the Mosque into a maze of gray-and-white-swirled marble columns, each flowering into delicately carved arches that framed the structure. It was seemingly round, the arches symmetrically repeating themselves in a harmonious curve to the right and to the left of me. The light was muted, hovering in those hollowed arches, softening the heat against us. There were pilgrims everywhere, some standing, some sitting, and some lying down on their sides. I fastened hands with other pilgrims and zigzagged through the crowds that carpeted the mosque floor. My heart raced with anticipation as I made my way toward the courtyard. Hurrying down steps that my feet have no memory of touching, I glanced up to see the corner of the Ka'bah peeking through the rows of arches in front of me. I clasped my hand against my mouth, trying to hold in the outpouring of emotion that burst forth from my heart. My shoulders shook as I stepped into the splendor of the full sight!

There it stood, like a majestic black jewel, rising out of the center of a lake of cool white marble—the Ka'bah, more magnificent than my imagination could ever have fathomed. Head turned upward, my hungry eyes reverently canvased the holy edifice. A simple cubic structure, solid and upright, its noble shoulders solemnly draped in gold-trimmed black cloth. To the west of the Ka'bah, encased in glass, are the imprints in stone of the feet of its builder, prophet Abraham. Still further west is a short arched wall, which guards the grave of the woman at whose breast the noble prophet Ishmael was fed, and at whose skirt he was taught the love of God. She is Hagar, an African woman, the only woman buried in these holy precincts. I momentarily closed my eyes against the sun, offering a prayer of thanks to be standing on such sacred ground.

Gracing the eastern corner of the Ka'bah, suspended within a silver casing, is a special stone. It marks the starting point for encircling the hallowed House, its shiny meteoric blackness calling to mind the undeniable innocence and colorlessness of our common human nature. It was here, at the Black Stone, that I began to move—slowly, thoughtfully, incredulously, tearfully, lovingly, prayerfully. Around the Sacred House. Seven times, counterclockwise in a slow human whirlpool, against time and place and lines that divide one human soul from another. Around the Sacred House. Shoulder to shoulder, tear to tear, hope to hope, we all toiled in a teeming, rotating cycle of Oneness. Around the Sacred House. Past Abraham's footprints, past Hagar's skirt, multitudes of men and women, rich and poor, Arab and non-Arab, black and white, from every corner of the globe. Around the Sacred House. Now somehow all an equal part of this divine human equation, forging forward toward the promise of God's forgiveness. Around the Sacred House. With the simplest words and the deepest devotion, in every human tongue, in one grateful human voice we answered God's call as we made the sacred circle a final time. Around the Sacred House. When the seventh circuit was complete, I performed the commemorative prayers near the Station of Abraham. I felt connected to humanity in a way that I had not known was possible. My soul was so joyful, so thankful, and so thirsty for more. And it was now ready for the Sacred Waters of Zamzam.

I descended the stairs that lead down beneath the courtyard floor into the area of the Well of Zamzam. I passed streams of women with containers of Zamzam water gripped tightly in their hands or balanced perfectly on their heads, carefully carrying them away for safekeeping until they returned to their respective homes. Of all the gifts that a returning pilgrim can bring to their loved ones, Zamzam water is the most requested and the most beloved gift of all. The Well is enclosed behind marble walls. Its waters pour forth from faucets and is savored from silver cups loosely chained to the faucet handles. As I patiently waited in line for my turn to drink, I savored in my mind the history of the Sacred Well's beginnings.

It is reported that God ordered Abraham to take his wife Hagar and their infant son Ishmael to a desolate place in a desert valley and to leave them there. With only a few dates and a bucket of water from which to drink, he left them, praying to God for their protection and safety. As Hagar watched him walk away, she cried out, "How can you leave us here? We will soon have nothing to eat or drink!" She repeated her question to him many times. He did not answer her. Finally, she thoughtfully inquired, "Is this God's will, or is it your own decision?'' "It is God's command," he confirmed. And with remarkable faith she replied, "Then God will not neglect us!"

She drank the water and ate the dates, nursing her son with the nourishment they provided. But soon the provisions were gone. Hagar's heart ached at the sound of her son's thirsty cries. Knowing full well the symbiotic relationship between faith and work (God helps those who help themselves), Hagar knew that she had to get busy. In an act of unconditional faith, she left her child, there on the floor of that lifeless valley, and began her quest.

Back and forth, back and forth, seven times between the hills of Safa and Marwa, she ran—searching, groping, scanning, seeking to find whatever help she could to relieve her thirsty child. But there was neither a bird, nor a blade of grass, nor any living thing in sight that could give them any aid. There was only the hot sun on that lonely, silent wasteland. When she returned to Ishmael, he lay there on his barren desert bed, kicking his feet in the sand. As his tiny toes pierced the dry earth, a small cool spring began to bubble up from the ground. Feverishly, Hagar dug her hands into the sand, corralling the water, keeping it from dissipating. She then drank from it and suckled her child, praising and thanking God for His infinite Grace. This marked the beginning of the Well, and the beginning of the City of Mecca, to which her husband would one day return, and with the aid of Ishmael, construct the Holy Ka'bah. And it is here, at the endless, life-giving waters of this ancient well, that every pilgrim must lovingly and gratefully remember Hagar—the black slave woman, the beloved wife of prophet Abraham, and the devoted mother of prophet Ishmael, a model of faith for all of humanity.

It was with love and gratitude that I took my first sip of the ancient water. It was cool and fresh, almost thick, its mineral-laden richness lying heavy on the tongue. I drank my fill, remembering Hagar and praying that I would one day be as faithful.

From the relief of the Well, I ascended the stairs, back into the heat of the day. Continuing the rites of Hajj, I made

my way through the mosque, up the sloping mount, to
the site of Hagar's ancient drama. It was now time to perform the ritual search between the two hills in the same
faithful manner as she had done. The crowd stretched into
two throbbing human streams, slowly plodding forward
to the distant mount ahead, then diligently laboring back.
I locked arms with other pilgrims and melted into the
masses starting down Mount Safa. There I was, among the
throngs of men and women moving forward, onward to
Mount Marwa. Sometimes it was not even in our view.
Only the sides and backs of pilgrims sweating, surging forward. It was such a struggle—back and forth between the
hills, seven times. Just as Hagar had done alone, in search
of help for her crying son, we now did en masse, in search
of peace for our crying souls. And the Divine relief was
near, but not before she had exerted and exhausted all of
her own human resources. She had lived what we were
now clearly learning, as we struggled on.

After descending Mount Marwa for the last time, we
spilled out, one by one, onto the pavement outside the
doors. Realizing that we had triumphantly completed the
first rites of Hajj, we instinctively raised our hands and
slapped each other five in our own ritualistic touch of victory. I cried and praised God out loud through my smiles
and tears. Although I couldn't put it all together then, I
knew that I had experienced something that would change
me inside forever. I couldn't have known then how I would
live that experience every day for the rest of my life. With
every challenge I now face, I am again at Safa, ready to
struggle through to Marwa, knowing that the relief of
Zamzam is near. With every prayer I again face the
Ka'bah, knowing that I stand shoulder to shoulder with
human beings everywhere, forming one solid circle of
praise around the Sacred House. Because of Hajj, I would
never again desire to be held above or accept to be held
behind another human being. I stand gratefully beside humanity in the dignity of the Circle. This is what my soul
was longing for. This gift my soul received at Hajj.

Sandy Boucher

Into the Silence:
A Tale of Seven Sisters

Here in the nunnery the afternoon is for sleep, study, contemplation. The night before, Ayya Khema suggested that we imagine we are going to die shortly and then see what we cling to. I find I am sad to lose my possibilities—for achievement, and, yes, for liberation. Why am I here, after all, if I do not believe in my capacity to be enlightened?— though we are made so uneasy by this idea that we make jokes. Sydney, a twenty-six-year-old Fulbright scholar from Florida, says that should sudden illumination awaken her, she will telegraph her family: "Bingo!"

Seven of us have come to study with German-born nun Ayya Khema on Parappuduwa Nuns' Island, in Sri Lanka: one Sri Lankan woman, two Germans, one German-American from Hawaii, and three Americans. We are here not as nuns but as *anagarikas*, that is, women who wear white robes and agree to abide by eight precepts: (1) not to kill any living creature, (2) not to take what is not given, (3) to refrain from all sexual actions, (4) to refrain from false speech, (5) not to use alcohol or drugs, (6) not to eat after noon, (7) not to wear jewelry or use cosmetics or seek out entertainment, (8) not to sleep in a soft or large bed.

Pondering my death, I know I will miss my senses: eating (of course, I would think of that first); feeling the light breeze off the lake; the sight of plumeria blossoms so waxy and white, spider orchids like spotted scorpions; the

221

sound of that dinky train that hoots along between the
lake and the ocean; imagination, learning, discovery. All
this I would hate to lose. And love, surprises, effort. The
making of things.

My body I would miss. Old friend who's been with me
half a century. ("Remember, the body is the seat of the
soul," says Sydney, who has taken up weight lifting here,
hefting bottles filled with sand.)

Ayya Khema asks, "Do you really want to be born
again? Imagine learning to walk, to feed yourself, to use
the toilet. Imagine going through adolescence again! I
think, "Oh Goddess, no, not that." And I am ready to renounce my desires. But looking at my own death I see how
securely I am bound, like Gulliver, with a hundred little
threads, to sensations, things, thoughts, to my need to become again, each moment, this stable entity that I imagine
myself to be.

I set off to pace the paths of this jungle island, opening
my faded umbrella to ward off the brutal tropical sun. I
love the paths, which wind between thick, glossy foliage,
then open to a view of the lake.

At moments I stand locked in surprise that I am here on
an island in a lake on the larger island of Sri Lanka in the
Indian Ocean. I think of my existence back in Oakland,
where as a writer, teacher, and longtime member of a community I live a complicated daily round of work and relationships. The telephone, the computer, the automobile are
stalwart friends. How odd this seems, here where there is
no electricity, not even a road to drive on. The island is so
tiny that I can walk its length in less than ten minutes, past
the nuns' dwellings, little cottages of white stucco with red
clay tile roofs set on high ground.

There are no real nuns on the island now. Those who
have been here, it is said, quarreled with Ayya Khema, or
they simply wanted to try another monastery or to practice alone. Sometimes we speculate on the reasons why
they left. The extreme heat and humidity together with the

civil unrest that wracks Sri Lanka make living here difficult and sometimes dangerous. Where Western nuns are concerned, a woman must be very independent and strong-willed to become a Theravada Buddhist nun, an extreme path not supported by our culture, and she may not be able to manage the obedience required of her in a monastic setting. It is also true that women sometimes find it hard to take direction from a female teacher, programmed as we are to take orders from men and to resist women's authority. And Ayya Khema, as we *anagarikas* well know, is a person of definite views and opinions, as well as utter self-confidence. Where the dhamma (Theravada Buddhism uses the Pali *dhamma* rather than the Sanskrit *dharma*) is concerned, she brooks no objection. Then there is the stress of being in a culture so different from our own. But all this is only speculation. We cannot know what transpired here with the women who once took the brown robes and shaved their heads and lived as nuns. Their cottages stand blank-windowed, empty.

Ayya Khema comes from a background that could have mired her in negativity. Of German-Jewish birth, she was imprisoned with her parents during World War II in a concentration camp, where her father died. Later she was rescued by the United States Army, was nurtured by the San Francisco Jewish community, became a U.S. citizen, and raised a family in Australia. She told me that she made a conscious decision as a young woman not to harbor bitterness against the Germans. Now she travels to teach for some months each year in Germany.

At 4:15 A.M. the digital clock that Barbara has brought from our house in Oakland beeps discreetly. From our beds against opposite walls we switch on flashlights to examine the floor for spiders. Ten minutes later, swathed in white sarongs, long-sleeved blouses, and white robes draped over the left shoulder, we walk to the meditation hall. Vasantha, who is the one Sri Lanka *anagarika*, walks ahead of us. The *bhavana sala*, or meditation hall, is set up high and open on three sides, commanding a view of the lake and the coconut grove as well as a small, steep hillside bright with potted plants.

Meditation begins at 4:30 A.M and lasts until 6:00. When we arrive, Ayya Khema is already there, seated at the front of the hall. We enter and arrange ourselves in order of age. Soon we are immobile white figures sitting cross-legged in the dim light of a hanging kerosene lantern. Beside each woman glows the red dot of a mosquito coil.

At first my mind occupies itself with logistics: Are my legs securely crossed, the flat pillow situated squarely under my buttocks, my back straight and tilted at the exact angle that will allow me to sit without moving for at least forty-five minutes? Then my body settles down. I feel my weight pressing on the pillow, the touch of my hands one laid on top of the other. Now my mind leaps about—"monkey mind," they call it. Predictably, I exist either in the past or in the future. As patiently as possible, I observe these gyrations and gently bring my attention to focus on my breathing. I follow the subtle stream of my breath, noting its pressure rhythmically lifting my belly. And then my mind goes off again.

In the trees massed near one open wall, the birds screech and chirp their excitement at the coming dawn. Today the time passes slowly, my mind skitters off into elaborate detours. I bring it back. Off it goes again, until I finally give up, as one must sometimes, and just let it think. I remember making the decision back in Oakland to come to the Nuns' Island.

A month before Barbara and I were about to leave home, civil disturbance broke out in Sri Lanka. The Sinhalese Buddhist majority and the Tamil Hindus had been committing acts of terrorism and repression against each other ever since the nationwide anti-Tamil violence of 1983. This time Tamil terrorists stopped a bus full of Buddhist monks and massacred them. Our friends took to stopping us on the street to beseech us, "Don't go to Sri Lanka!" We changed our minds every three days.

Now in the meditation hall, with the sun beginning to gild the coconuts on the palms across the lake, the water sloshing rhythmically against the shore, the possibility of violence seems a dream. Gradually my mind calms. Soon my legs ache, but my mind grows more still. It is this that I came for.

Breakfast is a *roti* (thick pancake), a slice of orange papaya, a cup of strong tea with milk, and a bowl of water for dipping one's fingers. This last is important, since in Sri Lanka no utensils are used: food is eaten with the fingers of the right hand. To eat with the left hand is a serious impropriety, since Sri Lankans clean themselves in the bathroom with their left hands. (No toilet paper here, only a bucket of water and a ladle set beside the hole in the floor that is the commode.) Butter and jam or *dahl* (boiled chickpeas) are passed down the line from Ayya at the head of the table to Sydney, our youngest. We eat in silence. Already it is so hot that as I drink the tea my whole upper body flushes and I feel the moisture coming out on my chest and forehead.

Then come the hours of "selfless service." Elisabeth and Rosemarie dig in the earth, weeding the garden, planting flowers and herbs. Sydney, who is bursting with turbulent energy, scrubs the floor and repairs anything broken. When she runs out of things to do, she invents more projects. She and Ricke, who room together, exhibit typical American irreverence (Ricke is a transplanted German), referring to Ayya Khema as "the coach" and our island as "Camp Convent."

Vasantha, by far the most decorous of the *anagarikas*, is an architect in lay life. She has taken on the job of repairing the leaks in the shallow footbaths at the entrance to each building. When I visit Vasantha on her porch I always find her bent over a book of Buddhist thought. In her self-effacing way, she subtly reminds me that a person who grows up and is educated in a Buddhist culture comes to this practice differently than a Westerner.

At the same time, we both understand that mastering the language of the sacred documents or memorizing the rules counts for nothing if one is not strongly grounded in meditation and moral conduct. Vasantha, I imagine, is puzzled by us Western women, but she never corrects or chastises us.

Ricke, Barbara, and I are the office crew this morning, working with Ayya Khema. Her short, round body draped in layers of brown cloth, her shaven head showing only the faintest gray fuzz, Ayya goes methodically from one helper to the next. She is succinct in her directions and so matter-of-fact as she corrects mistakes that I never feel personally censured or criticized. It is this directness that has drawn me to Ayya, and her down-to-earth Western woman's approach to Buddhism.

As a meditation teacher, Ayya emphasizes the goal of enlightenment and leads the student in the cultivation of deeply joyful and serene meditative states. To maintain oneself in a monastic discipline, which requires such extreme renunciation, Ayya asserts, one must experience deeply tranquil concentrated states that surpass and supplant worldly pleasure. She particularly stresses the impermanence of all things, including these pleasant states, and she affirms each student's ability to experience deep concentration. With Westerners she sidesteps the more devotional forms of Theravada observance (when Sydney, meeting her for the first time in Kandy, prostrated herself before her, as one would before an Eastern teacher, Ayya said, "Don't bother"), but she strongly maintains any practice that will protect and encourage the student. I appreciate Ayya Khema, also, because she honors the role of reason in Buddhist practice. She will suggest subjects for contemplation. She respects the student's need to read and study as well as to meditate and practice mindfulness.

We are here for the Rains Retreat, a convention dating

from the Buddha's lifetime twenty-five hundred years ago. The original monks and nuns had no fixed home; they wandered around the country receiving alms and meditating wherever they found themselves. During the rainy season, however, when the rice crop was planted and starting to grow, wandering mendicants were known to trample the new rice shoots, ruining the crop. So the farmers went to Buddha and asked him to keep his monks and nuns confined during those months. To accommodate the farmers, the Buddha instituted the Rains Retreat, three months during which his followers stayed in one place for study and practice. At the Nuns' Island, the Rains Retreat lasts from early July through early October, the hottest and wettest time of year in Sri Lanka.

At 10 A.M. we hurry back to the meditation hall where Ayya Khema reads the *suttas*, discourses of the Buddha. Each teaching from the Dighanikaya (collection of long discourses) that she has chosen begins always with a description of the particular village or park or mountain in India where the Buddha stopped to talk to the assembled people. Then the text describes the situation that prompted the discourse before going to the Buddha's actual words (memorized by his disciples and written down several hundred years after his death). She reads with great vigor, stopping to explain esoteric descriptions or to emphasize important doctrinal points. Her strong voice, erect body, and large eyes radiate enthusiasm.

At 11:15 the lunch bell clangs, and we proceed down to our last meal of the day. Arriving at the *dana sala*, or eating hall, we find that a group of people have come to bring our dinner. Usually this is prepared by Gunaseela, the cook, but on specified days people row across the lake from nearby towns to bring us food. In Asia one way in which *dana*, or generosity, is expressed is by feeding the monks and nuns. The people do this in order to build up good *kamma* (in Sanskrit, *karma*), to gain merit—

sometimes for themselves, sometimes for a relative who has died.

Six or eight people wait in a tight group, dressed in their very best clothes, beaming excitedly. They have brought bowls of special fish and vegetable curries; containers of rice, breadfruit, noodles, desserts of fruit and bowls of curd (yogurt) with *jaggery* (a coconut syrup) on top, sweets piled on small dishes; milk tea. It is a feast, the very best they can offer, and reverentially served. The cheap cloth of the old women's saris, the too-tight dresses of the young girls, missing buttons replaced by safety pins, tell how poor these people are. I am humbled by the care with which they ladle each serving into our bowls. We have no comparable ritual in the West. It is the look of joy on their faces that most affects me. To watch the ritual from the outside is one thing; to be the *object* of this awakens something deep inside.

In return for the meal, Ayya Khema offers a short talk on the dhamma. When Ayya speaks the Pali words for "May you be enlightened in this lifetime," our visitors bow in gratitude, placing their hands on the floor and touching their foreheads to the straw mats. I am overcome by the strangeness of my being here. Once in my room, I let the tears come.

It is early morning. Dressed in white robes, we sit in the meditation hall. The rain has stopped. Silence deepens the darkness. I rearrange my legs under the folds of cloth, wrinkle my nose against the bitter smoke of the mosquito coil. Opening my eyes a tiny bit, I see Ayya Khema seated like a rock before us, and I settle in to attend to the movements of my breath, the stillness inside me.

Gunshots echo across the water. I tense, my mind jumping to ask what they mean. Rosemarie had seen a bombed building in Colombo. She had tried to return to Germany when she learned that her son-in-law was being operated on for a brain tumor. Now there are no planes. A curfew has shut down all transportation. Telegraph and telephone lines have been cut; post offices have been bombed. Rosemarie can neither leave Sri Lanka nor communicate to her daughter what is happening here.

When Ayya Khema rings the bell, I get up quickly, looking around at the other women, seeing Rosemarie's worried face, wondering what the others are thinking. Barbara seems tired. We walk silently down the wet-dirt path, our sandals snapping against our heels. Ayya Khema seats herself, and after we say the lines that recall the purpose of this food (not for pleasure, not for beautification, etc.), she begins to speak, telling us that even though we may be afraid, we must simply go about the activities of our day as usual. She looks down the long table at us, her face grave, and a little annoyed. I remember that she has direct experience of war, of privation, of life as a prisoner.

"There is absolutely nothing we can do, for the moment," she says. "We will maintain our schedule. If information arrives that affects us, I'll tell you immediately."

We wait, hoping she will say more. But she looks down, her eyes calm. Lifting her bowl, she scoops up some of the yellow *dahl* and begins to eat.

Today I am struck by the incongruities of this situation. While people in the villages around this lake suffer, while some of them attack their institutions, destroy their shared property, and kill each other, all because there is not enough—food, medicine, opportunity, respect—while all this rages about us, we sit well nourished, physically safe from harm, possessing the leisure to pursue a meditation practice. Shouldn't we be doing something else? Helping to rebuild bombed buildings? Donating money for medicine?

I feel utterly helpless, defeated by what I have been reading in the nunnery library about Third World economics and by what I am observing. I experience a gnawing discomfort that it is I who walk about in this white-skinned, privileged body. Why am I here instead of being one of the women who looks out of a hut on the beach, a baby balanced on her hip? Why is my suffering less, or different? How do these things get allotted?

Distracted as I am now by events on the shore, still I have achieved sufficient composure to recognize the purpose of the many persistent thoughts that yammer at me. Worry, planning, discussing, inventing—all the continuous uncontrolled activity of the mind—the content doesn't matter. It arises only to solidify the "I," to convince me that I really do exist.

But sometimes in meditation the thoughts fall away like a chorus of voices sinking off to the left, and I am *alone with my breath*. I find myself suddenly in a different universe. So still here . . . so spacious.

Then, when my legs hurt, I am able to penetrate the pain so that I experience it as pulsation only. Not legs, just movement, just vibration. Fascinated, I attend to this with no desire to change position. And then I know that it is the "I" that tortures me, for if they were *my* legs hurting, I would be suffering. For minutes, I experience the commotion of cells and synapses fluttering there under my robe. I watch this in perfect comfort and equanimity. Then I "own" the legs again, saying these are *my* legs, and the sensations harden, coalesce into a nagging pain that sears down my thigh into my knee. When I am able to shift again, I plunge down deep inside the tissues where there is only motion, the unending movement of all that is. Here I stay in a precious balance, wondering, light.

When Ayya Khema rings the bell, I touch my head to the floor in gratitude.

LEAPS OF FAITH

God makes a way out of no way.

—SISTER HELEN PREJEAN

Carol Staudacher

Survivor

An old woman, cradling her apron,
feeds the snow; the birds gone,
there is nothing to witness
this act of believing.

Ellen Cassedy

The Things You Can't See

The Saturday after Easter, Anna was on her knees in the perennial bed on the north side of Aunt Clara's house. Beside her, Aunt Clara worked furiously with a trowel, uprooting dandelions and violets and chopping them to bits. "There's just enough room for my favorites," she told Anna. She meant the spiky woodruff with its tiny star blossoms, the purple columbines, the creamy foxglove, and the lupine. Everything else had to go.

Anna combed at the soil with a cultivator. To a bug or a worm, Aunt Clara would be a vast landscape in herself. Anna made her eyes creep upward from her aunt's fat knuckles to the distended freckles of her forearm, up the wrinkled elbow to the loose flap of upper arm and the big striped sleeve. From her collar emerged a neck as crinkled and faded as old crepe paper. Her earlobe was long and flat like part of a miniature cactus, and tendrils of wiry white hair curled around the strap of the red visor she always wore.

But now the terrain that was Aunt Clara heaved as she stood up and watched for the garden hose. Anna stayed on her knees and watched rainbows glimmer in the spray. She strained to hear what Aunt Clara was muttering under her breath. Sometimes she could recognize a passage from the New Testament and join in.

All at once the hose dropped to the ground and Aunt Clara's arms began to rise, palms up.

"I am the life," she called toward the birdbath. Her eyes were wide open, her teeth bared.

"The what?" Anna asked. "You're the what?"

"I am the LIFE!" Aunt Clara shouted, looking right through her. Half a dozen birds took wing and fluttered into the bushes. Anna stepped back a pace, then another. She wondered if she should call for help. Uncle Fred was down at the police station for the morning, drinking coffee with the sergeant. Dad and Brian were at the grocery store, and Mom wouldn't be able to leave the baby. Anyway, it wasn't clear Aunt Clara really needed rescuing. Her spell, or whatever it was, might be nothing more than a prayer, only louder. Anna backed up against the trunk of the weeping willow tree and waited.

Since the fall, when her family moved to Baltimore and her visits with Aunt Clara began, she'd become devoted to the willow. She liked the idea that a tree could cry, the whispering of the curtain of leaves, and the soft floor underneath. Her father refused to plant one next to their brand-new split-level in Greenview Park. "Those trees are evil," he said. "They're boa constrictors. They go looking for water pipes, and when they find one they wrap their roots around it and squeeze it to death."

When Aunt Clara lowered her arms to her sides and sat limp on the painted iron chair, Anna crept out and stood before her. Slowly the birds returned to the lawn—a chickadee, a sprinkling of sparrows. Aunt Clara reached for Anna's hands.

"God has called me," she said faintly. Her cheeks were drained of color. "I am going away."

Anna gripped her aunt's fingers. "Going away where?"

"Far away," Aunt Clara answered in a stronger voice. Her eyes focused on Anna's face. "I will help the poor little children to find the Lord. In India, or in Africa, my efforts will be welcome."

Unlike here. Aunt Clara didn't say the words but Anna heard them anyway. Mom and Dad had made it quite clear that they didn't appreciate Aunt Clara's attempt to save Anna.

Anna stirred the toe of her sneaker in the grass. "What about me?" she blurted miserably. She'd been trying to find the Lord for six months, and even with Aunt Clara's guidance she hadn't quite succeeded. Now she would never make it.

Aunt Clara took hold of her shoulders with firm hands. "God has plans for you, my dear," she said. "No matter what obstacles may be placed in your path, my time away will be a period of growth for you."

Anna stood a little straighter. "What does the call sound like?" she asked.

But her aunt merely looked up into the sky and smiled. "I shall fly," she said, and folded her hands in her lap.

From the moment she laid eyes on it, Anna hated Greenview Park. Even before she saw it, actually. She detested the shiny brochure full of smiling cartoon families which her father spread out on the dining room table the day the mortgage came through.

Dad poured champagne for Mom and himself, grape juice for Anna and Brian. "To life!" he said.

"Out in the country, no less," Mom said.

"Grass, trees, birds," Dad said. He drew an expansive arc with his glass. "You kids will love it."

Anna wouldn't touch her juice.

As the summer slipped by, the apartment became an alien realm with empty shelves and cardboard cartons lining the walls. Anna drifted in and out of her friends' apartments. She visited the concrete playground, where the chains on the swings were too hot to hold, and the cool basement laundry room with its rows of rattling washing machines. She peeked in the windows at the streaked blackboards and varnished floors of P.S. 132, where she wouldn't be going to sixth grade after all.

The day they left Brooklyn at dawn for the drive to Bal-

timore, she closed her eyes and called up rich natural land-
scapes she knew from books: lush river valleys, rolling
prairies, mountainsides strewn with wildflowers.

It was midafternoon when they reached the NOW AVAIL-
ABLE sign at the entrance to Greenview Park. They followed
the artificial curve of Collingdale Road and stopped in front
of the house with a moving van in the driveway. Anna was
horrified. All the houses looked alike. Every front lawn was
covered by a carpet of grass so new she could see the lines
where the rolls of sod had been laid down side by side. In
the center of each lawn, on a little man-made hill, stood a
tree no bigger than a bush, the bright green leaves clinging
tight to the stiff branches.

Anna climbed the concrete steps, glanced around the
empty living room with its gleaming white walls, and
went up the half flight of stairs to the bedrooms. She
wouldn't be sharing with Brian anymore. Bare box springs
sat in the middle of the blond wood floors. She wrinkled
her nose against the smell of paint and went back outside.
On one side of the tree in the middle of the lawn was a
stake with a rubber loop. She sat down on the other side
and drew her knees up to her chin.

She was still there when what appeared to be a Checker
cab painted robin's-egg blue pulled up in front of the
house. The woman in the driver's seat peered at the number above the door and checked it against the paper in her
hand. She sat with her lips moving before getting out and
starting right up the steep little hill, ignoring the concrete
steps. Her shoes were the kind Anna's Brooklyn grandmothers wore, black and stiff with broad heels and skinny
laces. They came through the cropped grass straight
toward Anna, then stopped.

"You must be eleven," the woman said. She carried a
shopping bag and wore a yellow housedress and a pink
cardigan sweater. Her blue eyes were watery behind rim-
less glasses and shaded by a red visor. She cocked her head.

"You look like your mother," she pronounced. "It's the eyes, not the nose."

With a groan she lowered herself to the ground and sat with her legs sticking out down the hill. Her stockings were rolled down to the knee. "Your grandmother wrote and said you were moving in today," she said. She took a cone of newspaper out of her bag. "I'm sure your dad loves flowers."

"He might," Anna said doubtfully.

"Louder," the woman commanded.

"I guess!" Anna yelled. She'd never seen either of her parents show any interest in flowers. It was bagels they'd squeezed between them on the front seat, a whole bagful from Freeman's Bakery.

"You'll run in and put these in a vase," the woman said. She thrust the package into Anna's hands. Wet stems poked through one end and a bouquet of purple blooms peeked out the other.

"Everything is still in boxes. There aren't any vases out yet."

"You'll find something. I'll wait." The woman faced the road. Anna let the screen door bang behind her.

She found her parents marveling over the giant refrigerator. It wasn't until she described the red visor that their faces lit up in recognition.

"Crazy Clara!" her mother said. "The one who read the Bible at our wedding."

"To herself," Dad said. "Nonstop. Even at the reception." He turned to Anna. "She's Grandma Edna's sister," he explained. "My aunt, the madwoman."

On the lawn, Aunt Clara received Dad's kiss and cooed over Brian and Susan, but when Anna's mother held out a hand she fumbled with her purse strap. "Help me up, Anna," she said. "I'm taking you with me."

Mom frowned, but Dad shrugged his shoulders and winked. "Go ahead," he said to Anna. "A couple of hours won't do you any harm."

Aunt Clara's neighborhood was only ten minutes away, but the houses were old, each different from the next, with tall trees and hedges. There were real hills, and a stone bridge where the road crossed a creek. Behind her modest clapboard house was a spread of pale green grass dappled with sun, raspberry bushes, a birdbath and a feeder, a shady side garden and a sunny one where she'd picked the purple flowers—asters, she said they were. Aunt Clara pointed out the willow tree. "Weeping for our sins," she said.

Inside was Uncle Fred with his checked flannel shirt and white crew cut. He grunted behind his unlit cigar and shuffled away up the stairs. At the picture window in the dining room, Aunt Clara introduced Anna to the birds. Nuthatch, titmouse, chickadee, blue jay—Aunt Clara made her repeat their names as they darted around the feeder until she knew them all. "You'll recite them again the next time you come," Aunt Clara said. "And now we'll have tea."

Anna wasn't allowed tea at home. She copied Aunt Clara, poured cream into the delicate china cup, watched white swirl into amber, and added two spoonfuls of sugar. She crooked her little finger and puckered her cheeks against the bitter taste. Her aunt took half a dozen brown-edged lemon wafers for herself and nudged the plate toward Anna.

"Tell me all about yourself," she said.

Anna counted off six cookies. "Well," she said, "I come from Brooklyn—"

"Came."

"Came from Brooklyn; I'm going into sixth grade; I'm really good at ball games; my best friends are Moira and Abby—"

"Were."

"Were Moira and Abby; I'm a pretty fast runner. . . ." She took a sip of tea.

"Very nice," her aunt said with a brisk nod. She leaned forward. "And what is your favorite holiday?"

Anna put down her cup and leaned back in her chair. "Well, for Christmas, we go to Grandma Edna's."

"My baby sister," Aunt Clara said. "The crazy one."

"Anyway, she has a Christmas tree, and our cousins come. She lets us take off our shoes and slide down the hall into a big pile of pillows." Anna bit into a wafer. Her aunt waited, both hands gripping her napkin. "And then, let's see. Chanukah is right around the same time of year. We're lucky because we celebrate both. We go to Grandma Minnie's and light the menorah—you know about that? With candles?"

Aunt Clara's mouth tightened. "Yes, of course." She tapped a spoon on the tablecloth.

"Well, Passover is pretty good, too. It has the same kind of songs as Chanukah, but it takes about two hours before you get to eat." Anna wiped her hands on her shorts. "I guess if I had to pick I'd say Halloween is the best. We start on the eighth floor and go all the way down to the lobby, and whenever we go into the stairwell we howl really loud, like banshees. This year Mom's making me a cat mask out of some fur that Mrs. Rosenbaum had left over from lining her coat."

Aunt Clara brushed crumbs into her hand. "Very nice," she said again. Her lips turned up in a smile. "Well, Anna, we've had an interesting conversation. We'll talk again next time." She pushed back her chair and laid her hand on Anna's head. "I've been waiting for you, my dear."

Dusk was falling when the blue Checker cab pulled up at the curb on Collingdale Road. Before Anna got out, Aunt Clara placed two parcels in her lap. The flat one contained pamphlets, she explained. "You'll take a look at them right away. You need them." Inside the other package were a dozen bulbs. "Daffodils and tulips for your own garden. But keep them apart. If you plant them together, neither will thrive." She put her mouth near Anna's ear. "Just like

Christians and Jews," she hissed, and touched Anna's knee.

Anna's mother exclaimed over the bulbs—"Little onions!"—and snorted at the pamphlets, which were part of a series called "My Weekly Bible." "Fundamentalist claptrap," she snapped. "Throw them out."

Dad reached for the pamphlets, but when Anna clutched them to her chest he dropped his hand and laughed. "All right, they won't kill you," he said. He moved a carton off a chair and sat down. "Clara was always after me to read the Bible when I was a boy, but I never would. She and my mother used to have big arguments about my liberal upbringing. 'Heathen,' she called it. She didn't let up until we moved to New York. Since your mom and I got married we've barely heard from her. I guess she hasn't changed a bit."

He unwrapped a glass and turned it around in his hand. "The funny thing is, we may think Clara is a little off her rocker, but from her point of view Grandma Edna is the nutty one because she stopped going to church and never sent her kids to Sunday school." He held the glass like a telescope and spied through it at Anna's face. "Who knows? Maybe there is a God, maybe there isn't. Some people like to pray, some don't. You'll make up your own mind someday."

Mom's back was still turned. Anna spirited the booklets up to her room and hid them under the mattress. Later, by the glow of her night-light in the strange new room, she pored over the stories about Jesus and the disciples, the wrath and the grace of God. The words had a rolling sound to them, like those she'd heard on the stage last summer when Mom took her to Central Park to see *A Midsummer Night's Dream*. That was about the last time she could remember having Mom to herself for more than five minutes. What with Susan crying and needing to be changed and fed and put down and picked up, and all the packing and moving, her mother hadn't paid any attention to her for months. Last year she could read Anna's mind, understand her down to the last molecule. Now she seemed like another person. Dad had changed, too. All summer he'd been busy wrapping up his old job at the high school and taking the train down to Baltimore to buy the house and get ready for his new position at the community college. He hardly ever sat out on the fire escape in his undershirt to watch the sun go down and play gin rummy with Anna and her friends the way he used to. When he did, half the time he had Susan fussing in his arms. It was as if he didn't belong to Anna anymore, or she to him. Sometimes at the breakfast table she couldn't stand looking at his blond whiskers and the hair curling out of his collar, or hearing the way he slurped his cereal.

Anna kept her heart closed against her new surroundings, opening it just enough to look forward to her visits with "the loony old lady," as Dad put it. Aunt Clara called for her every other Saturday. Together they banked the gardens and wrapped the raspberry bushes in burlap. They raked leaves, mounds and mounds of them. Uncle Fred emerged from his workshop in the basement, where he spent hours cleaning his hunting rifle and listening to the Orioles, to set fire to the piles in the gutter. After Thanksgiving they put out suet for the birds, and pinecones slathered with peanut butter. While Uncle Fred dozed with a fat copy of *Eisenhower: The War Years* on his lap, Aunt Clara sat Anna on the sofa and showed her old photo albums in which she appeared as a young woman in a pith helmet in Brazil, surrounded by naked children. "Look at all the souls I've saved," Aunt Clara said proudly.

Aunt Clara went to work on Anna's soul, too. At the beginning of every visit she quizzed her about the Bible pamphlets—had she read them, and what had she learned? Whenever they parted she gave Anna a new supply. "I'm praying for you, dear," she said. "I pray you will find Him." When Anna squeezed her eyes shut, she could see the blue gown and sometimes even the white beard. She hoped the face would be revealed to her before long. Sometimes she wondered why, if there really was a God, He was taking so long to answer Aunt Clara's plea for her. But she did her best to stifle the thought. It was just the kind of sly notion that might shoot down her aunt's prayers before they had cleared the treetops.

One evening Mom came into Anna's bedroom with a pile of clean clothes and caught her trying to hide a Bible pamphlet under her pillow. A few days later, Dad noticed her folding her hands at the dinner table and whispering a blessing, the way she did at Aunt Clara's. Soon after, she and Brian were summoned to the living room.

"In our family," Dad led off, "we believe in people. We don't worry too much about the things you can't see—God and heaven and so forth."

"A lot of folks in this neighborhood do," Mom chimed in. She jiggled Susan on her shoulder. "But you don't need to pretend to believe something you don't."

"On the other hand," Dad said, "you don't need to broadcast what you don't believe, either. If you eat at a friend's house and they say a prayer before dinner, just bow your head and wait."

"Another thing," Mom said. "We don't believe in prejudice. Dad and I want you to speak up loud and clear if you ever hear people saying something mean-hearted or unfair about someone of a different race or religion."

Anna picked at a thread on her sock. That very afternoon the boy next door had hooted and pointed when a dark-skinned family drove by. "At Sunday school they say God baked them longer," he'd said after the car turned the corner. "But they sure look burned to me. I bet they got that way you-know-where." Anna hadn't said a word.

In December, when nearly all the houses in Greenview Park and Aunt Clara's neighborhood sparkled with strings of Christmas lights, Anna's family celebrated, too. Dad took

Anna and Brian to buy a fragrant tree from a farm on Roll-ing Road. They all sat down at the dining room table with glitter and paste to make ornaments. There were rules, though. Snowmen and bells were encouraged; angels were not. Anna wasn't allowed to hang the cardboard crèche scene she'd made at Aunt Clara's on the outside of the front door—only on the inside, where it didn't count.

Dad invited Aunt Clara and Uncle Fred to Christmas dinner, but they declined. Aunt Clara had yet to sit down in Anna's house. On the Saturday morning before Christ-mas, she came to the door and stood uneasily on the threshold. The tree provoked a fleeting smile, but she shook her head when she caught sight of the brass menorah gleaming on the windowsill.

"My prayers for you will be more fervent this month," she remarked when Anna slid into the car. "Remember that God sees everything, young lady."

On Christmas Eve, Dad settled Anna and Brian into the sofa and told a cleaned-up version of the Nativity story. The shepherds were amateur astronomers witnessing a rare configuration of stars.

"What about the angel who appeared and said God's son had been born?" Anna prompted.

"Some people believe they saw an angel," Dad said. "All religions go through periods of upheaval and reform. His-torians speculate that back then there probably was some-one influential, some kind of leader, who may have called himself Jesus or something very similar."

For Chanukah they went downtown to a bookstore on a side street and bought a box of Israeli candles. The after-images of the flames burned on Anna's eyelids when she closed her eyes, and the smell of wax mixed with the aromas of sweet tangerines and chocolate coins in gold foil.

"The story goes that the Jews had just enough oil for one day," Mom said, "but it burned for eight. Maybe it was a very pure oil that could burn longer. Or maybe they just made up the whole thing. Every culture invents its own fairy tales. All over the world, people have a need to believe stories that couldn't possibly be true."

One cold, clear weekend in March, Anna and Aunt Clara stood near the raspberry bushes with their heads tipped back. High above them, a ragged V of geese traveled north. Anna would have missed their muted honking if Aunt Clara hadn't made her listen.

When the geese had passed, Aunt Clara kept her head tilted, searching the empty sky.

"Easter is coming," she said, her eyes still fixed on the heavens. "The rising of our Lord. The most important day of the year." She lowered her gaze to Anna's face. "I believe you're ready," she said finally. Her eyes seemed to bore through skin and bone into the very middle of Anna's skull. "You'll go to church with me on the holy day. We'll walk the aisle together, you and I." Her lips quivered. "You know, Anna, to most people I seem like a solitary old bird. Alone with my God and glad of it. Wrong, my dear! All my life I have treasured the joining of kindred souls in worship. Edna never once went to church with me—not after we were girls. Fred wanted no part of it. Your father—a lost cause." She sighed "The Lord has sent you to me, Anna, as a precious gift to an old lady who will soon be passing on."

Anna closed her eyes. She pictured herself floating toward the pulpit in a white gown while organ music swelled and long fingers of light shone onto the crown of her head like rays of sunshine streaming from behind a cloud bank on a hazy day. After months of preparation her moment was approaching. Aunt Clara was right. She was ready.

"We'll buy you an outfit at Hochschild's this afternoon," Aunt Clara said. They set out at once, and though Anna longed to linger in the bike department and fondle the handlebars of the three-speed she was saving for, she followed Aunt Clara up the escalator to the girls' department instead. Aunt Clara guided her away from the white dresses. "You're not an innocent babe in arms, my dear." She helped Anna into a severe navy dress of fine wool with white trimming and shiny red cherries at the collar. It came with a matching straw hat with a black elastic band and a purse with cherries at the clasp. Anna adored it. She wore her stretchy white gloves home in the car and sailed triumphantly into the house. Aunt Clara stood in the doorway while Anna lifted the dress out of its box to show her mother.

"How thoughtful of you!" Mom said, bobbing her head at Clara. She shifted Susan on her hip and fingered the soft wool of the pleated skirt. But then she caught sight of the navy hat and the white gloves.

"Honey!" she called urgently. Dad came out of his study with a journal in his hand, his glasses on top of his head. Mom murmured into his ear.

"What are you planning to do?" he asked Aunt Clara. He rested a hand on Anna's shoulder and glared. "I won't have you parading her into some church and passing her off as a Christian—do you hear me?" His mouth tensed into a thin line, then relaxed. "I'm sorry, Clara," he said. "I'm sure you remember we went through this twenty-five years ago. My mother didn't want me in church when I was Anna's age. It just wouldn't be right."

"Dad—" Anna began in a choked voice.

"Quiet!" Aunt Clara said harshly. Her eyes glittered. "May Jesus forgive you, Matthew," she spat as she turned to go, "and Lord preserve the child."

A few weeks after Aunt Clara heard the call in the perennial garden, Dad drove her to the airport. She was truly on her way—not to India or Africa, but to a Navajo reservation in Arizona, where her church sponsored a mission. Dad carried her two big leather suitcases. Anna had been permitted to wear her would-be Easter outfit for the occasion. Close by his wife's heels, Uncle Fred looked as bewildered as an earthquake survivor. Aunt Clara was dressed all in white, with a new white purse and a white shopping bag containing her red visor, sunglasses, a Bible, and a brown paper package Anna hoped was for her.

When the loudspeaker announced her flight, Aunt Clara sat down on a bench and drew Anna close. "Listen to me," she whispered fiercely. She reached into the shopping bag and pulled out the package in its brown wrapping.

"Take this and read it carefully," she said, "if it's the last thing you do." Her eyes darted from side to side. Dad was reading the departure board. "God will be watching. And Anna, you *will* find Him someday. It won't be long. Believe me."

Anna felt a surge in her chest as Aunt Clara pressed her lips to her forehead and released her. She was on her own, poised on the very brink of salvation, or redemption—she wasn't sure what was the right word.

"A queer duck, isn't she?" Dad said after they dropped off Uncle Fred. "Seventy years old and she leaves her husband and traipses off for a year in the Wild West."

Anna didn't answer.

"Well," her father said, glancing at her face, "what do you say we go get that new bike of yours? You've saved up almost enough, haven't you? Mom and I will chip in and make up the difference."

The Raleigh Speedster she had prayed for, the fancy one with hand brakes, thin wheels, and a black leather seat, just fit into the back of the station wagon. After lunch Anna wheeled it out of the garage, past the faded daffodils on the right side of the driveway and the remains of the tulips on the left. Still in her Easter best, she rode slowly around the block while her parents and Brian cheered from the front steps. Five times around the block it took before they finally went inside. And then she was retrieving Aunt Clara's package from the car, stashing it in her basket, and streaking down Collingdale Road. She turned up Kent to the boulevard, waited for the light to change, and made her way across six lanes of stopped traffic. Aunt Clara's house was farther than she'd expected. She rode for a long time beneath the pale new leaves of poplars and oaks before she came to the stone bridge and the library. Finally, after puffing up the big hill, she turned onto Cedar Street.

The Checker cab painted blue was parked in the driveway, but the house was closed up, its curtains drawn. Uncle Fred must have gone down to the police station as usual. The backyard was silent, as if frozen in a magic spell until Aunt Clara's return. Anna sat down under the willow tree, pulled off her gloves finger by finger, and untied the package.

Underneath a dozen "Weekly Bible" pamphlets lay a book with a brightly colored jacket. *How Jews Rule the World*, it was called, and the letters of the title were black and sinuous like the Hebrew letters on the box of Chanukah candles or the Passover Haggadah at Grandma Minnie's. It was a strange offering from Aunt Clara, who had never seemed interested in Jewish rituals. Anna studied the picture on the cover, a crude drawing of an ugly man with big black eyes and a long nose. He was pointing his finger and staring right at her.

With the tips of her fingers she turned to the table of contents. "Murderers of Jesus," she read. "The Blood of Christian Children on Their Lips. The Rothschilds and the Rape of Europe. The Myth of the Gas Chambers. Goldgrubbers and Greed: The Jerusalem Connection." Suddenly she sucked in her breath and pulled back her hand as if stung. The book cover slapped closed and the evil-looking Jew stared up at her once more. Hastily Anna hid his face under the brown wrapper, pushed the pamphlets into a pile, and shoved all of it away with her foot.

"Mean-hearted," she whispered as if tasting the words on her tongue. "Unfair." Slowly, with the heel of her shoe, without looking, she pushed dirt at the book and the pamphlets, shoving at them until the paper was smudged and torn. Finally she rested against the tree trunk. She waited for an ant or a worm to crawl into view, but none did. She looked over her shoulder at Aunt Clara's back door. The screen was blank. A sparrow splashed at the bath and the raspberry bushes stirred in the sun.

At last Anna got to her feet, hitched up her new dress, and climbed. The slender leaves brushed her face. She climbed high above the flower beds and the swath of pale green lawn. Higher and higher she went, until she could look into other people's backyards and see all the way down the hill to Greenview Park. Standing with her feet wedged in the space between two forking branches, she cried without making a sound. The tears ran down her cheeks until there were no more, and then she looked down at the ground and up at the sky. She breathed the blue air so sweet with spring blossoms and she could almost hold the scent in her hands. Off in the distance, the green hills melted into the clouds. She stayed so long the birds flew around her as if she were part of the tree, part of the sky.

Barbara Kingsolver

In the City Ringed with Giants

When God was a child
and the vampire fled
from the sign of the cross,
belief was possible.
Survival was this simple.
But the saviour clutched in the pocket
encouraged vampires to prosper in the forest.

The mistake
was to carry the cross,
the rabbit's foot,
St. Christopher who presides
over the wrecks,
steel cauliflowers
proliferating in junkyard gardens.
And finally, to believe in the fallout shelter.

Now we are left in cities ringed with giants.

The Titans in their secret slingshot burrows
encircled my city for half a lifetime
waiting for their subpoena,
or for a match to strike, touch
the first like a fuse, a crown
of liquid flame surrounding us, the coronated dead.

We are the children bereft of talismans
to hold against the promise
of those who would rub the lantern
and conjure fire. Conjure
darkness out of light.
We are bred to be God-fearing,
to stretch our frightened hands
to the magic lamp that someday will protect us.

We are the heretic children
who make all mistakes but this one:
we don't believe in the lantern.
Given time enough, we will
squander our inheritance of holocaust
in the small change of bonfires
and candles in the passageways.
We see beyond the phantasm
of mushroom shapes
to the mountains beyond. A simple green of trees.

We are the so-called blind.
And so we move
like white cave fish toward light,
along the path
of our only instinct,
to live as if our lives belonged to us.
On the forest floor
we dance in the fairy ring,
trample the root-cloth center
that sustains the mushroom circle,
dance until God
has found his second
childhood, and we have outlived the giants.

Akasha (Gloria) Hull

DreadPath/LockSpirit

Question: Why did I cut off (or, in Rastafarian parlance, "trim") a set of perfectly beautiful nine-year-old dreads only to commence locking again just one year later? The trimming actually began before that, in October 1988, almost immediately after I had made a cross-country relocation and assumed a new job. I radically pruned my locks, but did not completely divest myself of them until 1989, shortly after my December sixth birthday. I suspect that the move and the midlife birthday both contributed to a deeply felt sense of shedding the old and beginning anew. I was also extricating myself from a love relationship that was heavily associated with my hair: off with the hair, out with the lover! In general, this seems to have been a time to discard old, "locked-in" energy in order to make fresh starts. Just as clearly, though, I was loath to give up—in one fell swoop—so many years of cultivated beauty and my elder lockswoman status. Yet despite its fineness, this head of hair had reached—for me—a static state which was very different from the ever-changing dynamism which had helped attract me to dreadlocks in the first place. I have an even better understanding now of why people play around with various hairstyles "simply" for the sake of change.

After that one in-between year of no locks, I was eager to grow them again. I had spent those twelve months in total dissatisfaction with everything I did and did not do with my hair. The basic problem was that I could not make myself either comb it or cut it. Using the comb or pick was a laborious ordeal, and cutting it felt like a bloody amputation. So many years of not doing these things—fueled by the philosophies behind it—had thoroughly "ruined" me. Grooming my hair with my bare hands sufficed for quite a while, but when it grew beyond the shorter lengths, my black women friends wanted to know if I knew what I was doing with my hair, and one of them, Jamilah, volunteered to give me braids and a counseling session. This "neither fish nor fowl" state was obviously not working. With the well-earned relief of someone who has given an experiment a dogged try, I let my understanding son barber me a soft Afro from which I could neatly begin my second dread in December 1990.

By this time, I knew that I would be gridding in new growth and power and a transformed sense of self. One indication was my determination to lock exactly as I believed it should be done. This meant following what "roots" people in the know had always counseled: to simply stop combing the hair and let it go. That easy, that simple. Just put away the paraphernalia and allow nature to take its course. No parting and twisting, no "glueing" and no washing, none of those make-it-happen, hairstyling, hair management instructions that currently pass as the correct information about how to have locks. If there is "kink" in the genes and the hair is chemical-free, it will (eventually) ravel itself together in some way(s). My first time, I had twisted a bit and had encouraged a pattern of small, symmetrical separations. This time, I would do nothing except keep the clumps divided into the aggregations they themselves made so that I would not end up with huge "kungas" on my head. This possible outcome was the only thing which was not okay with me, and this management the only manipulation which did not feel inconsistent with an extremely natural approach.

From my years of consciously absorbing dreads of all

kinds (especially in Jamaica), I had really come to see that the healthiest, most beautiful sets of locks were those which evolved organically, growing out of the physicality and spirit of their individuals. I noticed the startling but always pleasing variety, the inexplicable resemblances to trees, roots, and other natural formations, the absolute rightness of each dread for its person—how the arch of the hair echoed the arch of the brows, eyes, or nose, or the thickness of lock paralleled the body's musculature, or the way texture and tint complemented the skin's own grain and tone. This, to me, was marvelous, magnificent—and I drank in these framed black faces with joy and appreciation. Yes, here was the way to truly have dreadlocks.

Unfortunately, preconceived notions about how a nice dread is supposed to look get in the way of this natural, laissez-faire approach. Most people seem to want to have (and see) locks which are thin and uniform, approximating as closely as possible the smooth regularity of braided styles, rather than deal with thick and/or thin, unpredictable organicism. And many prefer them long, still equating—for women—length with feminine attractiveness. When my first locks reached my shoulders, my mother finally accepted them, but told me—lovingly but baldly— that my new dread was "at that ugly stage." In similar fashion, Cheryl, a nationalist-minded, mid-thirties friend, all but turned up her nose at my "stubby-looking" hair even as she shared that she was contemplating letting her (thin and regular eight-inch) plaits go into locks.

We are still being influenced by cosmetic—and commercial—standards of beauty, still buying into the system in the ostensible act of repudiating it. How hard it is to shed this programming! Defensive, a little hurt, a bit angry (but outwardly cool), I found myself explaining to Cheryl that the locks only looked stubby at the ends and would grow out with a different appearance. As opposed to maintaining a centered, serenely immune attitude, I was desiring her approval and positive response. This was the reversed version of the ambivalence I used to feel when accepting compliments on my locks from folks who said, "I like yours"—*mine* being the exception to those other wild-looking things they had seen on Bob Marley and MOVE members in Philadelphia. All of this is not to say that we lockswomen do not receive clear-eyed admiration. We do— quite often and sometimes from unexpected quarters—and it is immensely affirming.

Even though dreadlocks primarily assert a racial message and are basically free of stereotypical sex-role signification (although something could probably be made of a wild-irregular-powerful-masculine versus thin-groomed-feminine equation), they yet make an emphatic, gender-related statement. I wish I really knew, for instance, in what ways wearing long hair reflects a black man's self-concept and image projections. I do know that for women, dreading is a rejection of a capitalistic, fetishized definition of female be-ing. Especially in the United States, strong, self-defining, and self-referenced women who have eschewed traditional notions of femininity—predominantly race/roots women and lesbians (often combined)—are the ones who dare to lock. Generally speaking, it still requires an ample measure of internal steadiness to walk this path of difference.

Dreading seems to also require at least a minimum level of comfort with the spiritual dimensions of existence. And if one is going to lock in what I earlier described as the most natural way (though I am humble about prescriptiveness and the possible range of what is natural), spiritual issues become even more obvious: really, truly giving up control and "going with the flow"; trusting process/this process to yield what is appropriate and best; and having patience. I have learned the hard way (and am still learning—though with less hardness) that these three desiderata—faith, patience, and surrender—are major keystones of an evolving spiritual consciousness and approach to life. Having them on any level, in any arena is not easy.

When trying to lock, one's patience is tested because it takes time, often a long time for the hair to aggregate and grow, not to mention its achieving full bloom. Faith waivers during those "ugly stages" and also when it looks as if what the hair is doing is headed in the wrong direction. Foregoing control is the hardest of all because one can so easily and summarily intervene (just reach up and twist or separate). The temptation to do so is also considerable, especially if one is susceptible to the ever-present pressure to always look "nice/good."

From this perspective, dreading can thus be viewed as a spiritual path/discipline. It can become a vehicle to enlightenment on an inner level comparable to the way it illuminates the external world via what we see/receive from wearing locks. If we are conscious and receptive, it functions as a full-time, built-in mirror that magnifies our realities. Having patience, faith, and the ability to surrender is an uplifting and liberating experience. Many of us women with locks say that we feel so "free." I believe this is not just because there is no combing, picking, teasing, styling, frying, fretting of our hair, but because there is likewise much less of that in our souls.

Related to this freedom is the opportunity that locking provides for a black woman to learn how she really feels about herself, to get in touch with her own true reaction to herself as she is. Here I mean internal feeling and not externally driven judgment or evaluation. Being so different forces us to really look at ourselves and ask/answer, "Hmm, what have we here?" Since the standard templates do not apply, it encourages the development of authentic/natural/original response. Regardless of what anybody says, I feel empowered to have discovered that I genuinely *love* the soft clumpings of hair at the base of my locks, or the tensile waviness of these tough, skinny ones, or the untamed way they all spring out when I am energized by sex or other fierce emotions.

Sometimes, though, I cannot be sure of how I feel.

Sometimes I have to admit that I do not always like everything I see. At one point, I was wrapping my locks with scarves. This is because I did not relate well to the flatness of my hair when it was freshly washed, to its bangs-and-skullcap silhouette which called up for me unpleasant images of men and wet-look curls. However, this was my own not liking, my own unique and private quirkiness, emanating from some personal aesthetic inside myself and not adopted from the outside/others. I was wrapping because *I* felt prettier with locks and scarf. Of course, the social aspect of this was that I wanted to look good in public. But I was the one deciding about that "good."

Finally, locking can be healing—for any African woman who has internalized a negative dismissal of herself as ugly, particularly as this relates to hair and color issues. The almost formulaic epithet "black and nappy-headed" had inflicted many a wound, for generations. In my case, this general experience was exacerbated by growing up with a light-skinned, "good-haired" sister with whom I was paired and compared. It was further amplified by the traumatic baby-girl ordeal of having all my hair shaved off for medical reasons and suffering from the resulting rejections at an age when I could only feel but not understand. Once, without even knowing this story, a chiropractic healer performing craniopathy on me said that I/my head had never gotten enough holding. The psychic, emotional, and physical embracing of my locks helps cure this long-standing deficiency. And its power is somehow so deep and complete that it withstands society's sometimes still negative appraisals. This mojo is stronger than their bad medicine.

HOLY GHOST

"Please state your name for the record."

"All of them?"

"Yes."

"Because I've had lots of names and they're all important like every human being is important. Did you know every name means something entirely different?"

"Sir, please state your name for the record."

"It might take forever."

"A bit too early in this custody battle to be found in contempt, son, isn't it?"

"Joshua Lafayette Chandler Wydell III. Sat Vikram Singh. Jelaluddin. Abba."

"Your current name, then, is Abba Wydell?"

"Just Abba. It's another word for 'God.' "

Joshua wasn't a guru when I married him, he was a tall man with good legs and thick blond hair that hung wild to his shoulders. He could stop a room, hold it there, and make the rest of the people in it look clumsy and wrong. For me, it was like discovering the most exciting human being on earth.

We were aggressive seekers of truth, and everybody with a story to tell or a soul to save passed through our door: sheikhs, Sikhs, Tibetan monks, twins from Duluth who spoke in tongues, a former student of Gurdjieff, Allen Ginsberg, a Sufi choir leader, Alan Watts and the psycho-

therapist who lived in the houseboat next to his, some der-
vishes, a storytelling rabbi, someone who knew Fritz Perls,
and a woman who never spoke but made dream-catchers
out of her own hair and teeth—stars, all of them. Masters
at relieving us from the everyday hum of our refrigerators.
They taught breathing, Zen, harmonics, posture, dream-
ing, letting go, getting to God, conscious cooking, chanting, bowing, pushing the *mala* beads around, bhakti,
shakti, cleansing the tongue, getting off the wheel of reincarnation, and pulling the *kundalini* energy right up your
butt.

There were mouth breathers, nose breathers, heavy
breathers—traveling men with smooth leather pouches
full of healing dust, ready with the gift of their sex to relieve the tightly wound American woman of her head-
aches, menstrual cramps, and the general blues. There
were goddesses with names like Zuleika, Rhada, and Dove,
all thin and yielding with clean white fingers and satin
shoes, letting their skin brush against yours as they danced
by, holding your eyes like practiced whores. There were
mountain-climbing, fire walking Buddhists who had
helped the Dalai Lama escape. And Ram Dass, and Yogi
Bhajan with his white-robed followers, and Timothy
Leary's first ex-wife (the French one), and an eighty-year-
old Hopi named David who carried the prophecy and sang,
"Honey, honey, let me take you to the rodeo. / Honey,
honey, let me take you to the picture show," with one
hand spread firmly on my thigh.

Joshua and I were holding nightly meetings at the
home of one of his students when I noticed a shy, thin guy
named Gary who clearly hadn't done much with his life. I
mean he was almost thirty and never had a girlfriend. And
Joshua (he now called himself Sat Vikram Singh) could
read it in the dark. *Thirty grand.* He could smell it. The
man's entire savings. What was he doing with it? Nothing.
It was just sitting around, like the man. Half the price of
a house back in the early seventies. My husband put an

incandescent arm around Gary's thin shoulders. For events like these, Joshua wore a long white robe, an Arab djellaba sewn by one of his students.

"You all know what this man has done?" Joshua asked the group.

A few people looked up from trances. Gary held the pose of "one who would soon be blessed."

"This man has given birth to possibilities. Like a woman, this man, this Gary man, has made a future for our little holy community here in Taos. With his generous gift, we will find and live in the House of Devotion and Fun. Forever. Together. Amen."

Joshua wiped his eyes. It wasn't easy to suck a man's soul from his body in a room full of people without breaking his spine or attracting the wrong kind of attention. My husband was good.

Gary leaned in slightly, seemed to be letting Joshua hold him up. Or maybe he just realized what he'd given away. Joshua shook him a little and the group formed a circle around them and sang: " 'Tis a gift to be simple" and my husband sang out: " 'Tis a gift to be poor," and everybody but the man without the savings account laughed and laughed.

With all the spiritual comings and goings, it took me a couple of years to see this particular talent of Joshua's. He took sacred teachings from everyone who stayed with us, reworked them, renamed them, called them his own. At first I thought it was learning or wisdom. Then it came to me: my husband was a ghost; he had nothing but what he could steal from people. He could take the things they cared about most. It was his great gift.

"Help me find our community house," Joshua said to me.

I knew he didn't mean hire a real estate guy. He made it sound ordinary, but he was asking me to *see* the house, something I was good at. Something I could do. What else could I do? Anything? Life before Joshua was difficult to remember. Things were coming back to me in bits. I could write, speak Italian, run things. I could get angry. I began making lists on napkins and stashing them with the money I was hiding in a black silk coin purse in the back of my underwear drawer.

"Will you help me, Annie?"

I closed my eyes and described what I saw: a white farmhouse on half an acre with a balcony, a chicken coop in back, and rows and rows of pink and red peonies. He wrote down every word, and in a month we had the place.

When we moved in, Joshua (he was now Jelaluddin) took the three biggest rooms for himself: a bedroom to sleep in "like a holy man," alone and naked on a blue futon; a sunroom where he could see people and eat sprout sandwiches; and the chicken coop for private sessions with pale blondes who had strong arms and missing fathers.

The first time I ever saw Joshua, he and his cold, clean girlfriend were teaching Sufi dancing, the two of them standing side by side on a stage, so tall and handsome that to see them together was to understand why kingdoms are formed.

I didn't marry for the usual reasons: love, money, biology. I married to stand beside him and become a kingdom. Not to be known by him, because, after all, what was there to know of me? Inside I was just a small bird, and he would never see inside me because he was always so busy leaning forward. His body pointed to the future. He would never really know me, and this I liked. Keeping my feathers to myself.

Why does anyone marry anyone beyond the patio talk of friendship or common ground or twinkle, twinkle, little love? Doesn't it come down to this: how hands look next to each other in the moonlight coming through a car window? And isn't it this: the animal smell that takes you back to wet forest floors and open sky, or back only as far as clean quilts and being tucked in by an aunt who loved you, with the window open, curtains moving slightly, and the noise of the night train coming through?

There are better reasons, sure, but I don't know them. I grew up in the House of Silence, Sorrow & Food. (The silence and food were for covering up the sorrow.) We did not read the Sunday paper as a family by the light of day. Instead, we stole sections for ourselves, read them in our separate rooms, and lied about having them when asked. And then the guests came, the relatives. We were a big, spread-out family, too cheap for hotel-motels. The guests got the good dishes, the good drinks, the good us. And when they drove away we pulled the cauls back over our eyes, the caper-colored walls went back up, and we set about not speaking to each other for months.

Isn't this why we marry? For the light on a hand, or the smell of the woods, or the memory of home, again and again?

As soon as Joshua and I moved into the farmhouse, I started seeing two children around us. I could feel them. The boy was older, fair, and had trouble keeping his attention in one place, but his heart was clear and open. The girl was dark, sweet, steady, a thinker.

"Do you ever sense any children when we're here together?" I asked Joshua. I figured whatever I could see, he could see better.

"Maybe. What do they look like? Are they here right now?"

"Yeah, they're here."

He walked over to the gas fireplace and pointed. "Where? Here?"

"Not exactly. Look, it's not like I can pinpoint them." He couldn't see a thing.

"More like an aura? An essence? I think I'm smelling something. Am I getting warm?"

"No. I don't know." I didn't want to tell him anymore, not about this. They seemed like my children already, and

I felt the need to protect them. The boy had big cow eyes, soft and thick-lashed, and odd, like a birthmark you come to find beautiful. The girl kept saying, "Don't worry about anything," which worried me tremendously.

"They're talking to you, aren't they? Annie. What are they saying?"

"Nothing."

He dropped down and put his ear against the uneven wooden floor, shutting his eyes. This would make a great evening lecture. He stayed in this position for a long time, using the full power of his concentration, waiting to hear something.

He never heard a thing.

That night, I was cooking for our group meeting: vegetable curry, mung beans, and basmati rice. I had three huge pots going and mustard seeds popping in an iron skillet so heavy it took two hands to lift it. Joshua's words floated in and out of the hot little kitchen.

"The gift of children will soon be with us. . . . I saw them, heard them myself . . . my own eyes and ears . . . like finding this house . . . my vision is complete."

Then there was applause.

I did not think about what came next. I stopped stirring and walked onto the meeting-room stage, my hands still yellow from the turmeric.

Joshua, I said, *Joshua, how could you take my vision from me?*

I saw a small disc of fear behind his eyes, and the barest of motions he made to his chief disciple, Akbar, who smiled, grabbed my arm hard, and pulled me back into the kitchen.

My husband preached the gospel of natural everything. His clothing and food and life were unadulterated. Pure wool, silk, and cashmere. Our sheets were three-hundred-count percale. We cooked in steel or iron—never aluminum—and rubbed French crystals under our arms instead of deodorant. I did not "paint" my face, and our living room had flats of wheatgrass where the couches should have been.

Sex, unfortunately, wasn't so natural for him. He needed it to be a ritual. Just once, I made the mistake of reaching under the sheets to touch him, to cup him in my hands, maybe get something going. He giggled like a girl and turned away as though we were doing something bad. Then he asked if I wanted anything. Like a cheese sandwich.

"Women are goddesses. I respect them all," he said, reaching for his pants.

"That's great, Josh, but we're married now. It's O.K."

"I respect you, my wife, most of all."

"But making love is—"

"We will never 'make love.' We will unite and raise the primal energy, the Tantric tail of all men and women."

Actually, I would have been happy just to come.

He lectured on, but I kept thinking of my thighs tightening, holding him, squeezing a little to let him know I knew his place in the divine hierarchy of *my* holy body. Pulling back, removing him, inserting him in my mouth with prayer, and sucking until he swelled to bursting. Cooling him. Heating him. Yeah, I still remembered a few things. I began to work him slowly with my hand.

"The woman should scrub her body with a stiff brush—oh god yes—then sesame oil to purify from head to toe—man oh man—then the flossing, the sandalwood, the sage to purify the air. Holy Jesus H. Mother."

"Uh-huh," I said.

"We are not doing this to get off—Annie my god—we are waiting to hear celestial . . ."

I had him.

I was moving down on him faster than words, moving in a rhythm he couldn't miss, a rhythm that couldn't be chanted or learned or talked away. I watched his eyes roll back in his head like an epileptic's and me coming like it would never stop, the rise and fall of the thin note inside me.

No. This time was different. This time I did not scrub up, oil up, and approach him with dried apricots and offerings to the gods. I did not lie down on him, grabbing under his long white robe, trying so hard to be content with the mashing of cotton on cotton.

Instead, I got fucked. Good and pregnant.

The baby came sliding down my back with a pain so intense I threatened to kill my doctor if she didn't shoot me up with something fast and serious.

"But you said natural all the way. I'm just being supportive," she said.

"Fuck supportive."

I labored for two days and two nights and there was nothing biblical about it.

Joshua was there in the beginning, but he got bored or busy and sent in various disciples to replace him. Like a tag team they'd come—the young, the hopeful, full of cheer and breathing techniques. Then they'd see me panting on all fours, my hospital gown spread open in back, ass up and howling. Lamaze, effleurage, decoupage, they all went out the window sometime around hour number twenty. Only my howling and the occasional fecal matter or body juices remained. The disciples sat frozen in aqua plastic chairs next to my bed, their "You can do it" lost in the forest of sounds and smells coming from my body.

Heaving of ribs, stretching of vulva, bending of backbone. The loss of body control. The dropping of gown as, naked, I pushed on all fours, fists pounding into bed, back raised like a cat. In between contractions I'd remember: *Joshua was bored. Nothing happening here. No new faces.*

I had my baby with a nurse whose name I did not know.

Before I drowned in drugs and exhaustion, I saw him. *His eyes.* I licked his face, counted toes, fingers, inspected his ears, his penis, the shape of his little head and the smell—*oh that smell*—of something that comes from deep inside you, something you know you will love more than life. And then I saw those eyes again, those cow eyes, unusually big, pale blue, thick-lashed.

"Somebody get Joshua. Tell him to come be with me and this baby."

"His name is Abba now," someone said.

I didn't see much of my husband after I insisted we move out of that House of Love & Lunacy to have a life and be a family. He spent all his time there anyway, with thin-lipped disciples who moved in bony silence. I stayed in our apartment and spent my time sticking a wet tit into a perpetually moving mouth. I was big and wore denim and baby excrement. Joshua was in his all-white phase, either a robe and turban, or a shimmery three-piece suit he'd found at the Salvation Army.

"But it's sharkskin," I told him. "A car salesman's suit. *Used* cars."

"You have no imagination," he said.

For an hour every afternoon he played with his son. This was our agreement. It was actually good seeing them together, bellies to the floor, playing with plastic toys, making Lego towers. Sure, he brought over some of the righteous ones to watch, but then he always did better with an audience.

I didn't gripe. I was too tired to gripe. I used the time to wash and mash and bleach. I kept my hands moving and I heard him talking to the baby.

"Hey, Buddha child, you wanna go on the road together? That's right, pal, me and you. You can teach the world. Sing your songs to the world. Soon. Soon."

Then I remembered: my husband could take things from people. The things they cared about most.

We made love only one more time. It was safe, the doctor said. I hadn't gotten my period back, and I was doing all that nursing. One time more and another child filled my belly.

One baby was enough. More seemed like trolling for danger. I'd get an abortion. And who could blame me? I had no money and a husband who left each morning with his clothes on inside out and came home each night the same way. Everyone adored his little quirks. Everyone loved him. I would get an abortion.

Soon after I stopped going to his House of Horrors, a group of holy women came over to set me right. They held up their skirts as they stepped delicately over pails of soaking diapers, piles of neatly folded baby clothes.

"Surrender to your female side," they said, practically in unison.

"How about a cup of coffee?" I asked.

"Abba says unless you become a spiritual woman you will not be able to raise spiritual children." Someone in the back coughed meaningfully. I could hear the baby crying.

"Tea?"

"You've got to start coming to group meetings. Surrender to your husband's teachings, like we all did."

Church ladies. Missionaries. Pirates dressed in white on a bad, bad ship. The baby was howling. The women were sitting so close to each other, there was no air between them. Someone smoothed her skirt. I stopped offering them things. I opened the door and held it open until the last prayer lady left my home.

That night I had one of those dreams you can smell and taste, and it was her. The dark child in my belly. She spoke simply and held my hand. "Don't worry. I'm with you."

Right before this second child was born, Robert Bly stayed at our apartment. He sat at my kitchen table all day making notes in a clothbound book. At night he'd read poems to Joshua and the disciples. Back then, Bly wasn't anybody famous, not the father of the men's movement or the author of *Iron John*. He was just a guy in a vest who combed his long gray hair to hide the bald spots and translated Sufi poetry.

"Let's the two of us talk," he said.

Loser, I thought. I mean where could you go translating Rumi?

"Come on. Sit with me awhile."

I made us a big pot of Earl Grey and sat across the table from him.

"Tibetan Buddhism is a heavy path," he told me. "Now, you take those so-called American Buddhists. How can they humiliate people, drink like fish, sleep around, and call themselves Buddhists?"

"I don't know." I lived in a small town and had a big belly. I was used to staying within my own four walls. "What are your thoughts on surrendering?" I asked.

"How do you mean?"

"A bunch of Joshua's women keep telling me I should give in to my female side or else I'm doomed. They want me to go to these group meetings and kneel before my husband."

"Oh, that."

"Should I surrender, Bly?"

"Not now. Not in a million years."

Joshua showed no interest in the birth of our second child. He put in brief appearances at the beginning and end of labor, but I didn't care. I forgot to need him. I knew what to do, and was not surprised at the quiet, serious girl who came and immediately curled her hand around my finger. And she would not let go of me, not even while she slept.

A child has been taken, but the mother does not know it yet. She goes through her day with vague symptoms of a cold or a stomach flu. She does not give it a name but senses that one of the major chords that make up her soul, a chord that moves her from task to task with purpose, has come undone.

A child is gone, but the mother does not know. She is out moving through the day, but something is not right with her belly. She prolongs the moment before she lifts the phone and asks the crippled baby-sitter to look in the boy's closet, where small clothes hang far above the floor. The husband always said he'd lower the pole so the boy could reach his little shorts and shirts, but he never did, and now there is the sound of the baby-sitter shuffling back to the phone, dragging her polio leg across the floor, the unbearable sound of something not right.

Everything is gone. His clothes, his toys, his shoes. The baby-sitter is crying. Her words fall on top of each other like badly shuffled cards. *He said he was taking him for a walk. I swear, that's all he told me.*

A child has been taken and no one will tell the mother where he is. She finds each disciple one at a time. They don't like her. She is not one of them. She does not go to group meetings. She has not surrendered. She and the girl child are adrift in their own little boat.

Each disciple says, *Leave it alone. He's gone now, praise be to Allah.*

The day ends and she still does not know where her child is and he has an ear infection that requires many steps of swabbing, dabbing, heating of oil. Who will do this? His bottom will get fiery from waist to knee if his diapers aren't changed often enough. Who will do this? He is gone from her.

That night, Annie sits on the couch in the light of the television drinking Wild Turkey. She feels every drop, from bottle to belly and all the roads in between, feels as though it's giving her whiskers, and she will need these whiskers to get her boy back. She drinks and the pain of separation and the whiskey cause the fog around her to lift. This is just a kidnapping. She will take him to court. She will win. She will get her boy back.

It is the moment a woman knows who she is and knows she will leave her husband. She will leave him, even if there is nothing to leave but a thief and a crazy man. Still, there must be this moment.

A woman may be folding her husband's socks for his next business trip—browns to browns, blues to blues—and she'll puzzle over a soaking-wet sock and then realize it is wet with her tears.

Or she will ask her man to come away from the dishes, talk with her a minute, and he will say, *Talk to you* and *do the dishes?* And that will be her moment.

Halfway through the Wild Turkey, Annie knows. The "Star-Spangled Banner" is on TV, stiff strangers saluting the flag, and she can think only of dead children in army-and-navy cottons rotting underground for their country. When the salt-and-pepper static with its electric buzz comes on the screen, she does not move to turn it off. She holds her girl baby to her breast, and waits for the next day when she will ask again of Joshua's people: *Where? Where?*

She will go right up the command chain of dirty angels until she reaches the top dog: Akbar. She walks slowly over to him in the store full of shoes he is selling and notices it is a summer day, warm and full of fragrance—a mixture of ether, leather, and cheap city flowers. She steps up close to him, big man, six-foot-something, and sees in his eyes the place where her son is. Those eyes shift away, won't catch hers.

What's it to you? he says.

Anger climbs up her spine. She is wild turkey mother, and grabs him by the throat, which is cooler than she expects, smooth and damp with intricate bumps of things just underneath the skin, things she will push and break if he does not tell her what she has come to find out.

He says she should meditate for answers, and this makes her tighten her grip on his air supply.

She is made of metal and cannot be shaken off.

She is prepared to die with her fingers, her nails, her wings, her jaws sunk into him, and she tells him this only once before he says what she has been waiting so long to hear.

Elizabeth Cunningham

Beyond Belief

It is beyond belief.

At least that is what I told myself when my son, Jay, called last month to ask me to arrange an opportunity for him to speak to the Meeting.

"My own Meeting, where I grew up," he had put it—rather sentimentally, I thought.

I could only too clearly recall him as a child, mindlessly kicking the bench or rolling his eyes at the Clancy children sitting opposite, thoroughly disrupting the perfunctory fifteen minutes of Silent Worship allotted to Quaker children in these slack modern times. When, as a somewhat older child, he finally managed to be quiet for that long, silence did not preclude heartless imitations of the poses—eyes closed or face buried in hands—struck by unsuspecting elders. While other Friends lamented the falling away of Quaker youth, I secretly rejoiced when Jay, at age fifteen, refused outright to go to Meeting anymore.

Now, some fifteen years later, Jay—or John, as he prefers to be called, as in John the Beloved Disciple—has become active again in the Religious Society of Friends—perhaps hyperactive. He has been granted a Minute for the Traveling Ministry from the Meeting in New Jersey he joined a year ago.

"I suppose late August is a good time for you to travel," I had commented in order to cover a vague sense of embarrassment. "I mean, everyone who is going to buy a swimming pool will have bought one by then."

Jay, a charmer from birth and a natural salesman, has done quite well for himself, changing products with the seasons.

"And people's gardens do tend to overproduce at that time," I'd blithered on. "They like to have guests to stuff with excess zucchini."

Jay had obliged me with a small laugh but had cautioned, "The timing may be convenient, but the message is timely—and timeless."

"Yes, well, I'll bring it up at Monthly Meeting," I'd swiftly promised to forestall a premature delivery of the Message on the phone. "I'm sure the Meeting will be willing to hear you, provided you submit to a potluck first."

In my mind I'd pictured twenty casseroles featuring zucchini in various guises.

"It can be tough for a prophet in his own country, you know," something foolish had prompted me to add.

There had been a brief silence. As I might have known, he was not biblically literate enough to get the reference. I have been playing this game with Friends since I became one—by convenience if not convincement—when I married Ed thirty-seven years ago, having been raised a Bible-believing Baptist. It was not very nice of me to turn the game on my son. God knows, it's not his fault no one knew what to teach in First Day School—a smattering of Quaker history here, a little nature study there, now and then the odd Old Testament tale, though most of these are too bloodthirsty for adult Friends to stomach.

"O.K., Mom. I know what you're doing. But guess what? I'm taking a course in Bible study this fall. Pretty soon I'll be able to play chapter and verse with you—and win!"

That's what I'm afraid of, I'd thought but did not say.

Now Jay—excuse me, John—is here. He arrived about an hour ago, my son the prophet, not barefoot and dusty from the road, but in a zippy little Mazda. He has to make a good impression on clients. No sackcloth but clean-cut clothes and short hair I can't quite get used to, having him fixed in my mind at a grubbier stage of development. Though it has been cool today with that nibble of fall in the air that I love in late August, he has gone upstairs to take a shower. He is, as he expressed it, "traveling under the weight of a concern." A hot and heavy business, I gather.

I can hear the water running as I stand in the kitchen slicing garden tomatoes to add to the salad. The sound makes a sort of barrier giving me a last moment of privacy in which to adjust to my son's presence in the house. I know that as a widow, the lone survivor in an empty nest, I am supposed to live for visits from my adult children. And it's not that I don't miss them. I do.

In fact, I have been missing my daughter for years. We are what I suppose must be called estranged—though not by my choice. I have a friend whose once estranged daughter has been returned to her twofold, now that her daughter is a mother herself and needs her own mother again—or perhaps at last understands the terrible love a mother can have for a child. I cannot even hope for such a reconciliation with Win.

I still think of her as Win—named Edwina for a father so overjoyed at having reproduced he could not wait for a boy to bestow his name—though on the rare occasions that I speak with her long-distance in India I must address her as Ma Prem Ananda. I miss Win most of all, more than Ed, who is merely dead—did my mother-in-law ever think what it would be like for her son's widow to have to say Ed is dead?—safely dead, my memory of him sealed and whole.

So, yes, I admit it. Of course, I'm lonely. But in the last year or so, of the three since Ed died, I am finding that my loneliness has a savor to it. I am exploring it, rolling it around on my tongue, relishing even the bitterness. I am reluctant to lose its subtle flavor in a strong infusion of company.

The thudding of the pipes as the taps are turned off gives me final warning to prepare myself, though for what and in what way I'm not sure. I put the salad in the refrigerator to chill for a few moments and turn my attention to the table in the dining alcove.

From the sideboard, I select an ivory-colored tablecloth and deep red cloth napkins, which bespeak not so much my standard of elegance as a recent commitment to avoiding excessive use of paper products. Still, I confess to having given some thought to the color scheme, a variation on the black and white dahlias I picked from my garden earlier this afternoon. Placing the vase on the table, I admire what I think of as the Zen-like rather than Quaker simplicity of the flower arrangement.

The white dahlias are lovely, but my eyes linger on the ones called black, they are so dark a shade of red. Sometimes I feel a fraud among the light-seeking Friends, and suspect I married into the wrong denomination. As a child, I had a fascination for the nearby Roman Catholic Church, a cavernous place, the light not blatantly revealed but distant and mysterious, filtered through gaudy bits of colored glass. The stacks of the college library where I continue to work have something of that quality of dim and musty sanctity.

"Smells delicious, Mom."

I turn from the table as Jay enters the room. With his damp hair slicked back from his face, he looks younger than he is, younger than he looked a few years ago, more like the child I remember: sleek and slippery from the bath, racing up and down the hall, daring me to get him into his pajamas. Such defenses as I have are all undone.

"We'll be ready to eat in just a minute," is all I can think of to say. "Why don't you get yourself whatever you'd like to drink."

I notice he pours himself a tall glass of milk, as if he has not outgrown his boyish craving for calcium. I continue to feel nostalgic but wonder if there will be enough milk left for breakfast.

"How 'bout you, Mom?"

"Oh, just water for me, thanks." I respond automatically, then feel annoyed with my tone; it seems falsely self-effacing and sacrificial. Was I like that as a mother?

After he's gotten our drinks, Jay sits down at the table to wait. I fetch the salad, then take the lasagna from the oven.

"Don't say I didn't warn you!" I laugh as I place the pan of lasagna on a serving tile to protect the tablecloth. "I'm unloading three of them on you. You see, I substituted zucchini for noodles. Frieda told me how to do it. You salt the slices first, then wring out the excess water before you bake. Very low-calorie, too. Not that you need to worry about that," I add out of force of habit. When I really look, I can see that he is developing the merest suggestion of a paunch, and his face looks fuller—I reject the word beefy, though it comes to mind—another reason, I suppose, that he looks a little younger.

Jay smiles but says nothing as I sit down, and I suddenly realize that he is waiting for me to be quiet. Our family always had a reverential moment of silence before meals. Living alone, I have been forgetting. I settle down, close my eyes briefly, my very real hunger making me both grateful and impatient. I am about to pick up a knife and spatula to serve the lasagna when Jay, eyes still squeezed shut, begins to speak.

"Lord—"

Lord?

"We thank you for this food we are about to receive. We know that you have said that whenever two or three are gathered in your name, you would be in their midst. Be with us now, Lord Jesus, and let this food strengthen us to do your work. We ask this in your name. Amen."

"Amen," I say politely, feeling that the wisest course is not to make any comment. It's an old maternal ploy to ignore certain behaviors rather than reinforce them with attention. And as a Friend, however fraudulent, I am comfortable with long silences.

"We're going to have to talk about it, Mother."

When he calls me Mother, I know that John is speaking.

"About what?"

I hand him his plate and take a smaller portion for myself. I should have served fish with a dark green vegetable, I think. The garish orange-red of the tomato sauce does not look right with the deep red napkins or the dahlias.

"Help yourself to salad," I prompt.

"About the change in my life now that I've met Jesus Christ."

"Surely you'd met before." I'm trying for a light touch, but my tone is sharp.

"I don't know why you'd think so, Mother, since no one ever introduced us."

Several smart remarks come to mind, further plays on the theme of introduction, but I take a bite of lasagna instead.

"I'm not sure what you mean, John," I say at last, since he seems to be waiting.

"You know very well what I mean, Mother. Liberal Quakers, most of your generation at Meeting, have trouble even pronouncing the word Jesus. You'd think it had four letters, the way most of you avoid it."

" 'There is one, even Christ Jesus, that can speak to thy condition.' " I repeat the famous quotation from George Fox that I picked up from the poster that has always been in the Meeting House. Bible-literate I may be, but I know only half a dozen Fox and Woolman quotes—the ones everyone uses in their Messages over and over. "Sound familiar?"

"That's exactly my point," he counters. "That's what's become of modern Quakerism: a few quotes on a bulletin board. George Fox and the Early Friends were alive with the Spirit of Christ, in direct contact. George Fox said, 'Christ has come to teach his people himself.' "

I think of a joke circulating among older Friends bemused by the growing evangelical fervor of the younger ones—Q: What do we have that the Early Friends didn't? A: The Early Friends.

"How do you know he isn't still teaching us?" I take a helping of salad.

"How do I know?!" John rather dramatically sets down his fork to confront me with a look I avoid. "When some Friends won't even acknowledge that Quakers are Christians—or are supposed to be? Look at your Meeting, Mother. How many people there can honestly say they belive in Christ? You know as well as I do that your Meeting has Jewish members, atheist members, homosexual members—"

"A homosexual person can believe in Christ, John," I interrupt him, appalled. "So can a Jew, if he wants to, and an atheist can follow the teachings of Christ as well as anyone—maybe better. There's always been a Universalist strain in Quakerism. Religious tolerance. Early Friends practically invented it."

"But liberal Friends have made a false idol out of tolerance as a way to excuse wishy-washiness, to cover up for the fact that Friends don't stand for anything anymore. Early Friends weren't a collection of self-satisfied, middle-class individuals, mistaking their vague thoughts in Meeting for Messages from God and congratulating themselves on their good works. They were seeking to know God's will for them as a unified people."

"Friends still attempt to do that."

"And fail, because they've lost their true center in Christ Jesus. They're pulling in ten different directions and getting nowhere."

There is some truth in what he says, I consider, picking at my lasagna, watching a string of mozzarella thinning in the middle as I lift my fork. Liberal Friends—as John calls them, pronouncing the word "liberal" as if it were a wad of partially chewed vegetables he might have spat out as a child—are worried about lack of Unity.

There have been dozens of weekend conferences and countless potlucks and discussions in the past few years on everything from the Bible to abortion, from homosexual marriage to what God likes to be called, as well as the history and how-tos of Quakers trying to figure out what God wants. That seems to be the one point of agreement among Friends: that God does have a definite opinion on all these subjects, and it's up to us to discover it. No easy task, given God's apparent tendency to self-contradiction.

"So what about you, Mother? You can quote up a storm, but I've never been sure of where you stand."

"Really? I thought you had me pegged as a self-satisfied, wishy-washy liberal."

The part about good works was a potshot at his father, I suspect. Ed was the director of Family Services until he dropped dead of a heart attack. But that wasn't enough. He was what you might call a volunteeraholic. The sick, the imprisoned, the hungry, the naked—he tackled the whole list of the least of Christ's brethren cited in Matthew 25. Too bad there is no mention in that passage of son or daughter.

"You sound so bitter, Mom."

We're back to Mom, and he is reaching across the table for my hands, an astute salesman changing tactics. And you'll know they are Christians by their love, I think to myself.

"It's just . . . It's just that I've been through this before."

I am horrified to hear my voice catch and to feel my eyes brimming with tears.

"What do you mean?" He is genuinely puzzled.

What do I mean?

"Mother." I can still hear Win's voice. "When you meet him face-to-face, you'll understand. You'll know! You won't be able to hide from yourself anymore. You'll have to face yourself."

Even as I remember, I wonder: Were those just words, the jargon of the devotee, or did she really see me that way, as someone hidden and self-deceiving? I have an image of myself concealed in the library stacks, where I love to be, all but disappearing, a mote of dust in a narrow shaft of light.

"He is one of the Masters, Mother, one of the perfect incarnations of God, like Buddha and Jesus. Just think, Mother! It will be as if you were one of the disciples meeting Jesus in the flesh! When you see him, you'll simply surrender."

Win didn't know, couldn't know the terror her words awoke in me. She did not have to listen, as a young, impressionable child, to numberless sermons on our preacher's favorite theme: If you met Jesus by the Sea of Galilee, and he said,———(fill in the blank with your name), follow Me! . . .

In sensual detail no Quaker, awash in an amorphous Ocean of Light, could ever conjure, the preacher would depict the scene: the smell of fish, the half-mended nets, the hot Mediterranean sun beating down on your head, and Jesus, his burning gaze fixed on you and you alone. Then, the moment of decision: Would you follow or would you fail? And failure meant not only damnation but failing Jesus, rejecting his love, lacerating his heart, crucifying him all over again. In short, he would take it very personally.

This scene became a nightmare obsession for me. I knew in the depths of my soul (which seemed to reside somewhere just below my navel and caused a good deal of indigestion) that if some strange man with smoldering eyes were to tap my shoulder and say, Follow me, I'd turn tail and run just as fast as I could.

"You've got to come to the ashram, Mother. I've arranged darshan for you. Do you know what darshan means? It means vision of God."

"Well," I'd answered cautiously, "naturally, as a Quaker, I believe there is that of God in everyone."

"That's just words!" she'd exploded. "That's all I ever hear at Meeting. Quakers don't mean anything by it anymore, except: Look at me, I'm such a nice, liberal, tolerant person. Mahavishnu Shree Shiva Ram is no platitude; he's the real thing!"

"Mom, listen." Jay is trying to reach me. "Jesus can help you. He can turn your life around. And you can meet him here. Now. Face-to-face."

I went to my darshan in an old borscht-belt hotel in the Catskills where Win's guru had an ashram before he decamped to India, fleeing charges of fraud and tax evasion. Despite my Win's scorn for Friends, I went determined to seek that of God in the guru—or at least to see what my daughter saw, what made her want to surrender. I wanted to understand, to ease my sense of loss through acceptance of what she called "her path."

My darshan was not an exclusive audience. Some twenty other people were there, most kneeling, some prostrate while the guru sat in an armchair on a slightly raised dais, flanked by two young women. If I'd had the nerve of an Early Friend, I would have remained standing while pointedly addressing the great one as "thee." Speaking truth to power, as it is still called among Friends. Instead my statement of radical equality was limited to sitting on the floor rather than kneeling.

He spoke for quite a long time in the most general terms; it all seemed very impersonal, and I did not understand the excitement he generated in his followers. Then, in one long silent moment, he turned his gaze on me. Meeting his eyes was one of the most profound exchanges in my life. It was a searing look, one that stripped away my liberal Quaker veneer, burned away the loose, flapping layers of open mind to reveal the hard, resistant core beneath.

There was no surrender—on either side; rather, a mutual recognition of the enemy. If there had been words for that moment we each might have said to the other: I know you. I've got your number. Others may be taken in. But not me.

I don't think either of us spoke aloud. I asked Win later, just to be sure. She told me she didn't know; she'd been too "blissed out." But at some level of my being, I heard him say quite distinctly: You must let her go. And I heard myself answer in loud silence: Never.

As if I had a choice, as if any mother ever did.

"You see, Mom," Jay continues patiently, "you may not want to face this, but there comes a time when you have to make a choice. You can't have it both ways. You're either for Jesus or you're against him. One of the biggest delusions of modern liberal Friends is that there are many paths to God. Now, we know in our hearts that's a lie. Jesus said: I am the Way. No man cometh to the Father except by me. The other paths don't lead to God; they lead to a wilderness of sin and self. This age is chock-full of false prophets, like that guru, who tell you that self is God. The only protection against their lies is to give yourself to Jesus."

I finally look at John. "You blame me for what happened to Win," I state flatly.

"Oh, Mom, it wasn't just your fault," he hedges. "Dad, too. Your whole generation. You were so permissive, so unclear about values, limits. Dr. Spock. . . ."

I almost have to laugh. My generation of parents, who weathered our children's hair-raising rebellion and experimentation in the late sixties and early seventies, now have to endure their repenting of their misspent youth and listen to their reproaches all over again. Is there no statute of limitations?

"But that's all in the past now."

Oh, what a relief, I think sarcastically.

"The wonderful thing about coming to Jesus is that you can lay it all down."

For my yoke is easy and my burden is light, I silently quote.

"We're all sinners, Mom, and we've all been saved through his sacrifice of himself on the Cross. Because of him, God forgives us."

Even as a willing believer, I never did quite understand how that worked. Before God couldn't forgive us, but now everything's all right, since we killed His son.

"God can forgive anything, Mom. Isn't that amazing? All you have to do is ask. Just ask."

"We have to forgive, Judith," Ed said to me.

But I never quite forgave Ed for refusing to recognize my right to outrage; for bobbing placidly on the gentle swells of the Ocean of Light, while in me the Ocean of Darkness rose: red, salty, bitter, howling in my womb.

It was not long after my darshan that the guru began urging his devotees, especially the female ones, to be sterilized. He convinced his young American followers that they were too "screwed-up" by their decadent, Western, materialist parents—(this from a man with thirteen Rolls-Royces housed in an air-conditioned garage)—to responsibly bring children into the world.

Win called me a few weeks after her twenty-fourth birthday when her tubal ligation was a fait accompli. She tried first for a bizarre breeziness, then resorted to angry defiance. But when I broke down and wept, her defenses crumbled and she sobbed, too. I can still hear her crying "Mama, Mama," like the lost child that she was. We each clung to the receiver instead of each other, understanding, without words, how brutally our bond had been severed. That was our last exchange of any depth. Ten years ago.

Win was right. The guru forced me to confront myself. The self no one else knows, or even suspects. I am no liberal Friend. I have no tolerance for religion. None. If there is that of God in Mahavishnu Shree Shiva Ram, I am blind to it. I do not love my enemy. Forgiveness strikes me as beside the point, even presumptuous. Who am I to forgive? If God loves this man and wants to forgive him, that's God's business. I want no part of it.

"Mom! Mom! Can you read me, Mom? Earth calling Mom."

I have been ignoring Jay, absorbed, as usual, in my anguish over Win. I always worried more about her. She was my first child, from the beginning so serious, so intense, though with a sweetness about her, a trustingness that made me fear for her. Inevitably, my mothering of my second child was different; it had an arrogant swagger to it. "I'm an old hand at this game. Besides," I'd say with pride, "this kid is tough. He bounces right back." No matter what trouble Jay got into, I fretted about Win more. At some level, I relished Jay's mischief, no doubt subtly encouraging it. Ed was also serious, earnest, and inaccessible in his goodness. I relied on Jay to be a pal, a fellow lightweight.

Now, although I am probably to blame in some way, I feel betrayed by his conversion. Abandoned. My loss is complete.

"I failed you all," I manage to say, meaning, equally: You all failed me.

"Come back to Jesus, Mom. He can heal your pain. You knew him once. Come back. Come home. Make that choice."

I squeeze Jay's hand and look at him, trying to give him—at least, at last—my undivided attention. Then I get up, go around the table, and put my arms around him, kissing his cheek. I can't help thinking of the kiss Judas gave Jesus. Judas—my own name is a female variation. When Jay was born, Ed suggested that we name our son after me, as our daughter was named for him. But even Jude and Judah seemed too close to Judas. So we just kept the first letter, nicknaming him Jay for John, the Beloved Disciple. And he is my beloved son. I want him to know that; I wish he could know that. Because, whether I want to or not, I am almost certain to betray him.

"Well, you have a choice to make, too," I say, straightening up. "There's peach cobbler for dessert or there's ice cream. Actually, you could have both."

He stares at me for a moment, startled, uncomprehending.

"Uh, no thanks, Mom," he says at last. "I'm watching my weight."

Alone, after Jay and I have given up on each other and gone to bed, I have difficulty sleeping. It is not just a fresh spate of grief for the loss of Win, or dismay at the change in Jay, or missing Ed, who could have shared some degree of blame. It is also wondering if John is right: that I have to make some ultimate choice for or against; some decision about the composition of the universe; about the identity and demands of God.

I fall into a fitful sleep, the kind where you dream but have no release from consciousness; the boundaries are all blurred. My dreams are vivid, sensory: the smell of rotting fish; something warm and salty in my mouth, tears or blood; glaring heat. There's a boat bobbing on the waves. The waves are light on the surface and dark where they curl. A man steps out of the boat, casually walking on the water. I recognize him as Jesus, from the pages of my Baptist child's Bible, blond and blue-eyed, a little sickly looking, with his cheeks hollowed out from suffering. Next time I look, he's changed into Mahavishnu, still walking toward me with his hot, contemptuous eyes.

But I'm not really interested in either of them or what they want. There's a baby crying somewhere. That's all I care about. I keep walking along the shore searching patiently, desperately, among the reeds for the basket I am certain holds an abandoned child.

At four in the morning, exhausted and drenched in sweat, I come all the way awake, and decide I've had enough of these dreams. I draw a bath and bathe in the dark, listening to the water lap at the shores of my body. I never bother to draw the bathroom shades. I can see stars through the window—dim, distant, mysterious, the way light should be.

When I'm done with my bath, I put on a fresh night-gown, an overcoat of Ed's, some winter boots, and go out-side to the garden. There I settle into an old wooden Adirondack chair near the dahlia bed. The white dahlias give back the ghostly gleam of stars, and the black ones blend with the night.

I am alone with my secret self in this secret time. It is a little like being alone in the stacks with the rich yet subtle smell of books and the dancing motes of dust—only more so. It is bigger, and I am even smaller. No doubt there are others awake and watching. I can hear the rustling of night creatures, the passing of an occasional car. Still, I have the sense of glimpsing the universe as it is when no one's looking. I had a similar feeling once, when, out for a walk in the woods, I got caught in a torrential downpour. So this is what trees do, I thought, when I'm not there.

I look up at the branches of the apple tree, defined by the absence of stars. In late summer, the tree is heavy with hard, ripening globes. From time to time I close my eyes and just listen. This is the proverbial darkest hour and the coldest, too cold tonight for the crickets and cicadas to sing. And yet it seems the night has a pulse, a rhythm of breath, and the stars and the trees, and the dahlias and I all partake of it.

Then, in the space of a heartbeat, I know: I do not have to decide. I am here, now, in this moment. Present. It is enough. This. I choose this. Anything else is too small.

The birds are waking up. I open my eyes to make my peace with light. Watching the sky, I see no sign of strug-gle, no darkness vanquished, no victorious light. Only the mystery of change, revelation succeeding revelation. The stars fade; the flowers come into focus. I can see the black dahlias again.

And I think, if I were to make up a story about darkness

and light, I would tell a different one. Dawn would not be a battlefield with the forces of good triumphant. Dawn would be a lingering caress, the union from which the world is born and born again.

I go back to bed and sleep deeply.

"Mother?"

Someone's knocking at my door.

"Mom?"

Jay opens the door and looks in.

"Hey, Mom. Since when were you such a late sleeper? It's after nine o'clock."

"I was up for a while in the night," I explain.

"Well, how about a little role reversal," he grins. "I've got pancake batter all mixed. If you can be down in a few minutes, I'll start cooking."

"Great."

After he's gone, I go to my closet and try to think what I should wear. Then I remember: I don't have to decide. I put on a bathrobe instead and go downstairs. Jay has made coffee, too. I pour myself a cup and sit down at the table to wait, while he flips pancakes.

"Hey, Mom," he says, catching sight of me as he finishes one stack and turns to get the bowl of batter. "Don't you think you should get dressed first? We really should leave for Meeting right after breakfast."

"I can dress later. I'm not going to Meeting today."

"What do you mean you're not going?!"

"I thought I'd stay home and harvest the basil."

"Mother! I'm speaking today."

"Yes, I know."

"Then what you mean is that you're rejecting Christ."

"He doesn't need to take it so personally," I say as gently as I can. "Neither do you."

"I don't believe this," he says. "You're beyond belief."

"Yes."

And I smile, enigmatically perhaps, a sort of postmenopausal Mona Lisa, pregnant with my unbelief.

Alison Luterman

The Largest Possible Life

For Ruth and Gladys

Building a fire, love;
  bent low
    over a flame

I am afraid of
  Coaxing passion
    from dry twigs

and dead leaves,
  the failures of the past, dirty fingers,
    and a moment of sunset

huge orange
  hangs in one eye—
    in my breast a sun

which, if I could see it, if I could
  know it, would
    light the world

with love. Then,
  an unexpected memory
    of my mother in the car, snow piled

along the gray streets
   of Massachusetts. It was my sixteenth year
     and we were fighting a life

and death struggle over my desire to give
   myself away completely to love before
     I had a self to give.

There she was, my block, my barricade,
   my iron grate, my broken door—our one shared
     passion, to hurt each other into truth, and

it was round two hundred million
   of our everyday war when she said
     "I don't know if I've ever loved anyone,"

and began to weep. Monks sit
   in the middle of fires
     they set themselves. They let

their bodies bloom
   into suffering,
     in the hope that, like this, they will open

someone's heart.
   What do we have to
     see, how close do we need to live by the

beautiful terrible flame of this world,
   flame of ourselves, which is
     the same thing?

How much anguish do we need to pour
   from cup to cup, drink of melted rubies,
     underwater food of the fevers that live

in our blood, in the light of our eyes
   where infinite tears are waiting and still
      you say, "Light a white candle," and I do, asking

whoever it is, Teach me to surrender
   this mind that grasps at shadows
      when the whole house is ablaze,
         when the only thing left

is to leap, carrying the impossible
   weight in my arms, into
      the heart of our fire, to melt and to bloom.

A White Woman's Burden

I'm sitting with the good Indian girl my husband's mother found for her second son—nine years ago, six years after I married her first son. We've been sliding a pair of aluminum and plastic lawn chairs, following the sun, across the courtyard of her house in New Delhi. Hawkers shout the names of fruits and vegetables behind the ten-foot wall that separates us from the alley (from the lower caste vegetable hawkers, from the beggars and the cows). My nephew squeals and runs out of the kitchen, a slight Nepali girl, his ayah, close behind. "It took me seven years to get a son," my sister-in-law says.

Two possibilities: she's trying to console me for fifteen years of happy, childless marriage; or she's trying to find out what her brother-in-law has been doing for so long instead of getting me pregnant.

"I never wanted to go through that kind of pain," she says.

"I'm more concerned about the feedings, diaper changes, toilet training, driving, and my privacy for eighteen years," I say, though for almost a year I've been downright cavalier about family planning. And to think about the trouble I have gone to for twenty years to keep from conceiving children!

"I had trouble," she says, "from the time I started taking the medicine."

"The pill?"

"Pills were supposed to make me fertile. They only made me sick."

"Fertility pills? You just told me that you didn't want any children."

She nods, undisturbed by what I see as a contradiction.

"What made you change your mind?"

"My mother-in-law was keen on a grandson."

Our mother-in-law, mutual. Thank God my husband had a brother, or his mother might have lived with us for fifteen years and died in an American hospital.

"We went to Goa on holiday," my sister-in-law said. "There is a church. One of your saints is displayed there."

"Francis," I say, not that he's exactly my saint. "I can never remember whether it's Assisi or Xavier."

"He was a missionary. When he died, the body did not decompose. You must go to Goa."

"Actually," I say, "we were more interested in Goa for the beach." We've gotten into the habit of going for a Third World vacation every year—Jamaica, Cancún, the American Virgin Islands; I couldn't let the rare trip to India deprive me of a few days in the sun.

"Goa has beautiful beaches," my sister-in-law says, "but you must see the remains of the saint. There is a box in front of his coffin. You must write your wish on a chit of paper, and the priest collects it with the rest and prays for your request to the saint."

"I'm not Catholic," I say. "I'm hardly even Christian."

"It does not matter. You could be Sikh like me. I thought, why not? And I wrote down my request for a son. When I came back, I conceived. I've got a lot of faith after that."

"In Christianity?"

"In general."

When we had called to tell my husband's brother when to meet us at the airport, Mona said that she would read her holy book until our plane touched down. With the circling, the layover in Bombay to refuel, and the wait for the fog to lift in Delhi, I figure twenty-four hours—half the time it takes to read the whole *Guru Granth Sahib* cover to cover, what the priest and his assistants do for holidays, a new house, a funeral, the birth of a son. It must have worked. Two days before we changed planes in Frankfurt, a bomb had blown the cockpit off a 747—same flight, same airline—and 259 people went down across a thirty-mile stretch of Scotland.

"The chance of a bomb going off on this flight is the equivalent of a meteor hitting the earth," my husband said.

Statistics have never helped me any more than praying. God knows I tried, but I only knew a handful of prayers anyway, and the prayer my mother taught me when she used to tuck me in at night—"if I should die before I wake"—has never been much help in going to sleep, especially on an airplane.

The plane was full of servicemen and their families, babies who screamed at takeoff, as if they could know something none of the rest of us could feel. At the back of the cabin, waiting for a toilet, where I spent most of the flight, I watched, out of the corner of my eye, a tall black American in an orange flak suit, chin taped with surgical adhesive, standing, for no apparent reason, in the aisle of the plane. My brain told me he was army, he'd got into a fight the night before, too much drinking; then the stereotype really kicked in, and I saw him brawling with his drunken dad. Thirty years of television and middle-class prejudice had me imagining him tearing through the cabin with a flamethrower. "This is a long flight," he said, to no one in particular; then, suddenly, I stopped suspecting him. The passengers applauded when the plane touched down.

In Frankfurt the black faces gave way to brown, Indians on their way, like us, to family and friends. Twenty years ago I had toyed with the idea of going to India like my friends—at least in their minds—but chanting mantras and avoiding meat did not suit me any better than singing

hymns or reading the responses in a Sunday morning service. But I could never concentrate enough to meditate, and
any college student will tell you that there's nothing that
can beat the flank of a holy cow for off-campus dining.
Intermarriage was a secular decision for me—even pro-
fane—and the only reason I have gone to India (twice: for
my husband's brother's marriage and my mother-in-law's
funeral, six years after that).

An African security guard passed me through the metal
detector. On the other side, I turned to see another guard,
blond, like me, running his palms up my husband's thighs,
down his rib cage. The man I fell in love with eighteen
years ago is brown enough to qualify as a person of color;
he might even pass for an Arab with his dark eyes and his
Semitic nose. But he and I are both Aryan, what they call
the tribe that migrated from Europe into India; our ancestors just happened to move in opposite directions.

An official in uniform herded us onto the plane, shouting, "Stay in line. Go directly up the stairs." I don't know
what it was, genetic guilt or what, but I did not feel comfortable letting a shouting, fair-haired German pack a
crowd of brown people on a vehicle. We taxied past El Al,
guards with their Uzis on the roof of the hangar, and I
almost wished we were leaving Germany for a country
that does not pretend the world has been achieving peace
since World War II ended.

Terrorism's just as bad in the land of Gandhi. We have
to open our purses for khaki-clad policemen, checking for
bombs outside the underground shopping center in the
middle of Connaught Place. Even on the gurdwara steps,
policemen check our bags. The priest sings sweetly and the
congregation bows in concentration. But I can't focus on
anything except the contact of the marble floor against my
buttocks. Mona bows, her palms pressed together, remembering my husband's mother and the father-in-law neither
of us had ever known, while her son runs from the wom-
en's side to the men's. She's lucky she's not Christian; she

would have to hold him to a pew and evoke the fear of God to keep him quiet.

Every time we go out with my husband's brother, who wears a turban to protect his uncut hair and pins his beard up underneath his chin, the police stop us, shine a flashlight into the car, and stare into my white face as if blond and blue-eyed people hadn't forced them into khaki uniforms and boots in the first place. Delhi maintains a more or less constant state of alert—police checks at the crossroads, the entire street to the prime minister's blocked. The day we fly to Goa, the government has hung two Sikhs for the assassination of Indira Gandhi. Our plane is held up all afternoon to wait for the arrival of Rajiv Gandhi's jet. Even for the domestic flight, we're being frisked on the chance that a Sikh terrorist might use our plane to avenge the executed zealots. My husband had cut his hair and shaved his beard long before we met. That may have made it easier to melt into an American pot, but in India, where unshorn Sikhs would know his religion by his name, he would be among the first accused of treason against the nonexistent nation some Sikhs are as willing as Palestinians to kill and die for.

"So much for a day in the sun," I say. A policeman, his rifle cradled in his arms, watches while we test the Arabian Sea in the moonlight. It's like a bath, amniotic, pulses throwing waves against our feet.

My husband says, "My mother always said that with the British at least you could count on trains coming and going on time."

"Nostalgia," I say. "Why do they have to have a guard? Terrorism this far from Delhi?"

"Hippies," he says. "This place is notorious for drugs."

"So this is where they looked for God."

It's beautiful, all right, with the sea working its inherent magic on our eyes and lungs. The longer I stare, the better I recognize the mother from which all of us have come. But as soon as I turn back to the hotel, I see the

guard with his automatic rifle, the tourists singing lieder in
the beachside café, a hundred years of well-trimmed grass,
flowering trimmed shrubs.

I drink my morning coffee on the private porch of our
five-star cottage, watching a gardener in his straw hat and
tattered pajamas clip a hedge into the shape of the fishing
boats that are, even now, bringing shrimp and pomfrets
for our tandooris and curries. Nearly all the shrubs are
blooming—yellow, red, at least white. I recognize the
ground covers as the plants we keep inside our house in
the suburbs, not far enough from New York to escape an-
nihilation if the bomb still hits. A six-foot woman, her
white hair glistening in the sun, emerges from the cottage
next to ours. *"Guten morgen,"* I hear her call to the other
tourists gathered at the pool, their broad backs red with
the sun. "Direct flights from Frankfurt," my husband
says, emerging from the bedroom.

"What's wrong with the Riviera?"

"Not warm enough, and Third World luxury is cheap."

"First Portugal," I say, "then England, then the Germans?"

"England never got a foothold in this part of India.
That's why Goans all have Portuguese names."

"Half-caste, interracial kids?"

"Converts. The missionaries changed their names to
make them sound more Christian."

"There's not a kid in this hotel," I say.

"That's because Indians can't afford it."

"And white people don't drag their kids across the
ocean when they go on vacation," I say, another reason
not to have a child I will have to drag across two oceans to
the relatives every several years. There were babies on that
plane from New York, army brats en route to the thawing
war in Europe, Indian children on the plane to Delhi,
speaking German like the natives that they are, teddy bears
in the wreckage of that jet that went down on the heath of
Scotland.

We spend the mornings in the water, afternoons in bed. We'd been so wiped out by the jet lag between New York and New Delhi that the first time we got up the energy to make a little love was two nights ago. For ten days we could hardly move under a pile of heavy blankets in my brother-in-law's concrete house, no heat, no hot water, the bathroom at the far corner of an open courtyard, a security gate and padlock between us and 40-degree elimination. It takes a private room with an attached bath and hot-water shower to bring out the erotic in us.

Our last day in the sun, I look through the *Goan English Daily* for news of riots, hijackings, or assassinations that might complicate our trip back to Delhi. I can't even find an article about the executions. But the language dispute between Karnataka and Maharashtra has turned violent. I realize that if constant war between the states had preserved the language of my ancestors, I'd be speaking German; I might even realize it's not Pennsylvania Dutch.

On the last page of the tabloid I see a headline: SPIRITUAL ENLIGHTENMENT SUPERSEDES PLEASURE. That's supposed to happen on a trip to India, but every time I've come, even for a funeral, I've only overeaten, exchanged presents, shopped, and sat for hours in a sun I won't see again for five more months. According to the editorial, in order to achieve the Hindu form of grace, a man must renounce pleasure: "The purpose of life is to avoid rebirths."

Abstinence is no difficult concept for a Protestant to grasp, even a lapsed Protestant. If I could renounce the pleasure of spending at least three days every winter in the sun, I wouldn't have to bear the guilt of being able to afford to risk my life for cheap, warm Third World luxury. But the second concept, "to avoid rebirths," is a tough one. Reincarnation has always looked good to me, anything that might offer a second chance in the face of eternal punishment for bliss. But the Hindu view of hell is life. I believe it every time I see a leper tapping on the taxi window with his stump.

I order breakfast while my husband showers, dresses, and shaves. We eat on the porch in the shadows of the crows cawing over the eaves. "I'm scared to death of flying out," I say.

"If the hotels weren't full," he says, "we'd stay another night."

"All you want is another warm night before the nights turn warm in New York. I want another day of life."

"Have a little faith."

The taxi takes us through the palm groves and cashew orchards lining the narrow country roads to the north coast, where the Portuguese first landed. Brick and stucco sanctuaries dot the road—a cross and Technicolor Jesus lit with candles and garlanded with marigolds inside. Goans walk along the dusty roads, their mustaches black against their brown faces. I have been raised to look for safety in the sunburned necks of the tourists we passed, but these white people had been born in Germany before the concentration camps were emptied.

In Old Goa, the street suddenly wide and lined with trimmed European hedges, the taxi stops between two Portuguese churches, stone and stucco, their baroque steeples exotic in a land of turrets, minarets, and domes. Hawkers peddle ice cream, balloons, and emaciated, jaundiced candles. I think about my sister-in-law, who told me she would light a candle if she ever brought her son to Goa, but I don't feel inclined to sentimentalize her faith, especially since I don't feel much of anything myself beyond the curiosity a tourist brings to a church in a land full of temples.

My husband, schooled by Irish brothers in New Delhi, dips his hand into the holy water and makes the sign of the cross. I'd never pull it off. He smiles. He sprinkles water on my head, the way he'd sprinkled me with holy water at the Sikh gurdwara. This is how he thinks he can protect me; he does not believe enough to do it for the mere sake of tradition.

The inside of the church is bare—for a Catholic house of worship—no pews on the uneven, cobbled floor, no Stations of the Cross below the dull, tinted windows high up in the wooden walls, no frescoes on the vaulted ceiling. The statue of some saint stares down, flanked by the Virgin and child, dressed up and white-faced, like the Hindu idols of Ram and Sita I have seen in temples. No German tourists here. A few Goan Christians wander in and stare at the Virgin and her child. A Punjabi couple, pale by my new South Indian standards, gaze into an alcove on the side of the altar. The young wife's hands and feet are still painted with elaborate paisleys and flowers, her neck and earlobes weighed down with marriage gold. A few more years and she might give birth to a son who will support her when she's old, if he never has to fight, suffer, and die before she's dead herself—or a daughter to amass a dowry for, to buy insurance that she will not be mistreated, beaten, burned to death.

A guide points out the body of Saint Francis, high on a platform twenty feet above the floor. Behind the glass of the casket I think I see a skullcap and hands pressed in prayer.

"That's the actual body?" my husband asks. "I can't see anything."

"Security is necessary," the guide says. "One lady bit off a toe. It bled, just as if the saint were still alive, after four hundred years."

"But they must have embalmed him," my husband says.

"They do nothing," the guide says. "It is a miracle."

I find myself more inclined to believe in this miracle than my statistician husband, but the preservation of even a good missionary's body strikes me as insignificant. All my life I have been wondering why God doesn't spend His time opening the hearts of the rich and powerful, to give everybody a world without war. What would make people happy enough to stop fighting? But I'm rich myself, in

India, a target not moving fast enough. I think of praying, but this Catholic shrine is no more my element than a Hindu temple with its graven images or a Sikh gurdwara with its incomprehensible scriptures.

Against the wall beside me is a box labeled "Requests for the Saint," a pen, and slips of paper on which my sister-in-law must have written her request for a son. I can't imagine writing to a spirit. Can't they read your mind? Life, I think, but I'm referring to my own, on the other side of the transatlantic flight I will entrust my body and my luggage to in two more weeks. It takes faith to bear a child, and I cannot feel it, not even in the church that's one-upped my sister-in-law's Sikhism. I look up at Saint Francis. How can I ask for anything? I have a nine-room house, a job I love, enough money to come to India whenever we want, health in the cancer belt of the United States, all the family I started out with, even the husband that I chose fifteen years ago. A baby is the last thing I need.

Give, I tell the saint. *Datta*. In Delhi a man called out "Sahib!"—so twisted that he had to walk on his hands and feet, his back permanently parallel to the ground. When my husband gave him a rupee, he held it to his forehead, kissed it, pressed it to his chest. My heart went out to him: *Dayadvam*.

Damyata, as if I were in control of my life.

I have never learned how to pray for the intercession of a saint. I don't dare pray for myself.

In a dusty courtyard I see the candles, stood up in an iron grate, burning in the blinding sunlight. I could have bought one on the street for a rupee, touched my candle to a flame someone had touched to another flame burning out in front of me, and fixed my candle into the lattice with the others. But I'm afraid. What if I don't feel anything? How important can my life be, neither Christian nor Hindu nor Sikh?

From the church we ride directly to the airport. The huge warehouse of a waiting room is full; we have to sit on the floor. All the flights are late. I watch the tourists smoothing their souvenir pajamas over their bellies. It's easy for them, Lufthansa; you never hear of one of them going down. A tall Sikh, rarer in Christian Goa than in Punjabi Delhi, walks past me, and I wonder what he's carrying in such a huge metal briefcase. I hope he isn't on our flight. I lean against my husband. "I'm scared," I say. "My stomach's already taking off and circling."

He shakes me off. I understand. For one thing, in India, in public, men and women do not touch. "Don't be stupid," he says.

"I'm not stupid. I feel doomed."

He walks away. What do you do after fifteen years of marriage? Take a lover or get pregnant? If you prize stability enough to stay married, in spite of in-laws, men, even boys, and midlife crises, you opt for the baby. Only a glutton for chaos cheats.

On the other hand, I cannot imagine controlling a child in that noisy warehouse. I don't see how the Indians do it, chasing down their toddlers before they can run into the khaki knees of the cops guarding the doors with their automatic rifles. The children should have reassured me: no terrorists would travel with a child.

"Do you want a sandwich?" my husband asks.

I've seen the sandwiches, a few slices of brownish chicken in a buttered hot-dog roll, the Goan equivalent of German cuisine. "I can't eat."

"A soda then," he says. "Campa Cola?" I shake my head. He buys me a bottle anyway.

By the time we board the plane, another sunny day has been wasted in the shade of the control Tower of Babel. Only one frisker, a man, stands at the foot of the plane, rubbing down the men with a metal detector that looks like the starter we use to light the charcoal grill at home. When a woman stops, he waves her on, his palm open and his head swinging laterally, a bashful smile on his face. The threat Pan Am ignored said that the bomb would be carried by a woman. I hold my breath when the airbus lifts me into the clouds, and every time it hits a pocket, my heart shoots through the stratosphere. I try to read, but the words dance around on the page. My husband urges me to eat the kabob or at least the rice pudding the stewardess has put in front of me. When the plane lands, my cold hands leave silver beads on the arms of my seat.

In a week we drive five hours with my brother- and sister-in-law because I can't have been to India twice without seeing the Ganges. The ashes of the executed Sikhs have been quietly immersed while we've been sunbathing in Goa. High above the holy city of Hardwar we climb the first foothill of the Himalayas. My heart beats too hard, too hard even for panic, and I have to stop for breath. My husband, a smoker, five years older than I, with heart disease on his father's side and cancer on his mother's, feels fine. Even my sister-in-law, who must be carrying thirty-five more pounds than she did before she had the baby, plods up the slope. I suppose I'll have to worry about my heart. I will stop eating oil, as soon as I get out of India. I'll see my doctor for a stress test. If I make it back.

I sit beside the path and watch the river, so swift that I can see the current, even from a mile away. So wide, it is no wonder people worship it. Far beyond the city I can see where Hindu worshipers have built steps down a deserted bank, only to be thwarted by Ganga meandering several hundred feet away. Now, this is a god, I think. I feel strangely inspired, in spite of my inability to breathe. The hill rises up behind me, the highest mountains in the world so far away, I will not see, not on this trip, but I know they are there, beyond me. Now anything seems possible, hope, life, even if some maniac propels us into the grave. I can almost see myself carrying my husband's child, like my sister-in-law, who has scooped up her toddler in her arms and is carrying him up the hill. If I can just stay away from cholesterol, carcinogens, toxic waste, terrorism, fear.

When I catch my breath, I turn and climb up to the

temple on the hill, where a holy man pours milk into my husband's hand. He sprinkles it over my head. "I think this is what you're supposed to do with it."

The holy man puts a smudge of carmine on my forehead and rests his brown hand on my blond hair. "What did he say?" I ask.

"All the usual blessings: good life, good family."

What I'll see my doctor for, two weeks later (the flight back home so uneventful that I will not even remember it), is a urine test to confirm the one I will do at home. I will leave the doctor's office not sure whether to give into the uncanny pride I want to feel or the fear I can't help feeling. It seems the greatest act of faith to carry a baby to term in this terrifying world. I'm thirty-nine. I'll have to have all the tests. When I take this kid to India to see half of its home, I'll be more frightened than I've ever been when the risks involved just my life and my husband's. But somewhere I will have to find the faith. At least, I'll have to fake it.

Jean Walton Wolff

Mary and the Maple Tree

On the deck outside is a small Japanese maple tree. As the days have warmed over the past few weeks, it has shyly produced green shoots tender as tea leaves. I bought the maple at Orchard Supply a few weeks after my mother's suicide, to soothe my seared soul. That first year it stayed bare as a black stick, never producing a single bud. Maybe it was the lack of light, or maybe it was empathetic to my sorrow, the way pets imitate their owners. At that same time I bought a graceful statue of Mary, 25 percent off. Mary holds her hands out and watches over the slender maple, day and night. She has a tiny smile on her face, warm as apples. I don't know which I love more, the tree or the statue. This is strange, because I am not Catholic.

I am a fallen Unitarian. It's not an easy thing to do, considering Unitarians are near the bottom of the spiritual food chain. Intelligent, educated people, certainly, but not ones to talk about God. Even in church. The last times I went to a Unitarian service, the topics were Salvadoran refugees and recycling. I come from a background not with a punishing God, but rather with a distracted bureaucrat in a gray suit hurrying down the hall, who cannot find my file and hopes I can figure this thing out on my own.

My ethnic group is constipated WASP. I come from people who do not believe in having much fun. They like to get up at 7:00 A.M. on weekends, have fried eggs, and then work, even if there is nothing to do. They'll stain the fence,

303

even if it doesn't need staining. That way they can qualify for a cool gin and tonic before lunch. In my family there are only a few sins: smoking, getting a divorce, and becoming Catholic.

So it was with great surprise that I found myself in a Catholic church last year. It took me a while to realize that you don't say you go to Catholic church. You go to Mass. This was only the first of many things I did not know. I was afraid if I went to Mass, I would become Republican. I don't have any intention of joining the Catholic church right now. The issues of abortion, the place of women, and other things keep me from taking that step. I see myself as dating rather than marrying the church. I had been looking for what I called spiritual heroin following the pain of my mother's suicide. After the first weeks and months of screaming, smashing dishes, and hanging up on most people I know, some of whom are kind enough to still be my friends, I knew I needed spiritual help. I had what I considered to be a solid spiritual life, but now I felt completely submerged. They say God never gives you more than you can handle. I don't think this is so. God sometimes does give us more than we can handle, and it is during those times we must turn to each other, or turn within: God comes to us when we are broken and alone.

In my church shopping I tried various Protestant churches, and usually wound up the only person in the congregation under sixty-five, and the only other thing going on during the week spaghetti feed on Wednesday for the truly desperate. I went back to Unity Temple, where I had gone off and on for years, and while I have some wonderful friends there, I kept looking for "Have a Nice Day" etched in the stained glass. I did not want to cheerfully pray for prosperity, and the happy songs just made me even more sad and angry. I needed a church where people talked about sorrow, where they knew about loss.

So out of desperation I tried the Catholics. My friend the ex-nun, who now lives with her boyfriend and a motorcycle, has always been a source of strength to me, and was one reason I went. She no longer goes to Mass, but her roots are deep and apparent, and I had gone with her to weekend retreats held in Catholic retreat centers. She introduced me to her friend the kind, avuncular priest, who was always willing to make time to talk to me. And my loving, earthy masseuse talks to me gently about Mary, the Divine Mother, while soothingly rubbing me with lavender oil.

On my first try, the priest, as handsome as Richard Chamberlain, mentioned with outstretched arms that his green vestment cost eight hundred dollars and, as the collection basket was being passed, that he saw his congregation more as a business than a family. I quietly slipped toward the door. But on my second try I found a down-to-earth priest who spoke from the heart. I found I could listen to him. Now I love everything about the service, as long as we don't talk about abortion, gay rights, or why there are no women priests. I love the men in the dresses, the tenderness on All Souls' Day, and Mary as Divine Mother. Sometimes when I pray I picture myself safe in Mary's Snugli. And above all, I love the candles. I was raised in Latin America, in Catholic countries, and grew up with the intoxicating and holy fragrance of candles and incense. Until recently I didn't know that these lovely eerie smells and lights flickering in the dark were used here. I feel relief for my searing grief when the coin drops in the noisy metal slot and I light a creamy white votive candle.

I love the procession into the church with what I call the domino book held high over the priest's head. My friend the ex-nun tells me the book is called the lectionary, but I think domino book more accurately describes this large book with dots. I am moved by communion, by the almost childlike quality of faith, everyone lining up quietly. The divine snack. Jesus's dime-thin wafers are shiny as hubcaps. I don't tell anyone I'm not Catholic, I just get in line. I figure it's between me and God.

*   *   *

I love that this church is available seven days a week. I need more than to sing nice hymns on Sunday while wearing clean socks. There is always a daily Mass somewhere, and I have gone often. Sometimes I go down to the weekday noon Mass at the tiny mission chapel and sit on the dark wooden pew, bathed in pink and red light from the stained glass. The two-hundred-year-old statues patiently gaze at the back of the priest's head, who is sometimes Italian and sometimes Irish. There is a solemnity and almost medicinal comfort in these small Masses, filled with housewives and carpenters on lunch break, that has often helped me get through the day. The trust among these strangers is touching; women leave their purses unattended on the pews while they step forward for communion.

In another parish, during the celebration in November of All Souls' Day, the photographs of the deceased in the back of the church for the month were another reminder that I was not alone, and that grief, as well as the departed, is holy.

Advent was especially comforting after my mother's suicide. I bought two Advent calendars, since I could not decide between the goofy one with the skating chipmunks or the serious one with donkeys in the hay. Even more than opening the little windows each morning over Grape-Nuts, I liked the homilies I heard those weeks. We were reminded that waiting during times of darkness is itself a sign of hope, and that our yearning is God expressing Himself or Herself. I saw that the constant ache of my grief did not mean there was something wrong with me, but that I was healing through a natural and predictable process.

During Mass for the feast of the Epiphany, a long way of saying three wise men, we were anointed with fragrant frankincense and myrrh. The halo of perfumed oil remained on my forehead for hours. It helped with my anger later that afternoon, when I received a long-distance call from my father, who called in a rage to blame me because he was alone, sick, and afraid in the rain, and his power was out. What do you expect me to do, I wanted to shout, jump in the car and drive one hundred miles with a light-bulb? I had a strong urge to call the Menendez brothers for help, but later decided against it. Surely it was the power of prayer in my life. I have been surprised not to have been more angry at God during this time. Maybe I had so much rage at my mother after she killed herself that I needed all the friends I could get.

Perhaps it has been the passage of time, or perhaps it is the power of prayer, in which I believe, but in any case the searing in my soul is somewhat less these days. In the days after my mother's suicide many people did not know what to say. Some were afraid to talk about it, some made strange comments like "Oh, I know just how you feel; I just broke up with my boyfriend." Others were wonder-fully and endlessly patient: I found special comfort from those who had suffered a similar loss. Others gave disqui-eting predictions, like the woman with the bad dye job who said, "Hey, this Christmas will be bad, but next year will be worse."

And she was right.

Others said I would find gifts in this tragedy, and of course I wanted to punch them in the nose. But despite the occasional heavy-handedness of these awkwardly loving encouragements, some have been accurate. There have been lessons and, yes, gifts in my mother's death.

I see how difficult it is to have or express sorrow in America. Anything but that, we tell ourselves. We are afraid to let our public figures fall apart and be human. We are afraid of that ourselves. We marginalize, and we want to push away those of us who mourn. We want to make sure that they are different from us. It happened to you because there is something wrong with you, but it won't happen to me. But loss touches us all. Everyone has had a lost dream, a broken heart. It is just not American to be sad. We convince ourselves it is better to be busy, productive, exhausted than sad, depressed, or grieving. And certainly don't take longer than a few weeks.

But grief takes time. Sometimes years, and often longer than we'd like. The soul mourns the way the seasons change. During these past months since my mother's death I am learning to embrace the raw and grieving parts of me, not discard them or try to flush them away out of shame. I feel I could not avoid them even if I wanted to, and sometimes envy people who seem to be over their grief quickly. Often I have felt, what is wrong with me, when is this going to be over, why am I so weak? Then I talk with someone else who has gone through it, before me or after me, or I see my own growth, and I am reminded that we cannot heal what we cannot feel, and that it will get better. Grief is a process to go through, not a foreign city to go around.

Anne Morrow Lindbergh, no stranger to grief, said, "Suffering . . . no matter how multiplied . . . is always individual." When I am hurting the most, I feel most misunderstood, most separate, and that my pain is unique. They say the worst pain is the one we each experience. In our solitary sorrows we are more alike than we know. "Oh, I know just how you feel" usually is not as helpful as "Oh, I'm so sorry, would you like to talk about it?" If I can embrace and heal through my own losses, I am less likely to blame you for yours. Modern life does not have room for being powerless, but sometimes we just are. Sometimes the waves are too big and the night too long to allow us to stay afloat on our own.

In the end, I don't know if I will find a permanent home in the Catholic Church, and I suppose it doesn't even really matter. I have found a solace in a deep and old spiritual tradition, to my surprise and comfort. It has enriched my spiritual path, reminding me that I find my answers within, and that there is not one perfect answer, or one perfect church. There are different imperfect ways to worship the Divine. God's comfort and direction also speaks to me through Zen Buddhist writing, through our "older brothers and sisters" the Jews, and, yes, sometimes even through Unitarians. I also find God in nature: mocking-birds, freesias, the ocean with its sun and solitary storms; in art and music: when I listen to gospel, I am in God's living room. And I have found I need not only comfort from God but the joy of celebrating life.

So this year as I prepared for Lent, and received a fore-headful of soot on Ash Wednesday, I thought less of what I could give up, and more of what I could add to life. I have given up enough: alcohol, cigarettes, men with tattoos, unhealthy eating habits, my mother. Instead of seeking one more place of darkness within me, I saw how I could add light. I let myself make a new friend, walk a different direction on the beach, wear a different color, travel to a new place, or simply spend more time on the couch. And I believed, even if I did not remember, that like Lent, spring always comes.

Today the tiny leaves on my dormant Japanese maple that Mary faithfully watches over have finally uncurled in the warmth of the sun, producing a delicate canopy of green. Each leaf has opened expectantly in trust, like the fists on a newborn child.

Gene Zeiger

The Little Bit

The little I want, you never bring it.
I miss it; that's why I lay claim to so much.
To so many things, to infinity almost. . . .
Because of the little bit that's missing, that you never bring.
—HENRI MICHAUD, trans. W. S. MERWIN

Because of the little bit that isn't there, that life refuses to bring; because of that moment of hesitation before getting wet, or born, or real; because of how you must lean away from the table as the full plate is set in front of you, because of the fullness of the plate, and the body's constant demands (Drink! Food! Sex!); because there is always the tiniest space between desire and its aftermath (more desire), between lips kissing, asking; between teeth, which require so much tending, flossing, rinsing; because of that tiny bit of space, that little absence, I once felt a longing so intense it made me cry. So I cultivated a kind of silence, which I believed would be the soil in which the little bit would grow and flourish. And occasionally it came and lit on my shoulder, or croaked in my throat, or threw me to my knees in a bright moment of ecstatic union, the little bit becoming everything and then *pop!* vanishing like the queen of hearts in a magician's hand, or the special piece of chocolate you try to keep hidden from your family, the little square of heaven that you squirrel away behind the jar of rice when no one is looking. Who the hell took it this time?

* * *

When you're a child, you have the little bit and it has you.
You throw it up and clap your hands. Your father momentarily catches it, but it is yours in your little animal eyes,
your tender knees, the way a banana unwraps in your
small hands, unzips as you slowly pull down the peel and
reveal the soft, pale fruit. You grow tall, taller, and the
little bit travels into new parts of your body, creating
breasts or a bigger penis, new hair in weird places, and you
know it's there because of the strangeness you feel. You
need another body, someone else's, to help tend the little
bit that hides in your sexed flesh. And it scares you, it over-
whelms you, it makes you strum the guitar and sing about
how "The Water Is Wide," or how "Tonight You Belong to
Me." And you try so hard to fix your hair up, to find the
right sweater or jeans so the little bit will be attracted back
to you and marry you and give you everything you ever
wanted, or lost.

But sadly, you learn that the little bit that's missing is
not found in other human beings. So what can you do?
You turn to nature, to flowers, to trees, who seem oblivious to the lost little bit. You stare at their hard sturdiness,
their green leafiness. And sometimes, if you stare hard
enough and walk among those great torsos long enough,
the little bit rubs off on you and you feel "tree-ness"
everywhere, especially in your chest and legs. But it
doesn't last, because the little bit that a tree has is its own
little bit, not yours.

Then you think: *Maybe the mind can find it*, and you
begin writing and talking about it, trying to strangle it,
that little bit, to circle it with words hooked together so
tight and fine that the little bit will choke on them and die.
But you realize that the little bit cannot be put into words.
So you try to fathom it in dreams, such as the one where
you are driving a car that is flying down a hillside out of
control, killing chickens, and your girlfriend is sitting be-

side you, gabbing and oblivious. You write down your dreams for years, believing they hold an important clue. Or you read about how Confucius, Jesus, Heraclitus, Buddha, Shmelke of Nikolsburg, Muhammad, or Rilke conquered or claimed the little bit with wisdom, and you believe that this wisdom, if grasped, will fill the space where the little bit lives. And while you read, or meditate on what you've read, you feel the little bit coming apart and you cry, and the salt seems to dissolve the wall behind which the little bit has been camping out. For a little while, you feel that you are a part of everything, but then the tears retreat and you get up to throw your soaked Kleenex away, and as you walk toward the bathroom, you notice how each object again retreats into its own specific space, then blurs into the same old shape in about two seconds flat, and the little bit—you hear it—chortles, *Ha!*

When I was working in suicide prevention, I once spoke to an incredibly fat man in my very small office. He came to see me because he wanted to die. He leaned forward over his massive belly and told me how he'd been dead once, during an operation for a problem related to his weight, and he had seen the famous light at the end of the tunnel, and it had been incredibly bright and alluring, the most wonderful thing he had ever felt. And then, wet-eyed, he leaned back and said he couldn't even describe it. Since that time, he said, he'd wanted to die, to return to the great light that welcomed all his weight and could lift him into itself as if he were a kid again. And every bit of me believed him, because of how he said it and because he was a car mechanic and never went to school and had never read *Life After Life.* And ever since I met him, I think of how the little bit that life holds back will, at least, be gloriously present in the vast beyond. I really like to believe that, don't you? I like to think of being absorbed by it, like the times you peered into your parents' bedroom through the slightly open door when you were scared by a bad dream, and they were both in bed reading and they smiled and invited you in between their warm bodies and said nice things. But now I can't really open that door for more than a few seconds at a time, and sometimes, though I don't want to, I think the bit about the bright light is really just a pretty illusion, like loving my first husband forever, and then so many bits of this and that intrude and I get really confused and don't know what I believe. That whole bit.

Linda Gregg

There Is a Sweetness in It

The sap rises in the maple each spring after
the squeeze and release, squeeze and release
of winter. The spirit rises up into the face
of a shepherd, light shining on his clothes
and legs, on his sheep, on the ground and on
the stranger standing nearby. Bodies, light,
sap, our language. The body and the spirit.
Would God put himself into the body of a man
if what he wanted was to escape from the body?
What if God wanted the tree to blossom simply
because it would be covered with purple flowers
without leaves as I remember seeing in Nicaragua?
The raised arms of a shepherd, the light
lighter at the horizon of black hills. Moonlight
falling passionately on the stranger passing
the roadside gravestone. God trying to get down
to squeeze him in the dark. God cannot stop.
God is there and always sees the black ball
the crescent moon is holding. Sees the old tree
bent over by the storm in a field of wheat
lit up like the ocean. His grip is suffering,
revelation is the release. The sap rises up
in man and beasts, and in all things vegetable.
Plants and animals do it even better, kneeling
or celebrating or shining more immediately
than men do. But God loves us more, because

314

of the dread and seeking we contain. He loves
our lostness because it is by loneliness
and sacrifice, our body and soul together, that
the thing God is can exist. We are the stone
that is sacred. The way we make love with each
other is the collision that makes His face shine.
Makes the sap rise. God squeezes and relents
like winter ending, and the sap rising.

SPIRIT BREAKS
INTO SONG

*Herein dwells the still small voice to which my
spiritual self is attuned.*

—MARY McLEOD BETHUNE

Janice Mirikitani

Tongues Afire

*Upon hearing Dr. Maya Angelou,
who moves us to remember*

You,
Your face like yellow roses,
you, honey colored,
nappy haired, curly, straight haired,
cropped, shaved, crimped, braided,
you remember the way women
walked in Dakar with baskets
on their heads, graceful
like palm trees swaying over
golden beaches.
You, earth red colored faces, comforting
as shade,
you, brown and electric,
boneblack as the sands of Kona,
living on the cheeks of craters,
you remember the heat of creation.
You, brilliant in red veils
from Bengal
even with lips blue from poison
indigo fields, plantations of death,
you remember rebellion, burning the slave holds.
You with long black thighs,
marching the roads of Selma,
opening entrance to buses and schoolrooms,

facing racism's gnashing teeth,
you remember to laugh.
     You with faces of white gardenias,
remember the maimed but independent women
whose hands, freed from knitting needles
and coat hangers,
kindle the pathways of choice.
     Our words like open wings
soar in spite of the pall of poverty,
the despair of shelters where lightbulbs
are missing, dim rooms of broken mirrors,
I look at you and see my possibilities
in your beautiful faces.
          We hold ourselves like candles.
          Whispers of light gather.
          Suddenly, we are blazing
          with tongues afire.

Flor Fernandez

Carmen

Carmen was our Afro-Cuban nanny. Her ancestors were slaves brought by the Spaniards to Cuba from Africa around 1800 to work on their sugar plantations and mills. Carmen lived with my grandparents for many years. I was told by my Grandfather José that when Carmen was young, maybe nineteen, she appeared one day at their door looking for work. My Grandmother Petra, who didn't believe in having maids, was hesitant at first to take the stranger into the family.

"*Señora*," Carmen said, with eyes that were pleading, "I have been knocking on doors all day long, and no one seems to need the working hands of this *negra*. Please give me a chance, I promise you'll be happy with my work."

"Look," Grandmother said, showing Carmen her strong and rough hands from her hard work in the house and the farm, "I have worked the land, I have cooked and taken care of all my children and husband without ever needing any maids in this house. My husband José thinks I'm a stubborn woman for not wanting any help, but I come from a place where my own mother raised all of us kids, all on her own and—"

"*Señora*," Carmen interrupted, "you have a good heart. You are not like the other rich ladies in town. You work like a man in the fields and like a *negra*, at home with your children."

"How do you know that?" Grandmother asked, some-

321

what perplexed by this young woman's knowledge of her life.

"This is a small town. People talk and they say what they see and that's what they say about you, *Señora* Petra," Carmen said, lowering her eyes, a little embarrassed by her disclosure. "Besides, *Señora*, your hands are just like the hands of my mother," Carmen said, very wisely stealing my grandmother's heart.

Carmen stayed with my grandparents, helping them with the chores around the house. She was an excellent cook who delighted the family with special recipes such as her *congri*, black beans and rice cooked in coconut milk, or her famous *ropa vieja*, shredded beef in a mild sauce of tomatoes, green peppers, garlic, onions, and other ingredients that Carmen never revealed to anyone, not even to Grandmother Petra. She became best friends with my mother, who was just a couple of years younger than her. When my mother married and I was born, Carmen moved into our household and became part of my family. She helped my mother take care of me, and later my brother.

My memories of Carmen are many. As a young child I remember her putting me to sleep with her ancient, sweet, and loving lullabies, *arru ru mi niña, arru ru mi amor duermete pedazo de mi corazón*, while she held me in her arms, close to her voluptuous, dark goddess body. It was like being embraced by the ocean, feeling the warm waves of love and tenderness from her skin on my tiny, fragile body.

"*Niña*," she used to say, "you better go to sleep now, because if you don't the moon is going to be upset, and she is not going to come around tomorrow night with her silver rays. It will be very, very dark."

I remember going to sleep and thinking about the moon and her powers. Yes, I thought of the moon as a woman. During the hot nights of the summer, Carmen used to tell my brother and me stories about the slaves that worked so hard on the sugar plantations, and how they kept themselves happy by drumming and singing at night. She also told us scary stories about ghosts and spirits that haunted old Spanish houses in the town where I grew up, and how when people go inside these houses they heard voices and sounds and they saw things being moved around by invisible hands.

"You are not supposed to disturb those spirits. People that go inside those houses end up suffering illness and terrible accidents," she said to us every time she told us the stories. "Like the man who went inside one of the houses, looking for old money buried in the ground. He found an old ceramic jar with many gold coins. He took them and a few months later he became very ill and the doctor in town was never able to diagnose his problem. He lost lots of weight and his skin turned yellow like the gold coins. He died slowly in great misery and pain. He died of ghost illness."

Carmen was very well known in our town for her healing powers and her capacity to be a medium. She was able to diagnose illnesses and prescribe herbs and remedies for those that sought her help. She was a *curandera*, or healer. Carmen had a special room in the back of our house where she practiced her ancient African Yoruba religion and medicine. I used to love going into Carmen's room when she was away, and exploring all the different magical plants that she kept for her practice. In one corner was an altar with her favorite saints—Saint Lazarus and Saint Barbara. For Saint Lazarus, she kept offerings of a large Cuban cigar and a little glass containing the best Cuban rum. For Saint Barbara, she kept a candle and a red apple. Every time I visited this sanctuary I felt an aura of protection and magic, as well as mystery, and sometimes I felt fear of the unknown powers Carmen professed to have.

My first experience with Carmen's practice as a medium was when I was seven years old. A woman from our neighborhood, Francisca, came to visit Carmen one morning. She had a look of worry on her face, and she was very pale and ill-looking to me. She was also coughing nonstop.

My brother and I were playing on the patio, near the water fountain across from Carmen's place, and I could see Francisca and Carmen engaged in what appeared to be a very secret conversation that immediately captured my attention. I heard Carmen say something like "The spirits will help us find out." That was more than enough for me to leave my game of army soldiers to figure out what was going on between the two women. Victor was disappointed and wanted to hide with me, but I sent him away with the promise that I would play with him later.

"The spirits," I said to myself, and quickly proceeded to a spot close to the window on the opposite side of the wall where Carmen had her altar. From my hideout behind the gardenia tree I could see inside. I was careful not to make any noise. My heart was beating very fast in anticipation and in fear that Carmen could see me. She had warned me many times not to go around this area when she was doing her healing work with friends or other people, but this time my curiosity was stronger than my fear. I wanted to find out once and for all what she was doing in there with the so-called "spirits."

I could see Carmen seated in front of the altar, and Francisca seated next to her. Carmen took one of the cigars from the altar and, after lighting it, proceeded to puff smoke everywhere around the room and over Francisca. Then she sat across from Francisca, and closing her eyes, softly sang words I couldn't understand—they were from another language. Soon Carmen began to sing louder and call out names and her face began to be transformed, as well as her voice. She looked and sounded angry—her frowning forehead, and mouth twisted with lips firmly pressed against each other. She got up from her chair and began to move around the room, again puffing on her big cigar and blowing smoke around, especially over Francisca. I couldn't figure out what was going on. I couldn't recognize any of the words. Carmen's voice became softer at this point, as she passed her dark hands over Francisca's body without touching her skin. It was as if she were cleansing something in the air and pulling some invisible thing from the woman's body.

At this point, Carmen's body started shaking and her words grew unintelligible. Words turned into deep sounds, like the roar of some wild beast. Carmen was sweating. She dropped to the floor, her body shaking all over.

At the same moment that Carmen fell, Francisca began to cry intensely, almost hysterically.

"Oh my God!" I whispered to myself, and I thought, What should I do, should I call my mother and get help? I was ready to run to the house when I heard a voice inside myself saying, "Stop and be quiet." I immediately began to feel calm, very calm and peaceful. It was as if a warm current of energy were moving like a wave from the bottom of my spine all the way to the top of my head. Almost as if Carmen's big arms were holding me and rocking me to sleep. At that moment I realized that all the time I had been there by the window, Carmen knew it. She knew it! Why didn't she send me away like other times? Having no answer, I stood there with my eyes fixed on the two women inside the room. Now things were quiet, Francisca was no longer crying or screaming. She was calmly seated in her chair, and Carmen was getting up from the floor with a soft smile on her dark, round face. When Carmen was up on her feet, the two women looked at each other, and then embraced in silence for a few seconds.

"*¿Dime Francisca, como te sientes?*" asked Carmen, looking into the eyes of her friend.

"Ay, *negra*, it was hard. I thought that I was going to die, but now I feel better, as if the whole world has been lifted from my shoulders," said Francisca, taking Carmen's hands into her own.

Carmen went to the altar and quietly picked some of the dry herbs she had placed inside a clay pot and gave some in a little bundle to Francisca with instructions on how to prepare tea with it. "*Mira*, Francisca, these are very healing herbs for your problem. Make a tea and drink it in the morning and at night before going to bed, and come back and see me in a couple of days."

Francisca thanked Carmen and left the room. I could see that she was no longer pale and she was moving more energetically than when she arrived. Then I saw Carmen coming toward my window. She stood there on the other side of the wall with her hands resting on her wide hips, looking right out at me. For a second I thought I was going to faint from fear. I was expecting the worst.

"Teresa," Carmen called me, "come inside, quick."

I thought about running away, but I knew I would have to face her sooner or later. As I walked slowly to the door, I saw that Victor was still gone, so it was just me and Carmen. I could feel my legs shaking and my heart racing faster and faster with every step I took.

"Teresa, what were you doing spying on this *negra* from that window?"

"I'm sorry, Carmen," I said in a very low voice. "I'll never do it again, I promise. I was just trying—" And before I could finish Carmen interrupted me.

"You are just a very curious child," she said, smiling. I was surprised she wasn't angry with me. "Come sit down, child."

"Aren't you mad at me, Carmen?"

"No, I am not, but I want to warn you that if I ever catch you again spying on me I will have to tell your mama, so she can decide how to punish you."

"No, please Carmen, don't tell Mami," I begged, knowing already she was not going to do anything. Carmen adored me and she had a heart the size of Cuba.

"*Mira*, Teresa, I want to say something to you. What you saw today is nothing to play with. These things I do are very sacred. You never want to upset the spirits that come to help me do my work with people. They don't like to be disturbed or annoyed in any way," Carmen said seriously, without taking her dark eyes off me.

"What would happen if they got upset? Who are they anyway?"

"They will come to your room at night and pull your toes when you're asleep. They will hide your toys and play tricks on you."

"Who are these spirits, Carmen?"

"They are ancient ones who have already passed on into the realm of the dead. They are good spirits who continue helping us on this earth when, and only when, we need them."

"What was happening to you when you had your eyes closed and you were talking some strange language and making scary sounds?"

Carmen shifted in her chair, as if she was beginning to get impatient with my questions. "Teresa, when I close my eyes in front of my altar, it is like when you white people go to church and pray to your favorite saints. I'm asking the spirits for help. They come and talk to me."

"How do they talk to you?"

"Just imagine my body being like a drum or a guitar. When they come, they play with my vocal cords, making the sounds I need to hear, or sometimes they even talk to the person I'm helping, like in the case of Francisca. That is how they communicate with me."

"How do you know when the spirits come?"

"You want to know everything, don't you?" Carmen said, smiling at me and patting me on the head. "Most of the time it's just a feeling. When they enter the room, I feel like a cool breeze is coming from the ocean. Other times, the vibrations of their essence are so strong that my body shakes. Occasionally, I can see their image. They may take the human form they had before they died."

Carmen learned much of what she knew from both her mother and her grandmother, who learned from their own people, *Africanos*, who brought to Cuba their spirituality and religion.

"My people," Carmen said, "were strong and wise.

They found ways to disguise their spirits or Yoruba deities by giving them names from the Catholic Church. That way, they were able to continue practicing their rituals."

I thought about the way Cubans call the name of Saint Barbara after seeing lightning in the sky during a storm. She is Shango, the main *orisha* of fire, lightning, and thunder. Carmen taught me about other saints and corresponding *orishas* such as: Oshun, equivalent to La Virgen de la Caridad del Cobre; Yemaya, to the Lady of Regla; Babalue, to our healing Saint Lazarus.

A few days after my experience with Carmen in her healing room, she invited me to go to a *Bembe* with her. A day before the *Bembe*, Carmen called me into the kitchen, where she was peeling plantains to make *tachinos* for lunch. The plantains are sliced, fried in hot oil till soft, then allowed to cool down so they can be pressed in between brown paper to form a kind of flat, round medallion shape, and then are thrown back in the frying pan until golden brown. The plantains are crunchy with somewhat of a sweet taste. Cubans eat *tachinos* plain or with black beans and rice.

Carmen was, as usual, having a good time by herself, singing along with the songs on the radio and dancing around as she picked up pots and pans from the cabinets. Carmen's hips were like ocean waves coming and going, or like the palm trees swaying to the gentle wind with softness and beauty.

"Sit down, *niña*," Carmen said as she handed me a knife. "Help me peel these plantains while we talk." She turned off the radio and sat next to me. "First of all, I want you to promise me to behave. I don't want you to be wandering off and disappearing from my sight," she said as she poked me on my right shoulder with her index finger.

"I promise, Carmen."

"This *Bembe* is to celebrate one of Rufino's children's birthday, his *santo*. What you're going to see is people drumming and dancing for the saints or *orishas*. I'm telling you this now, so you won't be asking all kinds of questions in the middle of everything." She paused and got up to check the rice she was cooking on the stove.

"Now let me tell you about the drums. These drums are used to call the *orishas* to come down and to inhabit the dancers' bodies. In this dance something very special happens, the *orishas* inside us come out to dance and a union of the human and the Divine takes place. This brings healing for the group." Carmen paused. She looked at me straight in the eye and proceeded in a very solemn tone. "You must not talk to anyone about this *Bembe*. The CDR has given Rufino permission to have a simple birthday celebration. Nothing about a *Bembe*, so you better seal your mouth, *niña*, otherwise we all end up behind bars."

"Why, Carmen? What's wrong with having a *Bembe*?" I asked.

"*Mira mija.* That *barbudo* doesn't want any kind of religion in this country," she said, referring to Fidel Castro and to his nasty beard. "*Bembe* is part of the Afro-Cuban religion. *Ese desgraciado*, he has declared," Carmen said slowly, emphasizing the word, "that religion causes anti-revolutionary attitudes among the people. So we are back to the times of slavery. Once more in the history of this country, we have to keep our deities well disguised."

I was very excited when Saturday finally arrived and Carmen and I walked down the street toward the outskirts of town. Rufino and his family lived in a modest white brick house, surrounded by palm, orange, avocado, lemon, and plantain trees. There was an atmosphere of celebration in the house. Rufino and his wife Caridad greeted us at the door. Several friends of Carmen had already arrived and were talking about the *fiesta* and expressing their hope and desire that the *orishas* would descend, and that the *milicianos* would stay away from that part of town.

Rufino invited everybody onto the patio, where some drummers were already tuning their drums. I was fascinated by the beauty of these drums, their differences in sizes and shapes and the smoothness of the wood and the skins. I was wishing deep inside that I could play them. Carmen said, reading my mind, "These drums are very special. It takes many years of training to play them. Each drum has a function. See that big drum there? That's the mother drum."

I walked to the mother drum, softly touching the stretched hide with my hands.

"Mother drum," Carmen continued, "does all the talking while the other, smaller drums keep the basic rhythms."

The drummer sitting behind the mother drum, a toothless black man with white hair, maybe fifty years old, smiled at me. "I'll let you play later," he said, and made a signal to the other two men. Carmen pulled me away from the drums to another side of the patio.

Soon, just as she said, the mother drum began to talk, followed by the other two drums, penetrating and loud. Carmen lowered her mouth to my ear and whispered, "The drums are asking Elegua to open the path for us. Elegua is the messenger, the Lord of the Roads, the gatekeeper. It is important to call Elegua first, otherwise he may get upset and not open the doors to the *orishas*."

The drums continued playing, calling the different *orishas* with changing rhythms, or toques, according to the saint being called. In the midst of all the pounding sounds and loud voices, Carmen tried hard to let me know what was going on.

"Now they're calling Ogun, the warrior of iron, the hunter," and she continued naming each one of them for me as the drums changed. "Obatala, the *orisha* of calm and clarity; Oshun, the goddess of the rivers; Babalue, Saint Lazarus the healer; Yemaya, the goddess of the sea."

People were moving their feet, hips, and shoulders rhythmically. Finally, Shango, the king of thunder, was called and some of the participants started to dance frenetically, as if they had been struck by lightning. They were jerking their bodies and throwing their arms into the air. Some were jumping and others were rolling on the ground. Rufino was shaking a rattle and chanting in a deep voice words I didn't understand. Carmen explained to me that he was greeting the *orishas* in the ancient Yoruba language. Several members of the crowd joined him. By then, the group of dancers were very excited and deeply involved in their dances, which are supposed to be an impersonation of the *orishas*.

An older black man moved across the patio as Ogun, pretending to be hunting in the forest. Next to him, Oshun moved softly in a sensuous dance of love. By her side was Yemaya, the *orisha* of the sea, with undulating hips that were inviting and provocative. I was fascinated by Yemaya's movements. I wanted to go and dance with her. I asked Carmen if I could and she said it was okay, so I moved shyly into the crowd. At first, I was very conscious of the way I was dancing, but slowly all my fears and self-awareness disappeared and I found myself right next to Yemaya and Oshun.

The more I danced the more I felt possessed by a deep wave of energy carrying me to a place in my imagination, somewhere by the ocean. My body was floating in the clear, warm waters of the Caribbean. There was no fear at all. The sea was like a safe womb, where I could relax and move effortlessly. "I am water, I am water," I heard my voice repeating. I'm a big wave crushing the shore in the winter, I thought. I am the calm surf caressing the coastline in the summer. In my belly, all kinds of colorful tropical fish were swimming and marine plants were growing.

In the midst of all the drums, I heard the voice of Yemaya singing to me, and she was rocking me in her watery arms. She was so beautiful in her white and blue cotton dress decorated with shells. Yemaya was singing ancient songs in the same Yoruba language Rufino had spoken earlier. I imagined Yemaya dancing in the waters with her body, radiating a rainbow of colors. She was dancing in the waters and laughing. I heard her say to me: "It is not magic! It is dancing with life, it is living . . . knowing death, it is walking the path of a woman." She smiled at me, and then continued. "Soon, you'll be a woman and you must

learn the ways of the waters.'' She paused. I saw her pulling out one of the shells from her dress, a tiny conch shell
that she handed to me.

"I'll tell you a story,'' she said. "Once there was a
woman who forgot her path. She got tangled in the old
pain of so many years and of so many generations. The
woman became old and her face filled with wrinkles. She
went to sit by the ocean, where she told her story over and
over, but no one listened. With time, tiredness occupied the
woman's mind and heart and her dark hair turned to salt
and her lips were sealed by the cold wind of the winter.

"Then . . . one day, a song was heard coming from the
sea. People ran to the shore trying to find who was playing
the music. To their surprise, a beautiful woman emerged
from the water. She was young, with dark long hair and
clear eyes. Her wet skin was brown like the earth and she
wore a dress made from silky silver threads from the
moon. The woman spoke to the people: 'I bring new
dreams and songs, I bring new dreams and songs . . .' "

The woman's voice was echoing in my mind when I
finally opened my eyes. I found myself in a corner of the
patio, still dancing to the beat of the drums. There were
people all around me moving and singing to the *orishas*. I
was confused by my experience with Yemaya. Did I fall
asleep? What happened? All I could remember was wanting to dance and then . . . Nothing made sense. I ran away
from the crowd and went inside the house. There by the
altar was Carmen lighting some tall white and blue candles. My first impulse was to go and talk to her, but then,
as I looked into the flame of the candle, I saw Yemaya dancing in the waters again. She said, "This is between you and
me. It is your dream and not Carmen's."

As Carmen and I walked home that evening, we were
quiet. I could feel that somehow Carmen knew about my
experience, but she also knew how important it was for
her not to ask me any questions. I figured it was going to
take me a very long time, if ever, to understand my encounter with Yemaya.

Chitra Banerjee Divakaruni

The Garba

The nine sacred nights of Navaratra
we dance the *garba*. Light glances
off the smooth wood floor of the gym
festooned with mango leaves
flown in from Florida. The drummers
have begun, and the old women
singing of Krishna and the milkmaids.
Their high keening is an electric net
pulling us in, girls who have never seen

the old land. This October night
we have shed our jeans
for long red skirts, pulled back
permed hair in plaits, stripped off
nail polish and mascara, and pressed
henna onto hands, kohl
under the eyes. Our hips
move like water to the drums.
Thin as hibiscus petals, our skirts
swirl up as we swing and turn.
We ignore the men,

creaseless in bone-white kurtas.
In the bleachers, they smile behind their hands.
Whisper. Our anklets shine
in the black light from their eyes.

Soon they will join us in the *Dandia* dance.
The curve and incline, the slow arc
of the painted sticks meeting red on black
above our upraised arms. But for now
the women dance alone,
a string of red anemones
flung forward and back
by an unseen tide. The old ones sing
of the ten-armed goddess.
The drums pound faster
in our belly. Our feet glide
on smooth wood, our arms
are darts of light. Hair, silver-braided,
lashes the air like lightning.
The whirling is a red wind
around our thighs. Dance-sweat
burns sweet on our lips.
We clap hot palms like thunder. And

the mango branches grow into trees.
Under our flashing feet,
the floor is packed black soil.
Damp faces gleam and flicker in torchlight.
The smell of harvest hay
is thick and narcotic
in our throat. We spin and spin
back to the villages of our mothers' mothers.
We leave behind

the men, a white blur,
like moonlight on empty *bajra* fields
seen from a speeding train.

Agate Nesaule

The Reciters

Once upon a time in Latvia, all women knew how to recite. As girls we memorized lullabies, folk songs, poems, and hymns. Safe in our own beds, warm under goose-down quilts and embroidered linen sheets, we whispered lines to ourselves as we drifted off to sleep. On Christmas Eve, standing in front of trees ablaze with real candles, we swayed back and forth to emphasize the rhythm of verses we had learned. If we recited correctly and loudly enough, we would be given creamy sweets wrapped in tasseled gold paper instead of bundles of switches reserved for bad children. During the brief white nights of summer, when along with visiting cousins we were allowed to sleep in fragrant hay in barns, we shouted verses we believed were uproariously funny, until gentle adult voices silenced us. On marketing days, in front of city shops or village stores, we turned our backs on boys who grinningly teased us. Holding hands, looking pleased with ourselves, reciting in unison, we skipped away.

Es meitia kā rozīte
Kā sarkana zemenīte,
Pienu ēdu, pienu dzēru,
Pienā muti nomazgāju.

I am a little girl like a little rose,
Like a red strawberry.

335

I eat milk, I drink milk,
And I bathe myself in milk.

Our feet, clad in fine white stockings and red shoes with
thin straps, moved rhythmically together. Our chants
might turn imperceptibly into song. We knew many melo-
dies too, of course, but above all we knew the words.

Women sang everywhere, in kitchens kneading rye
bread or slicing apples, in dairies skimming cream or
churning butter, in fields, raking hay or gathering grain.
Alone in parlors lit by kerosene lamps or newly installed
electric lights, on dark verandas scented by lilacs, on lonely
paths leading through forests, women sang to themselves.
Young women walked from one country church to another to look at the new ministers said to be handsome
and single, and then, having paid little attention to their
sermons, they walked home again, arms linked, laughing
and singing. Young men, dressed in dark suits and white
shirts, called out to them as they passed in polished wag-
ons pulled by lovingly groomed horses. On St. John's Eve
in midsummer, from hill to hill ablaze with bonfires,
women and men sang, first in competition, then in harmony. Old women sang together in churches, alone while
tending gardens and working at looms.

But always in addition to singing, women recited. On
postcards with photos of birches or roses, which women
sent for birthdays and namedays, they wrote lines they
had memorized. They inscribed poems in books given as a
school prize, in leather-bound albums presented to newly-
weds, on notes accompanying flowers for sick friends.
Women gave public speeches less often than men, but like
them they quoted the words of Latvian poets on ceremonial and political occasions.

Lines recited spontaneously were even more meaningful. So a woman might quote from a play by major Latvian
writer Aspazija to a friend passionately in love; she might
murmur a lyric about suffering and loss by the same poet

as she comforted her friend later. Women included stanzas from poems in hastily written letters to lovers and husbands away, to mothers welcoming new life, to old people marking the passing of years. That is how it was, once upon a time.

As the independence of Latvia was increasingly threatened by Nazis and Soviets both, lines from poems accompanied flowers laid anxiously at the foot of the Monument to Freedom in the center of Riga. Later, as women prayed to be saved from exile and war, they recited.

The reciting stopped abruptly in 1940, the Year of Terror under Russian occupation, when thousands of Latvians were imprisoned or deported to Siberia. Nazi armies overran Latvia the following year, and Soviet armies took forcible possession again in 1945. For almost half a century, Latvian language was discouraged and Latvian literature neglected. Girls and women who remained in their own country were forced to speak Russian. Those in exile learned other languages. Only fifty-two percent of the inhabitants of Latvia are now Latvians.

I was six when my family fled Latvia on one of the last ships sailing for Germany. In a camp circled with barbed wire, threatened by Nazi guards barely restraining leashed dogs, we whispered fearfully to each other. Flags with swastikas flew overhead, and nightly bombings continued. The following spring we were forced to watch as occupying Russian soldiers beat a retarded boy, executed a man, raped women without children. Dazed and afraid, we remained silent for a long time.

But as hunger turned into starvation, we had to speak. My mother taught me to recite in Russian. She washed my face, pinned an incongruously cheerful wreath of blue bachelor's buttons and red clover above my blond braids, and sent me away from the German village. Holding an empty bowl in my hands, I stood behind a barbed wire

fence, watching soldiers drinking, shouting, and stum-
bling. I waited for the briefest pause and then began, *"Petushok . . . petushok. . . ."*

I did not know the meaning of the Russian children's
rhymes I had learned by rote. I had to make the soldiers
notice me, so I used all my willpower to speak loudly and
distinctly. My legs and arms trembled, but my voice did
not fail. Usually the soldiers ignored the hungry children
behind the fence, they turned away from their comrades
and toward us only to vomit or urinate. Or they tried to
drive us off with furious gestures.

But sometimes a soldier would hear me and motion to
the others to listen. Surprised at me mouthing Russian
words, the soldiers laughed delightedly, as they might at a
goose singing or a dog dancing. They flung a chunk of
heavy dark rye bread or a piece of raw liver into my bowl.

Walking back to the village, I felt the envy and anger of
the other children scorching my back. I tried not to think,
I recited instead. Over and over again, I whispered the
meaningless sounds. I had to remember them for whatever
came next. I set the bowl on the ground in front of my
mother, turned away from her, ran to a tree, pressed
against it, prayed to grow into it, failed.

Later, in Displaced Persons camps in Germany, I recited
in Latvian for the last time. Without books or supplies,
Latvians started makeshift schools in every camp. Ac-
tresses, ministers, writers, historians, all lovers of words
recalled lines they knew and taught them to us. Every
week we had to recite "with appropriate feeling" a poem in
front of the whole class. We learned lines about the white
birches, fragrant grasses, and misty blue hills of Latvia.
We declaimed defiant speeches of ancient heroes who died
defending Latvia against foreign invaders. We chanted
hundreds of *dainas*, folk songs about brave girls and proud
women, and about the healing powers of nature and work.
Teachers repeatedly quoted a poem which included the line
"The riches of the heart cannot be destroyed." They said it

meant that we should study hard, because only our
knowledge could never be taken from us. We might lose
our family members, our country, and our possessions,
but the riches of the heart would remain ours.

Reciting in Latvian ended for me when I left the camps
in Germany for the United States. I learned English, won
scholarships, completed degrees at universities, taught
British poems to American students. I married an American and moved to a small town in the Midwest, away from
my mother, away from communities of exiled Latvians.
Slowly, through disuse, I forgot most of the Latvian poems
I knew.

But life, while harsh, is also miraculous. In 1991 Latvia
declared independence from the Soviet Union and was recognized as a sovereign nation. Although the shores of the
Baltic Sea are polluted, people now walk more freely on its
white sands and pine-bordered paths. They may even find
amber there, though they are cautious about picking it up.
Some of the lovely translucent yellow pieces are not crys-
tallized pine resin at all, but explosives carelessly disposed
of by Soviet military troops, many of whom are still sta-
tioned there.

I returned to Latvia last summer, after an exile of forty-
seven years. I eagerly looked forward to meeting relatives,
but of my father's family of six brothers and sisters, only
one of my cousins survived. After several painful encounters, I was forced to recognize that our relationship could
never be reestablished. Our lives had been too different, our
experiences too separate and painful.

Nor could the house where I had lived until I was six
give me the connection that I longed for. The large, comfortable country parsonage was now a run-down collective farm, so changed that I passed it three times without
recognizing it. Gone were the wide verandas and the sil-
very thatched roof, gone the apple trees, lilacs, and mock
orange, gone the flower beds filled with sweet william, iris,

and lilies. Even the pond, where storks used to wade, was dry.

Standing alone in the desolate rutted yard, I prayed not to give in to bitterness. If only I could stay open to experience, something else might happen. I had to believe that it would. I did not know yet that a stranger, an old woman reciting, would give me what I needed, and more.

Most people in Latvia have excruciatingly painful stories. They seize a visitor from the outside world by the hand, insist upon attention, prevent departure. They speak about the grim Soviet occupation, of Latvians being subjected to political repression and economic hardship, of being treated as second-class citizens in their own country, of being denied access to education and advancement. Latvians were imprisoned and deported, many died in Siberia, some committed suicide upon returning, others remain physically and psychologically damaged. In spite of the new independence, daily life in Latvia is still unbelievably harsh.

Listening to these recitations, I was rocked by conflicting emotions: sympathy for the people, anger at the devastation of the land, desire to help, guilt that I could never do enough. I wavered between high energy and absolute exhaustion. Desiring connection, I nevertheless found myself longing to be alone.

At an outdoor concert of Latvian folk songs, I allowed my mind to wander from a speaker who said that only in song did the spirit of Latvia still live undamaged. In January 1991, when Soviet Black Berets had killed five unarmed men, among them two prominent young filmmakers, Latvians had not turned to violence, but to singing. Indoors and out, in churches and concert halls, on street corners in Riga and Liepaja, Latvians sang in defiance of Soviet authorities. Journalists had been right in dubbing the independence movements in Latvia the Singing Revolution.

Too depleted to follow the rest of the speech, I watched the choirs arriving instead. Dressed in colorful costumes from various districts of Latvia, young men and old were lining up to sing. Women carried bunches of flowers, girls with wreaths of flowers in their hair walked by with arms linked. The fragrance of pines intensified as massed rain clouds parted for the late afternoon sun. Finally the singing began.

At first I strained to hear every word of songs I had known once. I tried to remember them. I had to repossess them. But gradually I realized there were too many songs completely unfamiliar to me, which had been composed during my long separation from Latvia. Try as I might, I inevitably failed to make out the words. Feeling separate from all the people and the common emotions the songs evoked, I closed my eyes.

When I looked again, my focus had shifted. The choirs had receded into the background, but individual people were now much more distinct. On the steps in front of a women's choir was a seven-year-old girl. She was sitting very still, looking past the audience to the line of birches across an open meadow. Her blue eyes had that clear, almost otherworldly gaze that one sometimes sees in children at moments when they feel absolutely secure. She made no movement to brush away a strand of blond hair escaping from her braids beneath a small wreath of red clover. Her hands rested lightly in her lap, over a long string of tiny, very dark amber beads. She wore an embroidered white linen blouse and a full red wool skirt, also embroidered. Her long legs and sturdy feet, clad in white thin stockings and highly polished shoes, were planted firmly on the ground.

A woman bent down to whisper to her, another woman brushed away the escaping tendril of her hair, and the little girl stood up. She was ready to sing. Complete in herself, she was also an essential part of the choir. Totally self-possessed, she was cherished and supported by the circle of women around her.

I felt an envy so surprising and so sharp I could hardly breathe. Holding onto myself, rocking silently back and forth, I concentrated on regulating my breathing until the pain began to subside. Shame followed quickly. How could I, a middle-aged, economically secure, politically privileged, well dressed and well fed university professor from America envy this little girl in Latvia? Hadn't I been paying attention as people told me repeatedly of extreme poverty, humiliation, hopelessness? Didn't I know the endless contriving and bribing and patching every mother had to do to send her child out fully clothed in the morning?

I forced myself to imagine the effort this mother had expended finding the string of amber beads, standing in line for a piece of unbleached linen to sew her daughter's blouse, collecting plants to make dye, saving and bartering for the polished black shoes. I could not know every detail, but I was touched nevertheless by the immense devotion and determination that must have gone into raising and clothing this little girl, who now looked as natural as a small berry.

Yet still I envied her. She was exactly where she belonged, in her own country, with people she had known all her life, singing in her own language. She knew all the words, and she could sing together with others. With courage and almost bravado the women were singing now:

> *Bēda mana liela bēda*
> *Es par bēdu nebēdāju*
> *Liku bēdu zem akmena*
> *Pāri gāju dziedādama*
>
> I had a great sorrow,
> But I didn't dwell on it
> I put it under a stone
> I stepped over it singing

Perhaps if one were so connected to other people and to the land, one could indeed put sorrow under a stone. But I was sentimentalizing the experience of the girls and women singing. I must stop feeling sorry for myself as well.

I tried to imagine the little girl making her way home to a shabby apartment or a run-down collective farm. But I could only see her walking on familiar roads past pine woods and banks of wild strawberries. She was holding her mother's hand and perhaps her aunt's. Tired but satisfied with the events of the day, they were talking softly together. The two women listened attentively as the girl recited a poem she had memorized for school, then lapsed into silence. But soon one of them began to hum, the others joined in. They seemed vulnerable now in the dusk, and I felt a tender protectiveness toward them. I wished fervently for their good fortune, and I regretted my envy once more. But something hard and rough, like a stone shard, remained in my heart.

Just outside the city of Riga lies Brīvdabas Muzējs, a large outdoor museum of farm buildings, churches, and mills dating back to the sixteenth century. Established during the brief period of independence between the two world wars, the museum has been kept open by Soviet authorities, though it seems sparsely attended, at least on weekdays. Walking on the wooded paths from one cluster of buildings to another, one can almost forget one is in a museum. The effect is of roaming about in the countryside, going from farm to flourishing farm, stopping by the side of a lake, climbing a hill to a Lutheran church.

I was surrounded by blossoming trees, swaying flowers, and ripe berries, several of which I remembered vividly from my childhood but had never seen growing outside of Latvia. Here and there a museum worker dressed as a farmwife encouraged me and the few other visitors to taste

the currants, to smell the chamomile, to pluck a blue bell-
flower to press in a book for remembrance.

I accepted everything so generously offered, but my
spirits did not lift. For the past two weeks I had heard people speak constantly about the war and its grim aftermath,
and I had listened, sympathized, offered help. But not one
person had asked me what had happened to my family or
me during the war, no one was interested in hearing about
the struggle of beginning life in a foreign country, no one
believed me when I said not everyone in the United States
lived in luxury. Having fought against my own envy, I recognized it in others as they spoke of all Americans as mil-
lionaires, without any experience of hunger or fear, totally
incapable of imagining hardship. I felt completely depleted,
the stone grated my heart.

I closed behind me the wooden gate of an orchard by an
eighteenth-century farmhouse, walked up a flower-
bordered path, and entered a dim barn. At first I could see
only a shadowy wagon, a few rakes and other implements,
some empty bins. Letting my shoulders sag, I leaned
against a wall. I wished I could stay in the restful darkness
forever.

"Come," a woman's voice called out, "come with me.
You look like someone who needs to hear me reciting."

A sturdy, small person, no more than five feet tall,
grasped my hand and guided me firmly out into the sunlight, then into the dappled shade under a white birch. She
was much older than I had first judged her by her decisive
movements. Hundreds of lines marked her round, weathered face, dozens of long white hairs grew on her chin, her
pale blue eyes were merry and knowing. For a brief moment I was confused, the person before me seemed to be a
woman and a man both, and yet neither. But then I saw
the gray braids secured at the nape of her neck, the long
skirt with its finely embroidered border, the worn gray
shawl pinned with a small amber pin. Judged by such ex-
ternals, she was clearly a woman. But being certain of her

gender seemed less important than usual. I felt as if I, though fully awake, had suddenly fallen into a dream.

"Listen," she said, "this is the poem for you."

She let go of my hand, stepped onto a slight elevation, closed her eyes, and started reciting. All my doubts about her being a woman vanished: her voice was melodious and strong, in a word, womanly. She had chosen "Sauciens Tālē," "Call into the Distance," a long poem of eight elaborate stanzas. I suddenly remembered that I too had memorized it once, when I was ten, in a Displaced Persons camp in Germany. But that had been more than forty years ago, so that now I could only feel the absolute rightness of each line as she spoke it, without being able to produce the next one myself.

"Sauciens Tālē," was written by Fricis Bârda for the Latvians who were driven into exile in 1905. Directly addressing a wanderer who has lost his country and everything else, the poet speaks of the pain of separation and the anguish of exile. He urges the wanderer not to forget Latvia and promises a final homecoming. On that distant joyous day of new freedom, trumpets will sound, flags and blossoms will lie in snowdrifts on rooftops, but the wanderer will bring with him the pain of his long years of exile. He will question what he can accomplish in the ashes and ruins of his country, he will be uncertain whether he has the strength to do anything at all. But return he must. He can at least offer to Latvia his heart which has suffered so much.

The professor inside me began by noting the formal characteristics of the poem, classifying it as romantic, criticizing it as too nationalistic, filing away words and metaphors I was glad to relearn. But by the second or third stanza none of that mattered.

The old woman had *recognized* me, and she was speaking directly to me about my depletion and alienation. She understood that even though I was now living a comfortable life in the United States, it had been painful for me to

separate from family members, to leave home, to experience exile and war. She knew too that returning at the beginning of new independence was more complex than
simply joyous.

I felt tears rising to my eyes, then flowing down my
face. By the time she finished reciting, I was crying freely.
The hard stone in my heart seemed to be dissolving and
flowing away, taking with it the pain of exile as well. I was
known and totally accepted. She had welcomed me home.
I felt connected to every tree and cloud and blade of grass.

She took my hand and waited in silence until I had more
or less finished crying.

"Thank you for that," I said when I could finally speak.

"That was good," she patted my hand. "Crying is healing, like some herbs that grow here."

She stepped away from me again, dropped her arms to
her sides, lifted her face toward the sky, and recited three
brief poems about the beautiful trees, hills, and roadsides
of Latvia. These too were poems I had once known well.

The feeling of being in a dream, the sense that the odd
and unusual was unsurprising and even fitting, persisted.
As if to make certain that I really was awake, I drew myself
up straight and rubbed my eyes, but the strangeness did
not dissipate.

"This has meant the world to me," I said.

"I know," she nodded.

We stood looking at each other, not quite willing to part
yet. And then suddenly I thought of it, a question I could
ask, almost a test I could give her. It would bring this significant exchange to a close, and it would certainly return
me to the everyday, rational world.

"Tell me," I said, "do you happen to know a poem which
contains the line 'the riches of the heart cannot be destroyed'?" For the last three years I had been searching for
the poem that teachers quoted to us in Displaced Persons
camps. I wanted to include it in a book I was writing, but I
was no longer sure I had it right. I had not found the line in

a collection by Kārlis Skalbe, which I had gone to great trouble to locate. I was not certain now of the author or the title or even whether I was quoting the line accurately.

I had asked every Latvian I knew in the United States about it: my father, old teachers, and women and men more or less my contemporaries, who had also spent part of their childhood in camps. Everyone said it sounded familiar, a few volunteered their approval or disapproval of the sentiment expressed, but no one could identify it precisely.

"What were those words again?" the old woman asked.

"The riches of the heart cannot be destroyed."

"Oh, yes," she murmured, "oh yes, that's the last line in a poem 'For Friends' by Kārlis Skalbe. But it's a little different. 'The riches of the heart do not rust,' is how it goes."

And of course, I knew it was so as soon as she said it. The riches of the heart were safe. Not only could they not be destroyed by displacement and war as I had been taught, but they could also not perish through disuse.

> Es nezinu, kas vakar bija,
> Es nezinu, kas rītu būs,
> Tik ausīs šalc kā melodija:
> Sirds bagātība nesarūs.
>
> I do not know what was yesterday,
> I do not know what will be,
> I only hear as a melody,
> The riches of the heart don't rust.

The past and the present were uncertain, but the riches of the heart were real. She had completed the poem and my return to Latvia for me.

Like so much in Latvia, the old woman seemed enchanted. Yet for me and for other exiles returning to the countries of our childhood, looking for clues as to how to face our coming old age, the angle of vision determines magic. For the present, I hope to see clearly without sentimentality.

In the years of independence between the two world wars, Latvia was indeed full of women reciting in safety and comfort. But nostalgia and envy had blotted out my memory of other reciters.

When she was seven years old, the future poet Aspazija recited to an examining Lutheran minister. Patting her on the head, he sighed regretfully. "It's too bad that you aren't a boy," he said. "Great things could come of you, but you're only a girl." My mother, who taught school-girls from orphanages to recite, had been told essentially the same thing when she was sent to a teachers college instead of the university.

Once, when I was five or six, a thin, almost emaciated old woman dressed in gray came to the back door of the comfortable country parsonage. Her lips blue with cold, she stood out in the muddy yard, on a low, round stump, reciting the Twenty-third Psalm. From the unhurried, matter-of-fact way the housekeeper gave her a bowl of porridge and a *centims*, I could tell that it was not unusual for old women to come begging to supplement their rations at the poorhouse in the next village.

The old woman ate very quickly, handed back the empty bowl to our robust housekeeper, and kissed her hand in gratitude. Then she lifted her face toward the sky and sang "Nearer, My God, to Thee" in a sweet, quavering voice. The housekeeper sighed in exasperation and ladled another serving of porridge, a half a bowl this time. "No more reciting now," she said as she handed the food to the old woman, who looked ashamed.

Once upon a time in Latvia, all women and girls knew how to recite. Reciting united us, hurt and divided us, reciting could heal us. Once upon a time in Latvia, there were so many kinds of reciters.

Linda Hogan

The Grandmother Songs

The grandmothers were my tribal gods.
They were there
when I was born. Their songs
rose out of wet labor
and the woman smell of birth.

From a floating sleep
they made a shape around me,
a grandmother's embrace,
the shawl of family blood
that was their song for kinship.

There was a divining song
for finding the lost,
and a raining song
for the furrow and its seed,
one for the hoe
and the house it leaned against.

In those days, through song,
a woman could fly
to the mother of water
and fill her ladle
with cool springs of earth.

She could fly to the deer
and sing him down to the ground.

Song was the pathway where people met
and animals crossed.

Once, flying out of the false death of surgery,
I heard a grandmother singing for help.
She came close
as if down a road of screaming.
It was a song I never knew
lived inside the muscle
of this common life.

It was the terror grandmother.
I'd heard of her.
And when our fingers and voices met,
the song
of an older history came through
my mouth.

At death, they say
everything inside us opens,
mouth, heart, even the ear opens
and breath passes
through the memories
of loves and faces.
The embrace opens
and grandmothers pass,
wearing sunlight
and thin rain,
walking out of fire
as flame
and smoke
leaving the ashes.

That's when rain begins,
and when the mouth of the river sings,
water flows from it
back to the cellular sea

and along the way
earth sprouts and blooms, the grandmothers
keep following the creation
that opens before them
as they sing.

Deborah Shouse

A Kaddish by the Sea

The Rabbi calls me collect from Miami Beach. Grand-mother Bibble has died and I am the only member of the family with a listed phone number.

"Chloe, is it?" he asks, as if disbelieving that the grand-daughter of a Jewish woman bears such a name. I could tell him it was inspired by my mother's dream after read-ing Edgar Cayce. I could say my father thought the name sounded like a train splitting the Nebraska prairie. I could reveal that my lover Arthur believes the name suits my terse blondness and insightful wit. But the news of Bibble's death makes me feel like a newspaper thumped hard on an empty porch. I am silent.

"Services tomorrow at three," the Rabbi says, his voice a brusque New York. I want to protest, to cry out with a mournful sound. Instead, I tear off a fingernail and say, "I'll be there."

I hang up the phone and pick up my cold cup of pepper-mint tea. If Arthur were here, he would hold me tight against his crisp white shirt and murmur, "Everything's going to be all right." I spill my tea reaching for a tissue. An umbrella pierces my foot when I fumble in the closet for a suitcase. I open the suitcase on the unmade bed and remember that tomorrow I was going to spend the whole night in Arthur's arms. Tomorrow, Arthur's wife, three children and dogs are leaving town. All week I have imag-ined Arthur's leg heavy over mine in the night, his hand

curled under his chin, his mouth slack in dreams. Arthur
fades as I pack the purple sequined sweatshirt Bibble sent
me for Chanukah. I think about Bibble's raucous laugh
and champagne-colored hair, which my mother Madelyn
called "impossible." I think of the year Madelyn flew to
Sweden and shipped me to Bibble in Miami. Friday nights,
I sat in dark clothes on the woman's side of the shul. I liked
the secret language Bibble used to find her God. I imagined
God with a decoder, understanding Bibble's mutterings,
my mother's chantings, my father's rantings and even my
whisperings. Saturdays, I kept quiet in Bibble's unlit living
room while ladies clacked teacups and gossiped. I remember coming home from school and checking the lemon tree
by the front stoop. I remember Bibble staring off toward
China as I romped in the ocean. Bibble's hair frothed
around her head, like fancy wrapping. Her legs stood
strong and smooth, as mine do now.

When I think of Bibble, I see sandpipers on a deserted
beach. Running, reaching, farther and then farther. Death
has nothing to do with my grandmother.

I scrape a spot off my black suit and wonder if Bibble
was ready to die.

Last Purim, on my yearly visit, I rented beach chairs so
Bibble could see the ocean. One was a sturdy chair, for Bibble's back, the other a slooping striped sling. I arranged the
chairs on the beach and prayed no one would steal them
while I helped Bibble shuffle across the parking lot. The
shifting sand jumped into her thick stockings and
scratched at her ankles. I held her cane while she settled.
Then I opened the thermos of martinis, made extra dry, the
plastic champagne glasses and the sack of barbecue potato
chips. All the things Bibble thought made a perfect picnic.

"I've always wanted to celebrate Purim like this," Bibble said. "I've had enough of hamantaschen, but you know
what the Rabbi would say."

I closed my eyes, heard the soothing heal of salt waters,
and listened as Bibble described her battles with the Rabbi.

354 Deborah Shouse

"He's a rebel caught in an old man's tradition," she explained. "I tell him, when I die, I want my ashes to dance across this ocean. I am profaning the Lord, he warns, and pops a piece of gum into his mouth. Can you believe, talking God and chewing Juicy Fruit?"

Was she preparing for death, I wonder, as I stumble over a tennis shoe and answer the phone. I can tell by Arthur's voice he is in the bedroom of his father-in-law's house.

"Oh God, I'm sorry," Arthur says. His voice is low, like a prisoner making an illegal call.

"You can't go a day late, can you?" he asks. I know he is lying on his in-laws' white bedspread, plucking balls of thread. He has excused himself from a game of hearts to call a client. "I don't know when we'll have another chance like tomorrow night," he says.

I remind him my mother is somewhere in the Andes, charting the course of UFOs.

"What about your father?" Arthur speaks as if he is plucking coffee grounds out of the garbage.

My father, Franklin, drives the back roads of Nebraska, peddling King James.

"He didn't love Bibble," I almost shout, angry that Arthur can't sense my sorrow. Soon Arthur will sit down with his family and eat the roast beef dinner his father-in-law's third wife prepared.

"Come with me," I suddenly urge.

"I'll try." Quietly, so no one except possibly I can hear, Arthur murmurs, "Iloveyou," slurred like melted heartbeats, and he is gone.

Madelyn taught me about men who leave.

"A man who's unattached expects too much," Madelyn had explained years ago, as she packed for her trip to the Esalen Institute. She was going to discover inner harmony with my biology teacher, Roger, a man attached to a thick wife and seven children.

"You've got to protect yourself from demands," Madelyn advised, motioning me to carry her luggage to the car. While Madelyn drove to California, Franklin traveled his territory, drifting from Scripture to Scripture. I dreamed my way through high school, a motherless child, and called Bibble every night. She always answered on the first ring.

"I miss you, darling," she'd say.

"I don't know when I'll be able to see you," I told her. I didn't want anyone expecting too much from me.

Arthur is not at the airport the next morning. I walk backward as I board the plane, hoping to see him. But I only see impatient faces wearing business suits. They want to hurry to their seats, plug in headphones, open briefcases.

I am the only mourner on the plane. I want to tell someone about Bibble's death, I want someone to say, "I know you feel the loss."

So far, all I feel is the harsh hustle, the bright blare of tourists carrying red net sacks of oranges through the Miami airport.

My purse spills as I stand in the rental-car line. I'd like to sit on the dirty floor beside the crumpled tissues, cheap pens, idle pennies, until someone arrives to help. Madelyn should be here, I tell myself, although she never got along with Bibble. Franklin would hold forth his New Testament and proclaim Bibble a heretic.

As I drive toward Bibble's, I wonder what Arthur is doing. His life seems as far away as Bibble's death. I imagine Arthur living on a planet where I cannot breathe, where the life-forms are alien creatures with their own language. Why do I love such a man, I wonder, parking in front of Bibble's house. He expects so little—I hope for so much.

"You don't like yourself much, do you?" Bibble had said, brushing the sand from her legs. "Otherwise you would not hook up with a married man."

Deborah Shouse

I had stared at a child trying to climb on a float against the waves.

"I was like that once." Bibble handed me her empty glass and struggled to stand. "Then Madelyn called and said she was dumping you in a boarding school while she ran off to Findhorn. I knew you needed to be with me. That year with you saved me."

I tasted the salt spray. I never knew I was the atonement for Bibble's sins. I never imagined who she gave up for me. Is that where she learned about martinis, I wanted to ask. But her face closed, as though a wind blew all the feelings out to sea.

"This is where I want to be buried," she said, as I helped her toward the car. "Say a Kaddish for me, will you darling?"

I don't know the prayer for the dead, I think, as I walk up the weedy sidewalk to Bibble's house. I don't know the language Bibble used for God. An old lady opens the door. She hugs me and pinches my cheeks for health. Like I was nine. I expect Bibble to be sitting in the rocker, amazed I believed her joke.

A wizened man mourns in Bibble's rocking chair. Brittle women take turns comforting me. They remember when I was this high.

"You haven't changed, bubbaleh," one of them whispers. But I have changed. I am sadder, and I settle for less.

Two men, white jowled faces and sunk black clothes, sit on metal chairs in the corner of the room. One stares at me as if I should know him. Is he the one Bibble gave up for me, I wonder. Here among Bibble's last friends, the clacking of coffee cups, the soothing chant of old voices, I feel the loss.

The funeral is short, packed with Psalms. I can't believe Bibble is inside the plain wooden coffin. I wish I knew Hebrew, so the prayers could take root in me. I wanted to ask

Bibble, how do you make a resting place for God? I used to imagine God as one of the old ladies who sat Saturdays with Bibble. God would know all the good gossip and know when to listen and when to talk. Ever since I'd tasted Bibble's God, I wanted Him for my own.

"She wanted to be cremated," I tell the Rabbi when the service ends.

"It was an old argument between us," he says. "An intellectual game." He holds the gray hairs at the end of his beard. Underneath a thick mustache, his lip quivers.

"She wanted to be scattered across the ocean," I say. When he turns away, I tug on his solemn black coat.

An old lady rattles up and puts her arm around me.

"It's against God's law," she whispers, and leads me out of the room.

I return to Bibble's. People bring apple cakes, briskets, strudels, kugel. Bibble would have loved such a party, but to me it's a series of thank-you notes to a series of strangers.

Every face blurs. I recognize only the Rabbi, as he hovers at the table, selecting a slice of kugel, a strong cup of tea.

"She wanted to be cremated," I repeat. I stand before him, like an avenging angel.

"You don't understand," the Rabbi says wearily, stirring sugar into his tea with a thick finger. "It was a joke, like coloring her hair. Inside, she wanted what God wanted."

Women clutter around, clearing me away from the holy man. I don't know what to do. Madelyn would close her eyes and check the vibrations from her quartz crystal. Franklin would clutch his golden cross and raise a warning finger against hell.

"You must be exhausted," an older lady worries. She hands me a cup of tea. My bones are limp with sadness, my heart beats in an empty cave. I wonder what Bibble expected of me.

I rush to the Rabbi as he moves toward the door.

"She wanted to be scattered across the ocean." I speak loud and hard, as though I were trying to convince a deaf and stubborn uncle.

"I don't want her cremated. I don't want to lose her that way," he says. He lowers his head, as if the words don't belong to him. A crumb of cake dances across his mustache.

I imagine Bibble burned to a pile of meager soot. I imagine pouring her ashes into a champagne glass and the wind stealing her from me.

"I don't even know how to pray for her," I want to tell the Rabbi. But he has walked off to deal with other sorrows.

The sunken old man is the last to leave. He kisses the mezuzah on the doorframe and disappears into the night. Alone, I realize I can call Arthur's house without worrying about his wife. I dial and picture Arthur, stretched out on his sofa, reading. His shirt is open at the neck, his silk tie draped across his loafers. He balances the telephone on his stomach, waiting for my call. I imagine him answering the phone instantly, his voice pleased and breathless.

Instead, I hear only endless ringing. As usual, I expected too much.

"I won't leave you," Bibble had said years ago, when Madelyn sent me to Miami. I followed Bibble like a sticky shadow, refusing friends, school.

"Go outside and play, and I'll be here waiting for you," Bibble commanded, putting the last hairpin in her French twist.

I went down the sidewalk, examined the lemon tree, ran to the corner and back, bursting into the house. Knowing it would be empty. And she was there, exactly as I left her.

Exactly as then, the black and white television gets only the Spanish channel. The sound treats me like warm milk.

I fall asleep in the rocker, clutching Bibble's crocheted pink pillow.

In the morning I dress in black and drink two cups of coffee before I remember the Kaddish. I dial the temple and the Rabbi answers.

"I promised I'd say Kaddish," I tell him. "I want to do it by the ocean."

I am surprised when he offers to meet me.

"I know a good beach," he says. He gives me directions in a voice sad as oatmeal.

I write his instructions on a napkin, then forget and wipe my mouth. Lipstick blurs the address, and I spend an hour lost in dead-end streets.

I barely recognize the Rabbi, leaning against a splotched red Volkswagen with a spray-painted peace symbol on its back. He wears sagging jeans and a battered University of Miami sweatshirt. I follow him and walk a long time before finding a stretch of beach not littered with people, pop cans and bulbous seaweed. I feel Bibble laughing at my black board-room suit and the Rabbi in the clothes of a sixties poet.

"*Yish Kadal*," he intones, and I repeat the heavy Hebrew words. Two teenage girls shouldering radios drift past, splattering rock music against the prayer. The wind slaps my hair into my face, the spray claims my legs. When the prayer has ended, when the music has faded down the beach, I feel alone, scared, unattached. I expected Bibble to live through my life with me.

I expected Arthur to cast off his family and move to my life. I expected Madelyn to return from California, lonely to see me. Yet I am alone. Madelyn, Franklin and Arthur are empty shells on the cluttered beach.

The Rabbi stands lighthouse-still, staring toward China.

"Let's go," he says, wiping his cheeks with the sleeve of his sweatshirt. Tears, like fleeting moments, are caught in his beard.

Was he the one she gave up for me, I wonder, as I follow him. Bibble would mock me for moving so slowly. I wonder what the Rabbi thinks as I take off my shoes and run ahead, racing against the sand and the tide, running fast as Bibble would have, leaping ahead just to catch up with her.

Horses on Calvary

It's raining hard and I feel like an escapee from the Ark when Bob and I pull into the wet driveway, grab our suitcases and make a dash for the front door of our house. The heat has been off while we were away. The living room is as cold and lifeless as the January landscape outside. I raise the blinds on the large, south-facing windows hoping to dissolve the pervasive melancholy that curls around me like a lapdog every winter whenever I slow down enough to think. Prodigal activity, my faithful substitute for sunshine, is in retreat.

California is moving toward breaking Noah's forty days and forty nights record. Two weeks ago we headed south down the interstate looking for some midwinter sunshine and warm weather. We got as far south as Newport Beach without the weather improving. The only sunny scenes we saw were on the pay-per-view movies we watched in our hotel room. Sheets of rain pounded the windows as we alternated movies with live TV newscasts of flooding rivers, mud slides and road closures all up and down the state. One afternoon we finally braved the storm and horrendous traffic jams to get out and buy a stack of paperback mysteries and car magazines from Barnes & Noble in the Fashion Island Mall. We had just dried off and settled down to spend the day reading when we received a long-distance call from the next-door neighbor who watches our house when we travel. He said there was serious flooding going on in our town.

Our house is sturdy. It's built on solid ground. Flooding water from the surrounding creeks has never reached us. No, our problem always comes from above: a leaky roof that defies all efforts to fix it. Our neighbor knows of the problem because he hears us swearing after every rainstorm when yet another "solution" fails to stop the leak. After an all-night deluge he checked inside the house for leaks. Sure enough, water was dripping in the upstairs bedroom, the ceiling sagging precipitously. He assured us he could handle the situation with tarps and buckets until we returned home.

Whenever we return from a trip, the first thing Bob does is check the messages on our telephone answering machine. It's something he looks forward to—a way to postpone the letdown of unpacking and cleaning up the car. While he listens to the tape full of messages, I decide to see how bad the leak is this time. Walking up the stairs, I wonder why my suitcase feels heavier than it did when I left, even though it contains exactly the same articles. Is it dirt or dread that adds to the weight?

I open the bedroom door and stop short. Our neighbor has wedged three T-shaped structures made of pine two-by-fours between the floor and ceiling to support the soggy Sheetrock threatening to crash down any minute like Armageddon. Crosses without headrests. Looks like Calvary, I think, then immediately segue into a fantasy about a troop of soldiers on horses coming over that hill. This short-circuiting of reason happens because a friend, who as a child escaped all religious indoctrination, told me she grew up thinking Calvary was a misspelling of the word "cavalry." Now those two words are forever bound together in my cowboys-and-Indians-saturated, Saturday-matinee mind.

I like the crosses in the bedroom. They give the room a certain center of interest it's always lacked. I'm in the middle of the second verse of "Jesus, Keep Me Near the Cross" before I realize what I'm singing. I try to change the subject matter and brighten my mood by humming an upbeat jazzy version of "You Are My Sunshine," the first love song I learned sometime between first grade, when my mother made up the imaginary Wilbur Chitwood, who she teased wanted to marry me, and fourth grade, when I really did want to marry fifth grader Buddy Jones. Buddy was my sunshine, the person I most looked forward to seeing every morning when I ran across the street to his house to walk to school with his sister, Mary. But I was never anything more to Buddy than his sister's best friend and a passable first-base player he recruited for his team once I proved to him I could throw, catch and hit a baseball. In spite of his hardly noticing me when off the diamond, he "made me happy when skies were gray."

They have a word for it now, agoraphobia, fear of open spaces, but in the 1940s, when I was growing up in Texas and my mother had it and cried all day and wouldn't leave her room for fear she would die, people called it plain old "being crazy" and I was afraid I would catch it. By the time I was eight years old I was obsessively preoccupied with disease and death, went long periods without eating because I was certain my mother was trying to poison me, and had panic attacks in Miss David's third-grade classroom after she caught me sucking a Smith Brothers licorice cough drop and told me if I ate too many of them I would die on the spot. I was so hungry I had eaten a whole box of them and kept expecting to fall over dead any minute. When I didn't die, I knew that to be saved from ending up like my mother I was going to have to get my fear under control and learn how to act normal. I began to watch other kids to see what normal was. For one thing, they went to church.

Meandering around the three crosses in the bedroom, I put away the contents of my suitcase and backslide into another old hymn from the large gospel repertoire I learned at the Cedar Crest Baptist Church during years of sitting through seemingly endless Sunday invitationals.

Brother Dansby prayed hard and loud that God's invisible messenger, the Holy Ghost, would make all us sinners come forward down the aisles to repent and accept Jesus as our one true Savior. I was shy and afraid when regular people spoke to me. The thought of a holy ghost talking to me brought me near panic. I sat in the back row of the sanctuary close to the door and prayed just as hard as the preacher did that the Holy Ghost wouldn't yank me up by the nape of the neck and make me walk down that long aisle between pews packed with Sunday-outfitted, mostly reborn believers. The thought of having to grab Brother Dansby's hand and give my testimony in front of the whole congregation made my heart pound and my hands sweat. It wasn't that I didn't want to be saved. I wanted more than anything to be saved from the fear and uncertainty surrounding me. I just didn't want anyone watching me when it happened.

It was too mortifying even to contemplate: making that interminable walk down the aisle, whispering Lord-knows-what into the preacher's ear to prove my repentance, then being totally dunked, hairdo and all, in that raised metal tank behind the pulpit. I was the only one in my family who went to church, so at least I could be saved in secret without my parents and brothers knowing about it. My mother may have been too afraid to leave the house, but when she wasn't crying she had a caustic sense of humor. So did my brothers. Because I was too timid to speak out and easily frightened, I was a good target for their teasing and scaring-to-death. I didn't trust that God would treat me any differently than they did. What exactly did the Holy Ghost have in mind for me, anyway? What would He do to me to give me the nerve to walk down that aisle and be welcomed into the Kingdom? Maybe I'd become temporarily blind like Saint Paul. Or maybe He'd make my mind go completely blank, which it sometimes did anyway without the Holy Ghost's help, when someone noticed me or asked me questions. As if this weren't enough to worry about, I had just learned about heart attacks when an old woman in our neighborhood had one and as I was constantly short of breath I knew I was on the verge of having one too, which made my breathing even more shallow.

I prayed hard that God wouldn't make my mind "go blank." One of the reasons my mother gave for never going outside was that when she did, her mind "went blank." I thought having my "mind go blank" was the first sign of "losing my mind," and the next step was being locked up in the state hospital in Terrell, Texas, the small town where my mother grew up, and where she learned all those "people going crazy" stories she told me, scaring us both half to death.

The summer before I went into sixth grade, Mrs. Nolan and the entire Sunday school class let me know that they were getting tired of praying for my soul every Sunday morning before and during the eleven o'clock worship service. Whether it was the Holy Ghost sent from God or just muscle fatigue, I'm not sure, but I finally loosened my tight grip on the back of the wooden pew in front of me and simply used my high-diving-board technique: don't think, just do it. I took a deep breath and plunged down the aisle like I was Moses passing through the parted Red Sea during the last verse of "Just as I Am." My mind didn't exactly go blank, but I don't remember what I said to Brother Dansby. The choir was singing so loudly he couldn't hear my repentance speech anyway. He smiled nicely and nodded his head. I was in! Baptized that night after Training Union, I was finally like everyone else in Mrs. Nolan's class. Being a baptized person would surely improve my odds of winning prizes in the Bible-quoting contests and make it easier for me to find rides to the girls' auxiliary roller-skating parties.

Now that I was a saved, registered 10-percent-of-gross-weekly-allowance tither, I wasn't prayed for anymore and that was a big relief. Being saved hadn't made me feel less afraid, but I was getting better at acting normal. I started talking more and found I loved to sing. I stole a hymnal (intending to take it back, but I never did) and learned how to read music by studying its pages. When I prayed, I prayed alone and kept my spiritual questions at a safe distance from church. Whether this wariness was from my own character weakness, or a healthy skepticism about the rigid fundamentalism surrounding me, or a budding feminist's questioning of why the God of most religions looks and acts like the men doing His describing, I don't know. Maybe I was holding out for a stronger partner with a better grip. I continued to dance with religion, learning all the steps for salvation, keeping the beat by humming beautiful hymns but ignoring most of the words: a converted-sincere-go-to-church-to-socialize type of Christian.

In the thirty years it's been since I left Texas and moved to California, I've filled up my dance card looking for that perfect partner. I've attended many churches: Episcopal, Presbyterian, Catholic, Quaker, Science of Mind and Christian Science to name a few. I've looked for God on the back of my eyelids, counted my breaths while seated in various uncomfortable positions, chanted mantras for better focus. I've made resolutions to upgrade both my philosophical outlook and musical taste by reading serious books I only half understand and listening to Bach and Mozart to expand my taste in music. I feel weighed down like Solomon in a tent of clay.

I seldom go to church anymore, but a friend of mine who is a nun recently pointed out that my house is full of more icons and statues of the Holy Family than the convent where she lives, that I have in my bookcase more translations of the Bible than she even knew existed, and enough hymnbooks collected through the years to outfit a church choir. She says I am the only person she knows who does Kegel exercises while saying the rosary, although she thinks it's a practice that might catch on in her order as more and more sisters and their bladders age. She doesn't exactly know where my collection of plaster Buddhas and wooden Balinese angels fits into my theology. I don't either but am thrilled that she thinks I have one—a theology.

I want to leave the three crosses up in the bedroom until the rainy season is over. I like the company. I slip into singing "On a hill far away, stood an old rugged cross" and only halfheartedly substitute, "Please don't take my Sunshine away." Memory is both my comforter and the shroud of regret. I let the past intrude too much on what I do and think about, but old habits and associations are harder to stop than the water from our leaky ceiling.

When Bob comes into the bedroom to unpack his suitcase, I stop humming. He tells me there is a week-old message on our answering machine from his brother that their Aunt Grace had died. She was ninety-four years old. We hadn't seen Aunt Grace since her younger sister Mabel, Bob's mother, died fifteen years ago. After Mabel's funeral, Grace watched Bob and his brother dismantle completely, in three days, the family house that she and Mabel had grown up in and that Mabel and Bob's dad had bought and lived in after they married. I had watched Grace grow pale, edging toward hysteria when she saw how fast a history could be so completely wiped out. Both Bob and his brother were in a hurry to get back to their busy lives and couldn't spend time agonizing over what to keep, what to sell and what to take to the dump. Grace had wanted to hold and tell a story about each item the brothers briskly pointed to, saying keep, sell or dump. In three days the house was emptied of three generations of furniture, china, silverware, memorabilia. The estate was quickly settled. The house sold. And Grace retreated from what we call the real world. She lived another fifteen years as a child, warehoused in a home for elderly children. Nothing remained: her family, her home, the religion she had once held on to so tightly meant nothing to her. She lived apart in a private world. All the books she had once read, all her life experiences, the beliefs, opinions and prejudices—everything was silenced by senility or sorrow.

No funeral; her ashes were returned to the small town where she grew up in Indiana and buried in the family plot. The psalmist said we're all creatures of flesh, given only an inch or two of life, a puff of wind that passes and does not return. An inch or two is about the length of those dashes sandblasted on granite tombstones between the birth and death dates. Within that inch or two is the story of a life, the dash between the two deep darknesses. Considering life's brevity, we should be called members of the human dash instead of the human race.

Many of my friends are involved in Eastern religions and most of my relatives are true believers in Christianity. My mother talks of dying and going to her reward like heaven is someplace just down the street that runs like Texas on Central standard time, where she will finally be unafraid and warmly greeted when she comes around after passing on. My ex-Baptist-now-born-again-Tibetan-Buddhist ex-husband also knows exactly what happens when you die and the true nature of all reality. It's a secret, so he can't tell me. I envy their certainty.

In spite of all the churches, therapies and self-improvement workshops I've tried, I seldom feel safe, never normal and have no certainty about the nature of God. My life is full of religious artifacts, relics of my past. Hymns, crosses, memories kept in the reliquary of my mind. I don't understand doctrines or trust dogmas. I am equally baffled by theories of the Eastern and the Western religions. Yet I can sit silently in a temple in front of a statue of Buddha or in an empty church staring at a crucifix and know there is a message here, something I want to learn. I can pick out hymns on the piano with simple I, IV, V chord progressions or listen to the complexities of Gregorian chants and know there is meaning beyond language. And I know that things are not always as they seem.

When I was nine or ten years old, I learned the song

"You Are My Sunshine" from a 78 record. I listened to Gene Autry sing it over and over until I had the words memorized.

That song gave me hope that a love like that awaited me. One day I would sing with the church choir "Love Lifted Me," and it would be true. It might be a love affair with God, or it might be with Buddy Jones. I would no longer feel afraid, abnormal, completely alone. The song proved it. Only recently did I learn that the former governor of Louisiana, Jimmy Davis, wrote that song, and he wrote it for his horse, Sunshine.

I'm grateful for horses on Calvary.

Marilyn Chin

Song of the Sad Guitar

In the bitter year of 1988 I was banished to San Diego, California, to become a wife there. It was summer. I was buying groceries under the yin and yang sign of Safeway. In the parking lot, the puppies were howling to a familiar tune on a guitar plucked with the zest and angst of the sixties. I asked the player her name.

She answered:
   "Stone Orchid, but if you call me that, I'll kill you."
I said:
   "Yes, perhaps stone is too harsh for one with a voice so pure."
She said:
   "It's the 'orchid' I detest; it's prissy, clichéd, and forever pink."

From my shopping bag I handed her a Tsing Tao and urged her to play on.

She sang about hitchhiking around the country, moons and lakes, homeward-honking geese, scholars who failed the examination. Men leaving for war; women climbing the watchtower. There were courts, more courts and innermost courts, and scions who pillaged the country.

Suddenly, I began to feel deeply about my own banishment. The singer I could have been, what the world looked

370

like in spring, that Motown collection I lost. I urged her to play on:

> Trickle, Trickle, the falling rain.
> Ming, ming, a deer lost in the forest.
> Surru, surru, a secret conversation.
> Hung, hung, a dog in the yard.

Then she changed her mood, to a slower lament, trilled a song macabre, about death, about a guitar case that opened like a coffin. Each string vibrant, each note a thought. Tell me, Orchid, where are we going? "The book of changes does not signify change. The laws are immutable. Our fates are sealed." Said Orchid—the song is a dirge and an awakening.

Two years after our meeting, I became deranged. I couldn't cook, couldn't clean. My house turned into a pigsty. My children became delinquents. My husband began a long, lusty affair with another woman. The house burned during a feverish Santa Ana as I sat in a pink cranny above the garage singing, "At twenty, I marry you. At thirty, I begin hating everything that you do."

One day while I was driving down Mulberry Lane, a voice came over the radio. It was Stone Orchid. She said, "This is a song for an old friend of mine. Her name is Mei Ling. She's a warm and sensitive housewife now living in Hell's Creek, California. I've dedicated this special song to her, 'The Song of the Sad Guitar.' "

I am now beginning to understand the song within the song, the weeping within the willow. And you, out there, walking, talking, seemingly alive—may truly be dead and waiting to be summoned by the sound of the sad guitar.

For Maxine Hong Kingston

Deena Metzger

The Bird in the Heart of the Tree

In honor of Reb Zalman Schacter

Seeing the movement down the tree, the descent of spirit into matter, or a singing bird, with blue feathers' leaping from branch to branch.

How spirit breaks into song, how it must break itself into pieces to sing, how a part of that which is indivisible enters the universe in a body, a feather, a color or a note.

Spirit entering into form, breaks off from itself, breaks itself, breaks itself into pieces, is broken. Wherever we see spirit, there is something broken.

Here the heart is broken, here the spirit enters. The prayers of a broken heart call the spirit in, inevitably heal, are therefore whole.

The song enters the world. Here, there is someone singing. And a different melody, exactly the same, coming from farther away than time. The two songs meet in a corner of the garden. Perhaps in the very heart of the tree. *Tepheret* is the place of their meeting.

Or *Tepheret* is the place where the prayer is spoken. Or it is the place where the prayer is heard. Is the meeting place.

The bird is always praying. Even when it is asleep, the song is alive in it. The heart of the bird is a small drum, and the drum is beating out its song. When the dawn comes, the melody is awakened by the light. Or if it is a nightbird, it sings all night long.

To be the bird is lonelier than to be the song. The song is never lonely, but the bird is always longing for the song. In the moment of song, there is prayer, or in the moment of prayer there is song. Everything has a home.

Each prayer is answered. The bird in exile sending a message to the song or asking for the dawn to break. In the moment of prayer, exile disappears. When we feel that we have prayed well, it is because we've come home.

When I pray, I do not know whether I am climbing a tree or making a ladder for the light to climb down. Whether I am calling the bird to my hand or flying to meet it among the leaves.

But if I am the bird, what am I calling to myself? Is it a song? Or is it light? Or is it to be broken?

Sometimes the bird turns away. Sometimes it does not open its mouth to sing. Sometimes it is afraid. Sometimes it is afraid of the dark. But when it forgets it is afraid and opens its mouth to sing, it fills with light.

There was a place where we expected the birds to disappear. But because the heart was broken, the prayers existed nevertheless. No matter how heavy the earth, the air can always bear the song of birds.

The light of prayer travels faster than the speed of light. It takes no time for the light of prayer to travel between the worlds. So even in that place, prayer existed, and reached its destination. Even in that place, And even in that place, there are bird songs now.

Prayer can exit from any opening. And the light can enter us everywhere. The prayer is the call and the light is the answer. Or the bird calls and the song appears. They are like day and night. They are inseparable. Or indistinguishable.

As the light can enter anywhere, keep all the doors open for the singing.

Sometimes the birds sing so sweetly, the tree itself is made of light.

There is a hollow in the heart of a tree which was pecked out by the bill of a singing bird. Who knows the grief the tree felt with the incessant pecking. But now when you pass the tree, you can see that the hollow is full of light or rather it is full of song. And the bird? It is gone. It has work to do. Its work is pecking and singing.

In the moment of prayer, light shines on the invisible, and everything is seen.

To pray, to make oneself so willing, one is transparent, or empty enough for the song to enter.

Sometimes we are so busy praying, we do not hear the light calling out to us, looking for a place to rest.

Sometimes we are so busy praying, we cannot see the singing, wanting to be heard.

The prayer and the response, the same: "I am here."

Sometimes gratitude, sometimes praise. Sometimes longing. A night owl on the one tree calling to another night owl in its branches.

A song without beginning and without end, breaking into notes, a light breaking into colors. All the pain of the breaking. And the beauty of it. The pain and the beauty. And that which is broken becomes whole. Prayer knows this.

Prayer is only the singing of one heart to another heart. And the beauty of it.

To get to it, to get to it, to get to it, prayer must travel so far in the dark to get to the light.

For the beauty of it. No prayer without beauty. And no beauty without prayer. And nothing without the heart of it. Beauty is the very heart of it. With all its brokenness, beauty is the heart of it.

In the Garden there is a Tree. And in the Tree is a Bird, a Bird with blue feathers. It sits in a nest it has carved into the very heart of the Tree. The Bird is singing. It is singing so sweetly, the Tree fills with Light. Perhaps the Song is the Light itself, perhaps the Light is the Song that the Bird with blue feathers has learned to sing.

A Song emerges from the Nest of Light in the Great Heart of the Tree. *Tepheret*. The Tree is full of Birds. Each Bird is full of Light. And the Light, it is also Singing.

The Long Journey Home

It is good to have an end to journey towards;
but it is the journey that matters in the end.

—Ursula K. Le Guin

Riane Eisler

The Long Journey Home:
Reconnecting with the Great Mother

I used to think of the divine as "God." Now, if I think in terms of a personalized deity at all, I think more of the Goddess than of the God. I feel very strongly that our society's denial of the feminine aspect of the deity, the Mother aspect, is one of the great obstacles to really having that personal relationship, that daily, direct connection with the divine.

I think of our whole life, from the time we're born, as a spiritual journey in search of the experience of oneness with the divine. There's been so much confusion about this; in me, too. I used to think the spiritual journey meant that you detach yourself from life, like the so-called wise men sitting on a mountain. Now I wonder, how wise can you be if you wrench yourself away from the human connection? If you negate nature, if you become very detached while people are starving all around you, is that wisdom? Is that really a path to God?

In the name of religion, we have detoured from the "partnership core" of our spirituality so terribly often. Why? This question was a major motivation for my research into prehistoric Goddess-based partnership societies. To answer it, I had to look at the whole of our history (including our prehistory) and at the whole of humanity (women and men). What emerged was a picture that affirms our spirituality and explains this detour. What I found was that, as a species, we have an innate potential for creativity, for caring, for awareness, for empathy.

My own path began, of course, in childhood. I was born into a Viennese-Jewish family, and when the Nazis took over we had to flee for our lives. We fled to Cuba, and my parents kept up the Jewish traditions there. Praying with my family gave me some of my most precious childhood memories. My mother used to bake bread for the Shabbat and light the candles. Have you ever seen a woman pray over the candles in Jewish tradition? She moves her hands in a beautiful way. When we move like that, we can access spirituality. That circular movement of benediction over the candles must have been part of a very ancient ritual that women, as priestesses, performed long before God became only male and before only men could be priests.

I also loved praying with my father to God—the Jewish God, of course. Every evening we said the "Shemah Israel" prayer in Hebrew, directed to "the Lord our God, King of the Universe." I had no clue what the Hebrew words meant, then; and now, with some sadness, I have to acknowledge the disempowerment inherent in those prayers. And yet they were magical because there was so much love between my father and me. When we prayed, we shared that spiritual moment.

Like any child under the circumstances, I added my own prayer at the end of it, in a very ritualized way. I was scared that if I forgot to say something, the prayer wouldn't come true. I always added a prayer for those of our family who had not escaped from the Nazis.

When the war ended I was fourteen. I saw the newsreels of what had happened in the concentration camps. The God of my childhood died then, a very painful death—not for God but for me. I had a lot of emotion invested in that relationship because of associations such as my mother baking bread for the Shabbat and lighting the candles. Now, of course, I understand that the lighting of the candles, which the Jewish prayer says is to the Bride, the

Kalah, must go back to much more ancient traditions, to the worship of the Great Goddess, and that the role of the woman in lighting the candles and baking the bread as sacred acts of light-giving and nurturing was preserved underneath the overlay of dominator religion that later became predominant in the Hebrew tradition. It was still a remnant of the old religion, where life-giving and life-nurturing were honored, where we were still empowered as priestesses and as women to directly partake in the divine, without a male intermediary.

But all I knew then was that the memory of those rituals, and my connection to the God of the Hebrew tradition, had been very meaningful. Yet because of the horror of what had happened in the war, it was over for me.

Actually, I had a very strange religious background. In Vienna I was a Jew, but in a very assimilated Jewish family so that my religion was only a supplement to our lives. In Cuba I was a Jew living in a Catholic country and attending a Methodist school. Like everyone else, I had to go to chapel. When they asked us, "Do you believe in Jesus Christ?" I raised my hand. Who wants to be the only kid on the block who doesn't raise her hand? So my father hired a rabbi to teach me that I was Jewish. I guess you could say I had a cross-cultural religious background.

I was immensely drawn to the Virgin Mary. This upset my parents and was a great embarrassment to me as a Jewish child. Now I understand that it was because she was the only remnant of the Great Goddess, the Mother who gives life to all of us, including a male divinity. She was still the Mother of God, wasn't she? But in Christian dogma She got demoted to become the only mortal figure in a religious pantheon where only the males are said to be divine. In retrospect, I really think it's funny that you should have a divine Father and a divine Son, yet the only one who isn't divine is the Mother.

Of course, I didn't understand any of this at the time,

only that the old familiar ideas I had been taught about what we call religion didn't make sense anymore.

So I began a very solitary spiritual journey. Often it was very painful, because I felt I had no connection. And yet I did.

I came to see that I didn't have to go to synagogue or church to take this journey. Gradually I tried different things. I tried meditation. I experimented with fasting. I began to understand that we are all both the center of the universe and its most insignificant part. I began to feel that I could establish a direct connection, through my own experiences, with this larger and totally mysterious reality out there that we'll never really understand with our reason, our brains—the equipment just doesn't receive it. But we can know it in a different region.

If I had stayed in an institutionalized religion, if I had never ventured out on my own, perhaps I never would have had that experience. Slowly, I also began to understand how, as a woman, you're in a miserable situation if you only have a God who's a Father, a King, and a Lord. It implies that the only relationship you can have with the male deity is indirect. If we as women are to access the Divine in us, a female deity, a Divine Mother, is essential. Of course, men need this connection to a Divine Mother too, but for women it's essential.

For the last five thousand years or so, society has been oriented primarily toward what I call a "dominator model." Because so much of our connection with divinity had to come through a hierarchy, its institutions and superimpositions interfered with our ability to have a really personal relationship with the divine. This religious hierarchy actually maintains itself in power by disempowering us. Presumably, we could not have any relationship with the deity without somebody (a man) who claimed that only he had a real relationship with God, and that we had to do it according to his orders.

Who are we to trust to guide our spiritual journey? Do

we trust what somebody else—an authority, a priest, whether Christian, Muslim, Buddhist, whatever—tells us? Or do we trust our own connection to the deity? How can we really own that relationship, internalize it, empower ourselves, and become part of the creative and healing power in the universe?

Through my research for *The Chalice and the Blade*, particularly in archaeology, myth, and art history, I began to see it wasn't always this way. Prehistoric societies saw the living world—the heavens, the earth, everything—as a Great Mother. But though they worshiped the Great Goddess, these societies weren't matriarchies, as has been mistakenly thought. She had both divine daughters and divine sons. These societies were oriented more toward what I've called a partnership model of society than toward a dominator model, the model that today may be taking us to an evolutionary dead end. That's one of the central themes of *The Chalice and the Blade*: that there is a viable alternative.

During those years of research and writing I also began to see how in these prehistoric societies it was much easier to be connected directly to the divine. Everything was divine, including nature. The Goddess gave life, and at death life returned to her womb, like the cycles of vegetation, to again be reborn. We didn't have the current artificial distinction between spirituality and nature, with man and the spiritual seen as above women and nature.

As I continued my research I also continued my own spiritual journey, and I began to see that the human spiritual impulse does not require an intermediary at all, but is inherent in the human condition. It's an evolutionary given, and its first expression was a very direct way of feeling real connection with the living world. You might think of this earlier partnership direction as "the childhood of our cultural evolution." When we shifted from it to the dominator detour of the last five thousand years, we lost our sense of connection.

I believe that the denial of our connection with the

Mother aspect, the feminine aspect of the deity, is one of the great obstacles to really achieving that meaningful and fulfilling personal relationship not only with the deity but with one another. We all can observe the element of the feminine, of the Mother, of the nurturer, from our own experiences of a mother. Not that all mothers can be so all-giving. That's the role of the Great Mother, not the human mother, and a lot of disappointment, anger, and guilt is connected with that. And of course the Great Mother also has a dark aspect, the transformative aspect of reclaiming life at death. But to have been deprived of that motherly dimension in the deity reflects something in our society—a deadening of empathy, a deadening of caring, a denial of the feminine in men, and a contempt for women and the feminine that is very characteristic of the dominator society.

But now, as we're beginning to shift toward a partnership society—as we're recognizing that one more war would be our last, that high technology and man's conquest of nature are a patently lethal mix—we are also beginning to recognize that this conquest mentality and the idea of a male God with men made in His image, who are to dominate over women, children, and the rest of nature, could be the swan song for us as a species. So naturally we're searching for something else.

I don't think it's accidental that today there's so much interest in spirituality. We're trying to reconnect. I think the search is very personal. It isn't abstract. Even though many of us don't think of spirituality in the context of social systems, so much of what's happening today is connected with the fact that we're rapidly approaching an evolutionary crossroads, a bifurcation, when we either move to a partnership future or we may have no future at all.

When the dominator model is no longer obstructing our search, then we can begin the *real* spiritual journey. The task of clearing the obstacles is just to get us to the point where we can explore our relationship to the Divine. The more we move toward a partnership model of society, the more we can search for what we think of as our higher potential. Humans have the capacity for creativity, for love, for justice, for searching for wisdom and beauty. All these are paths to the divine.

One of the greatest gifts to me of my work, of my research, has been to affirm that this feeling of connection with the divine that we seek is part of a primal human search. Of all the knowledge that we're reclaiming about these prehistoric societies, one of the most touching things to me is the knowledge of the sacral in everyday life—the understanding that what we think of as "sacred" can be, in fact is, present in everything we do every day. It tells us that we can build a society where all of life is imbued with that consciousness of our connectedness, our consciousness of the extraordinary miracle of life, of the beauty and mystery and sometimes tragedy of nature and ourselves as part of nature. It's imbued with a feeling of awe and wonder.

That knowledge of the inherent spirituality of life and of nature is something that came to us very early in our cultural evolution, as early as ten thousand or so years ago, in the Neolithic period, the first agrarian societies. It's revealed through the temple models unearthed by UCLA archaeologist Marija Gimbutas, where we see how what she calls the "civilization of Old Europe" was a more partnership-oriented society that worshiped the Great Goddess.

In these temple models, and in other archaeological remains, we see that the things that were traditionally "woman's work," like baking bread, were considered sacred. The temples had pottery kilns and looms for weaving cloth, because these were sacred acts. There were mortars for grinding wheat and ovens for baking bread. It's fascinating to me how even in the Bible, in Jeremiah, where we read of the people "backsliding" to the worship of the

Queen of Heaven, we learn how women still baked cakes as offerings to Her, just as they did in the Neolithic era.

What's important about this for us today is that we can imbue our daily life with that same sacral quality. And of course these women and men who worshiped the Great Goddess understood that giving birth is a sacred act, not the insanity that we later find in so many world religions that had so much dominator mentality superimposed on the original partnership core, the caring core. For example, in the Old Testament, women have to be purified by a male priest after they give birth, as if it were a dirty act.

The dominator model confused us all. Today's society calls for an unraveling process, and then a reweaving. We don't need to throw out the baby with the bathwater. For example, a lot of the Jewish teachings that I was brought up on, like the Christian teachings, have a real *partnership core* to them: a core of caring, respect. I want to keep that. What I don't want to keep is the dominator dogma that's been superimposed on that.

It's not only Western religions. We do a great injustice by only looking for spiritual wisdom in Eastern religions. They have a great deal of dominator superimposition as well. For example, in some forms of Buddhism, in the Hindu tradition, in the Muslim tradition, as well as in the Judeo-Christian tradition, there is this idea that women—half of humanity—don't have a soul, that the half of humanity that gives birth to life is somehow of a lesser order. Isn't that a strange way to look at life? Think about all the nonsense about authority that religions have preached, about the "divinely ordained" right of kings and husbands to rule. Think about crusades and inquisitions, and witch burnings, and persecutions of heretics, and public disembowelings, and tortures, all in the name of Christian love. These are all faces of a superimposed element that supports a dominator system over the partnership core.

But they couldn't get rid of the partnership core—it's the core of spirituality.

Real love is empathic. Real love is an act of service. We have to manifest the love of God in action as well as in thought and words. We need greater understanding, and this process is like unraveling and reweaving a sacred tapestry. But we also need the sacred acts: the sacred act of giving birth, the sacred act of making bread and of sharing that bread. These are all ritual acts in the sense of ritual as an act of love, not as an act of suffering.

Women are taught in patriarchal cultures that they're supposed to serve. But it's not enough to honor and serve others. You also have to honor and serve yourself. You have to nurture yourself. If you become a victim and a martyr, you're not serving anybody, as far as I'm concerned, because you deny your own divinity. You don't honor yourself, your own worth. There is a fine line between serving so that you maintain respect for yourself and your own dignity and serving so that you grovel and lose your dignity. The institutionalized religions, by and large, have not given us that balanced view, and we need to find it.

Some of the milestones of my own spiritual journey include knowing, and reclaiming, the long, long traditions where the sacred and the divine had a female form; and knowing that I am not cut off from it because I happen to have been born a woman.

In very tangible, concrete ways, I have redefined my understanding of what I mean by deity, by ritual, by sacred, by love. I now understand why, for example, I feel so connected with the Divine when I see beauty, when I look at a sunset. I understand that the artificial distinction between the spiritual and the natural is just part of the luggage that I can leave behind. I understand why I feel so good when I'm able to reach out a hand to someone. I don't do it as an artificial thing, because of a command from some remote punitive deity or some priest or pope or other man who's going to punish me if I don't.

Quite the contrary: I do it because it gives me pleasure.

And this pleasure is partly because such giving is innate in us.

How do you find the deity? Beware of advice about how to find the deity. Follow your own path. That's my only advice.

Dorothy Lazard

River and Shore

Spirituality, like maturity, comes in stages. It evolves. It is tailor-made to meet the needs of the soul as they arise. My spiritual quest evolved out of a need for family, an internal balance, an acknowledgment of the natural world and how I fit into it, and a clear affirmation of the gifts of my people.

Organized religion was my introduction to spirituality. Baptized into the Catholic faith, I learned quickly that religion and spirituality were two very different things. From my earliest days, as I participated in church ceremonies—communions, confessions, confirmations—I never felt spiritually connected to the Mass or the icons that adorned the church. No moment of life-altering conversion ever occurred. I processed its catechism as I would ghost stories: ancient tales of horror and torture and epiphany. A costume drama played out before my eyes. When I was young, the public display (religion) and the private emotion (spirituality) seemed to be mutually exclusive. I was hard-pressed to believe that a God I should fear, who could smite me at will and believed I was inherently blemished with sin, was a God I could worship comfortably. That God sounded dangerously like the embodiment of the racism my family and I faced on the streets and in the schools. In my parish churches, there was no discussion of issues that impacted my life: poverty, illness, prejudice. No one in these churches looked like me, offered me spiritual succor

389

to ease distress, or spoke my family's language. I felt alienated from the Church.

I began to recognize the development of my spirituality as I searched for a coping mechanism after my parents' deaths during my adolescence. Seeking answers as to why they were taken away from me, and, more importantly, how I could cope without them, led me on a search for internal resources I could draw upon to cope with the trauma.

I was on my way out the door, prepared for my first overnight camping trip, when the telephone rang. I ran into the bedroom my mother and I shared to answer it. It was my oldest sister, Mary, on the other end, asking me the usual questions about how I'd done in school that year. All A's, I said proudly, adding that I was going into the sixth grade. I glanced over my shoulder at my mother, whose eyes were closed, but who, I knew, wasn't asleep. It was a game she played, feigning sleep. She learned everyone's business that way. It was the advantage of being a shut-in, an invalid. People excused your presence in a room, no matter how private or incendiary the conversation. Mary, my father's oldest child, asked about my mother and brother, who was away at a boys' camp in Washington State. Then Mary briefly paused, which I found strange. Usually, after asking her typical questions she would give the phone to our father, who, in his old age, lived with her. But she held on to the line, asking about my grandmother, with whom my mother and I lived.

"Daddy died," Mary said finally.

"When?" I asked, looking out the window and into the bedroom of the Victorian next door.

"Sunday," she said. "You want me to tell Lavurn?" she asked, referring to my mother, her stepmother.

"No. I will." I glanced at the calendar from the neighborhood mortuary. Sunday was August 2, 1970.

As I placed the receiver back in its cradle, my mother

rolled over toward me and said, "Your daddy's dead, isn't he?"

Nodding, I turned to face her. "Do you want me to stay?"

I had no memory of when I hadn't taken care of my mother, doled out her medications, made sure she didn't hurt herself too badly when she was taken by a seizure, knew who could pick her up if she fell outside. I was willing to stay home with her.

"No," she said, "you go on your trip and have fun. I'll be all right."

I hoped she was right. I went to the bed and hugged her. Playfully as always, she swatted me away, saying she didn't want the hug. But her hands assured me that she did; she held on to my hands as I slowly drew away. We each tried to put smiles on our lips, and were mildly successful.

The ride from San Francisco to Mill Valley was a blur. As inner-city traffic gave way to quiet, tree-lined streets, I thought of my family dying as slowly and unceremoniously as my father had. What had happened to my family, I wondered. Just a few short years ago my parents, brother, and I had lived together in two adjoining cold-water flats over a grocery store in St. Louis. And now we were scattered all over the place. I wanted to remember us as being happy, but Mary's call had vaporized that fantasy. We were not a normal family. We had been uprooted and separated without rhyme or reason, without our mutual consent.

Once I reached the CYO camp, the reality of irreversible death had seized my mind. It would cover me like a shroud for the next four days. I tuned in and out of focus on the campfire stories that were told that first night at camp. At one point, quite spontaneously, I whispered to one of the camp leaders, "My father just died." It felt good to say it out loud.

She looked at me and blinked several times. "Oh. Sorry."

I was disturbed that she wasn't more shocked by what I had shared. Her expression didn't get close to what I was feeling. Was everyone used to death except me? All that weekend, I felt alone out in those woods, unprotected. I'm almost an orphan, I remember saying to myself. What role would that demand of me? How do I learn to feel reconnected to the world? I could think of no one who could help me out of this sorrow. At the neighborhood library I had read about things dying—ancient animals and old people who had no one to care for them. But I never expected it to happen to someone I knew and loved.

Lying in my sleeping bag under the stars that first night, I thought of death, wondered if my father had died alone, what ailment had taken the old man. I had forgotten to ask. Then all the things I had meant to ask him with my newly developed eleven-year-old curiosity came to me. All the things I never knew: his father's name, the school he went to, how he and my mother met, what it was like to cook for the railroads.

The successive deaths of my father, maternal grandmother, and, finally and most brutally, my mother set me on a quest to find a reason for living after my supports had been pulled from under me.

When my mother died, I was thirteen, still young enough to believe that the emotional storm of losing my geographically distant father and my emotionally distant grandmother was sufficient penance for whatever sin I had committed. What exactly had I done to make God so angry? I could never figure that out. Had I not believed in Him deeply enough or prayed to Him regularly enough?

After a period of numbing disbelief at my loss, I was overcome by bitterness toward God. On a good day I was deeply disappointed in Him; on a bad day, I was enraged. In private conversations with Him, I cursed His inadequacy as a supreme being. The church tenets that introduced me to Him seemed distressingly close to those I learned out in the world: that something was inherently wrong with me and my kind, and that I could be punished with impunity. Recalling sermons heard from Baptist preachers on Sunday morning radio and at my grandmother's church about the "taint of original sin" angered me more. At thirteen, I chafed at the ridiculousness of this idea. I could not accept God as a benevolent being, only as a capricious, destructive one. With youthful energy, I wanted to box with God, spit at the angels, deny them my attention and devotion. God had turned his back on me. And now it was my turn to turn my back on Him. I continued going to church, but felt more estranged than ever from what was being said. By the time I got to high school I had reduced my churchgoing to Midnight Mass on Christmas Eve. An activity performed like a required visit to a dying relative.

As a result of those three significant deaths in my youth, I became intrigued more by the finite nature of life than by the imposing threat of death itself. Like most children, I had never given much thought to death. It was something far off in the future. Something promised to old people. Life was all I had had and had known.

The seeds of a real spirituality in my life grew out of an acknowledgment of the wholeness of one's life. I began to look at each of our lives as individual eternities. The irony being that none of us knows exactly when our individual time clocks will tick to their inevitable end. That being the case, how will we choose to live? Does the bravery we admire in some come from an acceptance of that time clock? Does the kindness? The wisdom? I hadn't been able to bring myself to believe in God as He had been presented to me, but there was an instinct, a hope that there was something out there worth believing in.

In my early twenties, I railed against organized religion, charging that it was another form of oppression for African-Americans, and that, like idiot children, we had swallowed the poison without protest. Religion, in my opinion, was a salve that was used to placate and control us. I wanted none of it. I had to find my own way, create my own code of ethics, my own means of spiritual recovery. Three Hail Marys or a tear-inducing spiritual were not enough. I needed to go deeper. A spiritual game plan surfaced out of a need to survive my eternity with my head above water. There had to be some means of accepting what happens in a way that was not guilt-producing, of building a source of inner strength, and of finding a faith in my life that was affirming.

I tried a nondenominational church before abandoning the whole idea of organized religion. It was a middle-class congregation where the minister spent lots of time announcing which children were headed to college and which worshipers had been promoted or had begun their own businesses. There were all manner of events for the men's auxiliary and the women's auxiliary, the usher board and the youth group. Though I was mildly interested in the activities of this stratum of my community, it seemed that very little praying was going on. It made me wonder where God had gone. Had these people cast him aside, too, and were just congregating for the fellowship?

When I occasionally attended church as a child with my Baptist grandmother, God seemed to saturate the walls of that tiny storefront. The "spirit of the Lord" struck the white-gloved sisters at Pilgrims' Rest like lightning. Sweat rained from the minister's face, and the choir never stopped singing or humming or encouraging the sermon along with a throaty "Uhm-huh . . . yes, Jesus." To me, accustomed to the more subdued Catholic Mass, it seemed as though the Lord filled them, owned them. I wanted that kind of spiritual connection and emotional release. I wanted that kind of unshakable faith.

No such emotional displays were witnessed at the middle-class church of my early adulthood. And the curious part of my nature wondered why the people at this latter church seemed so distant from their God. For many more reasons than my grandmother and her friends had, these people, with their college-educated generations, had reasons to be truly thankful. As a result, I became very cynical about the idea of public worship. Maybe it was my religious orientation or my introspective personality, but I came to feel that if I were to communicate with God or any other supreme life force, it would have to be in private. That was the only thing that felt right to me.

Eventually I left the church, and for a time, whenever I was asked why, I felt a bit like a traitor, though I was never emotionally tied to religion enough to feel quite guilty about not going. More than anything I felt a cultural isolation for, at the time, I did not know many people who stayed at home Sunday mornings. I felt the burn of going against the grain. So much of our collective identity as African-Americans is connected with our oldest American institution, the church. Attending church was what black folks *did*, I was told, just as sure as we went to school or to work.

"Are you hanging out with white people now? Is that why you don't go to church anymore?" an aunt asked me once at a holiday dinner.

I was confused by what possible connection white people had with my sense of faith. "No," I said, "I just don't want to go anymore. It doesn't do anything for me."

"What's it supposed to do for you? You go to worship Him!"

"Why can't I worship Him here?" I said, skating on thin ice. This aunt, wild in her youth, was now a devoted usher board member. "If God is everywhere, why can't I pray to him here?"

She shook her head, not bothering to mask the disdain she felt for me. My decision to steer clear of God was not always easy. I feared that people thought my decision reckless, a result of my having no parents. But, on the other hand, I developed a bit of rebel cachet among my friends, which privately I liked. Without church to attend on Sunday mornings, I had more time to think and look for answers as to why things are the way they are.

I looked at the churches I had previously attended and found an equal measure of hypocrisy, racism, and gossip for every bit of fellowship and spiritual revival. Rarely had I seen a group of Christians live up to their ideals. But as I condemned it, I stumbled upon this idea. The church—any church—is not merely the edifice where people pray and repent and restore themselves. The church is the people themselves. And in accepting that idea, I found faith in my community. Not the ones who gather for worship each Sunday, but those people who trudge home, Monday through Sunday, tired from work, to cook meals and calm nerves and help with homework. These were the people who endeared themselves to me, the people I came to think of as ideal because they were constant, reliable. They taught me, by their example, that a higher form of being, of knowing was possible. Instead of moaning about their lot in life or waiting for "the sweet by-and-by," they simply worked to make their lives and, by extension, our communities stronger. My community, at its best, reinforced for me my newfound belief system. The greatest gift is to give not on the promise of thanks or reward, but because it is what is needed. To teach away ignorance, shout down hatred, celebrate one another's gifts. Against these people who work so hard and devotedly to make life better in the present, the amorphous God I learned about in church seemed painfully insufficient. Nevertheless, I thought a lot about Him and how we are introduced to religion in this country. I thought about how the notion of God had been used to promote all manner of war and mayhem and daily suffering. Yet we are told to look at Him as an ideal, to model ourselves after him. He became a myth to me; I was certain some demagogue had cooked up this whole theology to empower himself. As you can imagine, no one I

knew wanted to discuss this theory with me. It was blas-
phemous.

Then one day I came upon the mother of all blasphem-
ies: if we are only as good as our deeds, mustn't we also
only be as good as our God? Isn't God a manifestation of
the society that worships him instead of the other way
around? When we do good, I reasoned, God—the meta-
phorical body of our deeds—is good. And when we are not,
God is not around. I found this to be much more empower-
ing and spiritually connecting than what I was taught in
my various bits of religious schooling.

So I redirect my vision inward on my life, the process and
pace of it, instead of outward toward my death. A fresh
need to empower myself, after the hopelessness and helplessness of my parents' deaths, led me to search for something spiritual. Asking myself routinely, "Am I the person
I want to be?" "Am I treating people the way I want to be
treated?" forces me to contemplate more intensely my
time on this earth. It has taken me more than a few years
to learn not to take my clock for granted. Like most people,
I had what can be called my "lost years," in which little
spiritual growth occurred. But in the last decade, a new
series of family deaths, the nearby threat of AIDS and
urban violence, and a deeper, keener appreciation for true
friends have restored my faith in the possibility, the very
necessity of living a fully realized life.

I have resigned myself to the hard-bought deal that
death sells: the race is on and it holds the time clock. But
in that resignation there is also a determination to run the
race as well as I can. When I get too lazy to write, too
anchored in weltschmerz to be hopeful, too demoralized at
work to be creative, before long I remember that merciless
clock that screams, *Get your act together; time's a-wasting*.
Indeed it is.

The depth and quality of life are as important to me as
its length. My most consistent life goal has been to live

my life with arms and mind open to life's possibilities and realities. Fortunately, I realized early that the world stretched beyond the narrow margins of my first community. I can see myself, my goals and dreams, in the faces of others who do not look like me, were not reared like me, those who do not speak like me. They have reinforced an old notion I've held on to like a security blanket: people, as varied as they are, have something in common. There is a basis of commonality and, hence, a communion that we share. And at the same time, in our differences we find complements, yins to match our yangs.

With or without the church, there is an abiding need for community and the validation it brings, to build one where none exists, to nurture it where it does. Fellowship is the ground-root of my spirituality. I want to stand, not on the periphery of the circle, but as a link in it, hand in hand with other women, other African-Americans, other writers, other Midwestern-born Californians. I am enriched by the fact that I come from a people who have endured incredible hardships but have the vitality, hopefulness, and will to maintain the ability to smile, to be tender, to be responsible. For me my community is both river and shore. They give me what I need to survive in the world, and act as safe harbor when I crash against the emotional shoals of life.

The need for community has expanded to include the natural world, too. I am humbled to have a place in it, with such a unique and interesting vantage point. Nothing in that grand, Gothic Catholic church of my youth has moved me as much as a dew-saturated forest or the call of birds in the morning. No holy ceremony, fragrant with blessed incense, can pull from me emotions like seeing the sun burst through gray clouds, the burnished palette of trees in autumn, or waves crashing against a seawall. I am moved by the hell of a volcano and the heaven of a lush rain forest.

* * *

In these middle years of my life, I have become very comfortable with this tailor-made spirituality. It is inclusive, reverent, and not bred out of fear of any divine or vengeful being. We all hold within us the ability to be divine. I believe what is truly sacrosanct in this life is that which I can hold in my hand, touch with my heart, see with my eyes, and, as a result, be transformed by. My life has taught me that spirituality is transcendent beyond the religious dogma one inherits. We are the sowers of our own spiritual destinies, which can either atrophy in the arid climate of organized religion or, like liberally cast seeds, take root and bloom, vining in and around our individual eternities.

Ellen Grabiner

Oy Gevalt

Susan and I sit side by side in our matching, colorful tallisim (prayer shawls) listening to Dennis. It is Shabbat Together, a recent monthly innovation at our temple designed to make the services more accessible. Our son Alex and his friend Isaiah have found a tiny attic room above the bimah, filled with old prayer books and other dusty relics of years gone by. It is their secret place. Now he no longer fights with us when we want to go to services.

As Dennis leads the Torah discussion I become aware that Susan and I are holding hands. This, in and of itself, does not surprise me. We often hold hands in our own home, watching TV, or lying in bed, talking. Or at the movies, where it's dark and no one can see. We hold hands in Provincetown, or at lesbian bars, or gay-owned restaurants. At the Gay Pride March. That our list of "places we can hold hands" is short is also not a surprise. In the real world, if you are queer, you don't flaunt it. So mostly we don't.

But this is not the point. The point is that I don't even realize we are holding hands; I'm not worried, or even consciously surreptitious. I am that comfortable. As Dennis goes on, I shift my focus away from my amazement at my comfort and toward what he is saying.

"I wish that God would speak as directly to me as God did to Abraham," he laments. "I, too, want to know, want to hear that voice that tells me exactly what it is that God wants me to do." Members of the congregation respond to his plea:

"I have a friend who writes me. He says he hears God's voice. I say he's crazy, he should see a shrink"; and

"The Bible is metaphor. You can't take it literally. It must be taken as metaphor"; or

"I think God doesn't necessarily speak to us, but inside, what is guiding us, our core or our center, that's what is divine"; and from Phil, the spiritual leader of our shul,

"I hear God speak to me often. Usually in the voices of Morrie and Ada."

I play with the image of Morrie and Ada as God's mouthpieces. It seems fitting. They are husband and wife, both in their eighties, and are the grandparents of our congregation. During the sixties and seventies, and even the early eighties, as the older members of the congregation died and younger ones moved away, the membership dwindled. When Phil first began going to B'nai Brith, he said it always felt like a funeral. The numbers kept shrinking, and often there wasn't even a minyan, the number of people necessary to recite certain prayers. There was serious doubt that the temple would continue to exist. But Morrie, Ada, and a handful of determined, faithful members kept the books, and ran the board meetings, and paid for the oil to heat the building. And they waited. Slowly but surely, younger people came. People like Phil, who had been steeped in his Judaism. And people unlike Phil, ignorant and hungry, began to come. Morrie and Ada handed over their legacies, the wisdom of how it had all been done in the past. They were able to listen to the new ideas these younger people had, and most importantly, they were willing to make the changes to keep the shul that they had nurtured so lovingly for so long a vibrant, growing organism.

As the discussion goes on, I sit quietly, smiling. I do not join in the discussion, I do not share the fact that I had recently heard the voice of God. She had led me on a meandering and agonizing path ending right here, at Temple B'nai Brith, Somerville, 02144. She had brought me home.

When Alex turned three, Susan and I were concerned about his Jewish education. We began a process of "shul shopping." It wasn't going to be easy, we knew. We wanted a progressive congregation, a feminist egalitarian congregation. Yet we had both grown up in Conservative temples, and had memories of the more traditional liturgy. We sampled the local temples. One that had a large and vocal gay contingent played organ music during services. We agreed that that felt too much like church. A block away from our house, we found a small, historic synagogue, which from the outside felt just right. We had visited their festive Simchat Torah celebration, well known in our community. The members take to the streets, dancing and singing, carrying their Torahs high, celebrating the Five Books of Moses. However, when we asked about joining this shul, we were told that only the man of the family was allowed to be a full member of this temple. Fortunately, our next stop was B'nai Brith and we knew almost as soon as we entered that this one was just right. No single attribute clinched it, but rather a constellation of people and events that unfolded visit after visit, making it clear to us that we had discovered a treasure.

Our lives, like those of many of our contemporaries, suffer from the lack of an extended family on which our ancestors or even our parents relied. We are the generation that went away to college, moved out to the coast, the generation that left home. So when we walked into services on Rosh Hashanah and saw, scattered among our peers, real live old people, shades of our much-missed grandparents, we knew we wanted in. But that was just the appetizer. The main course was the power and soulfulness of the chanted prayers. It was partly the comfort of the familiar strains of our childhood, but this was not a congregation of mumblers. The members of this congregation belted it

out, they harmonized, their voices danced around each
other, drawing their prayers upward to fill the large, cavernous sanctuary. Here was a congregation that loved to
sing. And for dessert, there on the bimah was Phil, philosophy professor and bearded hippie spiritual leader. Gazing
down at us through his wire-rim glasses, he could have
been any of our friends. We were stuffed, we were satisfied.
But, we wondered, would *they* want *us*?

Susan courageously set about the task of composing a
letter to the president of the congregation, telling him that
we were two lesbians looking for a Jewish community in
which to raise our son. We were not about to pretend to be
otherwise. Would the congregation of B'nai Brith welcome
us? We received a letter from the president's wife, then the
head of the congregation's now defunct sisterhood. We pictured a matronly, middle-aged woman with tight curls
and bifocals, married to the balding, paunchy guy in a
white shirt and tie from our childhood temples. The petite,
powerhouse woman who runs a dance complex, writes
poetry, and who, with her pediatrician-musician husband,
raises their two children and has become our friend, was
nowhere in our imaginations. She welcomed us unre-
servedly. Yes, please, please come.

Once, God was at the center of my life. Our relationship
has been an off-again, on-again thing. I found God in my
unwavering connection to the earth, my earliest and most
direct experience of the Divine, alternately comforting and
fierce, solid and piercingly beautiful. And ultimately in my
Judaism, gleaming as a beacon, sometimes brilliant, sometimes obscured by impenetrable mists, to which I could finally return.

Until I was almost eleven, I assumed Jewishness. My
whole family was Jewish, my parents' friends were Jewish, my friends at school were all Jewish. Although I lived
in a Christian world, being Jewish was normal. So much so
that I had come to associate the Yiddish my grandparents

spoke, and the foods they ate, not with Jewishness but with "grandparent-ness." It wasn't until my first Protestant friend, Kathy, came to visit while my grandparents were there that I realized that *my* grandparents were different. That they had accents. The rich Russian-Yiddish that shaped their English and that had been music to me suddenly stood out in relief as I heard them through my friend's ears. Yet I felt no shame. I was proud to be a Jew, proud of what little I knew of my heritage. I had somehow, with no formal Jewish education, gotten the idea that I was special.

As first-generation Americans, my parents were concerned primarily with assimilating, separating from the alien and conspicuous ways of their parents. To them, being Jewish meant simply that they had Jewish friends, that they would swim at a certain swim club in summer, but it did not include building a spiritual life.

If there was to be a spiritual dimension to my life, it was up to me to create it. I was lucky to have help from Sarah, my childhood friend. When I first began to accompany Sarah to services, I went only to be with her. The children's services were held downstairs in one of the classrooms. There we were given beautiful stickers that we put in a booklet, much like the one my grandmother had for her S&H Green Stamps. But at services we got one stamp for each Torah portion read. This way we had a pictorial record of the services we'd attended, as well as a reminder of the stories. When we were old enough, we began to go upstairs to the regular service. I had learned no Hebrew, but my ear was good. When we weren't sneaking out to the rec room to practice our running leaps across the slippery, newly polished floor, and when there was transliteration, I sang along. I understood little of what was going on, but in the beams of light streaming through the windows, and in the harmonies, I sought the feeling I called "holy."

Early on I began to pray. My needs were simple and my prayer nondenominational.

> *I pray the Lord my soul to keep.*
> *God bless Mommy, Daddy, Steven, and Liz.*
> *And don't let anything happen to Daddy.*

Why this was my particular prayer is a mystery. Did I know that my father was going to die? Was I afraid that life would be dangerous without him to soothe and nurture me, to protect me from my mother's wrath? Or was this a guilt prayer to cover up how much I wanted him to stop being so intrusive, to go away? I felt that paradoxical combination of all-powerfulness and helplessness. I believed that God heard me, and that I was a good person. At least I tried desperately to be good, so that God would *have* to listen to me. I did pour a kettle of boiling water on the millions of ants congregating on our walk, but only because my mother told me to. And I did tease my brother mercilessly. And I lied, but only occasionally, and only little white ones, except for that time I broke the shade in the bedroom and blamed it on Steven, only two years old and sound asleep in his sofa bed across the room. And there was the time I made that little fat girl, Leah, be quiet all the way to the Sweet Shop, the day our parents forgot to pick us up from Sunday school. We waited and waited but nobody came. I called home and there was no answer. Her parents weren't home either. I must have been five or six, but I knew the way to my grandparents' store, just a mile or so down Broadway. It was straight, no turns, no way for Leah to get lost, but she didn't know that. I made her promise that she would keep quiet the whole way there, or I would run away and she would be lost. She tried to keep still, but soon she'd forget and start yammering or whining, which drove me crazy, which is why I wanted her to shush in the first place and why finally I couldn't stand it anymore and I started to run. She couldn't keep up, and by the time she made it to the store she was sobbing, and I lied again and said I didn't know why she was crying, but I did know why and maybe that's why God punished me and didn't listen to my prayer, but He sure waited long enough to get the punishment together, so long in fact that I had forgotten all about poor little Leah and how I had mistreated her, and I thought instead that God let my father die just to be mean. Just because I had asked Him not to.

At first, I clung to God. After I lost my father, God was all I had. And in my child's mind, He represented my link to my father. Much like the father in *Carousel*, I saw mine in heaven, at God's side, taking a break from polishing his cluster of stars, and asking the Big Guy if everything was O.K. down on earth with his family. I imagined that he felt guilty for having left each of us at a critical juncture in our lives; me in the middle of adolescence, my brother soon to be Bar Mitzvahed, my sister just six. And my mother, widowed at thirty-seven, young, beautiful, unskilled, with three children. Surely he would worry how it had all turned out? He would know that we wouldn't starve, he had provided for us. He was, after all, an insurance sales-man, a district manager, successful because he believed in his product. We were covered. What he couldn't have known was about the double indemnity clause. The one that said you get double the amount of money under cer-tain circumstances. Like accidental death, for instance. Like, for instance, if the doctors accidentally punctured your heart with the catheter they were using to measure your valves. That would qualify, under the policy's double indemnity clause. There was no way he could have fore-seen that. Or the malpractice settlement, either, although my mother insists we were gypped on that one. She says we never should have settled out of court, now, but then, she didn't know any better. And after seven years in litiga-tion, well, she'd just as soon the case was over. So he needn't have worried about money. My mother turned out to be a speed typist, an efficient secretary who worked her way up into the administrative management ranks of IBM, so we got by. But still, maybe he was curious. About our lives, our choices. Maybe he just wanted to see what we would look like grown-up.

I'd imagined my father watching me at first, knowing everything I did, all my bad thoughts transparent to him, all my lies laid bare. After a while, though, I couldn't live my sixteen-year-old life with my father perched on my shoulder. So I squelched the notion that he was with God, and ultimately I squelched God altogether.

I hadn't planned it. I don't even think I realized how furious I was, at the time, or to what extent I had taken my father's death as an assault that colored my sense of what kind of a place the universe was. I always expected the worst. When the phone rang late at night in my college dorm, someone was dead. In relationships, I expected to be discarded. I walked with shoulders up around my ears, awaiting blows that would come at any moment. I was afraid of the night, of the dark. After graduating from college, I lived alone above a pizza parlor, in a terribly safe suburb of New York City. I took a butcher's knife to bed with me each night, and lay awake, listening to the creaks of the building, to imagined intruders tiptoeing up the stairs, pausing at my door.

For a decade, I wandered rootless in my life, eventually coming face-to-face with the gaping hole at my center. At that point I embarked on my long and circuitous trek in search of meaning. Could I dare hope that I would, in the process, also find my way back to God? A God that I could accept, that would suture my severed connection with the universe? I never doubted that such a being existed. Rather, I believed that I would forever be denied that ultimate knowledge. The scars my father's death had left were still raw, and I ached to soothe them with some spiritual balm.

For years I stumbled about. I read books on meditation,

on "women's spirituality," on Buddhism. I tried to meditate, I lit candles; crystals, fertility medallions, and goddess
beads dangled from my neck. I lit incense, I went to retreats and cried and screamed and writhed on the floor and
shared and opened my heart. I learned Hindu and Native
American chants and Sufi dances. I invoked the four directions, I lit smudge pots and purified the space and
drummed until my hands were covered with blisters. My
lesbian sisters and I railed against the patriarchy that had
excluded us from seeing ourselves in the image of God; that
knew only God, He; that raised only men to the status of
priest, of rabbi, of shaman; that would accept prayers only
from beings endowed with a penis and balls.

Yet after all the retreats, rituals, and ceremonies, after
the ecstasies that accompanied my heart cracking ever
wider open had worn off, I was left alone, without the
faintest idea of who I was or how to transform my life.

Angered by traditional patriarchal Judaism and frustrated by my inability to connect deeply with any of the
many other practices I had been sampling, I was willing
to try anything. In the relatively sleepless year and a half
following Alex's birth, I was blissed out enough (no spiritual practice has ever touched as deep a joy and wonder as
Alex's birth) and tired enough to take a chance. Julie, our
massage therapist, told me and Elaine, my good friend and
neighbor, that a guru was coming to town. A woman
guru, Deva Deva. Elaine went to see her and fell in love at
first sight. Deva Deva was performing an initiation ceremony the following day, did I want to go? Why not?

The ceremony took place in a small Cambridgeport
apartment. Deva Deva led us through a series of purifica-
tion rituals preparing us to receive her grace. We were told
to close our eyes and meditate, and Deva Deva would come
around and touch us on the head with a peacock feather,
or on our forehead, and tell us that we should just keep
meditating and let whatever happens happen.

I tried to concentrate, but I was too nervous. Finally I

heard the soft rustling of her sari, a sound that in years to come would fill me with both longing and dread. I felt her touch my forehead, my ears, felt the brush of the feather across the top of my head. Almost immediately I was sobbing. Deep, racking sobs, my teeth chattering like a three-year-old's, my features contorting as if everything ugly inside of me had leapt out onto my face. Something serious was happening and I thought that meant I had better partake. If this was real, then I supposed it was meant to be.

After the whirl of the Shaktipat ceremony, I truly felt as if I had awakened in Oz. This was a beautiful, glistening country, visually rich and opulent, at the head of which sat a woman. Her disciples prayed to the feminine aspects of god for peace for all people. They valued the power of sound to transform and heal, extolled the virtues of food as sacred. It seemed almost too good to be true.

In the years that followed, I learned the Hindu chants and prayers. I threaded the silken sandalwood beads through my fingers and repeated the mantras they had taught us. I delighted in those moments during which I was once again actually praying, something I hadn't been able to do for years. Chanting with Deva Deva, whose lovely voice could fill spaces you didn't even know you had, often moved me to tears. So often, in fact, at retreats and meditation programs, all I did was cry. I took this to mean "it" (whatever "it" was) was working. From the beginning, I understood my reluctance to bow down to the guru as my resistance, a superficial remnant of my Jewish past. Something I would, in time, get over. In our small group discussions, designed to provide an opportunity for support and sharing, I often wondered why, as disciple after disciple spoke of how their lives had been transformed, how the waves of bliss traveled up and down their spines, I primarily felt agony and despair. The outsider. The Jewish one. Did no one understand? Yet I kept on, hoping that this was just karma I was working through, and that eventually those waves of bliss would crash over my head too.

The ranks of the disciples swelled, carrying more lesbians and gay men than the traditionally assigned 10 percent, seeking out the guidance of a woman spiritual leader. But the queerness of these disciples was never spoken of explicitly. On some level, we all must have known that when push came to shove, Deva Deva was no different from any of her male counterparts when it came to being queer. So we never pushed, never asked what the Hindu line on homosexuality was. We believed that she must know, and that she still loved us so it was O.K.

Until Laurie. Call her brave or call her stupid, but in the middle of a weekend retreat, Laurie approached the guru and asked her if she would perform a wedding ceremony for Laurie and her lesbian lover. Deva Deva had married heterosexual couples, so Laurie figured, why not? Neither she nor any of us were prepared for the response she got. Deva Deva told her it was not good for her spiritual development to be with a woman in "that way," and that she and her lover should look carefully at their relationship and their life and figure out if this was right for them. And of course she patently refused to marry them. Laurie ran from the room in tears, and we, a bevy of lesbian disciples, followed her, to witness her tears, to support her rage, to try to help one another understand the real, spiritual meaning of all this.

In the past Deva Deva had often spoken about each person's karma being an individual thing. When she handed out *prasad*, blessed fruit, we had learned that you couldn't trade, even if you preferred the banana that your friend had been given, and she, your nectarine. Because the fruit was blessed especially for you; what was a blessing for you might be deadly for your friend. So at first we thought maybe this was just about Laurie. But any confusion we may have had was cleared up when the guru published her position in the monthly newsletter. Being queer was not considered a desirable choice. Of course, she loved us as she loved all her disciples, and "not a desirable choice" was clearly a step up from "a sin for which you would burn in hell." The news, which I believe shocked no one, affected us all, perhaps relative to our karma, differently. Laurie, rebounded from her rejection with renewed devotion, and now joined by her lover who also took Shaktipat, has remained heavily involved with the guru. Elaine ended her nine-year relationship with her lesbian lover and married a disciple, a man, from California. I did nothing quite so dramatic, initially. It seemed clear to me that there was no major religion, no matter what the sex of its religious leaders, that sanctified homosexual unions. Why should Hinduism be any different?

I always had trouble believing that the guru was god incarnate. This just proved it to me. She was, in my opinion, a wise, beautiful, loving soul who had much to teach, but who, like the rest of us mortals, was human, and as such had some cultural baggage. India is not a place that is especially tolerant of homosexuality. Yet it was not her rejection of my lesbian lifestyle that posed the problem for me. I was used to that. Instead, it was something older, deeper, more primal.

In Hindu mythology, there is in each of us a snake lying dormant at the base of our spines. This snake, or Kundalini, is our divine energy. Through spiritual practice, through the touch or gaze of a realized master, through devotion, the Kundalini can be awakened and the spiritual journey begins. The snake unwinds and works its way up the spine, through the chakras, or energy centers, until it reaches the third-eye center, and realization occurs. The Shaktipat ceremony is one method of awakening the Kundalini. Although I believe my spiritual journey began before I took Shaktipat, I do think my snake was awakened at that point. But I suspect that She remained unfocused, drowsy, clinging to sleep, as one does when one awakes from a particularly deep and compelling dream, for several years. For when She finally awoke, and I now know the exact moment of Her awakening, She bellowed, "Oy ge- valt, what am I doing here?" with all her might and with all her heart, and with all of her fierce Jewish soul. She looked around Her at the annual retreat of the full moon held every July to celebrate all the gurus, and though She could appreciate the beauty and the power and the love of this path and of these people, She knew suddenly, and without a doubt, that it was not Hers.

It took Her a while to convince me. I did feel as if I were waking up from a dream. My senses were on overload: the crowded retreat room filled with chanting Westerners, candles, portraits of gurus, gods, and goddesses decorating the walls and altars, the incense and brilliantly colored spices used in the puja ritual, left no room for even my breath. I fled to the field behind the conference center and cried into the weeds. I knew it was time to go, and I was frightened. I didn't want to leave the magical protection of Deva Deva, or the lovely story that I had arrived there, karmically speaking, for a reason, that I had earned in some past life the grace of the guru. Just like in the dream where you find yourself taking a final exam in a class you can't remember attending and you have no idea what the material will be, I wondered how I had gotten there. And I longed for something I could unequivocally call my own.

I didn't know then where, or if, I would ever find a spiri- tual home. I only knew that I could no longer find myself in this strange place. I mourned over the next couple of years: the loss of Deva Deva, of the community, of the wonderful food, of those moments of being swept up in the frenzy of the chanting. However, there was also relief. I no longer felt that I was trampling the tender sprouts of my spirituality as they tried to find their way to the light, their Jewish roots running deep. Maybe with care and at- tention they could flourish. Maybe if there was such a thing as karma, it was my karma to be a Jew. I knew it wouldn't happen overnight, as much as I wanted it to. And I knew that it wouldn't be magic.

Before I had completely separated from the guru, I began going to services. I was trying to squeeze out a Shabbat when our crazy, jam-packed lives would permit it. I took a beginning Hebrew class. I had cracked the code. Suddenly, what had only been beautiful calligraphy in the past had meaning. Words, prayers that I had learned by heart, by repetition, now began to have a visual shape. And the many parts of the service where I had been hopelessly lost were beginning to open up for me. I was softening, tentatively embracing a Jewish legacy. As I sat there following along, my Hebrew improving by tiny increments, recognizing fragments of melody, I felt enveloped by the energy of the prayer and Phil's voice, as if they, and not just the tallis, were wrapped around me, holding me fast. It was as if I had been given something quite valuable and yet at the same time something that was rightfully mine.

Several years ago, in the throes of my confusion about Hinduism, Buddhism, and Judaism, I had cornered Phil in the parking lot of the temple and asked him something about God. I don't remember my exact question. It may have been about the judgmental, punitive qualities that I was uncomfortable with in the Old Testament God. What I was searching for was another way of experiencing "the Jewish God." While I don't remember my exact question, I do remember his exact answer. "You've never experienced the Jewish God because you've never prayed as a Jew," he said. And I do remember that I was pissed. I wanted him to give me something easy, something that would allow me to embrace Judaism, circumventing the parts of it that were so troubling to me. Instead what I heard in his answer was more judgments. I hadn't done it right, so I didn't get the goodies. And what really pissed me off was that I knew what he was saying was true. I *had* never prayed as a Jew. Except, perhaps, in whatever way I felt I had a direct line to God as a Jewish child. It is only recently that I am beginning to understand what he meant. Now, as my Hebrew improves, as we make it to Shabbat services more frequently, as we carve out a Jewish space in our lives, I feel how much being Jewish is a part of me.

In my world, my friends, for the most part, do not talk about God. They speak of their work, of relationships, of children, of the frightening changes in the political climate, their new computer, their upcoming vacation, of the ballet, their new book, of the exhibit at the MFA, the movie they saw last Saturday night. How could I talk about my spiritual life with them without sounding like a Hallmark card or the hopelessly inadequate English translations on the left-hand side of the prayer book? What words could I use to describe how the casing in which my shriveled up raisin-heart dwells had cracked open? I was determined to find a way.

When I was three or four, I learned that I had a vagina. My mother valued using the correct terminology for body parts and functions. When I visited friends' houses and they said they had to "make a number two," I had no idea what they were talking about. In our house it was a "bowel movement." I came to think that naming things was a sign of knowledge and maturity. Learning the name of this particular hidden part of me, this grown-up word, filled me with power and pride. I skipped into my grand-parents' luncheonette singing, "I have a vagina, I have a vagina," at the top of my lungs. My mother (and probably everyone else in the place) was too surprised to silence me. I was smart and now they all knew it.

Now this little girl skips up and back in the halls of my psyche with the same abundant pride, finally, finally knowing what she has known all along, and singing, "I'm Jewish, I'm Jewish," to all who will listen.

On Saturday mornings I chant the ancient prayers with the others, who, for as many reasons as there are numbers of us, come week after week to Shabbat services. I had known the healing power of sound, of music, before. But in shul, as our voices intertwine, they unknot the tangle of longing that forever blocked my chest, and fill it with their spaciousness. Floating freely, the galaxies of my Jewish head and my Jewish heart now reach out to each other. When I enter the tiny chapel in the basement of our shul where the weekly Shabbat services are held, I am as certain of the connection to this legacy as I am of my own two feet. They are far from perfect, my feet. Daily, they come more and more to resemble the feet of my grandfather, bunions and all. I know that I will always be able to find them, even though they are stuck in what should have been, on a more elegant leg, the middle of my shin. This is where the thick, peasant ankles of my grandmother join them to the rest of my body. I have often been ashamed of my feet, as I have been of wanting a spiritual life, of wanting a relationship with God. And I have hidden them away, as I have my longing, in the sand, inside of socks, under my thighs as I sit cross-legged on the floor. In spite of my shame, they have always carried me where I needed to go.

Perhaps "feet" are not the most poetic metaphor available, but they are, for the time being, the one that suits me. They link me in a concrete way to my parents, grandparents, *l'dor v'dor* (to generations and generations). Emboldened by the traditions through which they have walked, they step confidently onto the new ground being broken by our congregation and others like us, as we reshape our heritage to include the "her."

Now as I stand on these tired and well-traveled feet, praying in Hebrew, a language more layered and sweet than any baklava, I no longer feel that I am being denied access to the world of spirit. I am as surprised as anyone to find, that like one of those shapes in the Tetris game which come barreling out of the sky turning this way and that, finally with luck or skill or perhaps grace, I turn just the right way and slide gratefully into the space that is my Judaism.

After the frantically exotic ecstasies of the "energy" of

the Kundalini, I sigh and rest in the familiar arms of Judaism. My Jewish snake, now fully unfurled and basking in this warm, sweet comfort, is growing fat on Jewish prayer, and strong within our unique community.

It is wonderful to see Morrie and Ada. They have both been sick, and it is a rare treat to see them, even though this is not a happy occasion. As they took their turns in and out of the hospital and the rehab center, we, the younger members of the congregation, found ourselves scrambling to find ways to help ease their burdens. That they are healing and gaining strength seems no less a miracle to me than the tiny bit of oil lasting eight nights in the menorah.

That they are able to join the rest of the congregation at the cemetery for Esther Rome's funeral is bittersweet. Esther, founding member of the Women's Health Book Collective, and one of the earlier members of this new wave of our congregation, died of breast cancer at forty-nine. I am sure that neither Morrie nor Ada expected that they would outlive her, nor that they would find the strength to lift shovels full of dirt to cover the plain pine coffin in which Esther was buried. Phil tells us that to accompany someone to her grave, to cover her coffin with the freshly turned earth, is a great mitzvah, because the favor can never be returned. Yet as each of us had done our part, whether it was preparing food or stacking the dishwasher for the Romes in those last months of Esther's illness, or sitting with the body the night before the funeral, or making a bridge of people for Esther's family to walk through as they left the cemetery, we recognize that Esther's death has cemented whatever tentativeness there had been among us. We have become a community, in the fullest sense of the word. It is fitting that Morrie and Ada should be there to seal the bond.

It has started to drizzle again. As mourners take turns filling in the grave, I can't help but smile at Morrie and Ada, standing across from Susan and me, under their umbrella. I am remembering that time two years ago, before Morrie's heart attack, before Ada had that mysterious problem that none of the physicians could figure out when she lost circulation, and her fingers and toes and the tip of her nose turned black and fell off.

I remember that Susan and I approached the large round table where Morrie and Ada sat, eating their bagels after the Shabbat Together service. As the spiritual grand-parents of the shul, they were always surrounded by their heirs, the children. Ada, in spite of the pain she suffered even then from the cancer that is in her bones, had cro-cheted yarmulkes with the children's names on them. The children wear these to services. It was time for us to go home, but since we didn't know when we would see them again, it felt important just to say good-bye. Ada looked up at me with wide, wondering eyes. I realized that she was staring at my eye. I had recently had a skin cancer removed from my eyebrow. In the healing process, the blood had settled beneath my eye, giving me one helluva shiner. She subtly shifted her gaze to Susan. She is a mis-tress of the dramatic.

"Did you do that to her?" she asked Susan, barely cracking a smile. We were all silent for a split second. Then Morrie first, me, then Susan all laughed.

My heart is breaking. There is no place like home.

Vicky Phillips

Snake Woman's Hands

for Cindy

Not a few in Little Town believe that the venom of a copperhead snake—if survived—will cure all medical and spiritual evils known to mankind. Onie Cumberland believed
in the curative power of snakes. A bite to the neck had
cured her father of drunkenness. A puncture to the right
thigh had spirited the sex pox from her Cousin Brownie.
Great-aunt Getts had been twice cured of the gout in her
poor ugly feet. All this thanks to snakes. The power of
them as used by God Almighty. It was faith in this power
that Onie Cumberland, and most in Little Town, clung to
without question. Most, but not all.

Judith Ottie had heard the hymns of snakes many
times, first from her family, who handled as religiously as
anyone in Little Town, then from Onie, every time they'd
get close or serious about loving each other. But Judith
was what Onie called a mental mule. Judith had her own
ideas about snakes and God and faith and life. Whenever
Onie began insisting on the snake thing, especially the handling of them during the church revivals in the summer,
Judith would split. Faster than a snake, Judith would be
gone, disappeared out of Little Town, hitchhiked the forty
miles to the state highway, then out into the world at
large. Judith earned two college degrees and had a lot of
worldly adventures for no other reason than the one that

418

she could not side with Onie and sit still for the snake handling.

The urge to handle, as Judith saw it, was primitive. Illogical. Who would swing a stupid poisonous creature by
its tail in this day and age? Dancing with snakes and drinking kerosene from wide-lipped canning jars: these urges
sprung from some deep ignorance. Like prejudice itself,
these were not things that Judith cared to claim as her heritage. Ignorant and unthinking. Snake handling was something, like Little Town itself, that Judith had always hoped
to leave behind. But Judith wanted to keep Onie, and Onie,
her dear, dear Onie, would not let go of her snakes.

Onie, though not formally educated, had Judith's number.
It wasn't that Judith had no faith in God Almighty, as
some liked to mumble. It was that Judith hated to have
faith in anything that she could not lay her mind on. Not
her hands, *her mind*.

Judith liked it away from Little Town, in the city, because there was so much to be had in the city with her
mind: distractions everywhere, much that one was asked
to rebut or reveal as nonsense every minute of the day.
Think. Think. Think. Judith had absolute faith in words
and her power to reason. Judith read and absorbed words
like a starving baby sucks a sugar teat. Always had. Judith
had faith in her documentary films too, ghostly light
forms that she insisted she did not create, only captured.
Judith made documentary films for her living; they, in
turn, made her.

Judith did not have faith in the curative power of snake
venom, or that a dead man named Jesus did not lie rotting
in his grave. Judith was wilder than all that nonsense. Judith was an old woman, with two film Oscars, few teeth,
and two college degrees. She had not shaved her legs since
the first time she had taken Onie in her mouth, long before
record players could make music on their own without
being wound. As Judith liked to tease when she had

downed too much tequila, *once you have kissed a woman like Onie, what the hell need is there for any smaller version of God?*

Judith believed in one thing other than her long-standing love for Onie. She believed in her cameras. Judith's faith lay in the predictable yet magical science that allowed light to etch a ghostly living record which would outlast mankind. Judith's documentary films held most of her faith, like celluloid cups, constantly brimming beyond themselves. To Judith's mind, film succeeded where all religion promised, but failed. Her films brought people back in haunting bursts long after they were gone to their graves. Beyond life and death or any crazy question of God in his robelike pajamas or the devil in his best horns, danced Judith's stories, captured in light forever.

Film was the power, Judith liked to argue, that drew people to the movies. The power of sitting with others in the dark catacomb of life, watching as what we thought had passed came to sit on our knees and laugh in our faces again. Judith's films were bouncing angles of pure light, lost beyond God's reach. Judith had absolute faith in only two things: the immortality of her films and that Onie loved her in ways she would never begin to understand.

Though Onie preferred things she could lay her hands on to things of her own mind, she came to understand across the years how to hunt Judith with her own deadly weapons: logic and rational thinking. Onie liked to argue at Judith about the absolute logic of snake handling, whenever the topic came up between them, which was not infrequently.

There was a logic to it. A pure logic. What about the new attempts to cure AIDS? Weren't doctors injecting malaria into the collapsing veins of junkies, hoping that the malaria would shock the virus into retreat? Was that not illogical, to inject a dying man with a deadly thing and hope therein to encourage his salvation? Was this not snake handling of another kind?

Voodoo in the cities? Hadn't medical science come full circle from an arrogance in itself to a belief that faith in desperate measures might be the best solution after all? And if medical doctors could let go of their rationality and take hold of faith, careening across the caverns of the unknown on spiritual vines no stronger than old-fashioned hope, why could not Judith, smart as she was, take hold of a basic faith in God and the Hereafter, and swing herself to worldly safety?

Because, went Judith's carefully prattled part, *the universe is indifferent. Praying otherwise won't save a one of us from sliding out of our bodies and into the shadows that wait for us on the other side.*

All the more reason why Onie was not sure what to think or say when Judith, returning early one summer from a film shoot on crack-addicted babies, insisted on trying the snakes. Not filming the snakes, as she had been thinking about doing for a documentary. No. This time Judith wanted to feel the snakes, take them to her breast. Judith wanted to perform a snake dance.

Whatever does it feel like? Judith asked Onie after they had loved each other for the first time in months and Onie was curled like a sleepy child against Judith's small soft breasts. *Whatever is it like?*

Onie knew the feeling well, since childhood, countless times. The way it was to have a thick, five-foot snake in your hands, around your body, alive, breathing for you, like a knowing second skin. Onie knew the feeling, the trust with which she gave way and felt special because of it.

It's like holding the Hereafter that close to you. Like realizing that you are nothing more than a skin to be shed. It's like the first time you were inside of me. Something like that is as close as I can come.

Onie wanted to say something, something more. But the only thing that came to mind was to ask Judith if this sudden curiosity was because she truly believed there was something for her with the snakes or because she needed something to help her make sense of her own dying. If it was the latter, Onie wanted to tell Judith that there was no sense in dying.

Let go. Have faith. Don't look back! Reach out to what is coming.

What else could one do?

Judith had returned from the city this time with more than Ethan's bagels. She had returned with a carpenter's bag of pastel pills and the urge to throw up every two hours. For weeks, in the city, Judith had endured chemotherapy. Chemotherapy: medical science's hope that if you killed a person's diseased cells little by little, the whole of that person might wake up, fight back, and survive. Poison and kill all that is bad inside one . . . then get on your knees and pray like hell that something better grows back in its place. The irony of this kind of treatment against death was not lost on Judith when she returned to Little Town and Onie's sure arms.

Snakes can't move unless they are hot. Drop the temperature to below 50 and snakes tangle into one another, seeking the warmth that their own bodies lack by nature. Once heated, snakes don't move, they skim-spring around the earth, barely touching the ground. A snake can run faster than any human, twenty miles an hour on a hot summer day. People run from the sun, wild for shelter. Snakes take the sun's radiation, drinking it through their thin skin as lifeblood.

It was 91 degrees when Onie and Judith crawled into the old chicken coop where Onie kept her clan of copperheads, most of whom she had raised from the egg for several generations. Ninety-one degrees in late August, harvesttime. Everyone but Onie had complained all week about the heat.

Snake weather. Just right for reptiles. Maybe the last good handling of the season. They'll be hibernating soon. Onie was happy as she crawled up the coop ramp on her knees to feed her snakes, Judith right behind her.

Inside the coop, Judith stayed on her knees behind Onie, blinking, crawling, blinking, feeling ahead like a blind person, her palms spread out searching for snakes across the mud-caked, slatted floor. All these years she had not come into Onie's snake hut. It smelled like moldy feathers. Hot, unpleasant things. Chicken and bird nests, collected over the years by Onie, rested in ragged rows inside, barely visible, more like shadows suggesting themselves than anything solid and real.

Onie crawled around inside, her head bent for lack of clearance, laying fresh chicken eggs, a snake's most favorite treat, into the empty nests.

Judith followed, feeling small and blind, like a legless creature lost underground. *What did a living snake feel like? Like something you never wanted to take hold of to begin with, but once you had hold like an electrical wire that could not be forced back where it belonged no matter how hard you tried? And where were they? Where were they now? The snakes.*

Putting her tongue to the back of her few front teeth, Onie made a clucking sound as she crawled from nest to nest, shelling the eggs from the basket of her long cotton work shirt, settling them into the nests. She began to cluck a hymn. Rock of ages.

Not under your hands and knees, honey. No matter what the Good Book says. They don't stay on the ground this kind of weather. Heat rises. Snakes too.

Judith looked up. As her eyes adjusted to the peculiar way the August heat made the shadows dance and wave, she saw dozens of snakes, hanging like tangled clusters of copper and yellow grapes from the high corner eaves of the shed. *Medusa's head in the corner, in the half-light.*

Judith felt something. It wasn't fear, as she had expected, more an awe at the unexpectedness of the way the snakes clung to each other, wringing their bodies tightly together like hands in a worry; maybe just incredulity that she had not yet been bitten.

People who have never witnessed a handling cannot usually experience anything beyond the impulse to try *not* to imagine what it must be like. Even those who have been raised with handling as much a part of their religion as taking dry sacrament soda wafers at the altar can quickly drift from the tradition, finding shelter in a safer and more socially acceptable manner of devotion. Why Onie never took up a quieter way of worship with the Methodists down the mountain had always puzzled Judith. *Why?*

Onie did not puzzle over this herself. Onie never explored any religion but handling because handling pleased her so. Other than being with Judith, nothing excited Onie and brought her to a peak of aliveness like handling. Once the music started and people began to take up the snakes and dance with them eye-to-eye, Onie never wished to be anywhere but where this was happening, willingly lost to the uncertainty of her own actions.

Onie had been bitten twelve times, and while she knew what it was to be sick from a snake, no snake had yet dragged her the full way to heaven's gate. Onie attributed her salvation to her steadfast faith. Onie liked the feeling of using the will that God had given her. Really using it in an active way. Judith lived most of the year in the city, photographing the hellish streets. Onie stayed on the mountain and danced with her snakes, one generation of them after another. *Was there really that much difference between them?*

Judith attributed Onie's salvation to the fact that while snakes bite, not all bites have the true blessing of venom. Judith had done not a little research on the subject over the years as she had watched Onie laid up by snakes. Judith had a scientific understanding of the way snake poisoning *really* worked. If a snake does not hit into a human just right, the venom is not ejected or may be completely lost to the side. A direct hit into a vein will be deadly *only* if the snake is mature and strong enough. But snakes are not perfect marksmen. They do not "know" to aim for an artery, though instinctually their heat sensors—most snakes "see" by means of heat sensors in their heads, not through their eyes—can lead them to target an artery as the warmest part of the anatomy. The human heart makes the perfect target since it holds so much blood so close to the surface. Snakes can sense that much blood in one place and will strike at it.

Why a snake strikes or does not, no one knows. It is believed by scientists that snakes are complete cowards, more afraid of all that is around them than any human could ever be. Even being picked up and squeezed, or slung above the head, as wild young handlers who have drunk too much kerosene often do, does not guarantee that a snake will strike. More likely the snake will get its neck snapped this way. Snakes are all neck. They are very easy to kill. One quick snap will suffice. The fear modern people have of snakes is largely irrational.

Even though Judith had asked Onie to prepare her for Sunday's handling, the last of the season, she couldn't help but babble several times at the kitchen table that *snake bite recovery or cure had little of the miraculous attached to it once examined and much of the imperfectness of nature to thank for its power over the people of Little Town.*

Onie let Judith babble on, attacking her and Little Town, and her own mixed feelings about why she should want to handle after all these years.

Silly. Illogical. Won't help. Could hurt. Damn nonsense.

Onie saw no need to respond to Judith as she talked things out with herself. Supper finished, Onie helped Judith to bed, undressed her, and tucked her in.

Judith was becoming very shallow, like one of her own light images, existing slightly on some emulsion, not quite solid, as one expects a human to be. Onie was careful of touching Judith firmly because each day she seemed less of bone and flesh. More an image of herself.

Judith did not go to sleep as Onie instructed. Instead she ordered Onie to prop her up on the thick green pillows with yellow geese stampeding across them, pillows that Judith's mother had made for the girls years ago when she realized that they were not to be spinsters, as she had thought at first with her blinders on and her expectations unexamined. That they married each other never bothered anyone in Little Town. Even the uneducated know to step back from the unpredictable path of love.

Judith brought her hands to her face and clumsily lit and began to smoke a cigarette. As she held the cigarette to her mouth with both hands, Onie imagined—or did she?— that she could see the hurricane lamp shining through Judith's elegant fingers. Judith's hands, as she smoked, looked like white angel wings spread clumsily around her small mouth. Then, just as quickly, Judith's hands looked like nothing more than hands. A trick of light.

As Judith became herself, thicker and stronger, or perhaps just denser with the smoke, she complained more about what was the need to have faith anyway. So long she had gone with so little, if any, of that kind of stuff.

And God, what was He or She all about, just fear of there being nothing at all and that not being negotiable for any of us? None of us could stand the thought of being that trapped in the end, could we? God was a name for the place decent people went with their fear, no? God had many names, but the fear was always the same. No?

It was the heart of the night, rain pounding like a thousand righteous fists on the tin roof of Onie's house, when Judith decided to get up. She lifted Onie's sleeping arms from around her waist and expertly slipped her slight body aside.

Judith, the escape artist! Onie had called out loud many

times in the night, with good reason as Judith had been
gone or going much of their sixty years together.

But this night, Judith's restlessness was not about escape. At least not about an escape from Onie or Little
Town. Lately, Judith had not been able to sleep through a
night. Judith was dying and restless about it. Something
in her, knowing where she was headed, wanted to go as
quickly as possible. Something else, equally as powerful,
was calling her back. Judith imagined that the way she felt
was how the Apollo astronauts had explained to her on
film the feeling of leaving the earth's gravitational pull for
the very first time.

*Letting go of all that anchors. New and fast, reeling and
spinning toward forever! what a feeling! until some part of
you realizes . . .*

There is no fancy ceremony that stands as prelude to a
handling. About a dozen people, often related to each
other, many afflicted, not a few already dangling fingers
or arms left partially crippled by previous poisonings,
gather in what few would mistake as a church in this day
and age. In Little Town, the old abandoned general store by
the railroad tracks served as the established meeting place
for summer revivals.

A makeshift lectern, fashioned from wooden splints
hammered together with tin rivets, commanded the front
of the room, with a picture of Jesus cut from a Sunday
school magazine, framed in elaborately braided aluminum
foil hanging from crude twine around the lectern. No han-
dler cared what their place of worship looked like. A
muddy riverbank, just as God had made it, would have
suited them all, just as it did John the Baptist. Handling
was as much about what religion ought not to be as it was
anything else. God was not impressed by gold leaf. Did not
Jesus overturn the tables of the money changers who came
greedily into his temples? No money changed hands in this
religion. The only offering the handlers of Little Town ever

brought was themselves, some kerosene to spice things up and call the Holy Ghost quicker, and their baskets of snakes, of course.

Because it was Judith's night, Onie had brought her best copperhead snake with her. The big snake was coiled into a tight sleep inside the picnic basket that Onie carried on the crook of her right arm as she helped Judith uncertainly up the steps of the church with the other. This same snake had bitten Onie twice over the years, and was in his prime. He'd slipped four chicken eggs down that night for supper. Uncoiled, full of eggs, he was as thick and long as the leg of a grown millworker.

There was no minister or selected one to speak to the small group. Communion of spirit, for the handlers, came from within, not from one of their own threatening them into mortal submission, then taking their hard-earned money. They would get up and speak as the Holy Spirit, God's own unseen spiritual hand, moved them. Cousin Brownie had brought his spoons and would, predictably, offer a steady beat once someone began the devotions in earnest. Talking in tongues would happen for some, notably the twin Wineagar sisters, though not for Onie, as she was not so inclined.

As people began to pray among themselves, and Cousin Brownie got up and started to scream with the Ghost and beat his spoons against the lectern, Onie's snake was taken up by a skinny teenage boy named Hank. Hank had always been sickly. His face and arms were covered with pimples and sores, some sort of pox he'd had since a baby. He'd been handling for a year, but never been bitten. This disappointed him and his folks, who were not there this night. They were hoping for some sign, a trial of faith that would push Hank to fight for himself in some new way. God was leaving Hank be. This was not what they were hoping for.

Hank had the copperhead wrapped mostly around his left arm and was hopping around the room on the heels of his cowboy boots, petting the snake between the eyes with his right middle finger. *God Almighty, Jesus, we are One with You.* Hank singsonged into the mouth of the snake as he hopped. *Jesus Almighty, son of God, test us and find us with You.*

Judith sat and watched. Her mind was empty like never before. Judith said nothing, even when Onie got up and unwrapped the snake from Hank's arm like it was a bolt of lace and draped it gently around Judith's own thin, pale neck.

Onie took Judith by the hands and danced around the room with her. Judith soon had one end of the snake balanced and bouncing in each of her hands, as though it were a feather boa or a decorative shawl. She felt nothing but light. Onie had told her the whole truth. *Like realizing that you are nothing more than a skin to be shed.*

Though Judith was aware of the snake, its head dancing close to her heart, though she felt the power and the ecstasy of being so close without fear to something which all her life she had shunned as without logic, what Judith really felt was not the handling. Not the thing that had so attracted Onie all these years.

What Judith gave way to, and began to trust, was the simple way Onie's hand had·hold of the small of her back. Onie was gliding her expertly through a light that Judith had never seen before. A light that was quickly making shadow of them all.

Jane Kenyon

Let Evening Come

Let the light of late afternoon
shine through chinks in the barn, moving
up the bales as the sun moves down.

Let the cricket take up chafing
as a woman takes up her needles
and her yarn. Let evening come.

Let dew collect on the hoe abandoned
in long grass. Let the stars appear
and the moon disclose her silver horn.

Let the fox go back to its sandy den.
Let the wind die down. Let the shed
go black inside. Let evening come.

To the bottle in the ditch, to the scoop
in the oats, to air in the lung
let evening come.

Let it come, as it will, and don't
be afraid. God does not leave us
comfortless, so let evening come.

Martha Gies

A Heart of Wisdom

So teach us to number our days, that we may get us a heart of wisdom.
—PSALM 90:12

There was no religion in our family. My parents believed salvation lay in keeping the romance alive in their marriage, and in maintaining a high economic standard of living.

They had four children, each exactly three years apart, which I always took as a sign of my mother's superior sense of organization. I was the oldest, then came my brother, Michael, then a sister, Julia, and finally the baby, Toni. I was nine years old when Toni was born. I had special responsibilities as the oldest child: in some ways, I functioned more as a governess or a nanny. Michael, Julia, and Toni were like my own kids.

My father had a successful law practice and my mother had inherited land. We lived in the countryside, west of Salem, Oregon, near the Willamette River, with few neighbors to play with. This made the four of us very close as children. Also, our parents were extremely wrapped up in each other. They traveled together—to New Orleans, the coast, Diamond Lake, Mazatlán—and they enjoyed going to cocktail parties.

Three years after I left for Reed College, Father died unexpectedly of a heart condition. His death changed the family, violently and irrevocably. My mother was only

431

forty-one at the time, and she thought her own life was over. She did a lot of drinking and driving. When Michael departed for Antioch University and, two years later, Julia for Bennington, Toni was left at home alone with Mother, terrified and lonely. At this point, I was living in Montreal and didn't realize how chaotic the situation at home had become.

This was the sixties, so in addition to the disruptions caused by my father's death, we were also experiencing the aberrations of the age. I was in French Canada with a boyfriend who didn't want to be sent to Vietnam. At Antioch, Michael spent as much time dropping acid as he spent in class. At Bennington, I think Julia had quit shooting speed, but she dropped out of college after two years.

Then Toni became a Christian. All of us, Mother and the three siblings, were appalled. It would be many years before I had any insight into that period of Toni's life.

Toni was nineteen, and very shortly after her conversion she married a young man who shared her faith. She was taking herself as far as she could get from the pain she felt in her own family. Years later, she told me she had been desperate as a teenager. We were talking about conversion experiences at the time, and about what I had read as the three stages of faith: receptivity, mental assent, total surrender. "Boy," she said, "I moved through all three of those in about a week!"

Toni and Eugene, her husband, lived in the country and were farmers. Two children were born to them, a girl, Hope, in 1975, and a boy, Jess, in 1979. In the winter of 1980, Toni and Eugene signed on with Wycliffe Bible Translators to go to the Peruvian jungle on their guest helper program. Missionaries! This made our family even more hostile to her religion.

After four and a half months in Peru. Toni and Eugene decided to be missionaries for real. Their plan was to come home, liquidate their few assets, raise the money for their ministry, and sign on for a long-term program.

But instead, Toni ended up in the intensive care unit of Dallas Hospital. Salmonella had invaded her bloodstream. She lived, but was stuck with a gigantic hospital bill. They'd gone to be missionaries, after all: God was being unfair. She later said that her illness taught her she had two choices: she could stay stuck in her anger or she could move into acceptance.

At that time, I remember seeing this Scripture verse posted on her bathroom mirror: "We are afflicted in every way, but not crushed; perplexed, but not despairing" (II Corinthians 4:8).

It took Toni and Eugene four years to pay off the hospital bill. Finally, in December 1984, they were free of debt and looking forward to returning to the mission field.

That Christmas, while she was sitting at her kitchen table addressing Christmas cards, she felt a lump in her breast.

The phone rang one Wednesday night just as I walked through the door of my apartment in Seattle. It was Toni telling me the doctors had found a mass which they assumed was fibrocystic breast disease, but that they wanted to do a lumpectomy on her right breast and biopsy it. She said it was nothing to be concerned about, but not to tell Mother because she didn't want to worry her.

Mother was very alcohol-dependent at that point. The three of us older siblings had pretty much dismissed her as someone whose life wasn't going to show much movement. But Toni took a more aggressive and hopeful approach to Mother.

Things happened very quickly after that. Toni was told the lump was cancerous, and she was scheduled for a mastectomy. I said I'd meet her at the hospital in Salem on Monday morning.

I was struck by the number of friends, neighbors, and church members who showed up at the hospital to keep vigil with her. Toni's earliest instinct was to let others share in her journey, to not keep it a secret. People who couldn't come to the hospital to pray with her wrote letters. One friend sent her a box of nine presents to open, one day at a time. Each was labeled with one of the names of God from the Hebrew Scriptures. I remember glancing at them, observing the difference between Jehovah Raha, the Lord my shepherd, used in Psalm 23, and Jehovah Shalom, the Lord send peace, from Judges 6.

Two days after the mastectomy, Toni's tests came back from pathology: she had cancer in the lymph nodes. It was 1985. She was thirty-one years old.

Toni's original interview with the oncologist was tape-recorded, at his suggestion. I still have that tape. "Of course, we don't really ever know for sure, but statistically, we find that if there is cancer involvement in the lymph nodes, we're looking at maybe two years at the outside," the oncologist's deep voice says. "That's if two or three of the lymph nodes are involved."

And then, on the tape, a soft little voice asks, "How many lymph nodes did I have?"

"Sixteen."

With her husband Eugene, Toni prayed about whether or not to take chemotherapy. She, like everyone, had heard that with cancer, the medicine can be worse than the disease.

Eugene always regarded the cancer as something that had happened to *both* of them. "You know, you having cancer is really a gift," he told her early on, "because now we will never again have the opportunity for complacency in our lives."

That was to be true for the rest of us, though we did not know it at the time. The family was still very fractured at this point. Mother was living in Salem, drinking steadily. I was in Seattle, writing fiction and producing the "Motion Picture Seminar of the Northwest." Michael was in Portland, making great career leaps in the TV products division at Tektronix. Julia had gone back to graduate school and was practicing poverty nursing somewhere in Appalachia.

For us, Toni's cancer would become a redemptive catastrophe.

When Toni finally decided she would take the chemo, she made it clear to her oncologist that she had certain basic bottom-line concerns about the quality of life. First, she wanted to die at home. Her oncologist said he would respect that, but that she would have to do *her* part not to get into the emergency medical system. He suggested she post "Do Not Call 911" on all her phones.

She said she didn't ever want to become bedridden, and he said that it would become a matter of not treating her beyond a certain point.

She said, most importantly, she did not want to lose her mind. He said he couldn't make that promise to her.

She said, in her wry way, that's what she figured, but she was going to pray for it anyway.

So in April 1985, she began six months of chemotherapy. The chemicals made her nauseous, and it was a record hot summer in the Willamette Valley. She couldn't take the antinausea medication, because it gave her grand mal seizures. Yet her courage was extraordinary. She began to talk of running a 10k race in July.

"People say to me, You are so strong," she wrote in her journal, "but I am not. I am so weak! My strength is in the Lord. He is my rock, my fortress, my deliverer."

I wrote in my journal that summer, "Toni's faith organizes the experience for her, and gives it meaning."

The Post-it on her bathroom mirror that summer read: "Patience is accepting a difficult situation without giving God a deadline to remove it."

The family began to look at her Christian faith in a new light.

On the Fourth of July, Toni and Michael went to the Independence races. He entered the bicycle race and took first place. Then Toni's foot race began, and he cheered her at the start. He was there at the finish line, to see her place seventy-third out of seventy-seven runners, and he was still cheering, her victory clearly more stunning than his own.

In the fall, Toni had radiation for six weeks. After that, all of her tests were clean: her bone and blood scans, her mammogram. She'd done it; she'd licked it; the cancer was gone.

But in Tennessee, Julia was reading Toni's letters describing the degree of lymph involvement, and was able to stage Toni's cancer from her medical books. Although Toni had gone into remission, Julia foresaw the probable course of the disease and moved back to the Northwest, where she had not lived in seventeen years. She joined me in Seattle, took a job at a skid road clinic—and waited.

In January 1987, after Toni had gone a full year without cancer, a small nodule was removed from her right breast. She was told the results of the biopsy over the phone. She was angry, anticipating another round of doctors, humiliation, X rays, being poked at, shuffled around, and tested.

She went to see her oncologist, who recommended a stronger chemotherapy this time around. She was against it because she knew that would mean another round of nausea, vomiting, weakness. She just didn't think she could take it. Adriamycin was one of the chemicals he was recommending, and that meant hair loss. She said no way. She went to Oregon Health Sciences University for a second opinion. That was the first time she ever heard the term "Stage 4 Cancer, Incurable."

This is what Julia had feared all along: now she moved home to Oregon and took a job as a nurse practitioner with Multnomah County.

When I listened to the tape recording of Toni's second interview with the oncologist, I couldn't believe I was hearing so much resistance focused on hair loss. I called her up and exercised an older sister's authority. "Take the damn Adriamycin," I told her.

"That's fine for you to say," she told me. "You're not going to lose your hair."

I went out that day and had my head shaved to about a quarter of an inch of peach fuzz all over it. Then I sent her a photograph. On the back I'd written, "Chemotherapy solidarity."

Toni's thinking evolved from *Why is God doing this to me?* to *Why is God letting this happen to me?* and finally to *What does God want me to do about this?*

When she finally realized she would go ahead with the chemo, she planted four acres of strawberries. We were astonished. The thousands of tiny plants that she put into the ground in May wouldn't be ready for harvest until the following year.

"My feeling is: we go for the long haul," she wrote in her journal. "We learn to live with cancer, we learn to live with chemotherapy. We learn to adjust our lifestyle. We pace ourselves. We draw on the help our friends and family offer, and we are careful that no individual gets burned out—because we will probably need to go through this again. We pray for healing. But whether this is the last time, or only the second in a series, Jesus is still Lord. We will continue to praise Him and give glory to God. We *do* pray for healing, but most of all we pray for the Healer Himself to come and make our lives meaningful."

Her chemotherapy lasted six months. Halfway through, she had a port-o-cath installed to receive the chemicals on a slow drip. She lost her hair completely. Photographs of her that summer show her hoeing the young strawberries wearing a variety of wigs, turbans, and scarves.

Toni's case was becoming known. People came to interview her, to photograph her. She'd usually try to have her husband and her children—Hope now eleven, Jess seven—

present. Once a young reporter said to her, "I guess something like this makes you rethink your priorities." "Not really," Eugene said. "Ever since we got married, seventeen years ago, we have spent one January weekend, just the two of us, at the beach, praying and writing and talking about what is important to us. When the cancer hit, we were already trying to live the life we wanted."

Meanwhile, Mother had been available to her for every emergency, even to the point of going one or two whole days in a row without a drink. "This is changing our relationship," Toni wrote in her journal. "Suddenly she has shown me so much compassion and mothering and care."

In the fall of 1987, Toni asked two things of me. She wanted to know if I could be available in June and July of the following year to help her harvest the strawberries. And she asked me to put my writing skills to use and help her compile a manuscript that she would leave as a testimony for her family and friends.

When I moved back to Portland from Seattle, Toni offered to help me pack and move. "No way," I told her. "This time it will be a professional mover." "Well," she said, "you'll need some help on this end, cleaning and unpacking." And I was thinking, But it's not going to be you, kid.

She came back with one of the most important lessons I learned from her. "When I was sick and my friends came into my house and cleaned the toilets," she told me. "I didn't think I could stand it. And one time I came home from the hospital and looked out my bedroom window and saw an eighty-year-old man from our church weeding my strawberries! Oh, no, I thought. He'll kill himself! But Martha," she said, "sometimes you have to let people help you."

In March 1988, Toni began to experience symptoms of extreme thirst. A CAT scan showed thirty little BB-size tumors in the brain. "They're small," Toni told me on the phone, "but they're trouble." The doctor said she might be looking at a matter of months left in her life.

This was one of many terminal diagnoses which she outlived. After five weeks of radiation to the brain, she had another scan: the tumors were no longer detectable. She would live another two and a half years beyond that prediction.

In June, we began preparing for the first strawberry harvest. A neighbor pulled a trailer into Toni and Eugene's driveway, and I moved into it. Five days before we began the first pick, we learned that the cancer had metastasized to her lungs. "If Jesus Christ is not who He says He is," Toni said, "then now would be a really good time to find out."

Yet we had a wonderful summer, up at five each morning and starting the crew at 6:00. Toni had about sixty pickers out there, many of them Mexican people. That's a culture we both loved. I had painted the outhouses white and labeled them *Damas* and *Caballeros*.

Every afternoon, after the pickers went home and the buckets were picked up from the field, washed, and stacked for the next day, and Eugene had left to drive the berries to the cannery, Toni and I would shower, and lie down, and talk about her manuscript project. We tape-recorded seven interviews that summer, and these, along with her letters home from Peru and the journals she had kept for years, became our primary material.

"Toni has made a sacrament of her life," I wrote in my own journal that summer.

And I wrote: "Toni is not in control of her life: God is. She does not try to wrestle that control away from God, but to accept and to praise."

And I wrote: "Toni's only 'victory' is surrender."

And later that fall I wrote: "Toni's hair is growing back!" The following Easter (1989), she was asked to give her testimony in front of her congregation, the McMinnville Covenant Church.

"I wish I could tell you that the cancer has been totally removed," she said that Easter, "but I cannot. God is still working. Since the beginning of this year, we have learned that my lungs are a little worse and they found two small spots of cancer on my bones. What does this mean?

"I think it means, Ask not that it be lifted, but rather ask for God's grace to fulfill the task. Ask for sufficient grace to come closer to God, that you may be lifted above the circumstance."

This was to be the beginning of a public-speaking career.

The family began to wake up to something about Toni. Julia mentioned it first. She had been driving Toni around on some errands, and when they stopped to put gas in the car in Sheridan, all the attendants came out of the station and went around to Toni's side of the car, wanting to talk to her, wanting to be in her presence. Julia said it was the same at the post office, and the same at the hospital. All these people were getting something from Toni. The impossible had happened. The sibling order had been reversed: now we were the little ones. Toni had become our teacher.

One day in July 1989, when I had been planning to drive out to Toni's to spend the day putting up blueberry jam, she phoned me early in the morning to say she'd had a coughing spell during the night and snapped a rib. "Don't come," she said. "We can't get any jam made with this broken rib." I went out anyway, and we waited together for the doctor to return her call. She had a wrenching cough, along with the broken rib.

"Pain narrows vision," Toni wrote in her journal. "The most private of sensations, it forces us to think of ourselves and little else. That is why it is so important to me to keep my mind filled with Scripture and music, which focus my attention on God."

"God stands within the shadow, behind the dim unknown," I wrote in my journal.

In August, Toni and I put up pickles. She had oxygen then, which she used at night and when she wanted to do something strenuous during the day—like forty-two quarts of dill pickles. Fifty feet of clear plastic tubing snaked around the kitchen behind her, attached to the oxygen machine, which clanged and burbled down the hall.

Later that summer, we borrowed a wheelchair and took Toni to the Polk County Fair. I remember the cool poultry barns, the beauty of the white and polka-dot show chickens.

That summer, Eugene gave a sermon at McMinnville Covenant. "When doubt strikes," he said, "it is time for digging deeper into God's word, rather than closing the Bible and walking away. It is time for more praying and committing our will to Him. Doubt is not the opposite of faith, rather disobedience is. If we are choosing to be obedient to God . . . we are able to see how the process of doubt is woven into the process of faith."

That autumn, Toni had a health crisis. In a week she lost five pounds. She was fitted with a morphine infusion pump and needed several lung taps. The family began to take turns staying with her. This is when all the phones in her house were finally labeled "Do Not Call 911."

During my first shift, I phoned sixteen people and put together a chore network, two hours per week, mainly people from Toni's church. I was on the phone one afternoon when Toni called out for me. She wanted to take a nap, and she asked me to lie beside her and make sure she didn't stop breathing as she dozed.

After Julia took her shift, she told us Toni's metastatic brain cancer had probably returned.

Word was getting around that Toni was failing, and on Sunday night, the elders of McMinnville Covenant visited the house and laid on hands. Then they announced a weeklong prayer vigil, in which the whole congregation participated. I phoned the associate pastor and got my name on the list for the 10:00 A.M. slot. I'd never been part of a prayer vigil, and I prayed the nine names of God that Toni's friend had sent her four years before. ''Jehovah Raha, the Lord my shepherd, who leads me to water and sweet pastures, who counts me at night.''

By the end of the week, Toni rose off her bed, got her strength back, and even went the following month to be the keynote speaker at the 1989 Covenant Women's Retreat at Black Lake Bible Camp, in Tumwater, Washington.

I went along with her to push the cart that carried her eleven-pound portable oxygen unit.

There, in front of three hundred women, she gave her testimony, which said, in part:

''I remind myself, Let God be God. Don't demand healing; don't demand death on certain terms; don't demand closure. Be open to His will.''

The afternoon was set aside for small workshops, and Toni was giving one called ''Ministering to the Dying.'' We were told we'd get fifteen participants.

I walked her to her assigned meeting room after lunch and got her settled on a high stool at the front of the room, with her oxygen tank nearby. Then I scooped up her twenty handouts and went and stood by the door to greet people when they arrived. One hundred and fifty women walked through that door.

I learned something that day. In any crowd, no matter how unruffled they may look, or how serenely they are acting, there are always people harboring deep suffering, people who are ministering to the dying or caring for the sick, or praying about their own diagnosis, or weighing the worth of continuing to live.

One of the Scriptures Toni used for that workshop was II Corinthians 1:4.

He comforts us in all our troubles, so that we in turn may be able to comfort others in any trouble of theirs and to share with them the consolation we ourselves receive from God.

After the conference, Toni and I concentrated on finishing her manuscript. It was a book-length effort that went through five drafts. Now we spent three days together at the Embarcadero in Newport, line-editing. Her plan was to print a dozen copies, and have me deliver them to the designated recipients on the one-year anniversary of her death.

In December, Toni experienced loss of balance and vision problems. She had a myelogram that showed carcinoma meningitis, cancer of the spinal fluid. A new doctor, this time a neurologist, told her she had three months to live if she did nothing.

Toni was offered the option of a brain operation, a "bubble" implanted in the skull through which chemo could be poured directly. The neurologist said it might extend her life by as much as twelve months.

Toni was leaning *away* from the chemo. She was at the point where she was ready to live out her last quiet, normal three months at home, doing what she could do to be a wife and mom. "Even if I'm just defrosting dinner," as she put it.

Again, Julia read the literature. She determined that the chemo was *not* so likely to extend her life, but might block the progressive cranial nerve deterioration associated with meningitis: water on the brain, coma, death. Julia was registered for a monthlong language course in Nicaragua. She canceled her trip. If Toni refused the chemo she would need nursing care.

But someone, a nurse I think, talked Toni into the chemo. After a week of research and prayer, Toni told us she was scheduled for brain surgery. An Ommaya reservoir was implanted in her head, and a Groshong catheter in her chest, so she could take morphine without needles. After the surgery, Mother drove me to the Greyhound station and then doubled back to the hospital, where she sat and fed Toni chips of ice for two hours.

The next day, they dripped chemo down through the hole in Toni's head, directly into her spinal column. She was doing all right, so they released her from the hospital. Someone said of Toni's remarkable stamina, "It just goes to show, if you have the spiritual resources, how far modern medicine can help you."

On New Year's Day, Toni and Eugene made a resolution to date once a week.

Toni's great spiritual resources were stubbornness and a sense of humor. Once, when her oncologist put her on a new medicine, she was given a long list of signs to watch for, some of which, like vision and balance problems, she had already experienced from the cancer itself. The last of these symptoms to watch for was confusion. "So," she asked in a droll voice over the phone, "if you're confused, how in the world do you watch for confusion?"

When she developed double vision, she was told to put a patch over her eye and learn to live with it. Instead, she decided to get help on her own. She called Pacific University's Family Vision Center, and they replaced the eye patch with a prism on the inside of her right lens and started her on vision therapy. She went to the vision clinic every week for two months and did the prescribed exercises faithfully every day at home. When she was reevaluated, they found that both her vision and her eye coordination had improved. In fact, the opthalmologist told her he had begun writing an article on her case for a professional journal to show physicians that improvement can be made with vision therapy even in cases of cranial nerve damage from cancer.

In June 1990, Toni got a call from a television producer, asking her to appear on a local talk show. KATU-TV was planning an episode of "Town Hall" around the suicide of Janet Adkins. An Oregon woman, she had enlisted Dr. Kevorkian's help in giving herself a lethal injection in a Detroit motel room after learning she had Alzheimer's. The producer was casting about for someone who would be willing to go on the show and say they would *not* use Dr. Kevorkian's suicide machine—someone, that is, who was actually dying. Somehow KATU got Toni's name.

At that point, she weighed ninety pounds and had lost six inches of her height. She walked with a cane and with her neck bent at a 90-degree angle, her head facing the floor, her eyes peering up to the side to avoid bumping into things. But she went on the air, along with Derek Humphry, who is head of the Hemlock Society, and Ron Adkins, Janet's husband.

The show is staged arena-style, the host whizzing around the center platform on a swivel chair, making quips intended to incite debate. As an invited guest, Toni was seated in the front row of bleachers, frequently in view of the television camera. She didn't say much, but I could see that her frailty and poise affected people. She did not presume to tell anyone else what to do, nor was she interested in the issue of legal rights: she only knew God did not want her to take her life; that God had given this one gift, and that she would wait on Him to take it away.

Carol Remke, the girlfriend who had accompanied Janet Adkins to Detroit, was also on that show, and she came up to us in the corridor afterward, as Toni slowly made her way toward the exit. With tears in her eyes, Carol greeted Toni and touched her arm.

Two months later, Mother spent a week at Black Butte Ranch, taking care of Toni while Eugene and the kids rafted and swam. It was a beautiful September. Mother pushed Toni's wheelchair down cinder paths, crushing fragrant pine needles. The rest of us have never entirely known what took place there, but when they returned both Toni and Mother were calm about Toni's impending death.

After Black Butte, Toni declined radiation and contacted a hospice for in-home nursing care. Then, having made those arrangements, she spent a weekend at the beach with her best girlfriend, writing her own obituary.

A week before she died, Michael and I went to see Toni

on a Sunday night. She was so frail then; I remember thinking her head was like a heavy blossom on a broken stem.

At dinner, I cut up her food. She dropped two dosages of medications trying to get them out of her huge pill holder. They rolled around the kitchen table and onto the floor and it was a mess trying to sort them out.

The following Thursday night, Mother had a dream: she walked into Toni's house to find Jess (Toni's son, then eleven) lying on the couch, Eugene in the kitchen, and Toni dead in the bedroom.

The next day, when Mother actually drove out to Sheridan, she walked in on a scene that matched her dream, except that Toni lay half-conscious in the bedroom.

Mother phoned me. "I think Toni is dying," she said. "The hospice nurse is here, and she thinks so, too."

I called Michael, who left Tektronix and picked me up, and we drove to Sheridan. In the car, I was praying that Toni would live until we got there.

I went in to her as soon as we arrived. Her skin was hot and dry, and although she was wearing her oxygen mask, she was inhaling through her mouth and vocalizing each exhalation. She lay on her back and her eyes flickered open from time to time. She was conscious. I talked to her at length, held her hand, and prayed with her. That was Friday.

Julia was in Ann Arbor, where she had just begun a low-residency Ph.D. program in public health policy. We weren't able to make contact with her until Saturday, and she began hassling the airlines, trying to get home. By Sunday, Toni was in a light coma, but we kept telling her the exact hour that Julia's plane would arrive.

Late Sunday night, I was home in bed, having already said good-bye to Toni, when Julia called me from the Portland airport. Julia drove two hours to Toni's bedside. At one o'clock in the morning, Toni appeared unconscious, her breathing a shallow gurgle. Julia sat with her and told her everything she needed to say. Then she left the room.

Fifteen minutes later, when Eugene checked the room, Toni was dead.

Toni was granted all of her prayers: she died at home, she never became bedridden, she did not lose her mind.

She went through tremendous pain over a five-and-a-half-year period. Was it worth it to her?

"I would not trade anything that I have gone through or am going through in this battle with cancer," she wrote, "for what it has developed in my relationship with God and in a faith that will not let go of Him."

For me, it was a profound spiritual experience of sustained and unparalleled intensity.

I now think that when people refuse illness, dependency, and pain, they may be depriving themselves, and others, of a powerful transformation. "Sickness before death is a very appropriate thing," Flannery O'Connor once wrote to a friend, "and I think those who don't have it miss one of God's miracles."

Toni loved this Scripture from Habakkuk, and always quoted it whenever she spoke in public:

Though the fig tree does not bud and there are no grapes on the vines,
Though the olive crop fails and the fields produce no food,
Though there are no sheep in the pen and no cattle in the stalls,
Yet will I rejoice in the Lord,
I will be joyful in God my Savior.
The sovereign Lord is my strength;
He makes my feet like the feet of a deer,
He enables me to go on the heights.
                    (Habakkuk 3:17–19)

Patrice Vecchione

Toward the Only Sky

In memory of Rosmarie

West of east and south of north, where wind crosses
the miles of fences, loud all the way to the other side,
the silhouette of an angel stands,
same stance as always, one hip raised,
one foot slightly forward, snake beneath the feet.
The halo above her head is the full moon
glowing incandescent.
The tiny carmine lips, visible as she turns her head slightly,
her plaid wings woven from thin tree branches.

The map that leads here she carries under her dress,
the highways which move the blue blood
and the red blood.
She knows the world is round; where her heart used to be
there is water surrounded by a wall of stones,
moss covered, the bluest water.

Cherry Valley, Sun City, where the Mojave River forks,
south of Hesperia, north of Green Valley, White Water,
highway 10 and the small roads, tributaries that finger,
intersect. You have to follow the voice here, the only way
is to listen. But one doesn't always.

The ticket to heaven, it's hers, the woman
in the bed, in front of the window, across from and above
the new church steeple, shiny and black.

The one who lies in the bed dying kept hold of my eyes
with her eyes for minutes at a time.
I didn't know how to reassure her,
I just kept looking back. How long does dying take,
from the inside, how long?
"What does the ticket look like? How do I use it?" she asks
our bearded friend late in the night.
In his arms he holds a guitar, looks out toward
all the night,
as if to say, it's out there, the angels, not one
but many, who can take you there.
She describes a particular blue to me, like the Swiss Alps,
she says, not on top, underneath them, glacier blue.
How do you
die? You go underneath
the glacial blue and above it.
You take your press-on wings, insure them. Take flight,
make it yours for once and always.
Asking, is there another side?

In this canyon the wind comes up like a woman
not resigned to her dying. Saying, no, no, it isn't my time.
But then it is. Illness in the body says so,
how the bad cells destroy what is good. Her breathing
labors, pauses too long, labors again; in her hands
are scrunched fistfuls of sheet and blanket.

How do you die, relent, let go of what is known,
the familiar? How do you open the shutters
and allow the wind inside, the whole cold wind, let it in?
How do you do it? Doorway, path,
black church steeple outside the window,
and the bells chime on Sunday. She will walk
the tributaries, fingerings of water, past
where the river divides, up the frosted
northern slope, glacial blue, the underside.

Carole Maso

Night

This is probably the last love letter I will ever write.

Sing me a Yiddish song.

I kiss you.

Sing me a lullaby by Brahms.

You spoke once more of Trieste.

Queen of the Night.

I feel the Birdcatcher is near.

Thunder is heard.

Silver bells—for your protection.

A magic flute.

Sung in German.

I kiss you one hundred times.

On those evenings we saw forever.

The free world.

City of night.

He was always very tender with me.

I will.

A solitary night once.

A country road. A tree. Evening.

Louis and Louise and the giant poodle Lily.

In the winter do the trees still have the sensation of having leaves—though the leaves have fallen?

And I do not want to miss the cold.

Star light, star bright.

First star.

Your heart beating beneath my hand.

Make a wish.

Almost everything is yet to be written by women about their infinite and complex sexuality, their eroticism.

Ravishing, enchanting

Let me know if you are going.

Bearer of every kind of news.

What did she yearn for? What did she want? What were her hopes? Her unattainable goals?

Ninety, ninety-one, ninety-two, ninety-three. . . .

What did she dream?

Who was she?

And where is she going?

How we liked so much to go to the park. Father would do his funny walk. That made us all laugh so hard we fell in the grass. He'd call to me: Sophie, help! his arms outstretched.

Like the room in a dream.

Whisper in my heart. Tell me you are there.

Accuse me again, if you like, of overreaching.

The child learns her alphabet.

The mystery of your touch

Hovering and beautiful alphabet.

Of wanting too much.

After the masked balls, after the jokes—

I make no apologies. . . .

Look for this in my shoe.

Snow falls on Mozart's grave tonight.

It is given. It is taken away.

Feathered and bejeweled, masked, because in Venice in 1632 *the plague is over*.

To be sung.

It is given back. Sometimes, it is given back.

Our passion for pasta, focaccia, and every fish in the sea.

Use a wooden pestle not to crush, but rather to push the ingredients in a circular motion against the stone, which will grind them.

Bombs fell.

Children lived there.

Small paper boat.

Bolting between two subway cars in pursuit of a man who has grabbed her purse, she falls and is dragged by the moving train.

Open sea.

Her brother Paul: I do not think she will come here again. But I told my mother we had to go once.

The sound of guns is near.

Just once.

My sister was beautiful, he said. We are Buddhists. We believe that her spirit is alive and will have another life. I hope she will be beautiful again.

A place to collect things I don't want to forget:

Salamander. Praying mantis. Small horse. Star.

The way your hair caught the light.

So much desire.

She watches shooting stars.

Confetti. Quinze août.

Shortened—how can this—

Half-breathed response to your fingers, tongue.

Coming back from the place we've gone.

The tear in the curtain.

Veined ceiling.

Light.

Don't forget.

She screams.

The sea-soaked steps.

The souls being pulled out of the mouths of the dead.

By mistake—

I do not think she will come here again.

4. Sergei Nabokov (1900–1945) had, like his father, a passionate interest in music, especially

As we form our first words

Who knows where love goes?

The last movement begins with—

That night she dreamt of a shining marble city on a hill.

They hid in a red village.

French baby gifts: Salt for wisdom, an egg,

The next day, exploring, she found the cemetery.

Floating world.

La Régence: 18 July

A change in light, a tilt of the head, a repositioning of legs, the introduction of clouds. Fragments of conversation. A shift in intention. The light board. The cars and vans with their fleeting alphabets. Drama of tourists. Daily drama of lovers. Music in the square. . . .

Let me know—

He calls me with clicks and hisses.

Love, the stars are falling all around us.

I still think of you, after all this time.

The heat of July. I shall not forget. And dancing.

You held my hand.

Bernard

I do not think he will come again.

The last movement begins with a slow introduction in F# minor. There follows an allegro in A major. I intended for the high-spiritedness of this music to last throughout the movement, but I found that I was overtaken by sadness in the last few pages, and I let it stand that way.

Like a miracle in my arms.

I'm right here.

You spoke of Trieste, of Constantinople. You pushed the curls from your face. You thought of buying a hat, per- haps—it was how the days went.

I love you. Have always loved you. I have come, Ava Klein, many kilometers to tell you in person.

Careful of the intercom.

To this beautifully decorated box.

I miss the old days at the Academy—when we were all there together.

And we sang.

Brightly colored stitched messages. So many names. A quilt too big to display now. A quilt the size of the earth soon.

Green, how much I want you green.

Aldo Santini. Cherished—

Each occasion celebrated with verve.

Find a cure.

Well, auf Wiedersehen, as he said to me. Too late.

This is probably my last love letter

Find a cure.

But I remember, don't you, what it was like?

Find a cure.

How soon we become bright colors and stitches.

A few threads.

I will never see you again.

Find a cure.

One last glimpse. . . .

Well, auf Wiedersehen, as he said

His footprint in the ice.

Let me know if you are going. The nurses at their stations.

Central Park. I walked for a long time, wept bitter tears, brought you back

A ginkgo leaf. You smiled. Pet it with one finger. You had only hours to live then. We remembered the bridge, the color of rocks, the ginkgo trees

Sweet lavender and thyme.

Yes. You were quite burned by the sun.

And in another park: swan boats. Where we sang.

A bowler hat.

Father would do his funny walk

And how my own mother has always seemed a shadow

It was called *Precious Last Glimpses*.

It's getting late.

The touch of the sun

And how dusk and the moment right before the shapes are taken back by the night is erotic.

And the dark.

The look in your face as you turn away

And we follow it into forever, whispering, the too familiar.

The small light a candle can give.

Sitting here and counting the small beads of sweat on your face is erotic, and the way you toss your head, the curve of your shoulder, the circular garden, the late afternoon, and the memory of

And the dark.

We were all a little in love with her.

The drag and pull of the park.

She showed us how to dance.

The moan of roses.

In a circle holding hands.

I have been terribly lonely here. Not because I have been too much alone but because I simply have not had a kindred spirit (except for an Italian woman, on the train, who lives in Warsaw). It has been a strange experience, really difficult—but it has perhaps led to a kind of "transcendence" because my friends, amitié, has taken on such great value for me. I could almost grow teary-eyed simply writing the word.

I miss you.

The bread in braids.

Why did I think I would give in so gently?

Why did I imagine gentleness?

We used to take the rabbit path around the cliff.

And I find myself a little shakier than I used to be.

Ramon Fernandez, tell me, if you know
Why when the singing ended and we turned
Toward the town,

I know this letter will probably never get to you. But it is important and so I write it anyway.

How, then, to find the arabesque? The dancers?

A million swallows at sunset. Let's get lost in the pattern of rugs. A citadel. A minaret. The gate leading to the mosque. Open me.

How is this for an ending?

INVOCATION

Maya Angelou

Still I Rise

Just like moons and like suns,
with the certainty of tides,
just like hopes springing high,
Still I'll rise
Out of the huts of history's shame
I rise
I'm a black ocean, leaping and wide,
welling and swelling I bear in the tide.
Leaving behind nights of terror and fear
I rise
into a daybreak that's wondrously clear
I rise
bringing the gifts that my ancestors gave,
I am the dream and the hope of the slave
I rise
I rise
I rise.

Contributors

Maya Angelou is an author, poet, playwright, stage and screen producer, director, performer, and singer. Her many titles include *Kofi and His Magic*, *Phenomenal Women*, *All God's Children Need Walking Shoes*, and *I Know Why the Caged Bird Sings*.

Laurine Ark is the author of *Writing from the Exterior Dramatic Perspective: A New Vision for Literature*. She teaches creative writing nationwide and has been nominated for the Pushcart Prize. Her fiction and poetry have appeared in *Negative Capability*, the *Haight-Ashbury Literary Journal*, and many other small-press publications. She lives with her son, Ben, in Delaware and believes in never abandoning hope.

Sue Bender is the author of *Everyday Sacred: A Woman's Journey Home*, and *Plain and Simple: A Journey to the Amish*. An artist, lecturer, and former family therapist, she makes her home in Berkeley.

Becky Birtha is an African-American Quaker, lesbian, feminist poet and fiction writer, and the mother of a young daughter. Her books include *The Forbidden Poems* and a short story collection, *Lovers' Choice*. She also works as an adoption coordinator helping to find homes for children with special needs.

Sandy Boucher is a writer and teacher living in Oakland. She has a master's degree in religion from the Graduate Theological Union in Berkeley, and much experience in Buddhist practice and study. Her latest book, *Opening the*

Lotus: What Women Want to Know About Buddhism, was published by Beacon Press.

Ellen Cassedy has published in *Redbook*, *Woman's Day*, and the *Philadelphia Daily News*. She is a graduate of the creative writing program at Vermont College and lives near Washington, D.C. "The Things You Can't See" reflects elements of her own childhood struggle to find a spiritual home.

Melody Ermachild Chavis is a private investigator who works on trials and appeals for death row inmates. She lives with her husband in Northern California, is a mother and grandmother, and volunteers with a community gardening project for youth at risk. A student of Zen Buddhism, she is a member of the Buddhist Peace Fellowship.

Marilyn Chin is a poet and story writer. Her books include *The Phoenix Gone*, *The Terrace Empty* (Milkweed Editions), and *Dwarf Bamboo* (Greenfield Review Press). She teaches creative writing at San Diego State University and believes that Everywoman is a goddess and has her own occasional epiphanies.

Lucille Clifton is the author of many books of poetry, including *An Ordinary Woman*, *Next*, and *The Book of Light*. Her awards include the Juniper Prize for Poetry, an Emmy Award from the American Academy of Television Arts and Sciences, and two fellowships from the National Endowment for the Arts. She is presently Distinguished Professor of Humanities at St. Mary's College of Maryland.

Descended from nine generations of Episcopal priests, **Elizabeth Cunningham** is a Quaker and a pagan priestess, and is studying to be an interfaith minister of spiritual counsel. Mostly she writes novels and is the author of *The Wild*

Mother, The Return of the Goddess, How to Spin Gold: A Woman's Tale, and *Daughter of the Shining Isles*.

Originally from India, **Chitra Banerjee Divakaruni** lives in the San Francisco Bay Area, where she teaches creative writing at Foothill College. She is the author of *Black Candle: Poems About Women from India, Pakistan, and Bangladesh*. She has recently published her first novel, *Arranged Marriage*.

Robin Drury has given up teaching elementary school, cigarettes, Scotch, a weed-free garden, and husbands. She got her first hiking boots at fifty, her M.A. in education at fifty-one, and went on her first backpacking trip at fifty-two. With one foot in Santa Cruz and the other in the Sierra, she only comes home to feed the cat.

Riane Eisler is the author of *The Chalice and the Blade* and *Sacred Pleasure: Sex, Myth, and the Politics of the Body*. Born in Vienna, she was a refugee from the Nazis and at fourteen immigrated to the United States, where she obtained degrees in sociology and law at UCLA. She has taught at UCLA and at Immaculate Heart College, and has done pioneering work in human rights, developing a new, integrated model that includes the rights of women and children.

Anita Endrezze is a poet, short story writer and artist. She is the author of *at the helm of twilight* (Broken Moon Press), which won the Bumbershoot/Weyerhaeuser Publication Award. She recently completed a new manuscript of poems, *Life Hidden in a Small Room*, as well as a short story collection, *The Humming of Stars and Bees and Waves*.

Flor Fernandez is a transpersonal psychotherapist in private practice in Seattle. Born in Cuba, she is a ritualist, artist, and writer, as well as a member of Los Norteños, a

Latino group of writers, dedicated to the promotion of cultural awareness through storytelling and theater. She is presently working on a collection of essays about her spiritual journey as a Cuban exile.

Sally Miller Gearhart is a former professor, recovering political activist, lesbian feminist, child of the Great Depression, double Aries with Virgo rising, a student of yoga, tai chi, barbershop harmony, Spanish, and New Age metaphysics. She lives on a mountain of contradictions in Northern California.

Martha Gies teaches short story and personal essay writing at Marylhurst College in Portland, Oregon. Her essays and short stories have appeared in *Zyzzyva*, *Orion*, *Other Voices*, and *Left Bank*. In 1995 she was awarded an Oregon Literary Arts Fellowship. "A Heart of Wisdom" was a first-place winner in the 1996 Associated Church Press competition.

Ellen Grabiner, a native New Yorker, makes her home in Cambridge with her lover and their son. She paints, writes, sings, and dances in her studio in Allston, vacations in Truro, and prays in Somerville. She has just completed a collection of essays, *Piece of Cake: Memoir of a Lesbian Mother*.

Linda Gregg is the author of four books of poetry, most recently *Chosen by the Lion* (Graywolf Press). She is a bicoastal resident of Marin County, California, and Northampton, Massachusetts.

Joy Harjo is the author of several volumes of poetry, including *The Woman Who Fell from the Sky*. She has received awards from the National Endowment for the Arts and the Poetry Society of America. She is professor of English at the University of New Mexico, Albuquerque.

Judith Harris received her Ph.D. from George Washington University, where she presently teaches. Her poetry and essays have appeared in the *Antioch Review*, *Boulevard*, the *Women's Review of Books*, and *Her Face in the Mirror: Jewish Women on Mothers and Daughters*, among others.

Linda Hogan's volumes of poetry include *Savings* and *The Book of Medicines* and the novel *Mean Spirit*. Her work has received many awards, including the Guggenheim and an American Book Award. She teaches in the University of Colorado creative writing program.

June Hudson lives in Sonoma, but her pen often takes her back to Texas, where she grew up attending church and sweating through tent revivals. She's forgotten the theology but still loves singing the hymns. Her work has been published in *New Letters*, *Calyx*, *Poets On*, *Sun Dog*, and in several anthologies.

Akasha (Gloria) Hull is completing a book on spirituality in the lives and literature of African-American women. She meditates and studies ancient wisdom teachings with esoteric groups. A poet, scholar, and critic, she is a professor of women's studies and literature at the University of California, Santa Cruz.

Mary Karr, author of *The Liars' Club*, a memoir about her childhood, grew up in a swampy east Texas refinery town. Presently she lives in upstate New York with her son and teaches literature and creative writing at Syracuse University. She has won the Pushcart Prize for poetry and essays, and has published in *Ploughshares*, *Parnassus*, and *Granta*.

Jane Kenyon is the author of several volumes of poetry, including *Boat of Quiet Hours*, *Let Evening Come*, *Constance*, and *Otherwise: New and Selected Poems*. Married to the poet Donald Hall, she died of leukemia in 1995.

Barbara Kingsolver is a writer of fiction, nonfiction, and poetry. Her titles include *Pigs in Heaven*, *Animal Dreams*, and *High Tide in Tucson: Essays from Now or Never*. She lives in Tucson, Arizona.

Daniela Kuper has published a number of short stories and has been awarded time at the Djerassi Resident Artists Program to work on her novel, *Night Stands*. Her own spiritual journey was given a paved road the day she left a man like the one she wrote about in "Holy Ghost."

Dorothy Lazard resides in Oakland, California. She took her spiritual destiny into her own hands at the tender age of thirteen, having no tolerance for a bully God. Recently she completed her first novel, *Springs That Feed the Stream*.

Priscilla Lee has published poetry in the *Kenyon Review*, *Mid-American Review*, and *Zyzzyva*, and has received the James D. Phelan Literary Award from the San Francisco Foundation. She's an Aries-Firehorse, of the type they used to drown in China, who was raised by her unemployed Buddhist fortune-teller grandma. She prays to Kuan Yin every morning.

Madeleine L'Engle's many books include *A Wrinkle in Time* and *A Swiftly Tilting Planet*, and most recently she has published *A Live Coal in the Sea*, and *Glimpses of Grace: Daily Thoughts and Reflections*. She lives in New York City, where she is writer-in-residence at the Cathedral of St. John the Divine.

Alison Luterman grew up in Massachusetts, and in 1990 moved to California, where she is a poet-in-the-schools, HIV educator, and counselor. Her religion is Judaism, her spiritual practices are meditation, writing, hugging trees, and talking with the ocean. She has published in *The Sun*.

Joanna Macy is active as a speaker and workshop leader within the context of citizen action for justice, peace, and ecological survival. Her books include *World as Lover, World as Self* and *Mutual Causality in Buddhism and General Systems Theory: The Dharma of Natural Systems*.

Nancy Mairs's most recent book is *Ordinary Time: Cycles in Marriage, Faith and Renewal*. Her previous titles include *Plaintext, Remembering the Bone House*, and *Carnal Acts*. She makes her home in Arizona.

Carole Maso's fourth novel is *The American Woman in the Chinese Hat* (Dalkey Archive). Forthcoming from Dutton is *Defiance*. She lives in Manhattan and teaches at Columbia University. Maso is the recipient of a 1993 Lannan Literary Fellowship for fiction.

Brooke Medicine Eagle is a Native American earthkeeper, ceremonial leader, sacred ecologist, and author of *Buffalo Woman Comes Singing*. She is the creator of EagleSong, spiritually oriented wilderness camps, and FlowerSong Project, which promotes a sustainable, ecologically sound beauty path upon Mother Earth.

Deena Metzger is the author of *A Sabbath Among the Ruins* and *Looking for the Faces of God*, two recent collections of poetry (Parallax Press), and *Writing for Your Life: A Guide and Companion to the Inner Worlds* (Harper San Francisco). Coeditor of the anthology *Between Species: Women & Animals* (Ballantine), she lives in Topanga Canyon with writer Michael Ortiz Hill and the wolves Owl and Isis. Her spiritual journey is implicit in the chronology and titles of her books.

Brenda Miller is a writer and editor living in Salt Lake City. She received a Pushcart Prize in Nonfiction in 1994 and her work has appeared in many periodicals, including

Yoga Journal, the *Georgia Review*, and *Seattle Magazine*. She is completing a manuscript of essays, *A Thousand Buddhas*.

We, the Dangerous is **Janice Mirikitani**'s third volume of poetry. She has also edited several anthologies. Mirikitani is a Sansei, or third-generation Japanese-American, born in California and interned as an infant with her family during the Second World War.

Pat Mora's newest book of poetry is *Agua Santa: Holy Water* (Beacon Press). Her other titles include *Nepantla*, *Communion*, *Chants*, and *Borders*. Mora is the recipient of many awards, most recently a National Endowment for the Arts Fellowship. She is also a writer of children's books.

Agate Nesaule was born in Latvia, experienced war and camps in Germany, and immigrated to the United States in 1950. Her memoir, *A Woman in Amber: Healing the Trauma of War and Exile*, won a 1996 American Book Award. A former professor of English and women's studies at the University of Wisconsin, she lives, gardens, and writes in Madison.

An award-winning poet, **Kathleen Norris** is also the author of two books of prose: *Dakota: A Spiritual Geography* and *The Cloister Walk*. She has been an oblate of Assumption Abbey in North Dakota for ten years.

Naomi Shihab Nye is a poet, teacher, essayist, and anthologist. She is the author of three collections of poetry: *Different Ways to Pray*, *Yellow Glove*, and *Hugging the Jukebox*. *Words Under the Words*, a selection of poems from these three volumes, was published in 1995 by Far Corners Press.

Vicky Phillips based "Snake Woman's Hands" on the stories her grandmother told her about her great-grandmother, who was a noted faith healer. As she wrote the story, she realized that the two women were more alike in their faith than dissimilar, and that the most important spiritual element was the daily faith they had developed over the years in one another.

Robin Podolsky lives and writes fiction, essays, and poetry in Los Angeles, where she was born. Her regular column, "Pollyanna with a Hatchet," was featured in the *L.A. Weekly*. Among the anthologies that include her work are *Hers*, *Grand Passion*, and *Best Lesbian Erotica*. Her book, *Queer Cosmopolis*, is forthcoming from New York University Press.

Sarah Rabkin lives in the Monterey Bay Area, where she teaches writing and journalism at the University of California, Santa Cruz. Her work has appeared in the *Lavender Reader*, the *San Jose Mercury News*, *Health*, *Hippocrates*, and other publications.

Adrienne Rich's many books include *Dark Fields of the Republic: Poems 1991–1995*, *What Is Found There: Notes on Poetry and Politics*, and *An Atlas of the Difficult World: Poems 1988–1991*. She was awarded a MacArthur Fellowship in 1994. Ms. Rich lives in California.

Robbie Clipper Sethi has published stories in *Atlantic Monthly*, *Mademoiselle*, and a number of literary magazines. Her collection, *The Bride Wore Red*, was selected by Barnes & Noble for its Discover Great New Writers Program in 1996. She considers herself a religious eclectic and finds truth in several religions.

Deborah Shouse has published in *The Sun*, *Newsweek*, *Ms.*, and *Redbook*. "When I swim, I struggle to go underwater, to hold my breath, to touch the rough and rocky bottom. When I write, I face the same struggle, how to get deeper, beyond the safe, the ordinary, into the hidden parts of the psyche." She writes to give people forgotten parts of themselves.

Carol Staudacher is an author in the field of psychology, a fiction writer, poet, and editor. Her award-winning poetry has appeared in numerous journals and anthologies, including the *New York Quarterly*, *Poetry Flash*, *Cumberland Review*, *Five Fingers Review*, and *Grain*.

Claudia Sternbach is a freelance writer living in Northern California with her husband, daughter, and dog. She writes a regular column for the *Santa Cruz Sentinel* and has been published in various national magazines. She has completed a manuscript on life after a cancer diagnosis.

Amber Coverdale Sumrall has edited or coedited twelve anthologies, including *Catholic Girls*, *Lovers*, *Women of the 14th Moon*, and *Touching Fire*. She is codirector of WomenCARE, a women's cancer resource center in Santa Cruz. Her greatest spiritual teachers were her grandmother and grandfather, and her cat, Sam, companion for eighteen years.

Daa'iyah Taha, an African-American who converted from Catholicism to Al-Islam over twenty years ago, was raised in the San Francisco Bay Area and graduated from Mills College. She is an author, illustrator, and publisher of Islamic educational materials for children, as well as a magazine editor and freelance writer.

Poet and educational consultant, **Patrice Vecchione,** director of the Heart of the Word: Poetry and the Imagination, has taught poetry to children for over twenty years. She is the editor of *Fault Lines: Children's Earthquake Poetry*, and coeditor of *Catholic Girls* and *Bless Me Father: Stories of Catholic Childhood*.

Lisa Vice lives with her partner, the writer Martha Clark Cummings, in Thermopolis, Wyoming. Her novel, *Reckless Driver*, is a Plume/Penguin paperback. *Preacher's Lake*, her second novel, is forthcoming.

Helena María Viramontes is the author of the highly acclaimed *The Moths and Other Stories*, and the novel *Under the Feet of Jesus*. Raised in East Los Angeles, she graduated from the MFA program in creative writing at the University of California, Irvine.

Charlotte Zöe Walker is a professor of English and women's studies at the State University of New York, at Oneonta. She has a strong interest in the connections between feminism and environmental issues. Her novel *Condor and Hummingbird* was published by Alice Walker's Wild Trees Press. She often explores a theme of spiritual quest in her writing.

Anita Wilkins, a Pushcart Prize recipient, has published three collections of poetry. She writes, "The light of the unearthly has come most often through connection with the earth itself, a connection sometimes discontinuous while at the same time mysteriously continuous—loss and return, grief and abundance."

Terry Tempest Williams is naturalist-in-residence at the Utah Museum of Natural History. She is the author of *Pieces of a White Shell*, *Refuge*, *Desert Quartet*, and *An Unspoken Hunger*. She lives in Salt Lake City with her husband.

Jean Walton Wolff is a fallen Unitarian, who draws strength from nature, Emmet Fox, psalms, and daydreaming. Her writing has appeared in several magazines and anthologies, including *Sleeping with Dionysus* and *Milvia Street*. She lives and teaches writing in Northern California.

Gene Zeiger leads writing workshops in western Massachusetts. She is the author of two collections of poems, *Sudden Dancing* and *Leaving Egypt*, and a commentator for National Public Radio. At midlife, she feels she is now truly coming home spiritually.

The following pages constitute an extension of the copyright page.

"Still I Rise" from *And Still I Rise* copyright © 1978 by Maya Angelou is reprinted by permission of Random House, Inc., and Little, Brown.

"The Tappin" by Laurine Ark first appeared in *Negative Capability* and is reprinted by permission of the author.

Excerpt from *Plain and Simple: A Woman's Journey to the Amish* copyright © 1991 by Sue Bender is reprinted by permission of HarperCollins Publishers, Inc.

"Mythology" from *The Forbidden Poems* copyright © 1991 by Becky Birtha is reprinted by permission of Seal Press, Seattle, Washington.

"Into the Silence: A Tale of Seven Sisters" by Sandy Boucher first appeared in *Tricycle: The Buddhist Review* and is reprinted by permission of the author.

"Street Trees" by Melody Ermachild Chavis first appeared in *Sierra Magazine* and is reprinted by permission of the author.

"Song of the Sad Guitar" from *The Phoenix Gone, The Terrace Empty* copyright © 1994 by Marilyn Chin is reprinted by permission of the author.

"brothers, part 6" from *The Book of Light* copyright © 1993 by Lucille Clifton, Copper Canyon Press, is reprinted by permission of the author.

"The Garba" from *Black Candle* copyright © 1991 by Chitra Banerjee Divakaruni is reprinted by permission of Calyx Books.

"The Long Journey Home: Reconnecting with the Great Mother" by Riane Eisler first appeared in *For the Love of God: New Writings by Spiritual and Psychological Leaders*, edited by Benjamin Shield and Richard Carlson (New World Library, 1990), and is reprinted by permission of the author.

"The Medicine Woman's Daughter" from *At the Helm of Twilight* copyright © 1992 by Anita Endrezze, Broken Moon Press, is reprinted by permission of the author.

"The Pit Bull Opportunity" by Sally Miller Gearhart first appeared in *Reality Change*, Summer 1994, and is reprinted by permission of the author.

"A Heart of Wisdom" by Martha Gies first appeared in *Second Opinion*, April 1995, and is reprinted by permission of the author.

"There Is a Sweetness in It" copyright © 1994 by Linda Gregg from *Chosen by the Lion* is reprinted by permission of Graywolf Press, St. Paul, Minnesota.

"Eagle Poem" from *In Mad Love & War* copyright © 1990 by Joy Harjo, Wesleyan University Press, is reprinted by permission of University Press of New England.

"Wherever in the Language of Jewish Women a Garden Grows" by Judith Harris is reprinted from *Tikkun Magazine: A Bi-Monthly Jewish Critique of Politics, Culture, and Society*. New York, NY.

"The Grandmother Songs" copyright © 1993 by Linda Hogan is reprinted from *The Book of Medicines* by permission of Coffee House Press.

"DreadPath/LockSpirit" by Akasha (Gloria) Hull first appeared in *My Soul Is a Witness: African-American Women's Spirituality* and is reprinted by permission of the author.

"Houses of the Spirit" by Mary Karr first appeared in *Vogue* magazine, March 1995, and is reprinted by permission of the author.

"Let Evening Come" by Jane Kenyon, copyright © 1996 by the Estate of Jane Kenyon, is reprinted from *Otherwise: New and Selected Poems* by permission of Graywolf Press, St. Paul. Minnesota.

"In the City Ringed with Giants" copyright © 1992 by Barbara Kingsolver is reprinted from *Another America* by permission of Seal Press, Seattle, Washington.

"Holy Ghost" by Daniela Kuper first appeared in *The Sun* in a slightly different version and is reprinted by permission of the author.

"The Vision" by Priscilla Lee first appeared in *Konch*, 1992, and is reprinted by permission of the author.

"Whole, Healed and Holy" from *Walking on Water* by Madeleine L'Engle copyright © 1980 by Crosswicks is reprinted by permission of Harold Shaw Publishers, Wheaton, Illinois.

"Three Lessons in Compassion" from *World as Lover, World as Self* by Joanna Macy, 1991, is reprinted by permission of Parallax Press, Berkeley, California.

"From My House to Mary's House" from *Ordinary Time: Cycles in Marriage, Faith, and Renewal* copyright © 1993 by Nancy Mairs is reprinted by permission of Beacon Press, Boston, Massachusetts.

"Night" from *Ava* copyright © 1993 by Carole Maso is reprinted by permission of Dalkey Archive Press.

"The Rainbow Bridge" by Brooke Medicine Eagle first appeared in *Shamanic Voices: A Survey of Visionary Narratives*, edited by Joan Halifax (Dutton, 1979 and is reprinted by permission of the author.

"The Bird in the Heart of the Tree" by Deena Metzger first appeared in *Worlds of Jewish Prayer, A Festschrift in Honor of Rabbi Zalman M. Schachter-Shalomi*, edited by Shohama H. Wiener and Jonathan Omer-Man (Jason Aronson, Inc., 1993, and is published by permission of the author.

"A Thousand Buddhas" by Brenda Miller was first published in the *The Georgia Review*, Fall 1993, and is reprinted by permission of the author.

"Tongues Afire" from *We, the Dangerous: New and Selected Poems* copyright © 1995 by Janice Mirikitani is reprinted by permission of Celestial Arts, Berkeley, CA.

"Litany to the Dark Goddess" from *Agua Santa: Holy Water* copyright © 1995 by Pat Mora is reprinted by permission of Beacon Press, Boston, Massachusetts.

"The Reciters" by Agate Nesaule was first published in *Northwest Review*, 1994, and is reprinted by permission of the author.

"My Monasticism" from *Dakota* copyright © 1993 by Kathleen Norris is reprinted by permission of Ticknor & Fields/Houghton Mifflin Co.

"Grandfather's Heaven" from *Words Under the Words* copyright © 1995 by Naomi Shihab Nye is reprinted by permission of Far Corner Books/Eighth Mountain Press, Portland, Oregon.

Part II of "Sources," from *Your Native Land, Your Life: Poems by Adrienne Rich* copyright © 1986 by Adrienne Rich is reprinted by permission of the author and W. W. Norton & Company, Inc.

"A White Woman's Burden" by Robbie Clipper Sethi first appeared in *The New Review*, 1992, and is reprinted by permission of the author.

"A Kaddish by the Sea" by Deborah Shouse first appeared in *The Sun* and is reprinted by permission of the author.

"The Sacred Journey: The Gift of Hajj" by Daa'iyah Taha first appeared in *My Soul Is a Witness: African-American Women's Spirituality*, edited by Gloria Wade-Gayles (Beacon Press, 1995), and is reprinted by permission of the author.

"Toward the Only Sky" by Patrice Vecchione first appeared in *Porter Gulch Review* and is reprinted by permission of the author.

"What Faith Is" by Lisa Vice first appeared in *Grow Old Along with Me: The Best Is Yet to Be*, Papier-Mâché Press, and is reprinted by permission of the author.

"The Moths" by Helena María Viramontes from *The Moths and Other Stories* is reprinted by permission of the Arte Público Press.

"The Virgin of the Rocks" by Charlotte Zöe Walker first appeared in *Ms.*, November/December 1994, and is reprinted by permission of the author.

Excerpt from "Long-Billed Curlews" from *Refuge* copyright © 1991 by Terry Tempest Williams is reprinted by permission of Pantheon Books, a division of Random House, Inc.

"Mary and the Maple Tree" by Jean Walton Wolff first appeared in *West* magazine (*San Jose Mercury News*), June 1995, and is reprinted by permission of the author.

"The Little Bit" by Gene Zeiger first appeared in *The Sun* and is reprinted by permission of the author.